A Bibliographical Guide to
the Study of
Western American Literature

A Bibliographical Guide to the Study of Western American Literature

by
Richard W. Etulain

UNIVERSITY OF NEBRASKA PRESS
Lincoln and London

The paper in this book meets the guidelines for permanence and durability of
the Committee on Production Guidelines for Book Longevity of the Council
on Library Resources.

Library of Congress Cataloging in Publication Data

Etulain, Richard W.
  A bibliographical guide to the study of western American literature.

  Includes index.
  1. American literature—West (U.S.)—History and criticism—Bibliography.
  2. West (U.S.) in literature—Bibliography.   3. West (U.S.)—Bibliography.
  I. Title.
  Z1251.W5E8   1983   [PS271]   016.81'09'978   82-8579
  ISBN 0-8032-1801-X   AACR2

For
John Milton, Don Walker, Max Westbrook, Deb Wylder—
four pioneers of the American literary West

CONTENTS

Preface   1
BIBLIOGRAPHIES   5
ANTHOLOGIES   12
GENERAL WORKS   15
    Books, Dissertations, and Theses   15
    Articles   26
SPECIAL TOPICS   48
    Local Color and Regionalism   48
    Popular Western Literature:
      Dime Novels and The Western 53
    Western Film   60
    Indian Literature and Indians
      in Western Literature   64
    Mexican-American Literature and
      Chicanos in Western Literature 72
    The Beats   77
    Canadian Western Literature   80
WORKS ON INDIVIDUAL AUTHORS   84
    Abbey, Edward   84
    Acosta, Oscar Zeta   85
    Adams, Andy   85
    Adeler, Max   85
    Aldrich, Bess Streeter   86
    Alexander, Charles   86
    Allen, Henry Wilson   86
    Alurista   86
    Anaya, Rudolfo   86
    Antoninus, Brother   87
    Applegate, Jesse   87
    Arias, Ron   87
    Atherton, Gertrude   87
    Austin, Mary   88

Bailey, Margaret Jewett 89
Balch, Frederic Homer 89
Bancroft, Hubert Howe 90
Barker, S. Omar 90
Barnard, Mary 90
Barnes, Will Croft 90
Barrio, Raymond 90
Beagle, Peter S. 90
Bedicheck, Roy 90
Bennett, Emerson—Sidney Moss 91
Berger, Thomas 91
Berry, Don 91
Bierce, Ambrose 92
Blake, Forrester 93
Bliven, Bruce 93
Bly, Robert 93
Boatright, Mody C. 94
Bolton, Herbert Eugene 94
Borland, Hal 95
Bower, B. M. 95
Bradford, Richard 95
Brand, Max 95
Brautigan, Richard 95
Brett, Dorothy 96
Brink, Carol Ryrie 96
Brink, Frank 96
Browne, Charles Farrar 96
Browne, J. Ross 97
Burgess, Gelett 97
Burroughs, Edgar Rice 97
Bynner, Witter 98

Cain, James M. 98
Cantwell, Robert 98
Capps, Benjamin 98
Carmichael, Sarah Elizabeth 99
Case, Robert Ormond 99
Casey, Bill 99
Cassady, Neal 99
Castaneda, Carlos 99
Cather, Willa 99
Catlin, George 107
Chandler, Raymond 107
Chase, J. Smeaton 107

Church, Peggy Pond 107
Clark, Badger 107
Clark, Charles Heber 107
Clark, Walter Van Tilburg 108
Clark, William 110
Clemens, Samuel L. 110
Clyman, James 116
Coburn, Walt 116
Coggeshall, William T. 116
Comfort, Will Levington 117
Coolbrith, Ina 117
Coolidge, Dane 117
Cooper, James Fenimore 117
Corey, Paul 121
Corle, Edwin 122
Corso, Gregory 122
Crane, Stephen 122
Crawford, J. W. 124
Croy, Homer 124
Cunningham, Eugene 125
Cunningham, J. V. 125
Cushman, Dan 125

Daggett, Rollin Mallory 125
Dana, Richard Henry 125
Davis, H. L. 125
Day, Robert 127
Decker, William 127
Derby, George H. 127
De Vaca, Cabeza 127
DeVoto, Bernard 128
Dewlen, Al 129
Didion, Joan 129
Dixon, Maynard 129
Dobie, J. Frank 129
Doctorow, E. L. 130
Donnelly, Ignatius 130
Dorn, Ed 130
Downing, J. Hyatt 131
Dresbach, Glenn Ward 131
Dubie, Norman 131
Duncan, Robert 131
Duniway, Abigail Scott 131

Duval, John C.   132
Dye, Eva Emery   132

Eastlake, William   132
Eastman, Charles Alexander   132
Eastman, Elaine Goodale   133
Eggleston, Edward   133
Eiseley, Loren   133
Ellis, Anne   133
Ellison, Ralph   134
Erdman, Loula Grace   134
Eustis, Helen   134
Evans, Max   134
Everson, William   134

Faust, Frederick   134
Feikema, Feike   135
Ferber, Edna   135
Fergusson, Erna   135
Fergusson, Harvey   135
Ferlinghetti, Lawrence   136
Ferril, Thomas Hornsby   136
Fiedler, Leslie   137
Field, Eugene   137
Fisher, Clay   137
Fisher, Vardis   138
Fitzgerald, F. Scott   140
Fletcher, John Gould   140
Flint, Timothy   140
Flynn, Robert   141
Foote, Mary Hallock   141
Fraser, George C.   141

Gard, Wayne   141
Garland, Hamlin   142
Garrard, Hector Lewis   146
Gerstäcker, Frederich   146
Ghiselin, Brewster   146
Gilfillan, Archer B.   146
Ginsberg, Allen   147
Gipson, Fred   147
Glidden, Frederick   148
Gordon, Caroline   148

Goyen, William   148
Graves, John   148
Gregg, Josiah   149
Grey, Zane   149
Griffin, John Howard   150
Guthrie, A. B., Jr.   151

Haines, John   153
Haley, J. Evetts   153
Hall, Dick Wick   153
Hall, Hazel   153
Hall, James   153
Hamilton, Donald   154
Hammett, Dashiell   154
Harte, Bret   154
Havighurst, Walter   157
Hay, John   157
Haycox, Ernest   157
Hemingway, Ernest   158
Henderson, Alice Corbin   158
Henry, O.   158
Henry, Will   158
Higginson, Ella   158
Hill, Edwin B.   159
Hill, Ruth Beebe   159
Hillerman, Tony   159
Hoagland, Edward   159
Horgan, Paul   159
Hough, Emerson   160
Howard, Robert Erwin   161
Howe, Edgar Watson   161
Howells, William Dean   162
Hudson, Lois Phillips   162
Hugo, Richard   162
Humphrey, William   163

Inclán, Luis   163
Inge, William   163
Irving, Washington   164

Jackson, Helen Hunt   166
James, Will   167
Jayne, Michell F.   167

Jeffers, Robinson   167
Johnson, Dorothy M.   173

Kelton, Elmer   173
Kerouac, Jack   173
Kesey, Ken   175
King, Charles   178
King, Clarence   178
Kipling, Rudyard   179
Kirkland, Joseph   179
Kizer, Carolyn   179
Koike, Kyō   180
Krause, Herbert   180
Krutch, Joseph Wood   180
Kyne, Peter B.   180

LaFarge, Oliver   181
L'Amour, Louis   181
Langrische, John S.   182
Larson, Clinton F.   182
Lawrence, D. H.   182
Lea, Tom   182
LeMay, Alan   183
Lewis, Alfred Henry   183
Lewis, James Franklin   184
Lewis, Janet   184
Lewis, Meriwether   184
Lewis, Sinclair   184
Linderman, Frank B.   187
Lindsay, Vachel   187
Lomax, John A.   188
London, Jack   188
Long, Haniel   194
Lott, Milton   194
Luhan, Mabel Dodge   194
Lummis, Charles Fletcher   195
Lutz, Giles   195
Lyon, Harris Merton   195

McCarter, Margaret Hill   195
McClure, Michael   195
McDaniel, Wilma Elizabeth   196
Macdonald, Ross   196

McGrath, Thomas 196
McGuane, Thomas 196
Maclane, Mary 196
Macleod, Norman 196
McMurtry, Larry 197
McNichols, Charles L. 198
McNickle, D'Arcy 198
Mailer, Norman 198
Malamud, Bernard 198
Malin, James C. 199
Manfred, Frederick Feikema 199
Markham, Edwin 201
Marriott, Alice 202
Marryat, Francis S. 202
Mathews, John Joseph 202
Mayer, Tom 202
Mendoza, Rita 202
Micheaux, Oscar 202
Michener, James 203
Milburn, George 203
Miller, Cincinnatus Hiner 203
Mills, Enos 204
Milton, John R. 204
Moberg, Vilhelm 205
Momaday, N. Scott 205
Morris, Wright 206
Muir, John 209
Mulford, Clarence 210
Muro, Amado Jesus 210

Neihardt, John G. 210
Nichols, John 212
Norris, Charles 212
Norris, Frank 212
Nye, Edgar Wilson 217

Okada, John 218
Olsen, Tillie 218
Olson, Sigurd 218
O'Malley, D. J. 218
Ortiz, Simon 218
Oskison, John Milton 218

Overholser, Wayne D.   218
Owens, William A.   218

Parkman, Francis   219
Parrington, Vernon Louis   219
Patchen, Kenneth   220
Paulding, James Kirke   220
Peacock, Thomas Brower   220
Perry, George Sessions   220
Phoenix, John   221
Pike, Albert   221
Pokagon, Chief Simon   221
Porter, Katherine Anne   221
Porter, William Sydney   223
Portis, Charles   224
Powers, J. F.   224
Pynchon, Thomas   225

Quick, Herbert   225

Raine, William MacLeod   225
Read, Opie   225
Reid, Mayne   225
Remington, Frederic   226
Rexroth, Kenneth   227
Rhodes, Eugene Manlove   228
Richter, Conrad   229
Ricketts, Edward F.   230
Riggs, Lynn   231
Rivera, Tomás   231
Robbins, Tom   232
Roethke, Theodore   232
Rogers, Will   235
Rölvaag, Ole   235
Roosevelt, Theodore   237
Rothenberg, Jerome   238
Royce, Josiah   238
Runyon, Damon   238
Russell, Charles M.   238
Ruxton, George F.   239

Sabin, Edward L.   240
Sandoz, Mari   240

Santee, Ross	241
Saroyan, William	241
Scarborough, Dorothy	242
Schaefer, Jack	243
Schorer, Mark	243
Scott, Harvey	244
Seelye, John	244
Seltzer, Chester	244
Service, Robert W.	244
Shelton, Richard	244
Short, Luke	244
Silko, Leslie Marmon	244
Sinclair, John L.	245
Sinclair, Upton	245
Siringo, Charles A.	246
Smith, Jedediah	246
Snyder, Gary	246
Sonnichsen, C. L.	248
Sorenson, Virginia	248
Spicer, Jack	249
Stafford, Jean	249
Stafford, William	250
Stapleton, Patience	251
Steele, Wilbur Daniel	251
Stegner, Wallace	251
Steinbeck, John	253
Stephens, Allan	263
Sterling, George	263
Stevens, James	264
Stevenson, Robert Louis	264
Stewart, George R.	264
Stoddard, Charles Warren	264
Storm, Hyemeyohsts	265
Straight, Michael	265
Strobridge, Idah Meacham	265
Suckow, Ruth	265
Sukenick, Ronald	266
Summerhayes, Martha	266
Swallow, Alan	267
Swarthout, Glendon	267
Sweet, Alexander	267
Swett, John	267
Swisher, Bella French	267

Taylor, Bayard 267
Thomason, John William, Jr. 268
Thorpe, Thomas Bangs 268
Thurman, Wallace 268
Toomer, Jean 269
Torsvan, Berick Traven (B. Traven) 269
Townsend, John K. 269
Turner, Frederick Jackson 269
Twain, Mark 271

Udell, I. L. 271
Urista, Alberto 271

Victor, Frances Fuller 271
Villarreal, José Antonio 271

Wagoner, David 271
Walker, Stanley 271
Ward, Artemus 271
Ward, May 271
Ware, Eugene Fitch 272
Waters, Frank 272
Weathers, Winston 273
Webb, Walter Prescott 273
Weinstein, Nathan Wallenstein 274
Welch, James 275
Welch, Lew 276
West, Jessamyn 276
West, Nathanael 277
Wetjen, Albert Richard 277
White, Stewart Edward 277
White, William Allen 277
Whitely, Opal 278
Whitman, Walt 278
Wilder, Laura Ingalls 279
Williams, John 279
Wilner, Herbert 279
Wilson, Harry Leon 279
Winters, Yvor 280
Winther, Sophus K. 281
Wister, Owen 281
Wolfe, Thomas 285
Wood, Charles Erskine Scott 285

Wood, Stanley   285
Woods, John   285
Wright, David   285
Wright, Harold Bell   285
Wright, James Arlington   286

Young, Brigham   286
Young Bear, Ray A.   286
INDEX   287

PREFACE

The recentness of most listings in this bibliography illustrates the growing interest in western literature in the last decades. Although the first significant interpretations of the literary West by Ralph Leslie Rusk, Dorothy Dondore, and Lucy Lockwood Hazard appeared in the 1920s, Franklin Walker's notable works in the 1930s and 1940s, and Henry Nash Smith's indispensable *Virgin Land* in 1950, these pioneer studies did not spawn an immediate interest in western writing. Not until the 1960s did a growing number of students and scholars begin systematic study of western literature.

Much of this earliest commentary dealt with nineteenth-century writers like James Fenimore Cooper, Bret Harte, and Joaquin Miller and later interpretations with such authors as Owen Wister, Eugene Manlove Rhodes, and Sinclair Lewis. While interest in some of these writers has declined, critics continue to deal extensively with the life and writings of Hamlin Garland, Frank Norris, Willa Cather, and John Steinbeck. And an increasing number of essays and books have been written about Jack London, Robinson Jeffers, Larry McMurtry, N. Scott Momaday, and post-Beat writers Ken Kesey, Gary Snyder, Richard Brautigan, and Joan Didion.

At the same time, scholars have been paying increased attention to several topics. Regionalism, the formula Western, the Beats, and the Western film as literature are popular subjects; and women writers and western heroines, Mormons, images of Indians and Chicanos, and Canadian western literature are subjects receiving additional notice. While such well-known critics as John R. Milton, Don D. Walker, and Max Westbrook have advanced tentative overviews of western American literature, their broader interpretations are exceptions, for most western literary commentary is narrowly focused or limited to single works. In addition, several popular approaches in American literary criticism have not been applied to western writing and writers. This being the case, western American literature, though benefiting from the increased attention it has received in the last twenty years or so, remains a field ripe with possibilities for literary critics and historians.

To take into account the growing and diversified interest in western literature, this bibliography updates, enlarges, and reorganizes *Western American Literature: A Bibliography of Interpretive Books and Articles* (Vermillion, S.Dak.: Dakota Press,

1

1972). Intended as handy guides to the major interpretive works about western literature, as well as those on numerous individual authors, the following listings are not exhaustive, but they are comprehensive and bring together in one volume the most important research on the literature of the American West. Recent work is stressed, including material published through 1981.

This checklist is divided into five major sections: (1) bibliographies listing research on western American literature; (2) anthologies of western literature; (3) general works, divided into two categories: (a) books, dissertations, and theses; and (b) essays; (4) listings of research dealing with seven important aspects of western literature: (a) local color and regionalism; (b) popular western literature: dime novels and the Western; (c) Western films as literature; (d) Indian literature and Indians in western literature; (e) Mexican-American literature and Chicanos in western literature; (f) the Beats; (g) Canadian western literature; and (5) essays and books on more than three hundred fifty writers.

Limited primarily to those authors who were born and reared in the trans-Mississippi West or who spent large portions of their lives in the West, this listing also includes items on writers like Cooper, Washington Irving, Stephen Crane, Owen Wister, Nathanael West, and Thomas Berger, whose works have influenced western literature. Major emphasis is placed on writers of fiction and poetry, but some books and articles dealing with notable western historians and well-known nonfiction writers are also noted.

I have included listings on this large and varied region and group of writers because I want this bibliography to be as comprehensive as possible. To move in the other direction—to narrow the definition of "western," to omit the Beats and such contemporary writers as Kesey, Brautigan, and Tom Robbins, and to leave out non-Westerners who have written notable books about the West—is to become too exclusive and to amputate the meaning of the region. Still, authors such as Thomas Mann, Henry Miller, Ursula LeGuinn, and others who lived (or have lived) long periods in the West, are not included because they have not written about the West. Literary critics and historians must utilize definitions sufficiently broad and flexible to cover the varied kinds of literature written about the West, by insiders and outsiders. I have used this broader definition of the West and "western" literature in compiling this bibliography.

Users should note other aspects of the organization of this volume. Because so much has been written about Cooper, Clemens, Cather, and Steinbeck, these sections are particularly selective, although I have tried to include all major books and essays about these authors, as well as the most useful bibliographical references. Though the table of contents lists official and pen names of several authors, items are listed under their given names. Thus, for example, books and essays about Mark Twain are under Clemens, items about Max Brand under Frederick

2

Faust, and those about Artemus Ward under Charles Farrar Browne. On a few occasions autobiographical books and essays are noted when they add information not otherwise available on that writer's life and works. Finally, the index is a guide only to authors of books and essays listed here; it is not a subject index.

Scholars interested in additional bibliographical materials about western writers and writings should consult the yearly bibliographies in winter issues of *Western American Literature*. Also helpful are the annual *MLA International Bibliography*, bibliographical listings in *American Literature* and *Western Historical Quarterly*, and bibliographies appended to volumes and pamphlets in the Twayne United States Authors Series and the Boise State Western Writers Series.

A number of persons helped in the preparation of this volume. At Idaho State University, Sherrill and John Redd, Barb Herrbach, and Andy Dredge typed and doublechecked endless 4- by 6-inch cards. At the University of New Mexico, Avis and Jo Lou Trujillo and Annabelle Oczon typed the manuscript and helped prepare the index. My daughter, Jackie, proofread numerous entries. The Research Allocation Committee of the University of New Mexico provided partial funding for typing the manuscript. John R. Milton encouraged the preparation of the earlier version of this bibliography.

BIBLIOGRAPHIES

1. Adams, Ramon F. *Burs under the Saddle: A Second Look at Books and Histories of the West.* Norman: University of Oklahoma Press, 1964.
2. ———. *The Rampaging Herd: A Bibliography of Books and Pamphlets on Men and Events in the Cattle Industry.* Norman: University of Oklahoma Press, 1959.
3. ———. *Six-Guns and Saddle Leather: A Bibliography of Books and Pamphlets on Western Outlaws and Gunmen.* Norman: University of Oklahoma Press, 1954, 1969.
4. Adelman, Irving, and Rita Divorkin. *The Contemporary Novel: A Checklist of Critical Literature on the British and American Novel Since 1945.* Metuchen, N.J.: Scarecrow Press, 1972.
5. Alsmeyer, Henry L., Jr. "A Preliminary Southwestern Reconnaissance." *Southwestern American Literature* 1 (May 1971): 67-71. Lists literary guides of the Southwest.
6. *American Literary Scholarship: An Annual.* Durham, N.C.: Duke University Press, 1965-. Yearly collection that summarizes and analyzes literary scholarship.
7. *American Quarterly.* 1949-. An annual bibliography of American Studies is issued.
8. Anderson, John Q., Edwin W. Gaston, Jr., and James W. Lee, eds. *Southwestern American Literature: A Bibliography.* Athens: Ohio University Press—The Swallow Press, 1979. A very important listing.
9. Andrews, Clarence A. "The Literature of the Middle West: A Beginning Bibliography." *Great Lakes Review* 1 (1974): 35-67.
10. Andrews, Thomas F. "'Ho! For Oregon and California!': An Annotated Bibliography of Published Advice to the Emigrant, 1841-1847." *Princeton University Library Chronicle* 30 (1971): 41-64.
11. Baird, Newton D., and Robert Greenwood. *An Annotated Bibliography of California Fiction 1664-1970.* Georgetown, Calif.: Talisman Literary Research, 1971.
12. Bay, Jens C. *A Handful of Western Books.* Cedar Rapids, Iowa, 1935.

5

13. ——. *A Second Handful of Western Books.* Cedar Rapids, Iowa, 1936.

14. ——. *A Third Handful of Books.* Cedar Rapids, Iowa, 1937.

15. ——. "Western Life and Western Books." *Missouri Historical Review* 36 (1942): 403-11.

16. Blanck, Jacob. *Bibliography of American Literature.* New Haven: Yale University Press, 1955-.

17. Bragin, Charles. *Dime Novels: Bibliography, 1860-1928.* Brooklyn: C. Bragin, 1938.

18. Brenni, Vito Joseph. *The Bibliographic Control of American Literature 1920-1975.* Metuchen, N.J.: Scarecrow Press, 1975.

19. Bryer, Jackson R., ed. *Fifteen Modern American Authors: A Survey of Research and Criticism.* Durham, N.C.: Duke University Press, 1969. Contains sections on Cather and Steinbeck.

20. Bullen, John S., ed. "Annual Bibliography of Studies in Western American Literature." *Western American Literature,* 1966-. Issued each year in the Winter issue.

21. Bush, Alfred L. "The Princeton Collections of Western Americana." *Princeton University Library Chronicle* 30 (1971): 1-17.

22. Carson, W. G. B. "The Theatre of the American Frontier: A Bibliography." *Theatre Research* I (March 1958): 14-23.

23. Coan, Otis W., and Richard G. Lillard. *America in Fiction: An Annotated List of Novels that Interpret Aspects of Life in the U.S.* 4th ed. Stanford, Calif.: Stanford University Press, 1956.

24. Cole, Wendell. "Early Theatre West of the Rockies: A Bibliographical Essay." *Theatre Research* 4 (1962): 36-45.

25. Coleman, Rufus A., ed. *Northwest Books: First Supplement.* Lincoln: University of Nebraska Press, 1949.

26. Cracroft, Richard, ed. "Research in Western American Literature." *Western American Literature,* 1974-. Appears annually in the Winter issue and lists theses and dissertations completed or in progress on western American literature.

27. "Current Reading: A Scholarly and Pedagogical Bibliography of Articles and Books, Recent and Old, on Southwestern Literature and Culture." *Arizona English Bulletin* 13 (April 1971): 80-108.

28. Davidson, Levette J. *Rocky Mountain Life in Literature: A Descriptive Bibliography.* Denver: University of Denver Book Store, 1936.

29. Dobie, J. Frank. *Guide to Life and Literature of the Southwest.* Rev. ed. Dallas: Southern Methodist University Press, 1952.

30. Dondore, Dorothy Anne. *The Prairie and the Making of Middle America: Four Centuries of Description.* Cedar Rapids, Iowa: Torch Press, 1926.

31. Donelson, Kenneth L. "Some Adolescent Novels About the West: An Annotated Bibliography." *Elementary English* 49 (May 1972): 735-39.

32. Dougherty, Charles T. "Novels of the Middle Border: A Critical Bibliography for Historians." *Historical Bulletin* 25 (May 1947): 77-78, 85-88.

33. Dykes, Jeff C. *Western High Spots: Reading and Collecting Guides.* [Flagstaff, Ariz.] : Northland Press, 1977.

34. Eichelberger, Clayton L., comp. *A Guide to Critical Reviews of United States Fiction, 1870-1910.* 2 vols. Metuchen, N.J.: Scarecrow Press, 1971, 1974.

35. Emerson, O. B., and Marion C. Michael, comps. *Southern Literary Culture: A Bibliography of Masters' and Doctors' Theses.* University: University of Alabama, 1955, 1979. Lists theses on several southwestern writers.

36. Erisman, Fred. "American Regional Juvenile Literature, 1870-1910: An Annotated Bibliography." *American Literary Realism 1870-1910* 6 (Spring 1973): 109-22.

37. ——, and Richard W. Etulain, eds. *Fifty Western Writers: A Bio-Bibliographical Guide.* Westport, Conn.: Greenwood Press, 1982.

38. Etulain, Richard W. "The American Literary West and Its Interpreters: The Rise of a New Historiography." *Pacific Historical Review* 45 (August 1976): 311-48.

39. ——. *Western American Literature: A Bibliography of Interpretive Books and Articles.* Vermillion, S.Dak.: Dakota Press, 1972. First edition of this volume.

40. ——. "Western American Literature: A Selective Annotated Bibliography." *Rendezvous* 7 (Winter 1972): 67-78.

41. ——. "Western Literary History: A Brief Bibliographical Essay." *Journal of the West* 19 (January 1980): 71-73.

42. Flanagan, John T. "A Bibliography of Middle Western Farm Novels." *Minnesota History* 23 (June 1942): 156-58.

43. Fleck, Richard F. "Supplement to a Selective Literary Bibliography of Wyoming." *Annals of Wyoming* 47 (Fall 1975): 232.

44. ——, and Robert A. Campbell. "A Selective Literary Bibliography of Wyoming." *Annals of Wyoming* 46 (Spring 1974): 75-112.

45. Gaston, Edwin W., Jr. *The Early Novel of the Southwest.* Albuquerque: University of New Mexico Press, 1961, pp. 195-302.

46. Gerstenberger, Donna, and George Hendrick. *The American Novel 1789-1959: A Checklist of Twentieth-Century Criticism.* Denver: Alan Swallow, 1961.

47. ——. *The American Novel: A Checklist of Twentieth Century Criticism on Novels Since 1789. Volume II: Criticism*

Written 1960-1968. Chicago: Swallow Press, 1970.

48. Gohdes, Clarence. *Bibliographical Guide to the Study of the Literature of the U.S.A.* 4th ed., rev. Durham, N.C.: Duke University Press, 1976.

49. ———. *Literature and Theatre of the States and Regions of the U.S.A.: An Historical Bibliography.* Durham, N.C.: Duke University Press, 1967. Excellent listing for each western state and other lists for the Western and regionalism; very useful.

50. Griffith, Doris, et al. "A Regional Bibliography." *Western Humanities Review* 6 (1952): 207-12.

51. Hanna, Archibald. "Western Americana Collectors and Collections." *Western Historical Quarterly* 2 (October 1971): 401-4.

52. Harvey, Alice G. *Nebraska Writers.* Rev. ed. Omaha: The Author, 1964.

53. Haslam, Gerald. "Who Speaks for the Earth?" *English Journal* 63 (January 1973): 42-48. Ecology and literature. Includes selected bibliography of American Indian, western American, and nature literature.

54. Havlice, Patricia Pate. *Index to American Author Bibliographies.* Metuchen, N.J.: Scarecrow Press, 1971.

55. Hill, Gertrude. "The Southwest in Verse: A Selective Bibliography of Arizona and New Mexican Poetry." *Arizona Quarterly* 23 (Winter 1967): 306-12.

56. Hotchkiss, Jeanette. *American Historical Fiction and Biography for Children and Young People.* Metuchen, N.J.: Scarecrow Press, 1973.

57. Howard, Patsy C. *Theses in American Literature, 1896-1971.* Ann Arbor, Mich.: Pierian Press, 1973.

58. Jacobson, Angeline, comp. *Contemporary Native American Literature: A Selected and Partially Annotated Bibliography.* Metuchen, N.J.: Scarecrow Press, 1977.

59. Jones, Howard Mumford. *Guide to American Literature and Its Backgrounds since 1890.* 4th ed., rev. and enl. Cambridge, Mass.: Harvard University Press, 1972.

60. Keller, Richard. "Annual Bibliography of Studies in Western American Literature." *Western American Literature.* 1977-. Issued each year in the Winter issue.

61. Kherdian, David. *Six Poets of the San Francisco Renaissance.* Fresno, Calif.: Giligia Press, 1967.

62. Kimball, Richard R. "Beginnings of Literature Based on the American Frontier: Descriptive Bibliography." Master's thesis, University of Southern California, 1950.

63. Kirby, David K. *American Fiction to 1900: A Guide to Information Sources.* Detroit: Gale Research, 1975.

64. Kurtz, Kenneth. *Literature of the American Southwest: A*

Selective Bibliography. Los Angeles: Occidental College, 1956.

65. Leary, Lewis. *American Literature: A Study and Research Guide.* New York: St. Martin's Press, 1976.

66. ———. *Articles on American Literature, 1950-1967.* Durham, N.C.: Duke University Press, 1970.

67. ———. *Articles on American Literature, 1968-1975.* Durham, N.C.: Duke University Press, 1979.

68. Lepper, Gary M. *A Bibliographical Introduction to Seventy-five Modern American Authors.* Berkeley, Calif.: Serendipity Books, 1976.

69. Logasa, Hannah. *Regional United States: A Subject List.* Boston, 1942.

70. Lyon, Thomas J., ed. "Research in Western American Literature." *Western American Literature,* 1966-. Appears annually in the Winter issue and lists theses and dissertations completed or in program on western American literature.

71. McLean, Malcolm. "In the Beginning." *Southwestern American Literature* I (January 1971): 5-7.

72. McNamee, Lawrence F. *Dissertations in English and American Literature . . . 1865-1964.* New York: R. R. Bowker, 1968; *Supplement One . . . 1964-1968,* 1969.

73. Maguire, James H. "A Selected Bibliography of Western American Drama." *Western American*

Literature 14 (Summer 1979): 149-63.

74. Major, Mabel, and T. M. Pearce. *Southwest Heritage: A Literary History with Bibliographies.* 3d ed., rev. and enl. Albuquerque: University of New Mexico Press, 1972.

75. Meyer, Roy W. "An Annotated Bibliography of Middle Western Farm Fiction, 1891-1962." *The Middle Western Farm Novel in the Twentieth Century.* Lincoln: University of Nebraska Press, 1965, pp. 200-242.

76. Milton, John R., ed. "Selected Bibliography of Materials Relating to the Western American Novel." *South Dakota Review* 2 (Autumn 1964): 101-8; 4 (Summer 1966): 79-80.

77. *MLA International Bibliography.* Published annually in hard covers and includes a large section on American literature.

78. Nilon, Charles H. *Bibliography of Bibliographies in American Literature.* New York: R. R. Bowker, 1970. The best single source for general bibliographies.

79. *Northwest Books.* Portland, Oreg.: Binfords and Mort, 1942.

80. Oaks, Priscilla. *Minority Studies: A Selective Annotated Bibliography.* Boston: G. K. Hall, 1976.

81. Pady, Donald. "Annual Bibliography of Studies in Midwestern Literature." *Mid America,* 1975-.

82. Paluka, Frank. *Iowa Authors: A*

Bio-Bibliography of Sixty Native Writers. Iowa City: Friends of the University of Iowa Libraries, 1967.

83. Patterson-Black, Sheryll and Gene. *Western Women: In History and Literature.* Crawford, Nebr.: Cottonwood Press, 1978. Most useful for its extensive bibliographies.

84. Paul, Rodman W., and Richard W. Etulain. *The Frontier and American West.* Goldentree Bibliographies in American History. Arlington Heights, Ill.: AHM Publishing Corporation, 1977.

85. Polk, Noel, comp. "*Guide to Dissertations on American Literary Figures,* 1870-1910: Part One." *American Literary Realism 1870-1910* 8 (Summer 1975): 177-280.

86. Pollard, Lancaster. "A Check List of Washington Authors," *Pacific Northwest Quarterly* 31 (1940): 3-96; 35 (1944): 233-66.

87. Pownall, David. *Articles on Twentieth Century Literature: An Annotated Bibliography, 1954 to 1970.* 6 vols. New York: Kraus-Thomson, 1973-78. An ongoing, annotated listing taken from *Twentieth Century Literature.*

88. Powell, Lawrence Clark. *Heart of the Southwest: A Selected Bibliography of Novels, Stories, and Tales Laid in Arizona and New Mexico and Adjacent Lands.* Los Angeles: Dawson's Book Shop, 1955.

89. Robbins, J. Albert, et al., comps. *American Literary Manuscripts: A Checklist of Holdings in Academic, Historical, and Public Libraries, Museums, and Authors' Homes in the United States.* Athens: University of Georgia Press, 1977. Lists the major manuscript collections of the leading western writers.

90. Roemer, Kenneth M. "American Utopian Literature (1888-1900): An Annotated Bibliography." *American Literary Realism 1870-1910* 4 (Summer 1971): 227-54.

91. Rosa, Alfred F., and Paul A. Eschholz. *Contemporary Fiction in America and England, 1950-1970: A Guide to Information Sources.* Detroit: Gale Research, 1976.

92. Rubin, Louis D., ed. *A Bibliographical Guide to the Study of Southern Literature.* Baton Rouge: Louisiana State University Press, 1969.

93. Rundell, Walter, Jr. "Interpretations of the American West: A Descriptive Bibliography." *Arizona and the West* 3 (Spring 1961): 69-88; (Summer 1961): 148-68.

94. Rusk, Ralph Leslie. *The Literature of the Middle Western Frontier.* 2 vols. New York: Columbia University Press, 1925.

95. Sackett, S. J., comp. "Master's Theses in Literature." *Lit* 8 (November 1967): 45-174.

96. Schwartz, Narda Lacey. *Articles on Women Writers: A Bibliography.* Santa Barbara, Calif.:

ABC-Clio, 1977. A very useful listing.

97. Smith, Dwight L., comp. *The American and Canadian West: A Bibliography.* 3 vols. Santa Barbara, Calif.: ABC-Clio Press, 1979.

98. Streeter, Thomas W. "Notes on North American Regional Bibliographies." *Papers of the Bibliographical Society of America* 36 (1942): 171-86.

99. Stronks, James. "Supplements to the Standard Bibliographies of Crane, Dreiser, Frederick, Fuller, Garland, London, and Norris." *American Literary Realism 1870-1910* 11 (Spring 1978): 124-33.

100. Tonsfeldt, Ward, comp. "The Pacific Northwest: A Selected and Annotated Bibliography." *Northwest Perspectives: Essays on the Culture of the Pacific Northwest.* Eds. Edwin R. Bingham and Glen A. Love. Seattle: University of Washington Press, 1979, pp. 219-35. Lists primary and secondary literary items.

101. Uzendoski, Emily Jane. "A Handlist of Nebraska Authors." Doctoral dissertation, University of Nebraska, Lincoln, 1976. Bibliography of Nebraska authors.

102. Van Derhoff, Jack. *A Bibliography of Novels Related to American Frontier and Colonial History.* Troy, N.Y.: Whitston Publishing Company, 1971.

103. Wagner, H. R. *The Plains and the Rockies: A Bibliography of Original Narratives of Travel and Adventure, 1800-1865.* San Francisco, 1921.

104. Weber, F. J. "A Bibliography of California Bibliographies." *Southern California Quarterly* 50 (March 1968): 5-32.

105. West, Ray B. *Writing in the Rocky Mountains with a Bibliography by Nellie Cliff.* Lincoln: University of Nebraska Press, 1947.

106. Wheeler, Eva F. "A Bibliography of Wyoming Writers." *University of Wyoming Publications* 6 (1939): 11-37.

107. White, Barbara. *American Women Writers: An Annotated Bibliography of Criticism.* New York: Garland, 1977.

108. *Women and Literature: An Annotated Bibliography of Women Writers.* 3d ed. Cambridge, Mass.: Women and Literature Collective, 1976. American writers, pp. 1-93.

109. Woodress, James. *American Fiction, 1900-1950: A Guide to Information Sources.* Detroit: Gale Research Company, 1974.

110. ——. *Dissertations in American Literature 1891-1966.* Durham, N.C.: Duke University Press, 1968.

111. ——, ed. *Eight American Authors.* Rev. ed. New York: W. W. Norton, 1972.

112. Wright, Frances Valentine, ed. *Who's Who Among Pacific Northwest Authors.* 2d ed. Missoula: University of Montana Press, 1969.

11

ANTHOLOGIES

113. Apple, Max, ed. *Southwest Fiction.* New York: Bantam Books, 1980, 1981.

114. Babcock, C. Merton. *The American Frontier: A Social and Literary Record.* New York: Holt, Rinehart and Winston, 1965.

115. Becker, May L. *Golden Tales of the Far West.* New York: Dodd, Mead, 1935.

116. Bergon, Frank, and Zeese Papanikolas, eds. *Looking Far West: The Search for the American West in History, Myth, and Literature.* New York: New American Library, 1978.

117. Blacker, Irwin R. *The Old West in Fiction.* New York: I. Obolensky, 1961.

118. Botkin, Benjamin Albert, ed. *A Treasury of Western Folklore.* New York: Crown, 1944.

119. Boyer, Mary G. *Arizona in Literature.* Glendale, Calif.: Arthur H. Clark, 1934.

120. Carlson, Roy, ed. *Contemporary Northwest Writing: A Collection of Poetry and Fiction.* Corvallis: Oregon State University Press, 1979.

121. Caughey, John and LaRee, eds. *California Heritage.* Los Angeles: Ward Ritchie Press, 1962; rev. ed., Itasca, Ill.: F. E. Peacock, 1971.

122. Coggeshall, William T. *The Poets and Poetry of the West.* Columbus: Follett, Foster, 1860.

123. Coleman, Rufus A. *The Golden West in Story and Verse.* New York: Harper, 1932.

124. Collier, Ned, ed. *Great Stories of the West.* Garden City, N.Y.: Doubleday, 1971. Collected from *West*, a pulp magazine of the 1920s and 1930s.

125. Cummings, D. Duane, and William Gee White, eds. *The American Frontier.* New York: Benziger Brothers, 1968.

126. Davidson, Levette J. *Poems of the Old West: A Rocky Mountain Anthology.* Denver, Colo.: University of Denver Press, 1951.

127. ———, and Forrester Blake. *Rocky Mountain Tales.* Norman: University of Oklahoma Press, 1947.

128. ———, and Prudence Bostwick. *The Literature of the Rocky Mountain West, 1803-1903.* Caldwell, Idaho: Caxton Printers, 1939.

129. Day, A. Grove. *The Sky Clears: Poetry of the American Indians.* Lincoln: University of Nebraska Press, 1964.

130. Durham, Philip, and Everett L. Jones, eds. *The Frontier in American Literature.* New York: Odyssey Press, 1969.

131. ———. *The Western Story: Fact, Fiction and Myth.* New York: Harcourt Brace Jovanovich, 1975.

132. Elder, Gary, ed. *The Far Side of*

12

the Storm: New Ranges of Western Fiction. Los Cerillos, N.Mex.: San Marcos Press, 1975.

133. Flanagan, John T., ed. America is West: An Anthology of Midlewestern Life and Literature. Minneapolis: University of Minnesota Press, 1945.

134. Frederick, John T., ed. Out of the Midwest: An Anthology of Midwestern Writing. New York: Whittlesey House, 1944.

135. Gallagher, William D. Selections from the Poetical Literature of the West. Cincinnati: U. P. James, 1841.

136. Greenberg, David B., comp. The Land Our Fathers Plowed. Norman: University of Oklahoma Press, 1969.

137. Greenway, John. Folklore of the Great West. Palo Alto, Calif.: American West, 1969.

138. Gregg, John J. and Barbara, eds. Best Loved Poems of the American West. Garden City, N.Y.: Doubleday, 1980.

139. Griego y Maestas, José. Cuentos: Tales from the Hispanic Southwest. Trans. Rudolfo A. Anaya. Santa Fe: Museum of New Mexico, 1980.

140. Haslam, Gerald W., and James D. Houston, eds. California Heartland: Writing from the Great Central Valley. Santa Barbara, Calif.: Capra Press, 1978.

141. Hine, Robert V., and Edwin R. Bingham, eds. The Frontier Experience: Readings in the Trans-Mississippi West. Belmont, Calif.: Wadsworth, 1963.

142. Hoffman, Hans A. Poets of the Western Scene: Poems from Westward, a National Magazine of Verse. San Leandro, Calif., 1937.

143. Holbrook, Stewart H., ed. Promised Land: A Collection of Northwest Writing. New York: Whittlesey House, 1945.

144. Inge, M. Thomas, ed. The Frontier Humorists: Critical Views. Hampden, Conn.: Archon Books, 1975.

145. Jackson, Joseph Henry, ed. Continent's End: A Collection of California Writing. New York: Whittlesey House, 1944.

146. Kopp, Karl, Jane [Kopp], and Bart Lanier Stafford, III. Southwest: A Contemporary Anthology. Albuquerque: Red Earth Press, 1977.

147. Larson, Clinton, and William Stafford, eds. Modern Poetry of Western America. Provo, Utah: Brigham Young University Press, 1975.

148. Lee, Charles, ed. North, East, South, West: A Regional Anthology of American Writing. New York: Howell, Soskin, 1945.

149. Lee, W. Storrs, ed. California: A Literary Chronicle. New York: Funk and Wagnalls, 1969. See also Storrs's anthology of Colorado writing.

150. ———. Washington State: A Literary Chronicle. New York: Funk and Wagnalls, 1969.

151. Lomax, John A., coll. Cowboy Songs and Other Frontier

Ballads. New York: Macmillan, 1927.

152. Lucia, Ellis. *This Land Around Us: A Treasury of Pacific Northwest Writing.* Garden City, N.Y.: Doubleday, 1969.

153. Lyons, Richard, ed. *Poetry North.* Fargo: North Dakota Institute for Regional Studies, 1970.

154. Major, Mabel, and Thomas M. Pearce, eds. *Signature of the Sun: Southwest Verse 1900-1950.* Albuquerque: University of New Mexico Press, 1950.

155. Maule, Harry E., ed. *Great Tales of the American West.* New York: Modern Library, 1945.

156. Meltzer, David, ed. *The San Francisco Poets.* New York: Ballantine Books, 1971.

157. Meredith, Scott. *Bar 1: Roundup of Best Western Stories.* New York: Dutton, 1952.

158. ——. *Bar 2: Roundup of Best Western Stories.* New York: Dutton, 1953. Meredith later edited several other anthologies of this type.

159. Milton, John R., ed. *The Literature of South Dakota.* Vermillion: University of South Dakota Press, 1976.

160. Newman, Mary W., ed. *Poetry of the Pacific: Selections and Original Poems.* . . . San Francisco: Pacific, 1867.

161. Pearce, Thomas M., and A. P. Thomason, eds. *Southwesterners Write.* Albuquerque: University of New Mexico Press, 1947.

162. ——, and Telfair Hendon, eds. *America in the Southwest: A Regional Anthology.* Albuquerque: University of New Mexico Press, 1933.

163. Perry, George Sessions, ed. *Roundup Time: A Collection of South-Western Writing.* New York: Whittlesey House, 1943.

164. Powell, Lawrence Clark. *California Classics: The Creative Literature of the Golden State.* Los Angeles: Ward Ritchie Press, [1971].

165. Rowland, Connie M. Payne. "An Anthology of Western Literature for High Schools." Master's thesis, Idaho State University, 1972.

166. Schaefer, Jack. *Out West: An Anthology of Stories.* Boston: Houghton Mifflin, 1955.

167. Shockley, Martin, ed. *Southwest Writers Anthology.* Austin, Tex.: Steck-Vaughn, 1967.

168. Silber, Irwin. *Songs of the Great American West.* New York: Macmillan, 1967.

169. Sonnichsen, C. L. *The Southwest in Life and Literature.* New York: Devin-Adair, 1962.

170. Spence, Clark C., ed. *The American West: A Source Book.* New York: Thomas Y. Crowell, 1966.

171. Sterling, George, et al. *Continent's End.* San Francisco: J. H. Nash, 1925.

172. Stevens, A. Wilbur, ed. *Poems Southwest.* Prescott, Ariz.: Prescott College Press, 1968.

173. Strelow, Michael, et al. *An Anthology of Northwest Writing 1900-1950.* Eugene, Oreg.:

Northwest Review Books, 1979.

174. Targ, William, ed. *Western Story Omnibus.* Cleveland: World, 1945.

175. Taylor, J. Golden, ed. *Great Western Short Stories.* Palo Alto, Calif.: American West, 1967. Still the best collection available.

176. ——. *The Literature of the American West.* Boston: Houghton Mifflin, 1971. The most useful textbook anthology.

177. Thorp, N. Howard ("Jack"). *Songs of the Cowboys.* Eds. Austin E. and Alta S. Fife. New York: Clarkson N. Potter, 1966.

178. Trusky, A. Thomas. *Women Poets of the West: An Anthology, 1850–1950.* Boise, Idaho: Ahsahta Press, 1978.

179. Ward, Don, ed. *Great Short Novels of the American West.* New York: E. P. Dutton, 1946.

180. ——. *Wild Streets: Tales of the Frontier Towns, by Members of the Western Writers of America.* Garden City, N.Y.: Doubleday, 1958.

181. West, Ray B., ed. *The Rocky Mountain Reader.* New York: E. P. Dutton, 1946.

182. *A Western Sample: Nine Contemporary Poets.* Georgetown, Calif., 1963.

183. Winters, Yvor. *Poets of the Pacific, Second Series.* Stanford, Calif.: Stanford University Press, 1949.

GENERAL WORKS

BOOKS, DISSERTATIONS, AND THESES

184. Ahearn, Kerry D. "Aspects of the Contemporary American Western Novel." Doctoral dissertation. Ohio University, 1974.

185. Ahnebrink, Lars. *The Beginnings of Naturalism in American Fiction: A Study of the Works of Hamlin Garland, Stephen Crane, and Frank Norris.* Cambridge, Mass.: Harvard University Press, 1950.

186. Allen, Martha Mitten. "Women in the West: A Study of Book-length Travel Accounts by Women Who Traveled in the Plains and Rockies, with Special Attention to General Concepts that Women Applied to the Plains, the Mountains, Westerners and the West in General." Doctoral dissertation, University of Texas, Austin, 1972.

187. Alter, Judith. "The Western Myth in American Painting and Fiction of the Late 19th and Early 20th Centuries." Doctoral dissertation, Texas Christian University, 1970.

15

188. Andrews, Clarence A. *A Literary History of Iowa.* Iowa City: University of Iowa Press, 1972.
189. Bankston, Darena. "Pioneering on the Plains as Portrayed by American Women Novelists." Master's thesis, Texas Christian University, 1966.
190. Barnes, Robert. "Novels of the Oil Industry in the Southwest." *Southwestern American Literature* 2 (Fall 1972): 74-82.
191. Barnett, Louise K. *The Ignoble Savage: American Literary Racism, 1790-1890.* Westport, Conn.: Greenwood Press, 1975.
192. Barsness, John A. "The Breaking of the Myth: A Study of the Cultural Implications in the Western Novel in the Twentieth Century." Doctoral dissertation, University of Minnesota, 1966.
193. Berthoff, Warner. *The Ferment of Realism: American Literature, 1884-1919.* New York: Free Press, 1965.
194. Billington, Ray Allen. *Land of Savagery/Land of Promise: The European Image of the American Frontier in the Nineteenth Century.* New York: W. W. Norton, 1981.
195. Bingham, Edwin R., and Glen A. Love, eds. *Northwest Perspectives: Essays on the Culture of the Pacific Northwest.* Seattle: University of Washington Press, 1979. Includes several essays on Northwest literary culture.
196. Blaine, Harold A. "The Frontiersman in American Prose and Fiction, 1800-1860." Doctoral dissertation, Western Reserve University, 1936.
197. Blair, Walter, and Franklin J. Meine. *Half Horse, Half Alligator: The Growth of the Mike Fink Legend.* Chicago: University of Chicago Press, 1956.
198. Blatt, Muriel Rosen. "Making California American: Poetry and Culture, 1866-1925." Doctoral dissertation, University of California, Irvine, 1977.
199. Boatright, Mody C. *Folk Laughter on the American Frontier.* New York: Collier Books, 1961.
200. Bogard, William J. "The West as Cultural Image at the End of the Nineteenth Century." Doctoral dissertation, Tulane University, 1970.
201. Boynton, Percy H. *The Rediscovery of the Frontier.* Chicago: University of Chicago Press, 1931.
202. Branch, E. Douglas. *The Cowboy and His Interpreters.* New York: D. Appleton, 1926; New York: Cooper Square, 1961.
203. Brenner, Gerald J. "The New Western: Studies in Modern Western American Literature." Doctoral dissertation, University of New Mexico, 1969.
204. Bridges, Emily. *The Great West: In Fact and Fiction.* University of North Carolina Library Extension Publication 18 (January 1953).
205. Brier, Howard. *Sawdust Empire:*

The Pacific Northwest. New York: Alfred A. Knopf, 1958.

206. Brooks, Van Wyck. *The Confident Years: 1885-1915.* New York: E. P. Dutton, 1952.

207. Butler, Michael D. "The Literary Landscape of the Trans-Mississippi West: 1826-1902." Doctoral dissertation, University of Illinois, 1971.

208. Calder, Jenni. *There Must Be a Lone Ranger: The American West in Film and in Reality.* New York: Taplinger, 1974.

209. Campbell, Walter S. *The Book Lover's Southwest.* Norman: University of Oklahoma Press, 1955.

210. Chase, Richard. *The American Novel and Its Tradition.* Garden City, N.Y.: Doubleday, 1957.

211. Chittick, V. L. O., ed. *Northwest Harvest: A Regional Stocktaking.* New York: Macmillan, 1948.

212. Clark, M. Bruce. "The Desert in American Literature." Master's thesis, Sonoma State College, 1971.

213. Clevenger, Darnell Haines. "A Comparative Study of the Frontier in the Literatures of Spanish America and the United States." Doctoral dissertation, Indiana University, 1974.

214. Clifford, John. "Social and Political Attitudes of Fiction of Ranch and Range." Doctoral dissertation, University of Iowa, 1954.

215. Clough, Wilson O. *The Necessary Earth.* Austin: University of Texas Press, 1964.

216. Colquitt, Betsy F. *A Part of Space: Ten Texas Writers.* Fort Worth: Texas Christian University Press, 1969.

217. Crooks, Alan Franklin. "Walk-Down: A Play with Two Essays." Doctoral dissertation, University of Utah, 1972.

218. Crow, Charles L., ed. *Itinerary: Criticism, Essays on California Writers.* Bowling Green, Ohio: University Press, 1978.

219. Culmsee, Carlton F. *Malign Nature and the Frontier.* Logan: Utah State University Press, 1959.

220. Davis, Joseph Addison. "Rolling Home: The Open Road as Myth and Symbol in American Literature, 1890-1940." Doctoral dissertation, University of Michigan, 1974.

221. Deahl, William Evans, Jr. "A History of Buffalo Bill's Wild West Show, 1883-1913." Doctoral dissertation, Southern Illinois University, 1974.

222. DeMenil, Alexander Nicholas. *The Literature of the Louisiana Territory.* St. Louis: St. Lewis News, 1904.

223. DeShong, Charles Thomas. "Virgin Land Revisited: Imaginary Gardens, Real Toads." Doctoral dissertation, University of Tulsa, 1974.

224. Dickinson, Donald C., W. David Laird, and Margaret F. Maxwell, eds. *Voices from the Southwest: A Gathering in Honor of Lawrence Clark*

Powell. Flagstaff, Ariz.: Northland Press, 1976.

225. Dobie, J. Frank. *Guide to Life and Literature of the Southwest.* Dallas: Southern Methodist University Press, 1943, 1952.

226. Dondore, Dorothy. *The Prairie and the Making of Middle America.* Cedar Rapids, Iowa: Torch Press, 1926.

227. Durham, Philip, and Everett L. Jones. *The Negro Cowboys.* New York: Dodd, Mead, 1965.

228. Emmons, David M. *Garden in the Grasslands: Boomer Literature of the Central Great Plains.* Lincoln: University of Nebraska Press, 1971.

229. Erisman, Fred, and Richard W. Etulain, eds. *Fifty Western Writers: A Bio-Bibliographical Guide.* Westport, Conn.: Greenwood Press, 1982.

230. Etulain, Richard W., ed. *The American Literary West.* Manhattan, Kans.: Sunflower University Press, 1980. Reprints the ten essays appearing in *Journal of the West,* January 1980.

231. Evans, James Leroy. "The Indian Savage, the Mexican Bandit, the Chinese Heathen—Three Popular Stereotypes." Doctoral dissertation, University of Texas, 1967.

232. Ferlinghetti, Lawrence, and Nancy J. Peters. *Literary San Francisco: A Pictorial History from the Beginnings to the Present Day.* San Francisco: City Lights Books and Harper and Row, 1980.

233. Fiedler, Leslie. *The Return of the Vanishing American.* New York: Stein and Day, 1968.

234. Fielding, Lavina. "Attitudes Toward Experience in Western Travel Narratives." Doctoral dissertation, University of Washington, 1975.

235. ——. "The Frontier and Israeli Literature." Master's thesis, Brigham Young University, 1971.

236. Fishwick, Marshall. *The American Hero: Myth and Reality.* Washington: Public Affairs Press, 1954.

237. Fitzmaurice, James Earl. "Migration Epics of the Trans-Mississippi West." Doctoral dissertation, University of Maryland, 1974.

238. Fleck, Byron Y. "The West as Viewed by Foreign Travelers, 1783-1840." Doctoral dissertation, University of Iowa, 1950.

239. Folsom, James K. *The American Western Novel.* New Haven, Conn.: College and University Press, 1966.

240. ——, ed. *The Western: A Collection of Critical Essays.* Englewood Cliffs, N.J.: Prentice-Hall, 1979.

241. Franklin, Wayne. *Discoverers, Explorers, Settlers: The Diligent Writers of Early America.* Chicago: University of Chicago Press, 1979.

242. Frantz, Joe B., and Julian E. Choate, Jr. *The American Cowboy: The Myth and the Reality.*

Norman: University of Oklahoma Press, 1955.

243. Fussell, Edwin. *Frontier: American Literature and the American West.* Princeton, N.J.: Princeton University Press, 1965.

244. Galinski, Hans, ed. *The Frontier in American History and Literature.* Verlag Moritz Diesterweg, 1960.

245. Gard, Wayne. *Reminiscenses of Range Life.* Southwest Writers Series, No. 30. Austin, Tex.: Steck-Vaughn, 1970.

246. Gaston, Edwin, W., Jr. *The Early Novel of the Southwest.* Albuquerque: University of New Mexico Press, 1961.

247. Gottfried, Herbert Wilson. "Spatiality and the Frontier: Spatial Themes in Western American Painting and Literature." Doctoral dissertation, Ohio University, 1974.

248. Gurian, Jay. *Western American Writing: Tradition and Promise.* Deland, Fla.: Everett/Edwards, 1975.

249. Hafer, John William. "The Sea of Grass: The Image of the Great Plains in the American Novel." Doctoral dissertation, Northern Illinois University, 1975.

250. Hairston, Joel Beck. "Westerner's Dilemma: A Study of Modern Western Fiction." Doctoral dissertation, University of Minnesota, 1971.

251. Hardwick, Bonnie Skell. "Science and Art: The Travel Writings of the Great Surveys of the American West after the Civil War." Doctoral dissertation, University of Pennsylvania, 1977.

252. Harkness, David James. *The Literary Midwest.* University of Tennessee News Letter 37 (February 1958).

253. ———. *Literary Trails of the Western States.* University of Tennessee News Letter 34 (July 1955).

254. ———. *The Southwest and West Coast in Literature.* University of Tennessee News Letter 33 (October 1954).

255. Hart, James D. *A Companion to California.* New York: Oxford University Press, 1978.

256. Hazard, Lucy Lockwood. *The Frontier in American Literature.* New York: Thomas Y. Crowell, 1927; New York: F. Ungar, 1961.

257. Hazel, Erik R. "The Hollywood Image: An Examination of the Literary Perspective." Doctoral dissertation, Case Western Reserve University, 1974.

258. Herron, Ima Honaker. *The Small Town in American Literature.* Durham, N.C.: Duke University Press, 1939.

259. Hilfer, Anthony Channell. *The Revolt from the Village, 1915–1930.* Chapel Hill: University of North Carolina Press, 1969.

260. Hodgins, Francis E., Jr. "The Literary Emancipation of a Region: The Changing Image of the American West in Fiction." Doctoral dissertation, Michigan State University, 1957.

261. Howard, Richard. *Alone with America: Essays on the Art of*

Poetry in the United States. New York: Atheneum, 1969.

262. Hubbell, Jay B. *South and Southwest: Literary Essays and Reminiscences.* Durham, N.C.: Duke University Press, 1965.

263. Hudson, Ruth, et al. *Studies in Literature of the West: University of Wyoming Publications.* Laramie: University of Wyoming, 1956.

264. Humphrey, William. *Ah, Wilderness! The Frontier in American Literature.* Literature Series, Number Two. University of Texas at El Paso: Texas Western Press, 1977. A brief lecture by a well-known Texas novelist; primarily about the nineteenth century.

265. Huseboe, Arthur R., and William Geyer, eds. *Where the West Begins: Essays on Middle Border and Siouxland Writing, in Honor of Herbert Krause.* Sioux Falls, S.Dak.: Center for Western Studies Press, 1978.

266. Ifkovic, Edward Joseph. "God's Country and the Woman: The Development of an American Identity in the Popular Novel, 1893-1913." Doctoral dissertation, University of Massachusetts, 1972.

267. *Interpretative Approaches to Western American Literature.* Pocatello: Idaho State University Press, 1972. The contents of this book are identical to those of *Rendezvous* 7 (Winter 1972).

268. Jacobs, Elijah L., and Forrest E. Wolverton. *Missouri Writers: A Literary History of Missouri, 1780-1955.* St. Louis: State Publishing, 1955.

269. Jacobson, Harvey K. "A Study of Novels About North Dakota." Master's thesis, University of North Dakota, 1956.

270. Johannsen, Albert. *The House of Beadle and Adams and Its Dime and Nickel Novels.* 2 vols. Norman: University of Oklahoma Press, 1950; supplement, 1962.

271. Johnson, Kenneth. "The Lost Eden: The New World in American Nature Writing." Doctoral dissertation, University of New Mexico, 1973.

272. Jones, Howard Mumford. *The Frontier in American Fiction: Four Lectures on the Relation of Landscape to Literature.* Jerusalem: Magness Press, Hebrew University, 1956.

273. Jones, Joel M. "Everyman's Usable Past: The American Historical Novel." Doctoral dissertation, University of New Mexico, 1966.

274. Karolides, Nicholas J. *The Pioneer in the American Novel: 1900-1950.* Norman: University of Oklahoma Press, 1967.

275. Kay, Arthur M. "The Epic Intent and the American Dream: The Westering Theme in Modern American Poetry." Doctoral dissertation, Columbia University, 1961.

276. Keiser, Albert. *The Indian in American Literature.* New York: Oxford University Press, 1933.

277. Kennedy, Sister Patricia. "The Pioneer Woman in Middle

Western Fiction." Doctoral dissertation, University of Illinois, 1968.

278. Lamar, Howard R., ed. *The Reader's Encyclopedia of the American West*. New York: Thomas Y. Crowell, 1977. Includes entries on many western authors and subjects.

279. Leach, Joseph. *The Typical Texan: Biography of an American Myth*. Dallas: Southern Methodist University Press, 1952.

280. Lee, Lawrence L., and Merrill E. Lewis, eds. *Women, Women Writers, and the West*. Troy, N.Y.: Whitston, 1978.

281. Lee, Robert Edson. *From West to East: Studies in the Literature of the American West*. Urbana: University of Illinois Press, 1966.

282. Leisy, Ernest E. *The American Historical Novel*. Norman: University of Oklahoma Press, 1950.

283. Lewis, Merrill E. "American Frontier History as Literature: Studies in Historiography of George Bancroft, Frederick Jackson Turner, and Theodore Roosevelt." Doctoral dissertation, University of Utah, 1968.

284. ——, and L. L. Lee, eds. *The Westering Experience in American Literature: Bicentennial Essays*. Bellingham: Bureau for Faculty Research, Western Washington University, 1977. A collection of 23 interpretive essays.

285. Lyon, Peter. *The Wild Wild West*. New York: Funk and Wagnalls, 1969.

286. McDermott, John Francis, ed. *Travelers on the Western Frontier*. Urbana: University of Illinois Press, 1970.

287. McElhiney, Annette Bennington. "The Image of the Pioneer Woman in the American Novel." Doctoral dissertation, University of Denver, 1978.

288. McMurtry, Larry. *In a Narrow Grave: Essays on Texas*. Austin, Tex.: Encino Press, 1968.

289. Mahon, Robert Lee. "The Use of Adam and Eve as Conventions in the American Western Novel of the Twentieth Century." Doctoral dissertation, University of Notre Dame, 1975.

290. Marovitz, Sanford E. "Frontier Conflicts, Villains, Outlaws, and Indians in Selected Western Fiction, 1799–1860." Doctoral dissertation, Duke University, 1968.

291. Martin, Jay. *Harvests of Change: American Literature 1865–1914*. Englewood Cliffs, N.J.: Prentice-Hall, 1967.

292. Mattson, Jeremy. "The Conflict of Civilization and Wilderness." Doctoral dissertation, Ohio State University, 1972.

293. Meyer, Roy W. *The Middle Western Farm Novel in the Twentieth Century*. Lincoln: University of Nebraska Press, 1965.

294. Miles, Elton. *Southwest Humorists*. Southwest Writers Series, No. 26. Austin, Tex.: Steck-Vaughn, 1969.

295. Milton, John R. *The Novel of the American West*. Lincoln: University of Nebraska Press,

1980. The most important book on this large subject.

296. Mitchell, Lee Clark. *Witness to a Vanishing America: The Nineteenth-Century Response.* Princeton, N.J.: Princeton University Press, 1981.

297. Morgan, David Lee. "Frontier Themes in Science Fiction." Doctoral dissertation, University of Colorado, Boulder, 1977. Parallels between literature of the American frontier and science fiction.

298. Morgan, H. Wayne. *American Writers in Rebellion from Twain to Dreiser.* New York: Hill and Wang, 1965.

299. Morris, Wright. *The Territory Ahead.* New York: Harcourt, Brace and World, 1958.

300. Mossberg, Krister Lennart. "The Emigrant Voice as American Literature: Scandinavian Emigrant Fiction of the American West." Doctoral dissertation, Indiana University, 1979.

301. ———. *Scandinavian Immigrant Literature.* Western Writers Series, No. 47. Boise, Idaho: Boise State University, 1981.

302. Nash, Roderick. *Wilderness and the American Mind.* Rev. ed. New Haven: Yale University Press, 1973.

303. Nelson, Herbert B. *The Literary Impulse in Pioneer Oregon.* Corvallis: Oregon State College Press, 1948.

304. Nelson, Solveig Leraas. "Mountain Man: Fact and Fiction." Doctoral dissertation, Drake University, 1978.

305. Noble, David W. *The Eternal Adam and the New World Garden: The Central Myth in the American Novel Since 1830.* New York: George Brazillier, 1968.

306. Noel, Mary. *Villains Galore . . . the Heyday of the Popular Story Weekly.* New York: Macmillan, 1954.

307. Paine, Doris M., and Diana Martinez. *Guide to the Literature of the American West.* New York: Bantam Books, 1975. A 45-page booklet; primarily for high school students.

308. Parker, Robert Brown. "The Violent Hero, Wilderness Heritage and Urban Reality." Doctoral dissertation, Boston University, 1971.

309. Payne, Leonidas W. *A Survey of Texas Literature.* New York: Rand McNally, 1928.

310. Pearce, Roy Harvey. *The Savages of America: A Study of the Indian and the Idea of Civilization.* Baltimore: The Johns Hopkins Press, 1953.

311. Peterson, Levi. "The Ambivalence of Alienation: The Debate Over Frontier Freedom in the Quality Western Novel of the Twentieth Century." Doctoral dissertation, University of Utah, 1965.

312. Pilkington, William T. *Imagining Texas: The Literature of the Lone Star State.* Boston: American Press, 1981.

313. ———. *My Country's Blood: Studies in Southwestern Literature.*

Fort Worth: Texas Christian University Press, 1973.

314. ——, ed. *Critical Essays on the Western American Novel.* Boston: G. K. Hall, 1980. Collects 24 useful essays.

315. Pizer, Donald. *Realism and Naturalism in 19th Century American Literature.* Carbondale: Southern Illinois University Press, 1966.

316. Pohlmann, John Ogden. "California's Mission Myth." Doctoral dissertation, University of California, Los Angeles, 1974.

317. Potter, Richard Harold. "Rural Life in Populist America: A Study of Short Fiction as Historical Evidence." Doctoral dissertation, University of Maryland, 1971.

318. Poulsen, Richard Carl. "The Mountainman Vernacular: Its Historical Roots, Its Linguistic Nature, and Its Literary Uses." Doctoral dissertation, University of Utah, 1976.

319. Powell, Lawrence Clark. *California Classics: The Creative Literature of the Golden State.* Los Angeles: Ward Ritchie Press, 1971.

320. ——. *Southwest Classics: The Creative Literature of the Arid Lands: Essays on the Books and Their Writers.* Los Angeles: Ward Ritchie Press, 1974.

321. Powers, Alfred. *History of Oregon Literature.* Portland: Metropolitan Press, 1935.

322. Prince, Richard John. "To Arrive Where We Started: Archetypes of the American Eden in Popular Culture." Doctoral dissertation, University of Michigan, 1977.

323. *Prose and Poetry of the Livestock Industry of the United States.* Denver: National Live Stock Historical Association, 1905.

324. Pugh, David William. "A Study in Literary, Social, and University History: The Life and Often Hard Times of the *New Mexico Quarterly,* 1931-1969." Doctoral dissertation, University of New Mexico, 1975.

325. Quinn, Roland Joseph. "The Modest Seduction: The Experience of Pioneer Women on the Trans-Mississippi Frontier." Doctoral dissertation, University of California, Riverside, 1977.

326. Reddin, Paul Laverne. "Wild West Shows: A Study in the Development of Western Romanticism." Doctoral dissertation, University of Missouri, Columbia, 1970.

327. Reeve, Kay Aiken. "The Making of An American Place: The Development of Santa Fe and Taos, New Mexico, As An American Cultural Center, 1898-1942." Doctoral dissertation, Texas A & M University, 1977.

328. Robinson, Cecil. *Mexico and the Hispanic Southwest in American Literature.* Tucson: University of Arizona Press, 1977. Revised and enlarged edition of *With the Ears of Strangers,* 1963.

329. Robinson, Ruth Williard. "The

Montana Novel before 1914." Master's thesis, Montana State University, 1948.

330. Rodgers, John William. *Finding Literature on the Texas Plains.* Dallas: Southwest Press, 1931.

331. Rolfe, Lionel. *Literary L. A.* San Francisco: Chronicle Books, 1981.

332. Rosa, Joseph G. *The Gunfighter: Man or Myth.* Norman: University of Oklahoma Press, 1969.

333. Rosenzweig, Paul Jonathan. "The Wilderness in American Fiction: A Psychoanalytic Study of a Central American Myth." Doctoral dissertation, University of Michigan, 1972.

334. Rusk, Ralph Leslie. *The Literature of the Middle Western Frontier.* 2 vols. New York: Columbia University Press, 1925.

335. Ryan, Patrick Edward. "The American Frontier Narratives." Master's thesis, Idaho State University, 1970.

336. Saciuk, Olena H. "A Comparative Study of the Cowboy, Gaucho, and Kozak as Protagonists in Selected Novels." Doctoral dissertation, University of Illinois, Urbana-Champaign, 1973.

337. Savage, William W., Jr. *The Cowboy Hero: His Image in American History and Culture.* Norman: University of Oklahoma Press, 1979. The best study of this subject.

338. Schmitt, Peter J. *Back to Nature: The Arcadian Myth in Urban America.* New York: Oxford University Press, 1969.

339. See, Carolyn P. "The Hollywood Novel: An Historical and Critical Study." Doctoral dissertation, University of California, Los Angeles, 1963.

340. Silver, Marilyn Brick. "The Farmer in American Literature, 1608-1864." Doctoral dissertation, Ohio State University, 1976.

341. Simonson, Harold P. *The Closed Frontier: Studies in American Literary Tragedy.* New York: Holt, Rinehart and Winston, 1970.

342. Skårdal, Dorothy Burton. *The Divided Heart: Scandinavian Immigrant Experience Through Literary Sources.* Lincoln: University of Nebraska Press, 1974. Contains extensive bibliography.

343. Slotkin, Richard. *Regeneration Through Violence: The Myth of the American Frontier, 1600–1860.* Middletown, Conn.: Wesleyan University Press, 1973.

344. Smith, Caroline. "The Literary Image of Daniel Boone: A Changing Heroic Ideal in Nineteenth- and Twentieth-Century Popular Literature." Doctoral dissertation, University of Utah, 1974.

345. Smith, Henry Nash. *Virgin Land: The American West as Symbol and Myth.* Cambridge: Harvard University Press, 1950, 1970. A classic study.

346. Sonnichsen, C. L. *Cowboys and*

Cattle Kings. Norman: University of Oklahoma Press, 1950.

347. ——. *From Hopalong to Hud: Thoughts on Western Fiction.* College Station: Texas A&M University Press, 1978.

348. Spotts, Carl B. "The Development of Fiction on the Missouri Frontier (1830–1860)." Doctoral dissertation, Pennsylvania State University, 1934.

349. Stafford, William. *Writing the Australian Crawl: Views on the Writer's Vocation.* Ann Arbor: University of Michigan Press, 1978.

350. Starr, Kevin. *Americans and the California Dream: 1850–1915.* New York: Oxford University Press, 1973.

351. Stegner, Wallace. *The Sound of Mountain Water.* Garden City, N.Y.: Doubleday, 1969.

352. Stein, Rita. *A Literary Tour Guide to the United States: West and Midwest.* New York: William Morrow, 1979.

353. Sutton, Ann and Myron. *The American West: A Natural History.* New York: Random House, 1970.

354. Sweeney, J. Gray. "The Artist-Explorers of the American West 1860–1880." Doctoral dissertation, Indiana University, 1975.

355. Taft, Robert. *Artists and Illustrators of the Old West.* New York: Charles Scribner's Sons, 1953.

356. Tebbel, John. *Fact and Fiction Problems of the Historical Novelist.* Lansing: Historical Society of Michigan, 1962.

357. Tinker, Edward Larocque. *The Horsemen of the Americas and the Literature They Inspired.* Austin: University of Texas Press, 1967.

358. Todd, Edgeley W. "Literary Interest in the Fur Trade and Fur Trappers of the Trans-Mississippi West." Doctoral dissertation, Northwestern University, 1952.

359. Tooker, Dan, and Roger Hofheins. *Fiction: Interviews with Northern California Novelists.* New York: Harcourt Brace Jovanovich, 1976. Includes interviews with Stegner, J. West, Janet Lewis, and others.

360. Venable, William H. *Beginnings of Literary Culture in the Ohio Valley.* Cincinnati: Robert Clarke, 1891.

361. Von Frank, Albert James. "Frontier Consciousness in American Literature." Doctoral dissertation, University of Missouri, 1976.

362. Walker, Don D. *Clio's Cowboys: Studies in the Historiography of the Cattle Trade.* Lincoln: University of Nebraska Press, 1981.

363. Walker, Franklin. *A Literary History of Southern California.* Berkeley: University of California Press, 1950.

364. ——. *San Francisco's Literary Frontier.* New York: Knopf, 1939; Seattle: University of Washington Press, 1969.

365. ——. *The Seacost of Bohemia.* Santa Barbara, Calif.: Peregrine Smith, 1973. Adds new material to an earlier edition

published by the Book Club of California in 1966.

366. Walker, Robert H. *The Poet and the Gilded Age.* Philadelphia: University of Pennsylvania Press, 1963.

367. Watkins, Eric. "The Mississippi River as Image and Symbol in American Literature, 1820–1936." Doctoral dissertation, University of Minnesota, 1972.

368. Webb, Walter Prescott. *The Great Plains.* Boston: Ginn, 1931.

369. Weber, Harley R. "Midwestern Farm Writing in the Late Nineteenth Century: A Study in Changing Attitudes." Doctoral dissertation, University of Minnesota, 1968.

370. Wecter, Dixon. *The Hero in America.* New York: Charles Scribner's Sons, 1941.

371. "Western Literary History." *Pacific Historical Review* 45 (August 1976): 311–432. Special issue.

372. White, G. Edward. *The Eastern Establishment and the Western Experience: The West of Frederic Remington, Theodore Roosevelt, and Owen Wister.* New Haven: Yale University Press, 1968.

373. Wilson, Edmund. *The Boys in the Backroom: Notes on California Novelists.* San Francisco: Ridgeway Books, 1941.

374. Winston, Robert Paul. "From Farmer James to Natty Bumppo: The Frontier and the Early American Romance." Doctoral dissertation, University of Wisconsin, Madison, 1979.

375. Wolfe, Hilton John. "Alaskan Literature: The Fiction of America's Last Wilderness." Doctoral dissertation, Michigan State University, 1973.

376. Wu, William F. "The Yellow Peril: Chinese-Americans in American Fiction, 1850-1940." Doctoral dissertation, University of Michigan, 1979.

377. Wyman, Walker D., and Clifton B. Kroeber, eds. *The Frontier in Perspective.* Madison: University of Wisconsin Press, 1957.

378. Ziff, Larzer. *The American 1890s: Life and Times of a Lost Generation.* New York: Viking Press, 1966.

ARTICLES

379. Adams, Andy. "Western Interpreters." *Southwest Review* 10 (October 1924): 70-74.

380. Allen, John L. "Geographical Knowledge and American Images of the Louisiana Territory." *Western Historical Quarterly* 2 (April 1971): 151-70.

381. Altrocchi, J. C. "California Biography in Poetry." *Pacific Historian* 15 (Winter 1971): 1-12.

382. Anderson, John Q. "Scholarship in Southwestern Humor: Past and Present." *Mississippi Quarterly* 17 (1964): 67-86.

383. Armitage, Shelley. "Western Heroines: Real and Fictional Cowgirls." *Heritage of Kansas* 12 (Spring 1979): 12-20.

384. ——. "Rawhide Heroines: The Evolution of the Cowgirl and

the Myth of America." *The American Self: Myth, Ideology, and Popular Culture.* Ed. Sam B. Girgus. Albuquerque: University of New Mexico Press, 1981, pp. 166-81.

385. Armitage, Susan H. "Women's Literature and the American Frontier: A New Perspective on the Frontier Myth." *Women, Women Writers, and the West.* Eds. Lawrence L. Lee and Merrill E. Lewis. Troy, N.Y.: Whitston, 1978.

386. Arrington, Leonard, and Jon Haupt. "Community and Isolation: Some Aspects of 'Mormon Westerns.'" *Western American Literature* 8 (Spring-Summer 1973): 15-31.

387. ——. "Intolerable Zion: The Image of Mormonism in Nineteenth Century American Literature." *Western Humanities Review* 22 (Summer 1968): 243-60.

388. Ashliman, D. L. "The American West in Twentieth-Century Germany." *Journal of Popular Culture* 2 (Summer 1968): 81-92.

389. ——. "The Novel of Western Adventure in Nineteenth-Century Germany." *Western American Literature* 3 (Summer 1968): 133-45.

390. Athearn, Robert. "The American West: An Enduring Mirage?" *Colorado Quarterly* 26 (Autumn 1977): 3-16.

391. ——. *High Country Empire: The High Plains and Rockies.* New York: McGraw-Hill, 1960. Includes a chapter on literature.

392. Atherton, L. E. "The Midwestern Country Town—Myth and Reality." *Agricultural History* 26 (July 1952): 73-80.

393. Attebery, Louis. "The American West and the Archetypal Orphan." *Western American Literature* 5 (Fall 1970): 205-17.

394. Austin, James C. "Gold Dust, Dust Bowl and Gopher Prairie: The Story of Western Humor." *Revue Française d' Etudes Americaines* 4 (November 1977): 31-37.

395. Autor, Hans. "Alaskan Poetry." *Alaska Review* I (Spring 1964): 48-55.

396. Bangs, Carol Jane. "Women Poets and the 'Northwest School.'" *Women, Women Writers, and the West.* Eds. Lawrence L. Lee and Merrill E. Lewis. Troy, N.Y.: Whitston, 1978.

397. Banks, Loy Otis. "The Credible Literary West." *Colorado Quarterly* 8 (Summer 1959): 28-50.

398. Baritz, Loren. "The Idea of the West." *American Historical Review* 66 (April 1961): 618-40.

399. Barsness, John. "Creativity Through Hatred—and a Few Thoughts on the Western Novel." *Western Review* 6 (Winter 1969): 12-17.

400. Bashford, Herbert. "The Literary Development of the Pacific Coast." *Atlantic Monthly* 92 (July 1903): 1-9.

401. Baurecht, William C. "Romantic Male Deviance: Myth of Freedom in the West." *Southwest*

27

Images and Trends. Eds. Suzanne M. Owings and Helen M. Bannan. Las Cruces: New Mexico State University, 1979, pp. 160-70.

402. Beeton, Beverly. "The Frontiersman Before Leatherstocking." *Markham Review* 7 (Fall 1977): 1-5.

403. Billington, Ray A. "The Plains and Deserts through European Eyes." *Western Historical Quarterly* 10 (October 1979): 467-87. European literature about the American West.

404. Boatright, Mody C. "The American Myth Rides the Range." *Southwest Review* 36 (Summer 1951): 157-63.

405. ——. "The American Rodeo." *American Quarterly* 16 (Summer 1964): 195-202.

406. ——. "The Beginnings of Cowboy Fiction." *Southwest Review* 51 (Winter 1966): 11-28.

407. ——. "The Formula in Cowboy Fiction and Drama." *Western Folklore* 28 (April 1969): 136-45.

408. ——. "Thy Myth of Frontier Individualism." *Southwestern Social Science Quarterly* 22 (June 1941): 14-32.

409. ——. "Literature in the Southwest." *Sul Ross State College Bulletin* (June 1, 1953): 1-32.

410. Bouquet, Sarah. "Voices from the Southwest." *Voices from the Southwest: A Gathering in Honor of Lawrence Clark Powell.* Eds. Donald C. Dickinson, W. David Laird, and Margaret F. Maxwell. Flagstaff, Ariz.: Northland Press, 1976, pp. 33-44. Accounts by women.

411. Bracher, Frederick. "California's Literary Regionalism." *American Quarterly* 7 (Fall 1955): 275-84.

412. Brashear, Minnie M. "Missouri Literature Since the First World War: Part III—The Novel." *Missouri Historical Review* 41 (April 1947): 241-65.

413. Bredeson, Robert C. "Landscape Description in Nineteenth-Century American Travel Literature." *American Quarterly* 20 (Spring 1968): 86-94.

414. Brenner, Jack. "Imagining the West." *The Westering Experience in American Literature: Bicentennial Essays.* Eds. Merrill Lewis and L. L. Lee. Bellingham: Bureau for Faculty Research, Western Washington University, 1977, pp. 32-47.

415. *BYU Studies* 14 (Winter 1974). Special issue on Mormons and literature.

416. Brunvand, Jan Harold. "As the Saints Go Marching By: Modern Jokelore Concerning Mormons." *Journal of American Folklore* 83 (January-March 1970): 53-60.

417. Bryant, Paul T. "Western Literature: A Window on America." *CEA Critic* 40 (March 1978): 6-13.

418. Butler, Michael D. "Kansas Novels." *The Kansas Art Reader.* Ed. Jonathan Wesley Bell. Lawrence: University of Kansas, 1976, pp. 299-322.

419. ——. "Sons of Oliver Edwards;

or, The Other American Hero." *Western American Literature* 12 (May 1977): 53-66.

420. Byington, Robert. "The Frontier Hero: Refinement and Definition." *Publications of the Texas Folklore Society* 30 (1960): 140-55.

421. Carroll, John Alexander. "Broader Approaches to the History of the West." *Arizona and the West* I (Autumn 1959): 217-31.

422. Carstensen, Vernon. "Remarks on the Literary Treatment of the American Westward Movement." *Moderna Sprak* 51 (1957): 275-87.

423. Carter, Harvey C., and Marcia C. Spencer. "Stereotypes of the Mountain Man." *Western Historical Quarterly* 6 (January 1975): 17-32.

424. Carver, Wayne. "Literature, Mormon Writers, and the Powers that Be." *Dialogue* 4 (August 1969): 65-73.

425. Caughey, John W. "The American West: Frontier and Region." *Arizona and the West* I (Spring 1959): 7-12.

426. ——. "Shaping a Literary Tradition." *Pacific Historical Review* 8 (June 1939): 201-14. California literature.

427. ——. "Toward an Understanding of the West." *Utah Historical Quarterly* 27 (January 1959): 7-24.

428. Cawelti, John. "Cowboys, Indians, Outlaws." *American West* I (Spring 1964): 28-35, 77-79.

429. ——. "Prolegomena to the West-

ern." *Studies in Public Communication* 4 (Autumn 1962): 57-70.

430. ——. "Prolegomena to the Western." *Western American Literature* 4 (Winter 1970): 259-71.

431. Christensen, J. A. "Poetry in Its Western Setting." *Western Review* 7 (1970): 10-19.

432. Clark, Thomas D. "The American Backwoodsman in Popular Portraiture." *Indian Magazine of History* 42 (1946): 1-28.

433. Clark, Thomas L. "A Semantic Class in the Great Basin." *Names* 26 (March 1978): 48-57.

434. Clements, William M. "Savage, Pastoral, Civilized: An Ecology Typology of American Frontier Heroes." *Journal of Popular Culture* 8 (Fall 1974): 254-66.

435. Clough, Wilson E. "The Cult of the Bad Man of the West." *Texas Quarterly* 5 (Autumn 1962): 11-20.

436. Cohen, B. J. "Nativism and Western Myth: The Influence of Nativist Ideas on American Self-Image." *Journal of American Studies* 8 (April 1974): 23-40.

437. Cohen, Lester H. "Eden's Constitution: The Paradisacal Dream and Enlightenment Values in Late Eighteenth-Century Literature of the American Frontier." *Prospects: An Annual of American Cultural Studies.* Vol. III. Ed. Jack Salzman. New York: Burt Franklin, 1977, pp. 83-109.

438. Commanger, Henry Steele. "The

Literature of the Pioneer West." *Minnesota History* 8 (December 1927): 319-28.

439. Corning, Howard M. "The Prose and Poetry of It." *Oregon Historical Quarterly* 74 (September 1973): 244-67. Oregon writers in the 1920s and 30s.

440. Cracroft, Richard H. "The American West of Karl May." *American Quarterly* 19 (Summer 1967): 249-58.

441. Crowell, Chester T. "Cowboys." *American Mercury* 9 (October 1926): 162-69.

442. Cunningham, Keith. "The Respectability of Southwestern Literature." *Arizona English Bulletin* 13 (April 1971): 69-70.

443. Current-Garcia, E. "Writers in the 'Sticks.'" *Prairie Schooner* 12 (Winter 1938): 294-309.

444. Dale, Edward E. "Culture on the American Frontier." *Nebraska History* 26 (1945): 75-90.

445. ——. "The Frontier Literary Society." *Nebraska History* 31 (1950): 167-82.

446. ——. "The Romance of the Range." *West Texas Historical Association Year Book* 5 (June 1929): 3-22.

447. Davidson, Levette J. "Early Fiction of the Rocky Mountain Region." *Colorado Magazine* 10 (1933): 161-72.

448. ——. "Fact or Formula in 'Western' Fiction." *Colorado Quarterly* 3 (Winter 1955): 278-87.

449. ——. "Folk Elements in Midwestern Literature." *Western Humanities Review* 3 (July 1949): 187-95.

450. ——. "The Literature of Western America." *Western Humanities Review* 5 (Spring 1951): 165-73.

451. Davis, David B. "Ten-Gallon Hero." *American Quarterly* 6 (Summer 1954): 111-25.

452. Davis, Robert Murray. "Playing Cowboys: The Paradoxes of Genre." *Heritage of Kansas* 12 (Spring 1979): 3-8.

453. Davis, Ronald L. "Culture on the Frontier." *Southwest Review* 53 (Autumn 1968): 383-403. Western drama.

454. Day, Robert. "Some Western Fiction of the 1970s." *Kansas Quarterly* 10 (Fall 1978): 99-103.

455. Dessain, Kenneth. "Once in the Saddle: The Memory and Romance of the Trail Driving Cowboy." *Journal of Popular Culture* 4 (Fall 1970): 464-96.

456. Dippie, Brian W. "Bards of the Little Big Horn." *Western American Literature* I (Fall 1966): 175-95.

457. Ditsky, John. "'Directionality': The Compass in the Heart." *The Westering Experience in American Literature: Bicentennial Essays.* Eds. Merrill Lewis and L. L. Lee. Bellingham: Bureau for Faculty Research, Western Washington University, 1977, pp. 215-20.

458. Dobie, J. Frank. "Cow Country Tempo." *Texas Quarterly* 7 (Spring 1964): 30-36.

459. Donald, David, and Frederick A. Palmer. "Toward a Western Literature, 1820-1860." *Mississippi Valley Historical Review* 35 (December 1948): 413-28.

460. Dondore, Dorothy. "Points of Contact Between History and Literature in the Mississippi Valley." *Mississippi Valley Historical Review* 11 (September 1924): 227-36.

461. Donelson, Kenneth L. "A Fistful of Southwestern Books for Students and Teachers." *Arizona English Bulletin* 13 (April 1971): 71-76.

462. ——. "The Southwest in Literature and Culture: A New Horizon for the English Class." *English Journal* 61 (February 1972): 193-204.

463. Durham, Philip. "The Lost Cowboy." *Midwest Journal* 7 (1955): 176-82.

464. ——. "The Negro Cowboy." *American Quarterly* 7 (Fall 1955): 291-301.

465. Dykes, J. C. "Dime Novel Texas; or, the Sub-Literature of the Lone Star State." *Southwestern Historical Quarterly* 49 (January 1946): 327-40.

466. Eifner, Walter H. "The Kansas *Agora*: A Forum for Literature." *Markham Review* 8 (Fall 1978): 11-15.

467. Elliott, William D. "Poets of the Moving Frontier: Bly, Whittemore, Wright, Berryman, McGrath and Minnesota North Country Poetry." *Midamerica* 3 (1976): 17-38.

468. Erisman, Fred. "The Environ-mental Crisis and Present-Day Romanticism." *Rocky Mountain Social Science Journal* 10 (1973): 7-14.

469. ——. "Western Fiction as an Ecological Parable." *Environmental Review* 2 (Spring 1978): 14-23.

470. ——. "Western Writers and the Literary Historian." *North Dakota Quarterly* 47 (Autumn 1979): 64-69.

471. ——. "'Where We Plan to Go': The Southwest in Utopian Fiction." *Southwestern American Literature* 1 (September 1971): 137-43.

472. Erno, Richard B. "The New Realism in Southwestern Literature." *Western Review* 7 (Spring 1970): 50-54.

473. Eshleman, H. D. "A Grownup Western at Last." *Colorado Quarterly* 19 (Summer 1970): 107-12.

474. Etulain, Richard W. "The American Literary West and Its Interpreters: The Rise of a New Historiography." *Pacific Historical Review* 45 (August 1976): 311-48.

475. ——. "The Basques in Western American Literature." *Anglo-American Contributions to Basque Studies. . . .* Eds. William A. Douglass, et al. Reno: Desert Research Institute Publications in the Social Sciences, 1977, pp. 7-18.

476. ——. *The Closing Frontier.* Cassette. Deland, Fla.: Everett/ Edwards, 1976.

477. ——. "Main Currents in Modern

Western Literature." *Journal of American Culture* 3 (Summer 1980): 374-88.

478. ——. *The Modern Literary West.* Cassette. Deland, Fla.: Everett/Edwards, 1979.

479. ——. *The Mountain Man in Literature.* Cassette. Deland, Fla.: Everett/Edwards, 1974.

480. ——. "The New Western Novel." *Idaho Yesterdays* 15 (Winter 1972): 12-17.

481. ——. "Novelists of the Northwest: Needs and Opportunities for Research." *Idaho Yesterdays* 17 (Summer 1973): 24-32. Includes an extended bibliography.

482. ——. "Recent Views of the American Literary West." *Journal of Popular Culture* 3 (Summer 1969): 144-53.

483. ——. ["Recent Western Fiction."] *Journal of the West* 8 (October 1969): 656-58.

484. ——. "Research Opportunities in Western Literary History." *Western Historical Quarterly* 4 (July 1973): 263-72.

485. ——. "Western American Literature: The Colonial Period." *Journal of the West* 19 (January 1980): 6-8.

486. ——. "Western Fiction and History: A Reconsideration." *The American West: New Perspectives, New Dimensions.* Ed. Jerome O. Steffen. Norman: University of Oklahoma Press, 1979, pp. 152-74.

487. ——, ed. "Western Literature." *Idaho Humanities Forum.* Spring 1981, pp. 3-10. A special issue containing four essays.

488. Everson, William. *Archetype West: The Pacific Coast as a Literary Region.* Berkeley, Calif.: Oyez, 1976.

489. Fadiman, Clifton. "Party of One —The Literature of the Rockies." *Holiday* 34 (August 1963): 10, 12-17.

490. Fender, Stephen. "The Western and the Contemporary." *Journal of American Studies* 6 (April 1972): 97-108.

491. Fife, Austin and Alta. "Spurs and Saddlebags: Ballads of the Cowboy." *American West* 7 (September 1970): 44-47.

492. Fisher, Vardis. "The Western Writer and the Eastern Establishment." *Western American Literature* I (Winter 1967): 244-59.

493. Fishwick, Marshall W. "The Cowboy: America's Contribution to the World's Mythology." *Western Folklore* 11 (April 1952): 77-92.

494. Flanagan, John T. "A Half-Century of Middlewestern Fiction." *Critique* 2 (Winter 1959): 16-34.

495. ——. "Literary Protests in the Midwest." *Southwest Review* 34 (Spring 1948): 148-57.

496. ——. "The Middle Western Farm Novel." *Minnesota History* 23 (June 1942): 113-47.

497. ——. "Thirty Years of Minnesota Fiction." *Minnesota History* 31 (September 1950): 129-47.

498. Flores, Vetal. "Literature for Frontier Children." *Southwestern American Literature* 2 (Fall 1972): 65-73.

499. Folsom, James K. "English West-

erns." *Western American Literature* 2 (Spring 1967): 3-13.

500. ——. "*Shane* and *Hud*: Two Stories in Search of a Medium." *Western Humanities Review* 24 (Autumn 1970): 359-72.

501. ——. "'Western' Themes and Western Films." *Western American Literature* 2 (Fall 1967): 195-203.

502. Frederick, John T. "Early Iowa in Fiction." *Palimpsest* 36 (October 1955): 389-420.

503. ——. "The Farm in Iowa Fiction." *Palimpsest* 32 (March 1951): 124-52.

504. ——. "Town and City in Iowa Fiction." *Palimpsest* 35 (February 1954): 49-96.

505. Freeman, Martha Doty. "New Mexico in the Nineteenth Century: The Creation of an Artistic Tradition." *New Mexico Historical Review* 49 (January 1974): 5-26.

506. French, Carol Anne. "Western Literature and the Myth-Makers." *Montana: The Magazine of Western History* 22 (April 1972): 76-81.

507. French, Warren. "The Cowboy in the Dime Novel." *Texas Studies in English* (1951): 219-34.

508. ——. "West as Myth: Status Report and Call for Action." *Western American Literature* I (Spring 1966): 55-58.

509. Furness, Edna L. "Image of the Schoolteacher in Western Literature." *Arizona Quarterly* 18 (Winter 1962): 346-57.

510. Fuson, Ben W. "Prairie Dreamers of 1890: Three Kansas Utopian Novels and Novelists." *Kansas Quarterly* 5 (Fall 1973): 63-77.

511. Garland, Hamlin. "Literary Emancipation of the West." *Forum* 16 (1893): 156-66.

512. ——. "The West in Literature." *Arena* 6 (1892): 669-76.

513. Gaston, Edwin W., Jr. "Travel Accounts of the Southern Plains: 1800-1850." *Texas Journal of Science* 11 (March 1959): 3-16.

514. Geary, Edward A. "Mormondom's Lost Generation: The Novelists of the 1940's." *BYU Studies* 18 (Fall 1977): 89-98.

515. ——. "The Poetics of Provincialism: Mormon Regional Fiction." *Dialogue* 11 (Summer 1978): 15-24.

516. Gilliard, Frederick W. "Theatre in Early Idaho: A Brief Review and Appraisal." *Rendezvous* 8 (Summer 1973): 25-31.

517. Gillis, Everett A. "Southwest Literature: Perspectives and Prospects." *Southwestern American Literature* 2 (Spring 1972): 1-7.

518. Gillmor, Frances. "Southwestern Chronicle from Report to Literature." *Arizona Quarterly* 12 (Winter 1956): 344-51.

519. Goetzmann, William H. "Mountain Man Stereotypes: Notes and Reply." *Western Historical Quarterly* 6 (July 1975): 295-302. Reply by Harvey L. Carter, pp. 301-2.

520. Gohdes, Clarence. "The Earliest Description of 'Western' Fiction?" *American Literature* 37 (March 1965): 70-71.

521. Goodwyn, Frank. "The Frontier in American Fiction." *Revista*

Interamericana de Bibliografía 10 (1960): 356-69.

522. Gower, Calvin W. "Aids to Prospective Prospectors: Guidebooks and Letters from Kansas Territory, 1858-1860." *Kansas Historical Quarterly* 43 (Spring 1977): 67-77.

523. Graham, Don. "Is Dallas Burning? Notes on Recent Texas Fiction." *Southwestern American Literature* 4 (1974): 68-73.

524. Green, Douglas B. "The Singing Cowboy in American Culture." *Heritage of Kansas* 9 (Fall 1976): 3-9.

525. Green, Timothy, and Jack Schneider. "In Defense of the Southwestern Ethos: The Literature of Reaction." *RE: Artes Liberales* 5 (Fall 1978): 1-15.

526. Grover, Dorys Crow. "The Pioneer Women in Fact and Fiction." *Heritage of Kansas* 10 (Spring 1977): 35-44.

527. Gurian, Jay. "The Possibility of a Western Poetics." *Colorado Quarterly* 15 (Summer 1966): 69-85.

528. ——. "Sweetwater Journalism and Western Myth." *Annals of Wyoming* 36 (April 1964): 79-88.

529. ——. "The Unwritten West." *American West* 2 (Winter 1965): 59-63.

530. Guthrie, Alfred B., Jr. "The Historical Novel." *Montana Magazine of History* 4 (Fall 1954): 1-8.

531. ——. "Why Write About the West?" *Western American Literature* 7 (Fall 1972): 163-69.

532. Hale, Edward E. "The Romantic Landscape of the Far West." *Union College Bulletin* 23 (January 1930): 5-17.

533. Hansen, Klaus J. "The Millenium, the West, and Race in the Antebellum Mind." *Western Historical Quarterly* 3 (October 1972): 373-90.

534. Haslam, Gerald. "American Literature: Some Forgotten Pages." *ETC* 17 (June 1970): 221-38.

535. ——. "Predators in Literature." *Western American Literature* 11 (August 1977): 123-31.

536. ——. "Some New Classroom Vistas in Southwestern Literature." *Arizona English Bulletin* 13 (April 1971): 48-54.

537. ——, ed. *Western American Writers*. Cassette Series. Deland, Fla.: Everett/Edwards, 1974.

538. ——, ed. *Western Writing*. Albuquerque: University of New Mexico Press, 1974.

539. Hauptman, Laurence M. "Mythologizing Westward Expansion: Schoolbooks and the Image of the American Frontier Before Turner." *Western Historical Quarterly* 7 (July 1977): 269-82.

540. Heatherington, Madelon E. "Romance Without Women: The Sterile Fiction of the American West." *Georgia Review* 33 (Fall 1979): 643-56.

541. Heilman, Robert B. "The Western Theme: Exploiters and Explorers." *Northwest Review* 4 (Fall-Winter 1960): 5-14.

542. Hertzel, Leo J. "What About

Writers in the North?" *South Dakota Review* 5 (Spring 1967): 3-19.

543. "Historians of the Northern Plains," and "Historians of the Southern Plains." *Great Plains Journal* 18 (1979). Special issue devoted to brief essays about the major historians of the Great Plains.

544. Hitt, Helen. "History in Pacific Northwest Novels Written Since 1920." *Oregon Historical Quarterly* 51 (September 1950): 180-206.

545. Holbrook, Stewart H. *Far Corner: A Personal View of the Pacific Northwest.* New York: Macmillan, 1952, pp. 220-30.

546. Horgan, Paul. "The Cowboy Revisited." *Southwest Review* 39 (Autumn 1954): 285-97.

547. Hornberger, Theodore. "The Self-Conscious Wests." *Southwest Review* 26 (July 1941): 428-48.

548. Hough, Emerson. "The West, and Certain Literary Discoveries." *Century* 59 (February 1900): 506-11.

549. Howard, Leon. "Literature and the Frontier." *English Literary History* 7 (1940): 68-82.

550. Hubbell, Jay B. "The Frontier in American Literature." *Southwest Review* 10 (January 1925): 84-92.

551. Hunsaker, Kenneth B. "Mid-Century Mormon Novels." *Dialogue* 4 (Autumn 1969): 123-28.

552. Hutchinson, W. H. *The Cowboy in Literature.* Cassette. Deland, Fla.: Everett/Edwards, 1974.

553. ——. "Packaging the Old West in Serial Form." *Westways* 65 (February 1973): 18-23. Early twentieth-century literary treatments of the West in serial form.

554. ——. "Virgins, Villains, and Varmints." *Huntington Library Quarterly* 16 (August 1953): 381-92.

555. ——. "The 'Western Story' as Literature." *Western Humanities Review* 3 (January 1949): 33-37.

556. "Issue on Mormons and Literature." *BYU Studies* 14 (Winter 1974).

557. James, Stuart B. "Western American Space and the Human Imagination." *Western Humanities Review* 24 (Spring 1970): 147-55.

558. Jeranko, Mildred, and Jane Tyo. "Cowboys and Indians in the Classroom, Or a Shotgun Approach to Teaching American Literature." *Arizona English Bulletin* 13 (April 1971): 62-64.

559. Jewett, Isaac Appleton. "Themes for Western Fiction." *Western Monthly Magazine* 1 (December 1833): 574-88.

560. Jones, Harry H. "The Mining Theme in Western Fiction." *Studies in the Literature of the West.* Laramie: University of Wyoming, 1956, pp. 101-29.

561. Jones, Howard Munford. "The Allure of the West." *Harvard Library Bulletin* 28 (January 1980): 19-32. Early nineteenth-century narratives and travel accounts.

562. Jones, Margaret Ann. "The Cowboy and Ranching in Magazine Fiction, 1901-1910." *Studies in the Literature of the West.* Laramie: University of Wyoming, 1956, pp. 57-74.

563. Jorgensen, B. W. "Imperceptive Hands: Some Recent Mormon Verse." *Dialogue* 5 (Winter 1970): 23-34.

564. Josephy, Alvin M., Jr. "Publishers' Interests in Western Writing." *Western American Literature* 1 (Winter 1967): 260-66.

565. Juricek, John T. "American Usage of the Word 'Frontier' from Colonial Times to Frederick Jackson Turner." *Proceedings of the American Philosophical Society* 110 (February 18, 1966): 10-34.

566. Kaye, Frances Weller. "The Roles of Women in the Literature of the Post Civil War American Frontier." Doctoral dissertation, Cornell University, 1973.

567. Kedro, M. James. "Literary Boosterism: The Great Divide." *Colorado Magazine* 52 (Summer 1975): 200-224.

568. Keeler, Clinton. "Children of Innocence: The Agrarian Crusade in Fiction." *Western Humanities Review* 6 (Autumn 1952): 363-76.

569. Keim, Charles J. "Writing the Great Alaska Novel." *Alaska Review* 4 (Fall-Winter 1969): 47-51.

570. Keleher, Julia. "Los Paisanos." *New Mexico Quarterly Review* 15 (Summer 1945): 260-63.

571. Keller, Karl. "On Words and the Word of God: The Delusions of a Mormon Literature." *Dialogue* 4 (Autumn 1969): 13-20.

572. King, James T. "The Sword and the Pen: The Poetry of the Military Frontier." *Nebraska History* 47 (September 1966): 229-45.

573. Kittredge, William, and Steven M. Krauzer. "Writers of the New West." *TriQuarterly* 48 (Spring 1980): 5-14. Introduction to a collection of new western fiction.

574. Kizer, Carolyn. "Poetry: School of the Pacific Northwest." *New Republic* 135 (July 16, 1956): 18-19.

575. Klotman, Phyllis R. "The Slave and the Western: Popular Literature of the Nineteenth Century." *North Dakota Quarterly* 41 (Autumn 1973): 40-54.

576. Kramer, Mary D. "The American Wild West Show and 'Buffalo Bill' Cody." *Costerus* 4 (1972): 87-98.

577. Krause, Herbert. "Myth and Reality on the High Plains." *South Dakota Review* 1 (December 1963): 3-20.

578. Krupat, Arnold. "American Autobiography: The Western Tradition." *Georgia Review* 35 (Summer 1981): 307-20.

579. Kuhlman, Thomas A. "Warner's History of Dakota County, Nebraska: The Western County History as a Literary Genre." *Western Review* 9 (Winter 1972): 57-64.

580. Lambert, Neal E. Freedom and

the American Cowboy." *BYU Studies* 8 (Autumn 1967): 61-71.

581. ——. "The Representation of Reality in Nineteenth Century Mormon Autobiography." *Dialogue* 11 (Summer 1978): 63-74.

582. ——. "Saints, Sinners and Scribes: A Look at the Mormons in Fiction." *Utah Historical Quarterly* 36 (Winter 1968): 63-76.

583. Lambert, Patricia J. B. "The Western Hero Grows Narcissistic." *Heritage of Kansas* 12 (Winter 1979): 7-13.

584. Lavender, David. "The Petrified West and the Writer." *American Scholar* 37 (Spring 1968): 293-306.

585. Leach, Joseph. "The Paper-Back Texan: Father of the American Western Hero." *Western Humanities Review* 11 (Summer 1957): 267-75.

586. Lee, Hector. *The Roots of Western Literature.* Cassette. Deland, Fla.: Everett/Edwards, 1974.

587. ——. "Tales and Legends in Western American Literature." *Western American Literature* 9 (February 1975): 239-54.

588. Leithead, J. Edward. "The Saga of Young Wild West." *American Book Collector* 19 (March 1969): 17-22.

589. Lewandowska, M. L. "Feminism and the Emerging Woman Poet: Four Bay Area Poets." *Itinerary: Criticism, Essays on California Writers.* Ed. Charles

L. Crow. Bowling Green, Ohio: University Press, 1978, pp. 123-41.

590. Lewis, Marvin. "A Free Life in the Mines and on the Range." *Western Humanities Review* 12 (Winter 1958): 87-95.

591. Lindstrom, Naomi. "The Novel in Texas: How Big a Patrimony?" *Texas Quarterly* 21 (Summer 1978): 73-83.

592. Lyon, Peter. "The Wild, Wild West." *American Heritage* 11 (August 1960): 32-48.

593. Lyon, Thomas J. "Western Poetry." *Journal of the West* 19 (January 1980): 45-53.

594. McDowell, Tremaine. "Regionalism in the United States." *Minnesota History* 20 (June 1939): 105-18.

595. McKnight, Jeannie. "American Dream, Nightmare Underside: Diaries, Letters and Fiction of Women on the American Frontier." *Women, Women Writers, and the West.* Eds. Lawrence L. Lee and Merrill E. Lewis. Troy, N.Y.: Whitston, 1978.

596. McMurtry, Larry. "Take My Saddle from the Wall." *Harper's* 237 (September 1968): 37-46. The cowboy myth and the modern cattleman.

597. McReynolds, Douglas J. "American Literature, American Frontier, All American Girl." *Heritage of Kansas* 10 (Spring 1977): 25-33.

598. McWilliams, Carey. "Myths of the West." *North American Review* 232 (November 1931): 424-32.

599. ——. "The West: A Lost Chapter." *Frontier* 12 (November 1932): 15-24.

600. Manfred, Frederick. *Writing in the West.* Cassette. Deland, Fla.: Everett/Edwards, 1974.

601. Mann, Ralph. "The Americanization of Arcadia: Images of Hispanic and Gold Rush California." *American Studies* 19 (Spring 1978): 5-19.

602. Marchand, Ernest. "Emerson and the Frontier." *American Literature* 3 (May 1931): 149-74.

603. Marks, Barry. "The Concept of Myth in *Virgin Land.*" *American Quarterly* 5 (Spring 1953): 71-76.

604. Marovitz, Sanford E. "Bridging the Continent with Romantic Western Realism." *Journal of the West* 19 (January 1980): 17-28.

605. ——. "Myth and Realism in Recent Criticism of the American Literary West." *Journal of American Studies* 15 (April 1981): 95-114.

606. ——. "Romance or Realism? Western Periodical Literature: 1893-1902." *Western American Literature* 10 (May 1975): 45-58.

607. Meldrum, Barbara. "The Agrarian versus Frontiersman in Midwestern Fiction." *Heritage of Kansas* 11 (Summer 1978): 3-18.

608. ——. *Images of Women in Western American Literature.* Cassette. Deland, Fla.: Everett/Edwards, 1974.

609. ——. "Images of Women in Western American Literature." *Midwest Quarterly* 17 (Spring 1976): 252-67.

610. ——. "Western Writers and the River: Guthrie, Fisher, Stegner." *Pacific Northwest Forum* 4 (Summer 1979): 21-26.

611. ——. "Women in Western American Fiction: Image or Real Women?" *Idaho Humanities Forum*, Spring 1981, pp. 9-10.

612. Meyer, Roy W. "Character Types in Literature About the American West." *Opinion* 13 (December 1969): 21-29.

613. ——. "Naturalism in American Farm Fiction." *Journal of the Central Mississippi Valley American Studies Association* 2 (Spring 1961): 27-37.

614. ——. "The Outback and the West: Australian and American Frontier Fiction." *Western American Literature* 6 (Spring 1971): 3-19.

615. ——. "The Scandinavian Immigrant in American Farm Fiction." *American Scandinavian Review* 47 (September 1959): 243-49.

616. Miles, Elton. "Mencken's *Mercury* and the West." *Southwestern American Literature* 3 (1973): 39-48.

617. Miles, Josephine. "Pacific Coast Poetry, 1947." *Pacific Spectator* 2 (Spring 1948): 134-50.

618. Millbrook, Minnie D. "The West Breaks in General Custer." *Kansas Historical Quarterly* 36 (Summer 1970): 113-48.

619. Milton, John R. "The American Novel: The Search for Home,

Tradition, and Identity." *Western Humanities Review* 16 (Spring 1962): 169-80.

620. ——. "The American West: A Challenge to the Literary Imagination." *Western American Literature* 1 (Winter 1967): 267-84.

621. ——. "The Dakota Image." *South Dakota Review* 8 (Autumn 1970): 7-26.

622. ——. "Earth and Sky: Fiction of our Time." *Bulletin of Jamestown College* 49 (December 31, 1958): 1-4.

623. ——. "Fact and Fantasy in Western Fiction." *South Dakota Library Bulletin* 48 (December 1962): 126-30.

624. ——. "Inside the *South Dakota Review*." *Midcontinent American Studies Journal* 10 (Fall 1969): 68-78.

625. ——. "The Novel in the American West." *South Dakota Review* 2 (Autumn 1964): 56-76.

626. ——. "Two Wests." *Antaeus* 25/26 (Spring/Summer 1977): 93-98.

627. ——. "The Western Novel: Whence and What?" *Rendezvous* 7 (Winter 1972): 7-21.

628. ——. "The Writer's West." *Antaeus* 29 (Spring 1978): 76-87.

629. ——. "The Western Novel: Sources and Forms." *Chicago Review* 16 (Summer 1963): 74-100.

630. ——, ed. "Conversations with Distinguished Western American Novelists." *South Dakota Review* 9 (Spring 1971): 15-57.

631. ——, ed. "The Western Novel—A Symposium." *South Dakota Review* 2 (Autumn 1964): 3-36.

632. Monaghan, Jay. "The West in Fiction." *American Library Association Bulletin* 48 (February 1954): 94-99.

633. Morgan, Dale L. "Literature in the History of the Church: The Importance of Involvement." *Dialogue* 4 (Autumn 1969): 26-32.

634. Morley, S. Griswold. "Cowboy and Gaucho Fiction." *New Mexico Quarterly* 16 (Autumn 1946): 253-67.

635. Morrow, Patrick. "Some Old and New Voices in Western Poetry: An Essay Review." *Western American Literature* 8 (Fall 1973): 153-59.

636. Mossberg, Christer Lennart. "Notes Toward an Introduction to Scandinavian Immigrant Literature on the Pioneer Experience." *Proceedings of the Pacific Northwest Conference on Foreign Languages* 28 (1977): 112-17.

637. ——. "Shucking the Pastoral Ideal: Sources and Meaning of Realism in Scandinavian Immigrant Fiction About the Pioneer Farm Experience." *Where the West Begins.* Eds. Arthur R. Huseboe and William Geyer. Sioux Falls, S.Dak.: Center for Western Studies Press, 1978, pp. 42-50.

638. Nelson, F. C. "The Norwegian-American's Image of America." *Illinois Quarterly* 36 (April 1974): 5-23.

39

639. Nicholl, James R. "Dust in the Air: Narratives of Actual Versus Fictional Trail Drives." *Heritage of Kansas* 12 (Winter 1979): 14-24.

640. Nichols, Roger L. "Printer's Ink and Red Skins: Western Newspapermen and the Indians." *Kansas Quarterly* 3 (Fall 1971): 82-88.

641. Norell, Irene P. "Prose Writers of North Dakota." *North Dakota Quarterly* 26 (Winter 1958): 1-36.

642. Oliver, Egbert S. "The Pig-Tailed China Boys Out West." *Western Humanities Review* 12 (Spring 1958): 159-78.

643. Olson, James C. "The Literary Tradition in Pioneer Nebraska." *Prairie Schooner* 24 (Summer 1950): 161-68.

644. Owens, William A. "The Golden Age of Texas Scholarship: Webb, Dobie, Bedichek, and Boatright." *Southwest Review* 60 (Winter 1975): 1-14.

645. Packer, Warren M. "Color Me Gray, Dobie, or Sandoz." *Arizona English Bulletin* 13 (April 1971): 23-31. Teaching western American literature.

646. Paine, Gregory. "The Frontier in American Literature." *Sewanee Review* 36 (April 1928): 225-36.

647. Pearce, T. M. "The Un-Static Southwest." *Southwestern American Literature* I (January 1971): 1-3.

648. ——. "The 'Other' Frontiers of the American West." *Arizona and the West* 4 (Summer 1962): 105-12.

649. Peters, J. U. "The Los Angeles Anti-Myth." *Itinerary: Criticism, Essays on California Writers.* Ed. Charles L. Crow. Bowling Green, Ohio: University Press, 1978, pp. 21-34.

650. Peterson, Levi S. "The Primitive and the Civilized in Western Fiction." *Western American Literature* 1 (Fall 1966): 197-207.

651. ——. "Tragedy and Western American Literature." *Western American Literature* 6 (Winter 1972): 243-49.

652. Peyroutet, Jean A. "The North Dakota Farmer in Fiction." *North Dakota Quarterly* 39 (Winter 1971): 59-71.

653. Phillips, James E. "Arcadia on the Range." *Themes and Directions in American Literature: Essays in Honor of Leon Howard.* Eds. Ray B. Browne and Donald Pizer. Lafayette, Ind.: Purdue University Studies, 1969, pp. 108-29.

654. Pilkington, W. T. "Aspects of the Western Comic Novel." *Western American Literature* 1 (Fall 1966): 209-17.

655. ——. "The Recent Southwestern Novel." *Southwestern American Literature* 1 (January 1971): 12-15.

656. Pollard, Lancaster. "Washington Literature: A Historical Sketch." *Pacific Northwest Quarterly* 29 (July 1938): 227-54.

657. Polos, Nicholas C. "Early California Poetry." *California Historical Society Quarterly*

48 (September 1969): 243-55.

658. Pomeroy, Earl. "Old Lamps for New: The Cultural Lag in Pacific Coast Historiography." *Arizona and the West* 2 (Summer 1960): 107-26.

659. ——. "Rediscovering the West." *American Quarterly* 12 (Spring 1960): 20-30.

660. ——. "Towards a Reorientation of Western History: Continuity and Environment." *Mississippi Valley Historical Review* 41 (March 1955): 579-600. A major interpretive essay.

661. Porter, Mark. "Mysticism of the Land and the Western Novel." *South Dakota Review* 11 (Spring 1973): 79-91.

662. Poulsen, Richard C. "The Trail Drive Novel: A Matter of Balance." *Southwestern American Literature* 4 (1974): 53-61.

663. Putnam, Jackson K. "Historical Fact and Literary Truth: The Problem of Authenticity in Western American Literature." *Western American Literature* 15 (May 1980): 17-23.

664. Quantic, Diane Dufva. "The Ambivalence of Rural Life in Prairie Literature." *Kansas Quarterly* 12 (Spring 1980): 109-19.

665. ——. "The Revolt from the Village and Middle Western Fiction 1870-1915." *Kansas Quarterly* 5 (Fall 1973): 5-16.

666. Robinson, John W. "High Sierra Classics." *Book Club of California Quarterly Newsletter* 42 (Winter 1976): 3-20.

667. Rodenberger, Lou. "'The Gen-u-wine Stuff': Character Makes the Difference in the Trail-Drivin' Novel." *Heritage of Kansas* 11 (Winter 1978): 3-12.

668. Ronald, Ann. "The Tonopah Ladies." *Women, Women Writers, and the West.* Eds. Lawrence L. Lee and Merrill E. Lewis. Troy, N.Y.: Whitston, 1978.

669. ——. "Western Women Writing." Essay Review. *Western American Literature* 14 (Summer 1979): 171-74.

670. Rudolph, Earle Leighton. "The Frontier in American Literature." *Jahrbuch, für Amerikastudien* 7 (1962): 77-91.

671. Rundell, Walter, Jr. "Concepts of the 'Frontier' and the 'West.'" *Arizona and the West* 1 (Spring 1959): 13-41.

672. Rusch, Lana Koepp. "The American Dream in Selected South Dakota Novels." *South Dakota Review* 12 (Autumn 1974): 58-72.

673. Sage, Frances. "Contemporary Women Poets of Texas." *Texas Quarterly* (Summer 1978): 84-108.

674. Sage, Leland L. "Iowa Writers and Painters: An Historical Survey." *Annals of Iowa* 42 (Spring 1974): 241-70.

675. Saucerman, James R. "A Critical Approach to Plains Poetry." *Western American Literature* 15 (Summer 1980): 93-102.

676. Savage, William W., Jr. "Western Literature and Its Myths: A Rejoinder." *Montana: The Magazine of Western History* 22 (October 1972): 78-81.

677. Schlissel, Lillian. "Women's Diaries on the Western Frontier." *American Studies* 18 (Spring 1977): 87-100.

678. Schopf, Bill. "The Image of the West in the *Century*, 1881-1889." *Possible Sack* 3 (March 1972): 8-13.

679. Schroeder, Fred E. H. "The Development of the Super-Ego on the American Frontier." *Soundings* 57 (1974): 189-205.

680. Schwartz, Joseph. "The Wild West Show. 'Everything Genuine.'" *Journal of Popular Culture* 3 (Spring 1970): 656-66.

681. Scullin, George. "The Old Wild West." *Cosmopolitan* 145 (November 1958): 48-55.

682. Seelye, John. "Some Green Thoughts on a Green Theme." *TriQuarterly* 23-24 (Winter-Spring 1972): 576-638.

683. Sellars, Richard West. "The Interrelationship of Literature, History and Geography in Western Writing." *Western Historical Quarterly* 4 (April 1973): 171-85.

684. Seshachari, Candadai. "In Search of Literary Scalps: Some Observations on the Shortcomings of American Western Fiction." *Studies in American Literature*. . . . Eds. Jagdish Chandler and Narindar S. Pradhan. Delhi: Oxford University Press, 1976, pp. 127-33.

685. Shadoian, Jack. "Yuh Got Pecos: Doggone, Belle, Yuh're As Good as Two Men." *Journal of Popular Culture* 12 (Spring 1979): 721-36.

686. Shaul, Lawana J. "The West in Magazine Fiction, 1870-1900." *Studies in the Literature of the West*. Laramie: University of Wyoming, 1956, pp. 29-56.

687. Sherman, Caroline B. "The Development of American Rural Fiction." *Agricultural History* 12 (January 1938): 67-76.

688. ——. "Farm Life Fiction." *South Atlantic Quarterly* 27 (July 1928): 310-24.

689. ——. "Rural Literature Faces Peace." *South Atlantic Quarterly* 42 (January 1943): 59-71.

690. Simonson, Harold P. "Pacific Northwest Literature—Its Coming of Age." *Pacific Northwest Quarterly* 71 (October 1980): 146-51.

691. Singer, Barnett. "Toward the Great Northwest Novel." *Research Studies* 43 (1975): 55-69.

692. Skårdal, Dorothy Burton. "The Scandinavian Immigrant Writer in America." *Norwegian-American Studies* 21 (1962): 14-53.

693. Smith, Duane Allan. "Mining Camps: Myth vs. Reality." *Colorado Magazine* 44 (Spring 1967): 93-110.

694. Smith, Edwin B. "'The Confused West': A Literary Forecast." *Essays and Addresses*. Chicago: A. C. McClurg, 1909, pp. 360-76.

695. Smith, Goldie Capers. "*The Over-*

land Monthly: Landmark in American Literature." *New Mexico Quarterly* 33 (Autumn 1963): 333-40.

696. Smith, Henry Nash. "Can 'American Studies' Develop a Method?" *American Quarterly* 9 (Summer 1957): 197-208.

697. ——. "The Dime Novel Heroine." *Southwest Review* 34 (Spring 1949): 182-88.

698. ——. "The Frontier Hypothesis and the Myth of the West." *American Quarterly* 2 (Spring 1950): 3-11.

699. ——. "Kit Carson in Books." *Southwest Review* 28 (Winter 1943): 164-90.

700. ——. "Origins of Native American Literary Tradition." *The American Writer and the European.* Eds. Margaret Denny and William H. Gibson. Minneapolis: University of Minnesota Press, 1959, pp. 63-77.

701. ——. "*Virgin Land* Revisited." *Indian Journal of American Studies* 3 (1973): 83-90.

702. ——. "The West as an Image of the American Past." *University of Kansas City Review* 18 (Autumn 1951): 29-40.

703. ——. "Western Chroniclers and Literary Pioneers." *Literary History of the United States.* Eds. Robert E. Spiller, et al. 3 vols. New York: Macmillan, 1948.

704. ——. "The Western Farmer in Imaginative Literature, 1818-1891." *Mississippi Valley Historical Review* 36 (December 1949): 479-90.

705. ——. "The Western Hero in the Dime Novel." *Southwest Review* 33 (Summer 1948): 276-84.

706. Smith, Rebecca W. "The Southwest in Fiction." *Saturday Review* 25 (May 16, 1942): 12-13, 37.

707. Snyder, Gary. "The Incredible Survival of Coyote." *Western American Literature* 9 (February 1975): 255-72.

708. Sondrup, Steven P. "Literary Dimensions of Mormon Autobiography." *Dialogue* 11 (Summer 1978): 75-80.

709. Sonnichsen, C. L. "Fiction and History." *Mountain-Plains Library Quarterly* 13 (Summer 1968): 3-9.

710. ——. "The New Style Western." *South Dakota Review* 4 (Summer 1966): 22-28.

711. ——. "Tombstone in Fiction." *Journal of Arizona History* 9 (Summer 1968): 58-76.

712. ——. "The Two Black Legends." *Southwestern American Literature* 3 (1973): 5-21; with bibliography "Fiction of the Spanish-American Southwest, A Selection," pp. 22-26.

713. ——. "The West That Wasn't': Some Observations on Our Dual Citizenship in the Wests of Myth and Reality." *American West* 14 (November-December 1977): 8-15.

714. ——. "The Wyatt Earp Syndrome." *American West* 7 (May 1970): 26-28, 60-62.

715. Spinning, Bruce. "Notes Toward a Theory of Poetry in the

American West." *Possible Sack* 5 (January 1974): 29-38.

716. Steckmesser, Kent L. "Custer in Fiction." *American West* 1 (Fall 1964): 47-52, 63-64.

717. ——. "Paris and the Wild West." *Southwest Review* 54 (Spring 1969): 168-74.

718. Steensma, Robert C. "'Stay Right There and Toughy It Out': The American Homesteader as Autobiographer." *Western Review* 6 (Spring 1969): 10-18.

719. Stegner, Wallace. "Born a Square —The Westerner's Dilemma." *Atlantic* 213 (January 1964): 46-50.

720. ——. "Commentary: A Matter of Continuity." *American West Review* 1 (December 1, 1967): 12.

721. ——. "History, Myth, and the Western Writer." *American West* 4 (May 1967): 61-62, 76-79.

722. ——, and Page Stegner. "Rocky Mountain Country: Newcomers to the Suburbs of Eden." *Atlantic Monthly* 241 (April 1978): 44-64, 71-91.

723. Stevenson, Dorothy. "The Battle for Buckshot Basin." *New Mexico Quarterly* 33 (Autumn 1963): 315-24.

724. Stewart, George R. "The West as Seen from the East (1800-1850)." *Pacific Spectator* 1 (Spring 1947): 188-95.

725. Straight, Michael. "Truth and Formula for the Western Novel." *South Dakota Review* 2 (Autumn 1964): 88-93.

726. Swallow, Alan. "A Magazine for the West?" *Inland* 1 (Autumn 1957): 3-6.

727. ——. "The Mavericks." *Critique* 2 (Winter 1959): 74-92.

728. ——. "Poetry of the West." *South Dakota Review* 2 (Autumn 1964): 77-87.

729. Tate, George S. "Halldór Laxness, the Mormons and the Promised Land." *Dialogue* 11 (Summer 1978): 25-37.

730. Taylor, J. Golden. "The Western Short Story." *South Dakota Review* 2 (Autumn 1964): 37-55.

731. Taylor, Samuel W. "Peculiar People, Positive Thinkers and the Prospect of Mormon Literature." *Dialogue* 2 (Summer 1967): 17-31.

732. Tenefelde, Nancy L. "New Frontiers Revisited." *Midwest Review* 4 (1962): 54-62.

733. Todd, Edgeley W. "James Hall and the Hugh Glass Legend." *American Quarterly* 7 (Winter 1955): 363-70.

734. ——. "A Note on 'The Mountain Man as Literary Hero.'" *Western American Literature* 1 (Fall 1966): 219-21.

735. Torres-Rioseco, Arturo. "The Twenty-Five Year Anniversary of Don Segundo Sombra." *New Mexico Quarterly* 21 (Autumn 1951): 274-80. Deals with the South American cowboy novel.

736. Tynan, Kathleen. "Why They Live Here: Literary Letter from Los Angeles." *New York Times Book Review,* 18 November 1979, pp. 42-43.

737. Van Doren, Mark. "Repudiation of the Pioneer." *English Journal* 17 (October 1928): 616–23.

738. Venn, George. "Continuity in Northwest Literature." *Northwest Perspectives: Essays on the Culture of the Pacific Northwest.* Eds. Edwin R. Bingham and Glen A. Love. Seattle: University of Washington Press, 1979, pp. 99–118.

739. Veysey, Laurence R. "Myth and Reality in Approaching American Regionalism." *American Quarterly* 12 (Spring 1960): 31–43. In part a critique of H. N. Smith's *Virgin Land.*

740. Waldmeir, J. J. "The Cowboy, Knight and Popular Taste." *Southern Folklore Quarterly* 22 (September 1958): 113–20.

741. Walker, Don D. "Can the Western Tell What Happens?" *Rendezvous* 7 (Winter 1972): 33–47.

742. ——. "Criticism of the Cowboy Novel: Retrospect and Reflections." *Western American Literature* 11 (February 1977): 275–96.

743. ——. "Essays in the Criticisms of Western Literary Criticism." *Possible Sack* 2 (March 1971): 1–3; (August 1971): 1–4.

744. ——. "Freedom and Destiny in the Myth of the American West." *New Mexico Quarterly* 33 (Winter 1963–64): 381–87.

745. ——. "History and Imagination: The Prose and the Poetry of the Cattle Industry, 1895–1905." *Pacific Historical Review* 45 (August 1976): 379–97.

746. ——. "The Love Song of Barney Tullus." *Western Humanities Review* 26 (Summer 1972): 237–45.

747. ——. "The Meaning of the *Outlaw* in the Mind of the West." *Possible Sack* 2 (Summer 1971): 1–7.

748. ——. "The Mountain Man as Literary Hero." *Western American Literature* 1 (Spring 1966): 15–25.

749. ——. "The Mountain Man Journal: Its Significance in a Literary History of the Fur Trade." *Western Historical Quarterly* 5 (July 1974): 307–18.

750. ——. "Philosophical and Literary Implications in the Historiography of the Fur Trade." *Western American Literature* 9 (Summer 1974): 79–104.

751. ——. "Reading on the Range: The Literary Habits of the American Cowboy." *Arizona and the West* 2 (Winter 1960): 307–18.

752. ——. "Riders and Reality: A Philosophical Problem in the Historiography of the Cattle Trade." *Western Historical Quarterly* 9 (April 1978): 163–79.

753. ——. "The Rise and Fall of Barney Tullus." *Western American Literature* 3 (Summer 1968): 93–102. All students of western literature should read this essay.

754. ——. "Ways of Seeing a Mountain: Some Preliminary Remarks on

the Fur Trader as Writer." *Possible Sack* 3 (August-September 1972): 1-7.

755. ——. "Who Is Going to Ride Point?" *The Westering Experience in American Literature: Bicentennial Essays.* Eds. Merrill Lewis and L. L. Lee. Bellingham: Bureau for Faculty Research, Western Washington University, 1977, pp. 23-31. Reality in cowboy fiction.

756. Walker, Franklin. "On Writing Literary History." *Pacific Historical Review* 45 (August 1976): 349-56.

757. Walker, Robert H. "The Poets Interpret the Western Frontier." *Mississippi Valley Historical Review* 47 (March 1961): 619-35.

758. Walker, William S. "Buckskin West: Leatherstocking at High Noon." *New York Folklore Quarterly* 24 (June 1968): 88-102.

759. Warren, Sidney. *Farthest Frontier: The Pacific Northwest.* New York: Macmillan, 1949, pp. 242-74.

760. Weaver, John D. "The Antic Arts—The Western Hero." *Holiday* 34 (August 1963): 77-80, 91.

761. Webb, Walter P. "The American West: Perpetual Mirage." *Harper's* 214 (May 1957): 25-31.

762. ——. "The Great Frontier and Modern Literature." *Southwest Review* 37 (Spring 1952): 85-100.

763. West, Ray B., Jr. "Four Rocky Mountain Novels." *Rocky Mountain Review* 10 (Autumn 1945): 21-28.

764. Westbrook, Max. "The Authentic Western." *Western American Literature* 13 (Fall 1978): 213-25.

765. ——. "Conservative, Liberal, and Western: Three Modes of American Realism." *South Dakota Review* 4 (Summer 1966): 3-19.

766. ——. Essay review of *Towards a New American Poetics. Western American Literature* 14 (Summer 1979): 165-70.

767. ——. "The Ontological Critic." *Rendezvous* 7 (Winter 1972): 49-66.

768. ——. "Mountain Home: The Hero in the American West." *The Westering Experience in American Literature: Bicentennial Essays.* Eds. Merrill Lewis and L. L. Lee. Bellingham: Bureau for Faculty Research, Western Washington University, 1977, pp. 9-18.

769. ——. "The Practical Spirit: Sacrality and the American West." *Western American Literature* 3 (Fall 1968): 193-205.

770. ——. "The Themes of Western Fiction." *Southwest Review* 43 (Summer 1958): 232-38.

771. Westermeier, Clifford P. "The Cowboy—His Pristine Image." *South Dakota History* 8 (Winter 1977): 1-23. Late nineteenth-century treatments of the cowboy.

772. ——. "The Cowboy—Sinner or Saint." *New Mexico Historical Review* 25 (April 1950): 89-108.

773. Whetton, Betty. "A Very Personal View of Western Literature." *Arizona English Bulletin* 13 (April 1971): 59-61.

774. Whisenhunt, Donald W. "The Bard in the Depression: Texas Style." *Journal of Popular Culture* 2 (Winter 1968): 370-86.

775. White, Hayden. "Structuralism and Popular Culture." *Journal of Popular Culture* 7 (Spring 1974): 759-75.

776. White, Helen C. "The Writing of Historical Romance." *Wisconsin Magazine of History* 40 (Winter 1956-57): 83-86.

777. Wiget, Andrew. "Wonders of the Visible World: Changing Images of the Wilderness in Captivity Narratives." *The Westering Experience in American Literature: Bicentennial Essays.* Eds. Merrill Lewis and L. L. Lee. Bellingham: Bureau for Faculty Research, Western Washington University, 1977, pp. 69-84.

778. Wilgus, D. K. "The Individual Song: 'Billy the Kid.'" *Western Folklore* 30 (July 1971): 226-34.

779. Williams, John. "The 'Western': Definition of the Myth." *Nation* 193 (November 18, 1961): 401-6.

780. Willson, Lawrence. "The Transcendentalist View of the West." *Western Humanities Review* 14 (Summer 1960): 183-91.

781. Winther, Sophus Keith. "The Emigrant Theme." *Arizona Quarterly* 34 (Spring 1978): 31-43.

782. Wolf, Bobi. "Westerns in Eastern Europe." *Pacific Historian* 21 (Spring 1977): 29-35.

783. "Writing in the West and Midwest." *Critique* 2 (Winter 1959): 1-97.

784. Wylder, Delbert E. "Recent Western Fiction." *Journal of the West* 19 (January 1980): 62-70.

785. ———. "The Western Hero From a Strange Perspective." *Rendezvous* 7 (Winter 1972): 23-32.

786. Yoder, John A. "Miscegenation in Our Virgin Land." *South Dakota Review* 12 (Winter 1974-75): 102-10.

787. Young, Mary. "The West and American Cultural Identity: Old Themes and New Variations." *Western Historical Quarterly* 1 (January 1970): 137-60.

788. Young, Vernon. "An American Dream and Its Parody." *Arizona Quarterly* 6 (Summer 1950): 112-23.

789. Zanger, Jules. "The Frontiersman in Popular Fiction." *The Frontier Re-Examined.* Ed. John Francis McDermott. Urbana: University of Illinois Press, 1968.

SPECIAL TOPICS

LOCAL COLOR AND REGIONALISM

790. Allen, Charles. "Regionalism and the Little Magazines." *College English* 7 (October 1945): 10–16.

791. Anderson, David D. "Regional Reality: An Approach to Fiction." *Society for the Study of Midwestern Literature Newsletter* 7 (1977): 9–11.

792. Austin, Mary. "Regionalism in American Fiction." *English Journal* 21 (February 1932): 97–107.

793. Baker, Joseph E. "Four Arguments for Regionalism." *Saturday Review* 15 (November 28, 1936): 3–4, 14.

794. ——. "Provinciality." *College English* 1 (March 1940): 488–94.

795. ——. "Regionalism in the Middle West." *American Review* 4 (March 1935): 603–14.

796. ——. "Western Man Against Nature." *College English* 4 (October 1942): 19–26.

797. Beggs, Nancy Marie Kyker. "Development of the Regional American Short Story." Doctoral dissertation, East Texas State University, 1980.

798. Benson, Peter Edward. "Regional Realism and Regional Magazines in the American 1890s." Doctoral dissertation, State University of New York, Stony Brook, 1978.

799. Benton, Thomas H. "American Regionalism: A Personal History of the Movement." *University of Kansas City Review* 17 (Autumn 1951): 41–75.

800. Bernard, Harry. *Le Roman régionaliste aux Étas-Unis, 1913–1940.* Montreal: Editions Fides, 1949.

801. Botkin, Benjamin A. "Regionalism: Cult or Culture?" *English Journal* 25 (March 1936): 181–85.

802. ——. "We Talk about Regionalism—North, East, South, and West." *Frontier* 13 (May 1933): 286–96.

803. Boynton, Percy H. *The Rediscovery of the Frontier.* Chicago: University of Chicago Press, 1931.

804. Bracher, Frederick. "California's Literary Regionalism." *American Quarterly* 7 (Fall 1955): 275–84.

805. Brasher, Minnie M. "Missouri Literature Since the First World War: Part III—The Novel." *Missouri Historical Review* 41 (April 1947): 241–65.

806. Brodin, Pierre. *Le Roman Régionaliste Américain. . . .* Paris: G.-P. Maisonneuve, 1937.

807. Brooks, Cleanth. "Regionalism in American Literature." *Journal of Southern History* 26 (Fall 1960): 35–43.

808. Burke, John Gordon, ed. *Regional Perspectives: An Examination*

of America's Literary Heritage. Chicago: American Library Association, 1973. Contains essays on the Midwest, the Southwest, and the frontier; also includes a bibliography of commentary on regionalism.

809. Chametzky, Jules. "Regional Literature and Ethnic Realities." *Antioch Review* 31 (Fall 1971): 385-96. Provocative essay on the narrowness of regional literature.

810. Coleman, Rufus A. "Literature and the Region." *Pacific Northwest Quarterly* 39 (October 1948): 312-18.

811. Davidson, Donald. "Regionalism and Nationalism in American Literature." *American Review* 5 (April 1935): 48-61.

812. Dike, Donald A. "Notes on Local Color and Its Relation to Realism." *College English* 14 (November 1952): 81-88.

813. Dobie, J. Frank. "The Writer and His Region." *Southwest Review* 35 (Spring 1950): 81-87.

814. Dondore, Dorothy. "Points of Contact Between History and Literature in the Mississippi Valley." *Mississippi Valley Historical Review* 11 (September 1924): 227-36.

815. Dooley, Nelly. "Sectionalism and Local Color in the Short Stories of the Plains States, 1870-1938." Master's thesis, Fort Hays Kansas State College, 1940.

816. DuBois, Arthur E. "Among the Quarterlies: The Question of 'Regionalism.'" *Sewanee Review* 45 (April-June 1937): 216-27.

817. Eichelberger, Clayton. "Relation of Local Color to the Range Fiction of Wister, Lewis, and Rhodes." Master's thesis, University of Colorado, 1950.

818. Erisman, Fred. "Regionalism in American Children's Literature." *Society and Children's Literature.* Ed. James H. Fraser. Boston: David R. Godine, 1978, pp. 53-75.

819. ——. "Regionalism in Western American Literature." *Idaho Humanities Forum,* Spring 1981, pp. 7-8.

820. ——. "Western Literary Regionalism: A Status Report." *Regionalism and the Female Imagination* 4 (1978): 14-18.

821. ——. "Western Regional Writers and the Uses of Place." *Journal of the West* 19 (January 1980): 36-44.

822. Etulain, Richard W. "Comment." *Pacific Northwest Quarterly* 64 (October 1973): 157-59. Literary regionalism in the Pacific Northwest.

823. ——. "Frontier and Region in Western Literature." *Southwestern American Literature* 1 (September 1971): 121-28.

824. Everson, William. *Archetype West: The Pacific Coast as a Literary Region.* Berkeley, Calif.: Oyez, 1976.

825. Fisher, Vardis. "The Novelist and His Background." *Western Folklore* 12 (January 1953): 1-8.

826. Fishwick, Marshall. "What Ever

Happened to Regionalism?" *Southern Humanities Review* 2 (Fall 1968): 393–401.

827. Fiske, Horace S. *Provincial Types in American Fiction.* New York: Chautauqua, 1903.

828. Flanagan, John. "The Middle Western Farm Novel." *Minnesota History* 23 (June 1942): 113–47.

829. ——. "Middlewestern Regional Literature." *Research Opportunities in American Cultural History.* Ed. John Francis McDermott. Lexington: University of Kentucky Press, 1961, pp. 124–39.

830. ——. "Some Middlewestern Literary Magazines." *Papers on Language and Literature* 3 (Summer 1967): 237–57.

831. Geary, Edward A. "Women Regionalists of Mormon Country." *Kate Chopin Newsletter* 2 (1976): 20–26.

832. Gohdes, Clarence. "Exploitation of the Provinces." *The Literature of the American People.* . . . Ed. Arthur H. Quinn. New York: Appleton-Century-Crofts, 1951, pp. 639–60.

833. Hakac, John. "Southwestern Regional Material in a Literature Class." *Western Review* 7 (Spring 1970): 12–18.

834. Harkness, David James. *The Literary Midwest.* University of Tennessee News Letter 37 (February 1958).

835. Horgan, Paul. "The Pleasures and Perils of Regionalism." *Western American Literature* 8 (Winter 1974): 167–71.

836. Hubbell, Jay B. "The Decay of the Provinces. . . ." *Sewanee Review* 35 (October 1927): 473–87.

837. Jensen, Merrill, ed. *Regionalism in America.* Madison: University of Wisconsin Press, 1951, 1965.

838. Johnson, Thomas. "Regionalism and Local Color." *Literary History of the U.S.* Eds. Robert E. Spiller, et al. New York: Macmillan, 1948, Vol. 3, pp. 304–25; 3d ed., 1963, Vol. 2, pp. 304–25.

839. Kehde, Martha, comp. "Regionalism in American Literature: A Bibliography." *Regional Perspectives: An Examination of America's Literary Heritage.* Ed. John G. Burke. Chicago: American Library Association, 1973, pp. 307–10.

840. Keller, Richard Morton. "Regionalism in the Novels of the Northwest." Master's thesis, State College of Washington, 1938.

841. Kellock, Katharine. "The WPA Writers: Portraitists of the United States." *American Scholar* 9 (Autumn 1940): 473–82.

842. Kelton, Elmer. "Fact, Folklore and Fiction—Regional Writing." *Texas Library Journal* 52 (May 1976): 47–51.

843. King, Kimball. "Local Color and the Rise of the American Magazine." *Essays Mostly on Periodical Publishing in America: A Collection in Honor of Clarence Gohdes.* Ed. James

Woodress, et al. Durham, N.C.: Duke University Press, 1973, pp. 121-33.

844. Lawson, Benjamin S., Jr. "American Local Color in the British Isles." Doctoral dissertation, Bowling Green State University, 1972.

845. Mabie, Hamilton W. "Provincialism in American Life." *Harper's* 134 (March 1917): 575-84.

846. Mawer, Randall Ray. "Cosmopolitan Characters in Local Color Fiction." Doctoral dissertation, University of Pennsylvania, 1976.

847. Macleod, Norman, et al. "Regionalism: A Symposium." *Sewanee Review* 39 (October-December 1931): 456-83.

848. McDowell, Tremaine. "Regionalism in American Literature." *Minnesota History* 20 (June 1939): 105-18.

849. McWilliams, Carey. "Localism in American Criticism, a Century and a Half of Controversy." *Southwest Review* 19 (1934): 410-28.

850. ——. *The New Regionalism in American Literature*. Seattle: University of Washington Book Store, 1930.

851. Morrow, Patrick D. "Parody and Parable in Early Western Local Color Writing." *Journal of the West* 19 (January 1980): 9-16.

852. Neinstein, Raymond L. "Neo-Regionalism in America." Doctoral dissertation, State University of New York, Buffalo, 1977.

853. Odum, Howard W., and Harry Estill Moore. *American Regionalism*. New York: Henry Holt, 1938.

854. Oldham, John N. "Anatomy of Provincialism." *Sewanee Review* 44 (1936): 68-75, 145-52, 296-302.

855. Petry, Alice Hall. "Local Color Fiction 1879-1910." Doctoral dissertation, Brown University, 1979.

856. ——. "Universal and Particular: The Local-Color Phenomenon Reconsidered." *American Literary Realism 1870-1910* 12 (Spring 1979): 111-26.

857. Radke, Merle L. "Local-Color Fiction in Middle-Western Magazines, 1865-1900." Doctoral dissertation, Northwestern University, 1965.

858. Ransom, John C. "The Aesthetic of Regionalism." *American Review* 2 (January 1934): 290-310.

859. Raymond, Catherine E. "'Down to Earth': Sense of Place in Midwestern Literature." Doctoral dissertation, University of Pennsylvania, 1979.

860. "The Realities of Regionalism: A Symposium." *South Dakota Review* 18 (Winter 1981). A special issue containing comments by Lois Phillips Hudson, Gilbert Fite, Frederick Manfred, and William Stafford.

861. Reigelman, Milton M. *The Midland: A Venture in Literary Regionalism*. Iowa City: University of Iowa Press, 1975.

862. Rhode, Robert D. "Scenery and Setting: A Note on American

Local Color." *College English* 13 (December 1951): 142-46.

863. ———. *Setting in the American Short Story of Local Color.* The Hague: Mouton, 1975.

864. Rovit, Earl H. "The Regions versus the Nation: Critical Battle of the Thirties." *Mississippi Quarterly* 13 (Spring 1960): 90-98.

865. Saum, L. O. "The Success Theme in Great Plains Realism." *American Quarterly* 18 (Winter 1966): 579-98.

866. Simpson, Claude M., ed. *The Local Colorists: American Short Stories, 1857-1900.* New York: Harper and Brothers, 1960.

867. Skelley, Grant Teasdale. "The *Overland Monthly* under Millicent Washburn Shinn, 1883-1894: A Study of Regional Publishing." Doctoral dissertation, University of California, Berkeley, 1968.

868. "The Southwest: A Regional View." *New America* 3 (Spring 1979). Special topic issue.

869. Spencer, Benjamin T. "Nationality During the Interregnum." *American Literature* 32 (January 1961): 434-45.

870. ———. *The Quest for Nationality: An American Literary Campaign.* Syracuse, N.Y.: Syracuse University Press, 1957.

871. ———. "Regionalism in American Literature." *Regionalism in America.* Ed. Merrill Jensen. Madison: University of Wisconsin Press, 1952, pp. 219-60.

872. Stearns, Bertha-Monica. "Literary Rivalry and Local Books (1836-1860)." *Americana* 30 (January 1936): 7-19.

873. Stewart, George R. "The Regional Approach to Literature." *College English* 9 (April 1948): 370-75.

874. Suckow, Ruth. "Middle Western Literature." *English Journal* 21 (March 1932): 175-82.

875. Tate, Allen. "The New Provincialism. . . ." *Virginia Quarterly Review* 21 (1945): 262-72.

876. *Towards a Native Rural Culture: American Regional Literature.* . . . Madison, Wis., 1941.

877. Tuppet, Mary M. "A History of *The Southwest Review*: Toward an Understanding of Regionalism." Doctoral dissertation, University of Illinois, 1966.

878. Veysey, Lawrence R. "Myth and Reality in Approaching Western Regionalism." *American Quarterly* 12 (Spring 1960): 31-43.

879. Walcutt, Charles C. "The Regional Novel and Its Future." *Arizona Quarterly* 1 (Summer 1945): 17-27.

880. ———. "Regionalism—Practical or Aesthetic?" *Sewanee Review* 49 (1941): 165-72.

881. Walterhouse, Roger R. *Bret Harte, Joaquin Miller, and the Western Local Color Story: A Study in the Origins of Popular Fiction.* Chicago: University of Chicago Libraries, 1939.

882. Warfel, Harry R., and G. Harrison Orians, eds. *American Local-Color Stories.* New York: American Book, 1941.

883. Warren, Robert P. "Some Don'ts for Literary Regionalists." *American Review* 8 (December 1936): 142-50.
884. Weathers, Winston. "The Writer and His Region." *Southwestern American Literature* 2 (Spring 1972): 25-32.
885. Weigant, Leo Augustus. "The Manners Tradition and Regional Fiction in Nineteenth-Century America." Doctoral dissertation, Duke University, 1969.
886. Wells, Walter. *Tycoons and Locusts: A Regional Look at Hollywood Fiction of the 1930's.* Carbondale: Southern Illinois University Press, 1973.
887. Williams, Cecil B. "The American Local Color Movement and Its Cultural Significance." *Oklahoma State University Publications* 48 (September 30, 1951): 5-13.
888. ——. "Regionalism in American Literature." *Geist Einer Freien Gesellschaft.* Heidelberg: Verlag Quelle and Meyer, 1962, pp. 331-87.
889. Winther, Sophus K. "The Limits of Regionalism." *Arizona Quarterly* 8 (Spring 1952): 30-36.
890. Wood, Ann D. "The Literature of Impoverishment: The Women Local Colorists in America, 1865-1914." *Women's Studies* 1 (1972): 3-46.

POPULAR WESTERN LITERATURE:
DIME NOVELS
AND THE WESTERN

891. Agnew, Seth M. "Destry Goes on Riding—or—Working the Six-Gun Lode." *Publisher's Weekly* 162 (August 23, 1952): 746-51.
892. ——. "God's Country and the Publisher." *Saturday Review* 36 (March 14, 1953): 26-27.
893. ——. "The Literary Tumbleweed." *Saturday Review* 36 (March 27, 1954): 15 ff.
894. Arbuckle, Donald Redmond. "Popular Western: The History of a Commercial Literary Formula." Doctoral dissertation, University of Pennsylvania, 1977.
895. Barker, Warren J., M.D. "The Stereotyped Western Story: Its Latent Meaning and Psychoeconomic Function." *Psychoanalytic Quarterly* 24 (April 1955): 270-80.
896. Barsness, John A. "The Breaking of A Myth: A Study of Cultural Implications in the Development of the Western Novel in the Twentieth Century." Doctoral dissertation, University of Minnesota, 1968.
897. Bennett, M. H. "The Scenic West: Silent Mirage." *Colorado Quarterly* 8 (Summer 1959): 15-25.
898. Birney, Hoffman. "A Year-End Roundup on the Western Range." *NYTBR,* 4 December 1955, p. 38.
899. Bloodworth, William. "Literary Extensions of the Formula Western." *Western American Literature* 14 (Winter 1980): 287-96.
900. Bluestone, George. "The Changing Cowboy: From Dime Novel

to Dollar Film." *Western Humanities Review* 14 (Summer 1960): 331-37.

901. Boatright, Mody C. "The American Myth Rides the Range." *Southwest Review* 36 (Summer 1951): 157-63.

902. ——. "The Beginnings of Cowboy Fiction." *Southwest Review* 51 (Winter 1966): 11-28.

903. ——. "The Formula in Cowboy Fiction and Drama." *Western Folklore* 28 (April 1969): 136-45.

904. Boies, J. J. "Billy the Kid: The Myth and Its American Subliterary Treatments." *Markham Review* 6 (Spring 1977): 41-49.

905. Branch, Edward Douglas. *The Cowboy and His Interpreters.* New York: D. Appleton, 1926.

906. Brashers, Howard C. "The Cowboy Story from Stereotype to Art." *Moderna Sprak* 57 (1963): 290-99.

907. Burack, A. S., ed. *The Craft of Novel Writing.* Boston: The Writer, 1948, pp. 178-89.

908. Calder, Jenni. *There Must Be a Lone Ranger: The American West in Film and in Reality.* New York: Taplinger, 1975.

909. Capps, Benjamin. "The Promise of Western Fiction." *Roundup* 17 (October 1969): 1-2, 20; (November 1969): 2, 4, 14; (December 1969): 6, 8, 24.

910. Cawelti, John G. *Adventure, Mystery, and Romance: Formula Stories as Art and Popular Culture.* Chicago: University of Chicago Press, 1976, pp. 192-259.

911. ——. "Cowboys, Indians, Outlaws: The West in Myth and Fantasy." *American West* 1 (Spring 1964): 28-35, 77-79.

912. ——. "The Gunfighter and Society." *American West* 5 (March 1968): 30-35, 76-78.

913. ——. "Prolegomena to the Western." *Studies in Public Communication* 6 (Autumn 1962): 57-70.

914. ——. "Prolegomena to the Western." *Western American Literature* 6 (Winter 1970): 259-71.

915. ——. "Recent Trends in the Study of Popular Culture." *American Studies: An International Newsletter* 10 (Winter 1971): 23-37. Includes helpful bibliography.

916. ——. *The Six-Gun Mystique.* Bowling Green, Ohio: Bowling Green University Popular Press, [1971].

917. Cleary, Michael. "Saddle Sore: Parody and Satire in the Contemporary Western Novel." Doctoral dissertation, Middle Tennessee State University, 1978.

918. Clements, William M. "Savage, Pastoral, Civilized: An Ecology Typology of American Frontier Heroes." *Journal of Popular Culture* 8 (Fall 1974): 254-66.

919. Cronin, Con P. "Arizona's Six Gun Classic." *Arizona Historical Review* 3 (July 1930): 7-11.

920. Cunningham, Eugene. "Better Westerns." *Writer* 53 (April 1940): 105-8.

921. Curti, Merle. "Dime Novels and the American Tradition." *Yale Review* 26 (Summer 1937): 761-78.

922. Davidson, Levette J. "Fact or Formula in 'Western' Fiction." *Colorado Quarterly* 3 (Winter 1955): 278-87.

923. Davis, David B. "Ten-Gallon Hero." *American Quarterly* 6 (Summer 1954): 111-25.

924. Derleth, August W. "Romantic Story." *Writing Fiction*. Boston: The Writer, 1946.

925. DeVoto, Bernard. "Birth of an Art." *Harper's* 221 (December 1955): 8-9, 12, 14, 16.

926. ——. "Phaëthon on Gunsmoke Trail." *Harper's* 209 (December 1954): 10-11, 14, 16.

927. ——. "Horizon Land (1)." *Saturday Review* 14 (October 17, 1936): 8; "Horizon Land (2)." *Saturday Review* 15 (April 24, 1937): 8.

928. Durham, Philip. "The Cowboy and the Myth Makers." *Journal of Popular Culture* 1 (Summer 1967): 58-62.

929. ——. "Dime Novels: An American Heritage." *Western Humanities Review* 9 (Winter 1954-55): 33-43.

930. ——. "Introduction," to *Seth Jones by Edward S. Ellis and Deadwood Dick on Deck by Edward L. Wheeler: Dime Novels*. New York: Odyssey Press, 1966, pp. v-xiii.

931. ——. "The Negro Cowboy." *American Quarterly* 7 (Fall 1955): 291-301.

932. ——. "Riders of the Plains: American Westerns." *Neuphilologische Mitteilungen* 58 (November 1957): 22-38.

933. ——, and Everett L. Jones. "The West as Fiction." *The Negro Cowboys*. New York: Dodd, Mead, 1965, pp. 220-30.

934. Dykes, J. C. "High Spots of Western Fiction: 1902-1952." *Westerners Brand Book* 12 (September 1955): 49-56.

935. Etulain, Richard W. "The Historical Development of the Western." *Journal of Popular Culture* 7 (Winter 1973): 717-26.

936. ——. "Literary Historians and the Western." *Journal of Popular Culture* 4 (Fall 1970): 518-26.

937. ——. "Origins of the Western." *Journal of Popular Culture* 6 (Spring 1972): 799-805.

938. ——. "Riding Point: The Western and Its Interpreters." *Journal of Popular Culture* 7 (Winter 1973): 647-51.

939. ——. "The Western." *Handbook of American Popular Culture*. Vol. 1. Ed. M. Thomas Inge. Westport, Conn.: Greenwood Press, 1978, pp. 355-76.

940. ——. "Three Western Novels." *Journal of the West* 10 (April 1971): 389-90.

941. ——, and Michael T. Marsden, eds. *The Popular Western: Essays Toward a Definition*. Bowling Green, Ohio: Bowling

Green University Popular Press, 1974. Collects ten essays and a selective bibliography that appeared simultaneously in *Journal of Popular Culture* 7 (Winter 1973).

942. Fishwick, Marshall W. "The Cowboy: America's Contribution to the World's Mythology." *Western Folklore* 11 (April 1952): 77-92.

943. ——. "Daniel Boone and the Pattern of the Western Hero." *Filson Club Historical Quarterly* 27 (1953): 119-38.

944. Folsom, James K. *The American Western Novel.* New Haven, Conn.: College and University Press, 1966.

945. Frederick, John T. "Worthy Westerns." *English Journal* 43 (September 1954): 281-86, 296.

946. French, Warren. "The Cowboy in the Dime Novel." *Texas Studies in English* 30 (1951): 219-34.

947. ——. "West as Myth: Status Report and Call for Action." *Western American Literature* 1 (Spring 1966): 55-58.

948. Gardner, Erle Stanley. "My Stories of the Wild West." *Atlantic Monthly* 218 (July 1966): 60-62.

949. Garfield, Brian. "The Sun God Myth." *Roundup* 13 (July 1965): 9.

950. ——. "The Western Hero's Eden." *Roundup* 13 (September 1965): 9.

951. ——. "What Is the 'Formula'?" *Roundup* 13 (August 1965): 1-2.

952. Gibson, Michael D. "The Western: A Selective Bibliography." *Journal of Popular Culture* 7 (Winter 1973): 743-48.

953. Gleason, G. Dale. "Attitudes Toward Law and Order in the American Western." Doctoral dissertation, Washington State University, 1978.

954. Goulart, Ron. *Cheap Thrills: An Informal History of the Pulp Magazines.* New Rochelle, N.Y.: Arlington House, 1972. Contains chapters on dime novels and cowboy fiction.

955. Gregory, Horace. "Guns of the Roaring West." *Avon Book of Modern Writing No. 2.* New York, 1954, pp. 217-35.

956. Gruber, Frank. "The Basic Western Novel Plots." *Writer's Year Book.* Cincinnati: Writer's Digest, 1955, pp. 49-53, 160.

957. ——. *The Pulp Jungle.* Los Angeles: Sherbourne Press, 1967.

958. ——. "The 7 Ways to Plot a Western." *TV Guide* 6 (August 30, 1958): 5-7.

959. Hamilton, Cynthia A. "The Western Formula in American Literature." Doctoral dissertation, University of Sussex, n.d.

960. Harris, Charles W., and Buck Rainey, eds. *The Cowboy: Six-Shooters, Songs, and Sex.* Norman: University of Oklahoma Press, 1976.

961. Harvey, Charles M. "The Dime Novel in American Life." *Atlantic Monthly* 100 (July 1907): 37-45.

962. Horton, Andrew S. "Ken Kesey,

John Updike and The Lone Ranger." *Journal of Popular Culture* 8 (Winter 1974): 570-78.

963. Hutchinson, W. H. "Grassfire on the Great Plains." *Southwest Review* 41 (Spring 1956): 181-85.

964. ——. "Virgins, Villains, and Varmints." *Huntington Library Quarterly* 16 (August 1953): 381-92.

965. ——. "The 'Western Story' as Literature." *Western Humanities Review* 3 (January 1949): 33-37.

966. Jacobson, Larry King. "Mythic Origins of the Western." Doctoral dissertation, University of Minnesota, 1973.

967. Johannsen, Albert. *The House of Beadle and Adams and Its Dime and Nickel Novels.* 2 vols. Norman: University of Oklahoma Press, 1950; supplement, 1962.

968. Jones, Daryl E. "Blood'n Thunder: Virgins, Villains, and Violence in the Dime Novel Western." *Journal of Popular Culture* 4 (Fall 1970): 507-17.

969. ——. "Clenched Teeth and Curses: Revenge and the Dime Novel Outlaw Hero." *Journal of Popular Culture* 7 (Winter 1973): 652-65.

970. ——. *The Dime Novel Western.* Bowling Green, Ohio: Bowling Green State University Popular Press, 1978. The best study of this topic.

971. ——. "Of Few Days and Full of Trouble: The Evolution of the Western Hero in the Dime Novel." *New Dimensions in Popular Culture.* Ed. Russel B. Nye. Bowling Green, Ohio: Bowling Green University Press, 1972.

972. Knight, Damon, ed. *7 Westerns of the 40's: Classics from the Great Pulps.* New York: Harper and Row, 1977.

973. Kruse, Horst H. "Myth in the Making: The James Brothers, the Bank Robbery at Northfield, Minn., and the Dime Novel." *Journal of Popular Culture* 10 (Fall 1976): 315-25.

974. Leab, Daniel J. "The Western Rides Again." *Columbia University Forum* 7 (Summer 1964): 27-30.

975. Leach, Joseph. "The Paper-Back Texan: Father of the American Western Hero." *Western Humanities Review* 11 (Summer 1957): 267-76.

976. Leithead, J. Edward. "The Klondike Stampede in Dime Novels." *American Book Collector* 21 (1971): 23-29.

977. Marsden, Michael T. "The Modern Western." *Journal of the West* 19 (January 1980): 54-61.

978. ——. "Riding Drag: Or, Reflections from the Rear." *Journal of Popular Culture* 7 (Winter 1973): 749-51.

979. ——. "Savior in the Saddle: The Sagebrush Testament." *Illinois Quarterly* 36 (December 1973): 5-15.

980. Miller, Alexander. "The 'Western'—A Theological Note." *Christian Century* 74 (November 27, 1957): 1409-10.

981. Milton, John R. *The Novel of the American West.* Lincoln: University of Nebraska Press, 1980, pp. 1-40.

982. Monaghan, Jay. *The Great Rascal: The Life and Adventures of Ned Buntline.* New York: Bonanza Books, 1951.

983. Munden, Kenneth J., M.D. "A Contribution to the Psychological Understanding of the Origins of the Cowboy and His Myth." *American Imago* 15 (Summer 1958): 103-48.

984. Nelson, Mary Carroll. "Western Pulp Illustrators: A Touch of Romance." *New Mexico Magazine* 58 (February 1980): 34-39, 59.

985. Nussbaum, Martin. "The 'Adult Western' as an American Art Form." *Folklore* 70 (September 1959): 460-67.

986. ———. "Sociological Symbolism in the 'Adult Western.'" *Social Forces* 39 (October 1960): 25-28.

987. Nye, Russel. *The Unembarrassed Muse: The Popular Arts in America.* New York: Dial Press, 1970, pp. 280-304. The best account of the rise of the Western.

988. Pearson, Edmund. *Dime Novels; or, Following an Old Trail in Popular Literature.* Boston: Little, Brown, 1929.

989. Percy, Walker. "Decline of the Western." *Commonweal* 68 (May 16, 1958): 181-83.

990. Peverly, Carlos Francis. "The Cowboy in American Literature, 1853-1912." Master's thesis, University of Colorado, 1946.

991. Primeau, Ronald. "Slave Narrative Turning Westward: Deadwood Dick Rides into Difficulties." *Midamerica* (1974): 16-35.

992. Reynolds, Quentin. *The Fiction Factory.* New York: Random House, 1955.

993. Rosa, Joseph G. *The Gunfighter: Man or Myth?* Norman: University of Oklahoma Press, 1969.

994. Rosenberg, Betty. "The Poor, Lonesome, Unreviewed Cowboy." *Library Journal* 85 (December 15, 1960): 4432-33.

995. *The Roundup.* The monthly publication of the Western Writers of America. Each issue contains useful information on the Western.

996. Seshachari, Candadi. "Popular Western Fiction as Literature of Escape." *Possible Sack* 4 (April 1973): 5-8.

997. Settle, William A., Jr. "Literature as History: The Dime Novel as an Historian's Tool," *Literature and History.* Ed. I. E. Cadenhead, Jr. University of Tulsa Monograph Series No. 9. Tulsa: University of Tulsa, 1970, pp. 9-20.

998. Sharnik, John. "It's Go Western Young Men." *New York Times Magazine.* September 24, 1950, pp. 16, 18, 20, 22.

999. Simmons, Michael K. "The Dime Novel and the American Mind." *Mankind* 2 (October 1969): 58-63.

1000. ——. "The Dime Novel and the American *Zeitgeist*, 1860-1910: A Question of Influence." Doctoral dissertation, Indiana University of Pennsylvania, 1973.

1001. Sisk, J. P. "The Western Hero." *Commonwealth* 66 (July 12, 1957): 367-69.

1002. "The Six-Gun Galahad." *Time* 73 (March 30, 1959): 52-60.

1003. Skjelver, Mabel R. "William Wallace Cook: Dime Novelist." *Annals of Wyoming* 49 (Spring 1977): 109-30.

1004. Smith, Henry Nash. *Virgin Land: The American West as Symbol and Myth.* Cambridge, Mass.: Harvard University Press, 1950, 1970. See excellent chapters on dime novel heroes and heroines.

1005. Snell, Joseph W. "The Wild and Wooly West of the Popular Writer." *Nebraska History* 48 (Summer 1967): 141-53.

1006. Sonnichsen, C. L. *From Hopalong to Hud: Thoughts on Western Fiction.* College Station: Texas A&M University Press, 1978.

1007. ——. "Sex on the Lone Prairee." *Western American Literature* 13 (Spring 1978): 15-33.

1008. ——. "The Wyatt Earp Syndrome." *American West* 7 (May 1970): 26-28, 80-82.

1009. Steckmesser, [Kent] Ladd. "The Structure and Psychology of the 'Western' Novel." Masters thesis, University of Iowa, 1956.

1010. ——. *The Western Hero in History and Legend.* Norman: University of Oklahoma Press, 1965.

1011. Straight, Michael. "Truth and Formula for the Western Novel." *South Dakota Review* 2 (Autumn 1964): 88-93.

1012. Thompson, Thomas. "Strong, Silent and Stupid." *Writer* 66 (September 1953): 305-6.

1013. Topping, Gary. "The New Popular Western." *Idaho Humanities Forum,* Spring 1981, pp. 5-6.

1014. ——. "The Rise of the Western." *Journal of the West* 19 (January 1980): 29-35.

1015. Turner, E. S. *Boys Will Be Boys.* London, 1948; 2d ed., rev. London: Joseph Michael, 1957.

1016. Turner, William O. "Notes on Western Fiction." *Roundup* 16 (February 1968): 1-4; 17 (September 1969): 1-2.

1017. Walker, Don D. "Notes Toward a Literary Criticism of the Western." *Journal of Popular Culture* 7 (Winter 1973): 728-41.

1018. ——. "Wister, Roosevelt, and James: A Note on the Western." *American Quarterly* 12 (Fall 1960): 358-66.

1019. White, Trentwell Mason. *How to Write for a Living.* New York: Reynal and Hitchcock, 1937, pp. 106-11, 305-9.

1020. Williams, John. "The 'Western': Definitions of the Myth."

Nation 193 (November 18, 1961): 401-6.

1021. Wilson, Daniel J. "Nature in Western Popular Literature from the Dime Novel to Zane Grey." *North Dakota Quarterly* 44 (Spring 1976): 41-50.

1022. Wylder, Delbert E. "The Popular Western Novel: An Essay Review." *Western American Literature* 14 (Winter 1970): 299-303.

1023. ——. *Popular Westerns.* Cassette. Deland, Fla.: Everett/Edwards, 1974.

WESTERN FILM

1024. Alexander, William. "Frontier Films: Trying the Impossible." *Prospects: An Annual of American Cultural Studies.* Vol. 4. Ed. Jack Salzman. New York: Burt Franklin, 1979, pp. 441-57. Film group that made Pare Lorentz's important documentaries of the 1930s.

1025. Astre, Georges-Albert, and Albert-Patrick Hoarau. *Univers du Western.* Paris: Éditions Seghers, 1973.

1026. Barsness, John A. "A Question of Standard." *Film Quarterly* 21 (Fall 1967): 32-37. "Mythical" and "realistic" Westerns.

1027. Bazin, André. *What is Cinema?* Vol. 2. Trans. Hugh Gray. Berkeley: University of California Press, 1971. Includes three important essays by Bazin on the Western.

1028. Bluestone, George. "The Changing Cowboy: From Dime Novel to Dollar Film." *Western Humanities Review* 14 (Summer 1960): 331-37.

1029. Boatright, Mody C. "The Cowboy Enters the Movies." *The Sunny Slopes of Long Ago.* Eds. Wilson M. Hudson and Allen Maxwell. Dallas: Southern Methodist University Press, 1966, pp. 51-69.

1030. ——. "The Morality Play on Horseback: Tom Mix." *Tire Shrinker to Dragster.* Publications of the Texas Folklore Society, 34. Austin: Encino Press, 1968, pp. 63-71.

1031. Bogdanovich, Peter. *John Ford.* London: Studio Vista, 1967.

1032. Brauer, Ralph. "Who Are Those Guys? The Movie Western During the TV Era." *Journal of Popular Culture* 2 (Fall 1973): 389-404.

1033. —— (with Donna Brauer). *The Horse, The Gun and The Piece of Property: Changing Images of the TV Western.* Bowling Green, Ohio: Bowling Green University Popular Press, 1975. The only full-length study of this large subject.

1034. Brownlow, Kevin. *The War, The West and The Wilderness.* New York: Alfred A. Knopf, 1979. Well-researched study of the early Western.

1035. Bukalski, Peter J. *Film Research: A Critical Bibliography.* Boston: G. K. Hall, 1972.

1036. Calder, Jenni. *There Must Be a Lone Ranger: The American West in Film and in Reality.* New York: Taplinger, 1975.

60

1037. Cawelti, John G. *Adventure, Mystery, and Romance: Formula Stories as Art and Popular Culture.* Chicago: University of Chicago Press, 1976. Includes a long discussion of film and fictional Westerns.

1038. ——. "God's Country, Las Vegas and the Gunfighter: Differing Visions of the West." *Western American Literature* 9 (February 1975): 273–83.

1039. ——. "The Gunfighter and the Hard-boiled Dick: Some Ruminations on American Fantasies of Heroism." *American Studies* 16 (Fall 1975): 49–65.

1040. ——. "Reflections on the New Western Films: The Jewish Cowboy, the Black Avenger, and the Return of the Vanishing American." *University of Chicago Magazine* 65 (January/February 1973): 25–32.

1041. Clements, William M. "From Crow Killer to Robert Redford: The Pastoralization of Liver-Eating Johnson." *Markham Review* 8 (Spring 1979): 48–51.

1042. Deming, Caren Joy. "Education Films and the American Mythos: A Content Analysis Based on Norms Derived From Frontier Literature." Doctoral dissertation, University of Michigan, 1975.

1043. Esselman, Kathryn C. "When the Cowboy Stopped Kissing His Horse." *Journal of Popular Culture* 6 (Fall 1972): 337–49. Comparisons of TV and film Westerns.

1044. Evans, Max. *Sam Peckinpah: Master of Violence.* Vermillion, S.Dak.: Dakota Press, 1972.

1045. Fender, Stephen. "The Western and the Contemporary." [British] *Journal of American Studies* 6 (April 1972): 97–108.

1046. Fenin, George N., and William K. Everson. *The Western: From Silents to the Seventies.* New York: Grossman Publishers, 1973. The most comprehensive overview; updates the authors' *The Western: From Silents to Cinerama*, 1962.

1047. Fielding, Raymond. *A Bibliography of Theses and Dissertations on the Subject of Film: 1916–1979.* Houston: University Film Association, 1979. Lists nearly 1,500 unannotated items.

1048. Folsom, James K. "'Western' Themes and Western Films." *Western American Literature* 2 (Fall 1967): 195–203.

1049. Ford, Charles. *Historie du Western.* Paris: Editions Pierre Horay, 1964.

1050. Ford, John. "John Ford on *Stagecoach.*" *Action* 6 (September–October 1971): 10–12.

1051. Frayling, Christopher. *Spaghetti Westerns: Cowboys and Europeans from Karl May to Sergio Leone.* London: Routledge and Kegan Paul, 1981.

1052. French, Philip. *Westerns: Aspects of a Movie Genre.* Rev. ed. New York: Oxford University Press, 1977. Emphasizes recent Westerns.

1053. Friar, Ralph E. and Natasha A.

The Only Good Indian... The Hollywood Gospel. New York: Drama Book Specialists, 1972.

1054. Gallagher, Thomas Augustus, Jr. "The Movies of John Ford." Doctoral dissertation, Columbia University, 1978.

1055. Georgakas, Dan. "They Have Not Spoken: American Indians in Film." *Film Quarterly* 25 (Spring 1972): 26-32.

1056. Goldstein, Bernice, and Robert Perucci. "The TV Western and the Modern American Spirit." *Southwestern Social Science Quarterly* 43 (March 1963): 357-66.

1057. Harrington, John. "Understanding Hollywood's Indian Rhetoric." *Canadian Review of American Studies* 8 (Spring 1977): 77-88.

1058. Hart, William S. *My Life East and West.* Boston: Houghton Mifflin, 1929; New York: Benjamin Blom, 1966.

1059. Homans, Peter. "Puritanism Revisited: An Analysis of the Contemporary Screen-Image Western." *Studies in Public Communication* 3 (1961): 73-84.

1060. Hutton, Paul A. "From Little Big Horn to Little Big Man: The Changing Image of a Western Hero in Popular Culture." *Western Historical Quarterly* 7 (January 1976): 19-45. General Custer.

1061. Kaminsky, Stuart M. *Clint Eastwood.* New York: Signet Books, 1974.

1062. Karp, Walter. "What Western Movies Are All About." *Horizon* 17 (Summer 1975): 38-39. A very general piece.

1063. Kitses, Jim. *Horizons West... Studies of Authorship Within the Western.* Bloomington: Indiana University Press, 1969.

1064. Knight, Arthur. "*Stagecoach* Revisited." *Action* 6 (September-October 1971): 6-9.

1065. Koszarski, Diane Kaiser. *The Complete Films of William S. Hart: A Pictorial Record.* New York: Dover, 1980.

1066. Lahmen, Peter Robert. "John Ford and the Auteur Theory." Doctoral dissertation, University of Wisconsin, Madison, 1978.

1067. Lenihan, John H. *Showdown: Confronting Modern America in the Western Film.* Urbana: University of Illinois Press, 1980.

1068. *Le Western: Sources, Thèmes, mythologies, auteurs, acteurs, filmographies.* Paris: Union Général d' Editions, 1966.

1069. McBride, Joseph. *John Ford.* New York: Da Capo Press, 1975.

1070. ——, ed. *Focus on Howard Hawks.* Englewood Cliffs, N.J.: Prentice-Hall, 1972.

1071. ——, and Michael Wilmington. "Prisoner of the Desert." *Sight and Sound* 40 (Autumn 1971): 210-14. Analysis of John Ford's *The Searchers* (1956).

1072. McCarthy, John Alan. "Sam Peckinpah and *The Wild Bunch.*" *Film Heritage* 5 (Winter 1969-70): 1-10, 32.

1073. McKinney, Doug. *Sam Peckinpah.* Boston: G. K. Hall, 1979.

1074. McMurtry, Larry. "Cowboys, Movies, Myths, and Cadillacs: Realism in the Western." *Man in the Movies.* Ed. W. R. Robinson. Baltimore: Penguin Books, 1967.

1075. Manchel, Frank. *Cameras West.* Englewood Cliffs, N.J.: Prentice-Hall, 1971. For high school and college students.

1076. Marsden, Michael T. "Savior in the Saddle: The Sagebrush Testament." *Illinois Quarterly* 36 (December 1973): 5-15. Western fiction and western films.

1077. Mass, Roslyn. "Values in Film: A Comparison of Selected American Western Films of the 1940s and the 1970s." Doctoral dissertation, New York University, 1978.

1078. Meyer, William R. *The Making of the Great Westerns.* New Rochelle, N.J.: Arlington House, 1979.

1079. Money, Mary Alice. "Evolutions of the Popular Western in Novels, Films, and Television." Doctoral dissertation, University of Texas, Austin, 1975.

1080. Nachbar, Jack. "A Checklist of Published Materials on Western Movies." *Journal of Popular Film* 2 (Fall 1973): 411-28.

1081. ——, ed. *Focus on the Western.* Englewood Cliffs, N.J.: Prentice-Hall, 1974. Fifteen essays emphasizing the Western as a cultural document.

1082. ——, ed. *Western Films: An Annotated Critical Bibliography.* New York: Garland, 1975. The beginning place for research on Western films.

1083. Pauly, Thomas H. "The Cold War Western." *Western Humanities Review* 33 (Summer 1979): 257-73.

1084. ——. "What's Happened to the Western Movie?" *Western Humanities Review* 28 (Summer 1974): 260-69.

1085. Peary, Gerald. "Selected Sound Westerns and Their Novel Sources." *Velvet Light Trap* 12 (Spring 1974): 15-18.

1086. Pettit, Arthur G. "Nightmare and Nostalgia: The Cinema West of Sam Peckinpah." *Western Humanities Review* 29 (September 1975): 10-15.

1087. Pilkington, William T., and Don Graham, eds. *Western Movies.* Albuquerque: University of New Mexico Press, 1979. Collection of interpretive essays.

1088. Place, J. A. *The Western Films of John Ford.* Secaucus, N.J.: Citadel Press, 1974.

1089. Pogel, Nancy H. "Images of the Midwest: Cornfields in Poetry, Fiction, and Film." *Heritage of Kansas* 10 (Fall 1977): 17-28.

1090. Rieupeyrout, Jean-Louis. *La grande adventure du western: du Far West a Hollywood, 1894-1963.* Paris: Éditions du Cerf, 1964.

1091. ——. *Le western; ou, Le cinéma américain par excellence.* Paris: Éditions du Cerf, 1953.

1092. Sarris, Andrew. "*Stagecoach* in

1939 and in Retrospect." *Action* 6 (September-October 1971): 30-33.

1093. Schein, Harry. "The Olympian Cowboy." *American Scholar* 24 (Summer 1955): 309-20. Important essay of the 1950s.

1094. Seydor, Paul. *Peckinpah: The Western Films.* Urbana: University of Illinois Press, 1979.

1095. Silver, Charles. *The Western Film.* New York: Pyramid Productions, 1976. Brief, opinionated overview.

1096. Sinclair, Andrew. *John Ford: The Waning of the Great West, A Biography.* New York: Dial Press, 1979.

1097. Sonnichsen, C. L. "The West that Wasn't." *American West* 14 (November/December 1977): 8-15. Fiction and film.

1098. Spears, Jack. "The Indian on the Screen." *Films in Review* 10 (January 1959): 18-35.

1099. Trimmer, Joseph F. *"The Virginian*: Novel and Films." *Illinois Quarterly* 35 (December 1972): 5-18.

1100. Tuska, Jon. "The American Western Cinema: 1903-Present." *Focus on the Western.* Ed. Jack Nachbar. Englewood Cliffs, N.J.: Prentice-Hall, 1974. Reprinted from *Views and Reviews* 5 (Spring 1974): 1-15.

1101. ——. *The Filming of the West.* Garden City, N.Y.: Doubleday, 1976.

1102. ——. "John Wayne and the Indian." *Views and Reviews* 5 (September 1973): 9-17.

1103. Warshow, Robert. "Movie Chronicle: The Westerner." *The Immediate Experience.* Garden City, N.Y.: Doubleday, 1962, pp. 135-54. Another early influential essay on the Western; first appeared in *Partisan Review* 21 (March-April 1954): 190-203.

1104. Whitehall, Richard. "The Heroes Are Tired." *Film Quarterly* 20 (Winter 1966-67): 12-24.

1105. Willett, Ralph. "The American Western: Myth and Anti-Myth." *Journal of Popular Culture* 4 (Fall 1970): 455-63.

1106. Wood, Robin. *Howard Hawks.* Garden City, N.Y.: Doubleday, 1968.

1107. Wright, Will. *Sixguns and Society: A Structural Study of the Western.* Berkeley: University of California Press, 1975.

1108. Young, Vernon. "The West in Celluloid: Hollywood's Lost Horizons." *Southwest Review* 28 (Spring 1953): 126-34. Negative view of the Western.

1109. Zolotow, Maurice. *Shooting Star: A Biography of John Wayne.* New York: Simon and Schuster, 1974.

INDIAN LITERATURE
AND INDIANS
IN WESTERN LITERATURE

1110. Allen, Paula Gunn. "The Mythopoeic Vision in Native American Literature: The Problem of Myth." *American Indian Culture and Research Journal* 1 (1974): 3-13.

1111 ——. "The Sacred Hoop: A

Contemporary Indian Perspective on American Indian Literature." *Cross Currents* 26 (Summer 1976): 144-63.

1112. ——. "Symbol and Structure in Native American Literature: Some Basic Considerations." *College Composition and Communication* 24 (1973): 267-70.

1113. Allen, T. D. *The Whispering Wind: Poetry by Young American Indians.* Garden City, N.Y.: Doubleday, 1972.

1114. Astrov, Margot. *American Indian Prose and Poetry: An Anthology.* New York: Capricorn Books, 1962.

1115. Austin, Mary. *American Rhythm: Studies and Reexpressions of American Indian Songs.* 1930; New York: Cooper Square, 1972.

1116. Ballotti, Geno A. "The Southwest Indian in Fiction." *Studies in the Literature of the West.* Laramie: University of Wyoming, 1956, pp. 130-56.

1117. Barnett, Louise K. *The Ignoble Savage: American Literary Racism, 1790-1890.* Westport, Conn.: Greenwood Press, 1975.

1118. ——. "Nineteenth-Century Indian Hater Fiction: A Paradigm for Racism." *South Atlantic Quarterly* 74 (1975): 224-36.

1119. Beidler, Peter G. "Animals and Human Development in the Contemporary American Indian Novel." *Western American Literature* 14 (Summer 1979): 133-48.

1120. ——, and Marion F. Egge. *The American Indian in Short Fiction: An Annotated Bibliography.* Metuchen, N.J.: Scarecrow Press, 1979.

1121. Berkhofer, Robert F., Jr. *The White Man's Indian: Images of the American Indian from Columbus to the Present.* New York: Alfred A. Knopf, 1978. A major study; see especially pp. 71-111.

1122. Berkman, Brenda. "The Vanishing Race: Conflicting Images of the American Indian in Children's Literature, 1880-1930." *North Dakota Quarterly* 44 (Spring 1966): 31-40.

1123. Bevis, William. "American Indian Verse Translations." *College English* 35 (March 1974): 693-703. Includes a short bibliography.

1124. Bloodworth, William. "Neihardt, Momaday, and the Art of Indian Autobiography." *Where the West Begins.* Eds. Arthur R. Huseboe and William Geyer. Sioux Falls, S.Dak.: Center for Western Studies Press, 1978, pp. 152-60.

1125. ——. "Varieties of American Indian Autobiography." *MELUS* 5 (Fall 1978): 67-81.

1126. Brandon, William. *The Magic World: American Indian Songs and Poems.* New York: William Morrow and Company, 1971.

1127. Brenzo, Rich[ard Allen]. "American Indians vs. American Writers." *Margins* 14 (October/November 1974): 40-45, 88.

1128. ——. "Civilization Against the Savage: The Destruction of Indians in American Novels, 1823-1854." Doctoral dissertation, University of Wisconsin, Milwaukee, 1973.

1129. Brumble, H. David III. *An Annotated Bibliography of American Indian and Eskimo Autobiographies.* Lincoln: University of Nebraska Press, 1981.

1130. Buller, Galen Mark. "Comanche Oral Narratives." Doctoral dissertation, University of Nebraska, Lincoln, 1977.

1131. ——. "New Interpretations of Native American Literature: A Survival Technique." *American Indian Culture and Research Journal* 4 (1980): 165-77.

1132. Burns, Glen. "Indian Madness." *Amerikastudien/American Studies* 22 (1977): 90-106.

1133. Carey, Larry Lee. "A Study of the Indian Captivity Narrative as a Popular Literary Genre, ca. 1675-1875." Doctoral dissertation, Michigan State University, 1978.

1134. Chapman, Abraham, ed. *Literature of the American Indian: Views and Interpretations. . . .* New York: New American Library, 1975.

1135. Clark, LaVerne Harrell. "An Introduction to the Hopi Indians and Their Mythology." *Arizona English Bulletin* 13 (April 1971): 1-14.

1136. Davidson, Levette J. "White Versions of Indian Myths and Legends." *Western Folklore* 7 (April 1948): 115-28.

1137. Day, A. Grove. *The Sky Clears: Poetry of the American Indian.* Lincoln: University of Nebraska Press, 1964.

1138. DeFlyer, Joseph Eugene. "Partition Theory: Patterns and Partitions of Consciousness in Selected Works of American and American Indian Authors." Doctoral dissertation, University of Nebraska, Lincoln, 1974.

1139. Dillingham, Peter. "The Literature of the American Indian." *English Journal* 62 (January 1973): 37-41.

1140. Dockstader, Frederick J. and Alice W. *The American Indian in Graduate Studies: A Bibliography of Theses and Dissertations.* Parts 1 and 2. New York: Museum of the American Indian, Heye Foundation, 1973, 1974.

1141. Dorris, Michael. "Native American Literature in an Ethnohistorical Context." *College English* 41 (October 1979): 147-62.

1142. Easy, Peter. "The Treatment of American Indian Materials in Contemporary American Poetry." *Journal of American Studies* 12 (April 1978): 81-98.

1143. Espey, David B. "Endings in Contemporary American Indian Fiction." *Western American Literature* 13 (Summer 1978): 133-39.

1144. Evers, Lawrence J. "'Further Survivals of Coyote.'" *Western American Literature* 10 (1975): 233-36.

1145. ——. "The Literature of the Omaha." Doctoral Dissertation, University of Nebraska, Lincoln, 1972.

1146. ——. "Native American Oral Literatures in the College English Classroom: An Omaha Example." *College English* 36 (February 1975): 649-62.

1147. Fiedler, Leslie A. *The Return of the Vanishing American.* New York: Stein and Day, 1968.

1148. Fields, Kenneth. "Seventh Wells: Native American Harmonies." *Parnassus* 2 (Spring-Summer 1974): 172-98.

1149. Fisher, Laura. "All Chiefs, No Indians: What Children's Books Say About American Indians." *Elementary English* 51 (February 1974): 185-89. Includes a bibliography.

1150. Friar, Ralph E. and Natasha A. *The Only Good Indian . . . The Hollywood Gospel.* New York: Drama Books, 1973. Indians in Western films.

1151. Hamilton, W. I. "The Correlation between Social Attitudes and Those of American Authors in Depicting the American Indian." *American Indian Quarterly* 1 (1974): 1-26.

1152. Hamilton, Wynette, Lucy Snyder, and Robert Seal, eds. "Bibliography, Research and News: Recent Articles." *American Indian Quarterly* 2 (1975-76); 386-401; 3 (1977): 70-88, 175-90, 271-91; 3 (1977-78): 386-401.

1153. Haslam, Gerald. *American Indian Literature.* Cassette. Deland, Fla.: Everett/Edwards, 1974.

1154. ——. "American Indians: Poets of the Cosmos." *Western American Literature* 5 (Spring 1970): 15-29.

1155. ——. "American Oral Literature: Our Forgotten Heritage." *English Journal* 60 (September 1971): 709-23.

1156. ——. "The Light That Fills the World: Native American Literature." *South Dakota Review* 11 (Spring 1973): 27-41.

1157. ——. "Literature of *The People*: Native American Voices." *CLA Journal* 15 (December 1971): 153-70.

1158. Henley, Joan Asher. "Native American Life Stories: Problems and Opportunities for Literary Study." Doctoral dissertation, American University, 1976.

1159. Henry, Jeannette. *The American Indian Reader: Literature.* San Francisco: Indian Historian Press, 1973.

1160. ——, et al. *Index to Literature on the American Indian. 1970.* San Francisco: Indian Historian Press, 1972; *1971*; *1972*; *1973.* San Francisco: Indian Historian Press, 1972, 1974, 1975.

1161. Hirschfelder, Arlene B. *American Indian and Eskimo Authors: A Comprehensive Bibliography.* New York: Association on American Indian Affairs, 1973.

1162. Howard, Helen Addison. *American Indian Poetry*. Boston: Twayne, 1979.

1163. ——. "Literary Translators and Interpreters of Indian Songs." *Journal of the West* 12 (April 1973): 212-28.

1164. Hymes, Dell. "Particle, Pause and Pattern in American Indian Narrative Verse." *American Indian Culture and Research Journal* 4, No. 4 (1980): 7-51.

1165. *Index to Literature on the American Indian*. San Francisco: Indian Historian Press, 1971.

1166. Jamison, Blanche Noma Miller. "The Western American Indian: Cross-Cultural Literary Attitudes." Doctoral dissertation, East Texas State University, 1978.

1167. Kaufman, Donald L. "The Indian as a Media Hand-Me-Down." *Colorado Quarterly* 23 (Spring 1975): 489-504.

1168. Keiser, Albert. *The Indian in American Literature*. New York: Oxford University Press, 1933; New York: Farrar, Straus and Giroux, 1975.

1169. Larson, Charles R. *American Indian Fiction*. Albuquerque: University of New Mexico Press, 1978.

1170. Levernier, James A. "The Captivity Narrative as Children's Literature." *Markham Review* 8 (Spring 1979): 54-59.

1171. ——. "Indian Captivity Narratives: Their Functions and Forms." Doctoral dissertation, University of Pennsylvania, 1975.

1172. ——, and Hennig Cohen, eds. *The Indians and Their Captives*. Contributions in American Studies, No. 31. Westport, Conn.: Greenwood Press, 1977.

1173. Levitas, Gloria, and Frank R. and Jacqueline J. Vivelo, eds. *American Indian Prose and Poetry: We Wait in the Darkness*. New York: Putnam's, 1974.

1174. Lincoln, Kenneth. "Native American Poetries." *Southwest Review* 63 (Autumn 1978): 367-84.

1175. ——. "Native American Tribal Poetics." *Southwest Review* 60 (Spring 1975): 101-16.

1176. Linden, George W. "Dakota Philosophy." *American Studies* 13 (Fall 1977): 17-43.

1177. Littlefield, Daniel F., and Lonnie Underhill. "Renaming the American Indian: 1890-1913." *American Studies* 12 (Fall 1971): 33-45.

1178. Ludovici, Paola. "The Struggle for an Ending: Ritual and Plot in Recent American Indian Literature." Doctoral dissertation, American University, 1979.

1179. McAllister, H. S. "'The Language of Shamans': Jerome Rothenberg's Contributions to American Indian Literature." *Western American Literature* 10 (February 1976): 293-309.

1180. McTaggart, Fred. "Native American Literature: Teachings for the Self." *English Education* 6 (October/November 1974): 3-10.

1181. Marken, Jack W. *The American Indian: Language and Literature.* Arlington Heights, Ill.: AHM Publishing Corporation, 1978. A better-organized and more useful listing than the following volume.

1182. ——. *The Indians and Eskimos of North America: A Bibliography of Books in Print through 1972.* Vermillion, S.Dak.: Dakota Press, 1973.

1183. ——. "Some Recent Resources in Indian Literature." *American Indian Quarterly* 2 (Autumn 1975): 282-89.

1184. Milton, John R., ed. *The American Indian Speaks,* in *South Dakota Review* (Summer 1969); reprinted Vermillion, S.Dak.: Dakota Press, 1969.

1185. ——. *American Indian II,* in *South Dakota Review* (Summer 1971); reprinted Vermillion, S.Dak.: Dakota Press, 1971.

1186. Momaday, Natachee Scott. *American Indian Authors.* Boston: Houghton Mifflin, 1972.

1187. Morgan, Paul. "The Treatment of the Indian in Southwestern Literature since 1915: A Study in Primitivism." Doctoral dissertation, University of Texas, Austin, 1954.

1188. Nichols, Roger L. "Printer's Ink and Red Skins: Western Newspapers and Indians." *Kansas Quarterly* 3 (Fall 1971): 82-87.

1189. Oaks, Priscilla. "The First Gen-eration of Native American Novelists." *MELUS* 5 (1978): 57-65.

1190. O'Brien, Lynne Woods. *Plains Indian Autobiographies.* Western Writers Series, No. 10. Boise, Idaho: Boise State College, 1973.

1191. Oliva, Leo E. "The American Indian in Recent Historical Fiction: A Review Essay." *Prairie Scout* 1 (1973): 95-120.

1192. Pearce, Roy Harvey. *Savagism and Civilization: A Study of the Indian and the American Mind.* Baltimore: Johns Hopkins University Press, 1965. Appeared as *The Savages of America: A Study of the Indian and the Idea of Civilization,* 1953.

1193. Peterson, Richard K. "Indians in American Literature." *Bulletin of Bibliography* 30 (1973): 42-47.

1194. Porter, Mark. "Mysticism of the Land and the Western Novel." *South Dakota Review* 11 (Spring 1973): 79-91.

1195. Povey, John. "My Proud Headdress: New Indian Writing." *Southwest Review* 57 (Autumn 1972): 265-80.

1196. ——. "A New Second-Language Indian Literature." *Alaska Review* 4 (Fall-Winter 1969): 73-78.

1197. Ramsey, Jarold. "The Bible in Western Indian Mythology." *Journal of American Folklore* 90 (October–December 1977): 442-54.

1198. ——. "From 'Mythic' to

'Fictive' in a Nez Perce Orpheus Myth." *Western American Literature* 13 (Summer 1978): 119-31.

1199. ——. "The Indian Literature of Oregon." *Northwest Perspectives: Essays on the Culture of the Pacific Northwest.* Eds. Edwin R. Bingham and Glen A. Love. Seattle: University of Washington Press, 1979, pp. 2-19.

1200. ——. "The Teacher of Modern American Indian Writing as Ethnographer and Critic." *College English* 41 (October 1979): 163-69.

1201. ——. "The Wife Who Goes Out Like a Man Comes Back as a Hero: The Art of Two Oregon Indian Narratives." *PMLA* 92 (January 1977): 9-18.

1202. ——, ed. *Coyote Was Going There: Indian Literature of the Oregon Country.* Seattle: University of Washington, 1977. Anthology and commentary.

1203. Rans, Geoffrey. "Inaudible Man: The Indian in the Theory and Practice of White Fiction." *Canadian Review of American Studies* 8 (Fall 1977): 103-15.

1204. Redekip, Ernest. "The Redman: Some Representations of Indians in American Literature Before the Civil War." *Canadian Association for American Studies Bulletin* 3 (Winter 1968): 1-44.

1205. Rhodes, Geri Marlane. "Shared Five: Reciprocity in Contemporary American Indian and Related Literature." Doctoral dissertation, University of New Mexico, 1976.

1206. Roemer, Kenneth M. "Bear and Elk: The Nature(s) of Contemporary Indian Poetry." *Journal of Ethnic Studies* 5 (Summer 1977): 69-79.

1207. Rosen, Kenneth. "American Indian Literature: Current Condition and Suggested Research." *American Indian Culture and Research Journal* 3 (1979): 57-66.

1208. ——, ed. and intro. *The Man to Send Rain Clouds: Contemporary Poetry by American Indians.* New York: Vintage Books, 1975.

1209. ——, ed. *Voices of the Rainbow: Contemporary Poetry by American Indians.* New York: Viking, 1975.

1210. Rothenberg, Jerome. "American Indian Workings." *Poetry Review* 63 (1972): 17-29.

1211. ——, ed. *Shaking the Pumpkin: Traditional Poetry of the Indian North Americas.* Garden City, N.Y.: Doubleday, 1972.

1212. Ruppert, James. "The Uses of Oral Tradition in Six Contemporary Native American Poets." *American Indian Culture and Research Journal* 4, No. 4 (1980): 87-110.

1213. Saunders, Thomas E. "Tribal Literature: Individual Identity and the Collective Unconscious." *College Composition and Communication* 24 (October 1973): 256-66.

1214. ——, and Walter W. Peek, eds. *Literature of the American*

Indian. Abr. ed. Beverly Hills, Calif.: Glencoe; London: Collier Macmillan, 1976.

1215. Sayre, Robert F. "A Bibliography and an Anthology of American Indian Literature." *College English* 35 (March 1974): 704-6.

1216. Schneider, Jack W. "The New Indian: Alienation and the Rise of the Indian Novel." *South Dakota Review* 17 (Winter 1979-80): 67-76.

1217. ——. "Patterns of Cultural Conflict in Southwestern Indian Fiction." Doctoral dissertation, Texas Tech University, 1977.

1218. Shames, Priscilla. "The Treatment of the American Indian in Western American Fiction." Doctoral dissertation, University of California, Los Angeles, 1970.

1219. Smith, Dwight L. *Indians of the United States and Canada.* Santa Barbara, Calif.: ABC-Clio, 1974.

1220. Smith, William F., Jr. "American Indian Autobiographies." *American Indian Quarterly* 2 (1975): 237-45.

1221. ——. "American Indian Literature." *English Journal* 63 (January 1974): 68-72.

1222. Sonnichsen, C. L. "The Ambivalent Apace." *Western American Literature* 10 (August 1975): 99-114.

1223. Standiford, Lester A. "Worlds Made of Dawn: Characteristic Image and Incident in Native American Imaginative Literature." *Proceedings of the Comparative Literature Symposium* (Lubbock, Tex.) 9 (1978): 327-52.

1224. Stensland, Anna Lee. "American Indian Culture: Promises, Problems, and Possibilities." *English Journal* 60 (December 1971): 1195-1200.

1225. ——. *Literature by and about the American Indian: An Annotated Bibliography.* Urbana, Ill.: National Council of Teachers of English, 1973.

1226. ——. "Traditional Poetry of the American Indian." *English Journal* 64 (September 1975): 41-47.

1227. Sullivan, Sherry Ann. "The Indian in American Fiction 1820-1850." Doctoral dissertation, University of Toronto, 1979.

1228. Szasz, Margaret C. and Ferenc M. "The American Indian and the Classical Past." *Midwest Quarterly* 17 (1975): 58-70.

1229. Theisz, R. D. *Perspectives on Teaching American Indian Literature.* Spearfish, S.Dak.: Center of Indian Studies, Black Hills State College, 1977.

1230. Turner, Frederick W. *The Portable North American Indian Reader.* New York: Viking Press, 1973.

1231. Tyree, Donald W. "Northwest Indian Poets." *Portland Review Magazine* 20 (March 1974): 39-56.

1232. Van Der Beets, Richard. "The Indian Captivity Narrative as Ritual." *American Literature* 43 (January 1971): 548-62.

1233. Velie, Alan R., ed. *American*

Indian Literature: An Anthology. Norman: University of Oklahoma Press, 1979.

1234. Waters, Frank. "Crossroads: Indians and Whites." *South Dakota Review* 11 (Autumn 1973): 28–38.

1235. Wiget, Andrew W. "The Oral Literature of Native North America: A Critical Anthology." 2 vols. Doctoral dissertation, University of Utah, 1977.

1236. Wilson, Norma Jean Clark. "The Spirit of Place in Contemporary American Indian Poetry." Doctoral dissertation, University of Oklahoma, 1978.

1237. Witt, Shirley H., and Stan Steiner, eds. *The Way: An Anthology of American Indian Literature.* New York: Alfred A. Knopf, 1972.

1238. Zolla, Elémire. *The Writer and the Shaman: A Morphology of the American Indian.* New York: Harcourt Brace Jovanovich, 1969, 1973.

MEXICAN-AMERICAN
LITERATURE
AND CHICANOS
IN WESTERN LITERATURE

1239. Armas, José. "Role of Artist and Critic in the Literature of a Developing Pueblo." *De Colores* 3 (1977): 5–11.

1240. Blatt, Gloria T. "The Mexican-American in Children's Literature." *Elementary English* 45 (April 19, 1968): 446–51.

1241. Bruce-Novoa, John. "The Space of Chicano Literature." *De Colores* 3 (1975): 22–42.

1242. Bruce-Novoa, [Juan]. *Chicano Authors: Inquiry by Interview.* Austin: University of Texas Press, 1980. Collects 14 interviews with leading Chicano writers.

1243. ——. "Interview with José Antonio Villarreal." *Revista Chicano-Riqueña* 4 (Spring 1976): 40–48.

1244. ——, and David Valentin. "Revolutionizing the Popular Image: Essay on Chicano Theatre." *Latin American Literary Review* 5 (Spring-Summer 1977): 42–50.

1245. Cantú, Roberto. "Estructura y sentido de lo onírico en *Bless Me, Ultima.*" *Mester* 5 (November 1974): 27–41.

1246. Cárdenas de Dwyer, Carlota. "Chicano Literature, 1965–1975: The Flowering of the Southwest." Doctoral dissertation, State University of New York, Stony Brook, 1976.

1247. ——. "Cultural Regionalism and Chicano Literature." *Western American Literature* 15 (Fall 1980): 187–94.

1248. ——. "Westering and the Chicano Literary Tradition." *The Westering Experience in American Literature: Bicentennial Essays.* Eds. Merrill Lewis and L. L. Lee. Bellingham: Bureau for Faculty Research, Western Washington University, 1977, pp. 206–12.

1249. ——, ed. *Chicano Voices.*

Boston: Houghton Mifflin, 1975. An anthology.

1250. Carrillo, Loretta. "The Search for Selfhood and Order in Contemporary Chicano Fiction." Doctoral dissertation, Michigan State University, 1979.

1251. Castañeda Shular, Antonia, Thomás Ybarra-Frausto, and Joseph Sommers, eds. *Literatura chicana: Texto y contexto.* Englewood Cliffs, N.J.: Prentice-Hall, 1972.

1252. Castro, Donald F. "The Chicano Novel: An Ethno-Generic Study." *La Luz* 2 (April 1973).

1253. Chavez, John R. "The Lost Land: The Chicano Image of the Southwest." Doctoral dissertation, University of Michigan, 1980.

1254. "Chicano Literature and Criticism." *De Colores* 3 (1970). An important special issue.

1255. "La Cosecha: Literatura y la Mujer Chicana." *De Colores* 3 (No. 3). Special issue devoted to the Chicana.

1256. Dowell, Faye Nell. "The Chicano Novel: A Study of Self-Definition." Doctoral dissertation, University of Cincinnati, 1979.

1257. Elizondo, Sergio D. "Myth and Reality in Chicano Literature." *Latin American Literary Review* 5 (Spring-Summer 1977): 23-31.

1258. Fallis, Guadalupe Valdés. "Metaphysical Anxiety and the Existence of God in Contemporary Chicano Fiction." *Revista Chicano-Riqueña* 3 (Winter 1975): 26-33.

1259. Garcia, Ricardo. "Multi-Ethnic Literature in America: Overview of Chicano Folklore." *English Journal* 65 (February 1976): 83-87.

1260. García-Girón, Edmundo. "The Chicanos: An Overview." *Proceedings of the Comparative Literature Symposium* (Lubbock, Tex.) 9 (1978): 87-119.

1261. Garza, Mario. "Duality in Chicano Poetry." *De Colores* 3 (1977): 39-45.

1262. González, Sylvia A. "National Character vs. Universality in Chicano Poetry." *De Colores* 1 (1975): 10-21.

1263. Grajeda, Rafael Francisco. "The Figure of the Pocho in Contemporary Chicano Fiction." Doctoral dissertation, University of Nebraska, Lincoln, 1974.

1264. Hancock, Joel. "The Emergence of Chicano Poetry: A Survey of Sources, Themes, and Techniques." *Arizona Quarterly* 29 (Spring 1973): 57-73.

1265. Haslam, Gerald. "¡Por La Causa! Mexican-American Literature." *College English* 31 (April 1970): 695-709.

1266. Hinojosa, Rolando. "Mexican-American Literature: Toward an Identification." *Books Abroad* 49 (Summer 1975): 422-31.

1267. Jimenez, Francesco, ed. *The Identification and Analysis of Chicano Literature.* New York:

Bilingual Press, 1979. A collection of interpretive essays.

1268. Jordan, Lois B. *Mexican Americans: Resources to Build Cultural Understanding.* Littleton, Colo.: Libraries Unlimited, 1973.

1269. Langum, David J. "Californios and the Image of Indolence." *Western Historical Quarterly* 9 (April 1978): 181-96.

1270. Lattin, Vernon E. "The City in Contemporary Chicano Fiction." *Studies in American Fiction* 6 (1978): 93-100.

1271. ——. "The Quest for Mythic Vision in Contemporary Native American and Chicano Fiction." *American Literature* 50 (January 1979): 625-40.

1272. Leal, Luis. "Mexican American Literature: A Historical Perspective." *Revista Chicano-Requeña* 1 (1973): 32-44.

1273. [Lewis, Tom J., ed.] "Fiesta of the Living: A Chicano Symposium." *Books Abroad* 49 (Summer 1975): 422-58.

1274. Lomelí, Francisco A. "The Concept of the Barrio in Three Chicano Poets: Abelardo Delgado, Alurista, Richardo Sánchez." *Grito de Sol* 2 (October-December 1977): 9-24.

1275. ——, and Donaldo W. Urioste. *Chicano Perspectives in Literature: A Critical and Annotated Bibliography.* Albuquerque: Pajarito Publishers, 1976.

1276. Ludwig, Edward W., and James Santibanez, eds. *The Chicanos: Mexican American Voices.* New York: Penguin Books, 1971.

1277. McGinity, Sue Simmons. "The Image of the Spanish-American Woman in Recent Southwestern Fiction." Doctoral dissertation, East Texas State University, 1968.

1278. McKenna, Teresa. "Three Novels: An Analysis." *Aztlán* 1 (Fall 1970): 47-56. R. Barrio, *The Plum Plum Pickers*, F. Salas, *Tattoo the Wicked Cross*, and R. Vasquez, *Chicano.*

1279. Madrid-Barela, Arturo. "In Search of the Authentic Pachuco: An Interpretive Essay." *Aztlán* 4 (Spring 1973): 31-60.

1280. Mares, E. A. "Myth and Reality: Observations on American Myths and the Myth of Aztlán." *El Cuaderno* 3 (Winter 1973): 35-50.

1281. Martínez, Max. "Prolegomena for a Study of Chicano Literature." *De Colores* 3 (1977): 12-14.

1282. *Mestizo: Anthology of Chicano Literature.* Albuquerque: Pajarito Publications, 1978. Consists of Vol. 4, Nos. 1 and 2 of *De Colores: Journal of Chicano Expression and Thought.*

1283. Ortega, Adolfo. "Of Social Politics and Poetry: A Chicano Perspective." *Latin American Literary Review* 5 (Spring-Summer 1977): 32-41.

1284. Ortego, Philip D. "Backgrounds of Mexican American Literature." Doctoral dissertation, University of New Mexico, 1971.

1285. ——. "Chicano Poetry: Roots and Writers." *Southwestern*

American Literature 2 (Spring 1972): 8-24.

1286. ——. "Fables of Identity: Stereotype and Caricature of Chicanos in Steinbeck's *Tortilla Flat*." *Journal of Ethnic Studies* 1 (Spring 1973): 39-43.

1287. ——. "Which Southwestern Literature and Culture in the English Classroom?" *Arizona English Bulletin* 13 (April 1971): 15-17.

1288. ——, ed. *We are Chicanos: An Anthology of Mexican-American Literature.* New York: Washington Square Press, 1973.

1289. Ortego y Gasca, Felipe de. "An Introduction to Chicano Poetry." *Modern Chicano Writers.* Eds. Joseph Sommers and Tomás Ybarra-Frausto. Englewood Cliffs, N.J.: Prentice-Hall, 1979, pp. 108-16.

1290. Paredes, Américo. "The Folk Base of Chicano Literature." *Modern Chicano Writers.* Eds. Joseph Sommers and Tomás Ybarra-Frausto. Englewood Cliffs, N.J.: Prentice-Hall, 1979, pp. 4-17.

1291. ——. *"With His Pistol in His Hand": A Border Ballad and Its Hero.* Austin: University of Texas Press, 1958.

1292. ——, and Raymund Paredes. *Mexican-American Authors.* Boston: Houghton Mifflin, 1972.

1293. Paredes, Raymund A. "The Evolution of Chicano Literature." *MELUS* 5 (Summer 1978): 71-110.

1294. ——. "The Image of the Mexican in American Literature." Doctoral dissertation, University of Texas, Austin, 1973.

1295. Parr, Carmen Salazar. "Current Trends in Chicano Literary Criticism." *Latin American Literary Review* 5 (Spring-Summer 1977): 8-15.

1296. Pettit, Arthur G. *Images of the Mexican American in Fiction and Film.* Ed. Dennis E. Showalter. College Station: Texas A&M Press, 1980.

1297. Pino, Frank. "Chicano Poetry: A Popular Manifesto." *Journal of Popular Culture* 6 (Spring 1973): 718-30.

1298. ——. *Mexican Americans: A Research Bibliography.* 2 vols. East Lansing: Michigan State University, 1974. See especially Vol. 2, pp. 98-232.

1299. Pino, Frank, Jr. "The Outsider and 'el otro' in Thomás Rivera's *. . . Y no se lo tragó la tierra.*" *Books Abroad* 49 (Summer 1975): 453-58.

1300. ——, ed. "In-depth Section [on Chicano culture]." *Journal of Popular Culture* 13 (Spring 1980): 488-574.

1301. Rios-C, Herminio, Octavio Romano-V, and Estella Portillo. *Chicanas en la Literatura y el Arte.* Berkeley, Calif.: Quinto Sol, 1973.

1302. Rivera, Tomás. "Chicano Literature: Fiesta of the Living." *Books Abroad* 49 (Summer 1975): 439-53.

1303. ——. "Into the Labyrinth: The Chicano in Literature." *South-*

western American Literature 2 (Fall 1972): 90–97.

1304. Robinson, Barbara J., and J. Cordell Robinson. *The Mexican American: A Critical Guide to Research Aids.* Greenwich, Conn.: JAI Press, 1980. A very useful annotated bibliography.

1305. Robinson, Cecil. "The Extended Presence: Mexico and Its Culture in North American Writing." *MELUS* 5 (1978): 3–15.

1306. ——. *Mexico and the Hispanic Southwest in American Literature.* Tucson: University of Arizona Press, 1977. Updates his *With the Ears of Strangers: The Mexican in American Literature* (Tucson: University of Arizona Press, 1963).

1307. Rodríguez, Raymond J. "A Few Directions in Chicano Literature." *English Journal* 62 (May 1973): 724–29.

1308. ——. "Notes on the Evolution of Chicano Prose Fiction." *Modern Chicano Writers.* Eds. Joseph Sommers and Tomás Ybarra-Fausto. Englewood Cliffs, N.J.: Prentice Hall, 1979, pp. 67–73.

1309. Rojas, Guillermo. *Toward a Chicano/Raza Bibliography: Drama, Prose, Poetry.* El Grito Book Series, No. 2. Berkeley, Calif.: Quinto Sol Publications, 1973.

1310. Rollins, Myrth W. "The Role of the Mexican in Southwest Literature." Master's thesis, University of Texas, El Paso, 1972.

1311. Romano-V, Octavio I., ed. *El Espejo–The Mirror: Selected Mexican-American Literature.* Berkeley, Calif.: Quinto Sol, 1969.

1312. ——, and Herminio Rios-C. "Toward a Chicano/Raza Bibliography: Drama, Prose, Poetry." *El Grito* 7 (December 1973).

1313. Salinas, Judy. "The Image of Woman in Chicano Literature." *Revista Chicano-Riqueña* 4 (Fall 1976): 139–48.

1314. Salinas, Luis Omar, and Lillian Faderman, eds. *From the Barrio: A Chicano Anthology.* San Francisco: Canfield Press, 1973.

1315. Sanchez, George I. "Pachucos in the Making." *Common Ground* 4 (Fall 1943): 13–20.

1316. Sanchez, Rita. "Chicana Writer: Breaking Out of the Silence." *De Colores* 3 (No. 3): 31–37.

1317. Segade, Gustavo. "Toward a Dialectic of Chicano Literature." *Mester* 4 (November 1973).

1318. Simmen, Edward. "'We Must Make This Beginning': The Chicano Leader Image in the Short Story." *Southwest Review* 57 (Spring 1972): 126–33.

1319. Smith, Norman David. "Stereotypical Enemies: American Frontiersman and Mexican Caricatures in the Literature of an Expanding White Nation." Doctoral dissertation, Oklahoma State University, 1975.

1320. Sommers, Joseph. "Critical Approaches to Chicano Literature." *De Colores* 3 (1977): 15–21.

1321. ——. "From the Critical Premise to the Product: Critical

Modes and Their Applications to a Chicano Literary Text." *New Scholar* 5 (1977): 51-80.

1322. ——, and Tomás Ybarra-Frausto, eds. *Modern Chicano Writers: A Collection of Critical Essays.* Twentieth Century Views. Englewood Cliffs, N.J.: Prentice-Hall, 1979. A very useful anthology.

1323. Sonnichsen, C. L. "The Two Black Legends." *Southwestern American Literature* 3 (1973): 5-21. Novels in English about Mexican-Americans.

1324. "Special Issue of Chicano Literature." *Latin American Literary Review* 5 (Spring-Summer 1977): 5-141.

1325. Tatum, Charles M. "Contemporary Chicano Prose Fiction: A Chronicle of Misery." *Latin-American Literary Review* 1 (Spring 1973): 7-17.

1326. ——. "Contemporary Chicano Prose Fiction: Its Ties to Mexican Literature." *Books Abroad* 49 (Summer 1975): 431-39.

1327. ——, ed. *A Selected and Annotated Bibliography of Chicano Studies.* 2d ed. Lincoln, Nebr.: Society of Spanish and Spanish-American Studies, 1979.

1328. Trejo, Arnulfo D. *Bibliografía Chicana: A Guide to Information Sources.* Detroit: Gale Research Company, 1975. An excellent general listing.

1329. Ulibarrí, Sabine R., and Dick Gerdes. "Mexican Literature and Chicano Literature: A Comparison." *Proceedings of the Comparative Literature Symposium* (Lubbock, Tex.) 10 (1978): 149-67.

1330. Vaca, Nick Corona. "Sociology through Literature: The Case of the Mexican-American." Doctoral dissertation, University of California, Berkeley, 1976.

1331. Valdes, Ricardo. "Defining Chicano Literature, or The Perimeters of Literary Space." *Latin American Literary Review* 5 (Spring-Summer 1977): 16-22.

1332. Váldez, Luis, and Stan Steiner. *Aztlán: An Anthology of Mexican American Literature.* New York: Vintage Books, 1972.

1333. Woods, Richard D. "The Chicano Novel: Silence after Publication." *Revista Chicano-Requeña* 4 (Summer 1976): 42-47.

1334. Ybarra-Frausto, Tomás. "The Chicano Movement and the Emergence of a Chicano Poetic Consciousness." *New Scholar* 6 (1977): 81-109.

1335. Zamora, Bernice. "The Chicana as a Literary Critic." *De Colores* 3 (No. 3): 16-19.

THE BEATS

1336. Allen, Donald, ed. *The New American Poetry 1945-1960.* New York: Grove Press, 1960.

1337. Ardinger, Richard K., ed. *An Annotated Bibliography of Works by John Clellon Holmes.* Pocatello: Idaho State University, 1979.

1338. Bingham, June. "The Intelligent Square's Guide to Hippieland." *New York Times Magazine* 6

(September 24, 1967): 25, 68–73, 76–84.

1339. Butler, Frank A. "On the Beat Nature of Beat." *American Scholar* 30 (Winter 1960–61): 79–92.

1340. Charters, Ann, ed. *Scenes Along the Road: Photographs of the Desolation Angels, 1944–1960.* New York: Gotham Book Mart, 1970.

1341. Ciardi, John. "Epitaph for the Dead Beats." *Saturday Review* 43 (February 6, 1960): 11–13, 42.

1342. Cook, Bruce. *The Beat Generation.* New York: Charles Scribner's Sons, 1971.

1343. Everson, William. *Archetype West: The Pacific Coast as a Literary Region.* Berkeley, Calif.: Oyez, 1976.

1344. Feldman, Gene, and Max Gartenberg, eds. *The Beat Generation and the Angry Young Men.* New York: Citadel Press, 1958.

1345. Ferlinghetti, Lawrence, ed. *Beatitude Anthology.* San Francisco: City Lights Books, 1960.

1346. Fleischmann, Wolfgang B. "A Look at the 'Beat Generation' Writers." *Carolina Quarterly* 9 (Spring 1959): 13–20.

1347. Gebhardt, Eike. "Strategic Anomie and Contingent Valuation: Three Writers of Non-Political Dissent." Doctoral dissertation, Yale University, 1973. Deals with Kerouac, Burroughs, and Ferlinghetti.

1348. Holmes, John Clellon. *Nothing More to Declare.* New York:

Scribner's, 1952. Account by participant in the Beat Movement.

1349. Huebel, Harry. "A Study of the Beat Generation and Its Effect on American Culture." Doctoral dissertation, Washington State University, 1971.

1350. Kherdian, David. *Six Poets of the San Francisco Renaissance.* Fresno, Calif.: Giligia Press, 1967.

1351. Knight, Arthur Winfield and Glee, eds. *The Beat Book.* California, Pa., 1974. An anthology of essays, reminiscences, poems, letters, and photographs.

1352. —— and Kit, eds. *The Beat Diary.* California, Pa., 1977. A collection of essays, interviews, letters, and photographs.

1353. Krim, [Seymour]. "A Backward Glance o'er Beatnik Roads." *TriQuarterly* 43 (1978): 324–37.

1354. ——, ed. *The Beats.* New York: Fawcett Publications, 1960.

1355. Lipton, Lawrence. "Disaffiliation and the Art of Poverty." *Chicago Review* 10 (Spring 1956): 53–79.

1356. ——. *The Holy Barbarians.* New York: Julian Messner, 1959.

1357. Mailer, Norman. "The White Negro: Superficial Reflections on the Hipster." *Dissent* 4 (Summer 1957): 276–93.

1358. Meltzer, David, ed. *The San Francisco Poets.* New York: Ballantine, 1971.

1359. Ossman, David. *The Sullen Art.* New York: Corinth Books,

1963. Includes interviews with Rexroth, Ginsberg, and others.

1360. Parkinson, Thomas. "After the Beat Generation." *Colorado Quarterly* 17 (Summer 1968): 45-56.

1361. ——. "Phenomenon or Generation." *A Casebook on the Beat.* New York: Thomas Y. Crowell, 1961.

1362. ——, ed. *A Casebook on the Beat.* New York: Thomas Y. Crowell, 1961.

1363. Podhoretz, Norman. "The Know-Nothing Bohemians." *Partisan Review* 25 (Spring 1958): 305-11, 313-16, 318.

1364. *Poets of the Cities: New York and San Francisco, 1950-1965.* New York: E. P. Dutton, 1974.

1365. Rao, Vimala C. "Oriental Influence on the Writings of Jack Kerouac, Allen Ginsberg, and Gary Snyder." Doctoral dissertation, University of Wisconsin, Milwaukee, 1974.

1366. Rexroth, Kenneth. *The Alternative Society: Essays from the Other World.* New York: Herder and Herder, 1970.

1367. ——. "Disengagement: The Art of the Beat Generation." *New World Writing No. 11.* New York: New American Library, 1957.

1368. ——. "San Francisco's Mature Bohemians." *Nation* 184 (February 23, 1957): 157-62.

1369. Roy, Gregor. *Beat Literature.* Monarch Notes and Study Guides. New York: Thor Publications, 1966.

1370. Saroyan, Aram. *Genesis Angels:* *The Saga of Lew Welch and the Beat Generation.* New York: William Morrow, 1979.

1371. Schwartz, Marilyn M. "From Beat to Beatific: Religious Ideas in the Writings of Kerouac, Ginsberg, and Corso." Doctoral dissertation, University of California, Davis, 1976.

1372. Scott, James F. "Beat Literature and the American Teen Cult." *American Quarterly* 14 (Summer 1962): 150-60.

1373. Sheed, Wilfred. "The Beat Movement, Concluded." *New York Times Book Review,* 13 February 1972, pp. 2, 32.

1374. Sisk, John P. "Beatnicks and Tradition." *Commonweal* 70 (April 17, 1959): 74-77.

1375. Skau, Michael Walter. "Themes, Things, and Movements in the Literature of the Beats." Doctoral dissertation, University of Illinois, Champaign-Urbana, 1973.

1376. "Ten San Francisco Poets." *Chicago Review* 12 (Spring 1958).

1377. Tytell, John. "The Beat Generation and the Continuing American Revolution." *American Scholar* 42 (Spring 1973): 308-17.

1378. ——. *Naked Angels: The Lives and Literature of the Beat Generation.* New York: McGraw-Hill, 1976. The best scholarly work on the Beats.

1379. Walkover, Andrew. *The Dialectics of Eden.* Stanford Honors Essay in Humanities, Number 16. Stanford, Calif., 1974.

79

Deals in part with William Burroughs, Allen Ginsberg, Gary Snyder, Richard Brautigan, and Ken Kesey.

1380. Wallenstein, Barry. "The Beats." *Contemporary Literature* 18 (Autumn 1977): 542-51.

1381. Widmer, Kingsley. "The Beat in the Rise of Popular Culture." *The Fifties: Fiction, Poetry, and Drama.* Ed. Warren French. Deland, Fla.: Everett/Edwards, 1970, pp. 155-73.

1382. Wilentz, Elias, ed. *The Beat Scene.* New York: Citadel Press/Corinth Books, 1960.

CANADIAN WESTERN LITERATURE

1383. Baldwin, R. G. "Pattern in the Novels of Edward McCourt." *Queens Quarterly* 68 (Winter 1962): 574-87.

1384. Blodgett, E. D. "The Concept of the 'Prairie' in Western Canadian Fiction." *Proceedings of the VIIth Congress of the International Comparative Literature Association, Montreal-Ottawa.* Ed. M. V. Dimić. 2 vols. Stuttgart and Budapest, 1977.

1385. Brown, Russell M. "An Interview with Robert Kroetsch." *University of Windsor Review* 7 (Spring 1972): 1-18.

1386. Cameron, Donald. *Conversations with Canadian Novelists.* 2 vols. Toronto: Macmillan, 1973.

1387. Carpenter, David. "Alberta in Fiction." Doctoral dissertation, University of Alberta, 1973.

1388. Chambers, Robert. *Sinclair Ross and Ernest Buckler.* Toronto:

Copp Clark, 1975.

1389. Cherewick, Janice. "Elements of Romance in Selected Fiction of the Canadian West, 1920-1970." Master's thesis, University of Alberta, 1973.

1390. Djwa, Sandra. "False Gods and the True Covenant: Thematic Continuity Between Margaret Laurence and Sinclair Ross." *Journal of Canadian Fiction* 1 (Fall 1972): 43-50.

1391. ——. "No Other Way: Sinclair Ross's Stories and Novels." *Canadian Literature* 47 (Winter 1971): 49-66.

1392. Eggleston, Wilfrid. "Frederick Philip Grove." *Our Living Tradition.* Ed. Claude Bissell. Toronto: University of Toronto Press, 1957, pp. 105-27.

1393. ——. *The Frontier and Canadian Letters.* Toronto: Ryerson, 1957.

1394. Elder, A. T. "Western Panorama: Settings and Themes in Robert J. C. Stead." *Canadian Literature* 17 (Summer 1963): 44-56.

1395. Engel, Mary Frances. "Bankrupt Dreams: The Isolated and the Insulated in Selected Works of Canadian and American Prairie Literature." Doctoral dissertation, Kent State University, 1978.

1396. Greene, Donald. "Western Canadian Literature." *Western American Literature* 2 (Winter 1968): 257-80.

1397. Gross, Konrad. "'Looking Back in Anger': Frederick Niven, W. O. Mitchell, and Robert Kroetsch on the History of the Canadian West." *Journal of Canadian*

Fiction 3, No. 2 (1974): 49-54.

1398. Grove, F. P. *In Search of Myself.* Toronto: Macmillan, 1946.

1399. Hanson, Irene. "W. O. Mitchell and Robert Kroetsch: Two Prairie Humorists." Master's thesis, Idaho State University, 1976.

1400. Harrison, Dick. "'Across the Medicine Line: Problems in Comparing Canadian and American Western Fiction.'" *The Westering Experience in American Literature: Bicentennial Essays.* Eds. Merrill Lewis and L. L. Lee. Bellingham: Bureau for Faculty Research, Western Washington University, 1977, pp. 48-56.

1401. ——. "The Beginnings of Prairie Fiction." *Journal of Canadian Fiction* 4, No. 1 (1975): 159-77.

1402. ——. "The Mounted Police in Fiction." *Men in Scarlet.* Ed. Hugh Dempsey. Calgary: McClelland and Stewart West, 1974, pp. 163-74.

1403. ——. "Popular Fiction of the Canadian Prairies: Autopsy on a Small Corpus." *Journal of Popular Culture* 14 (Fall 1980): 326-32.

1404. ——. *Unnamed Country: The Struggle for a Canadian Prairie Fiction.* Edmonton: University of Alberta Press, 1977. The best study of western Canadian fiction; contains useful bibliography, pp. 224-42.

1405. ——, ed. *Best Mounted Police Stories.* Edmonton: University of Alberta Press, 1978.

1406. ——, ed. *Crossing Frontiers: Papers in American and Canadian Western Literature.* Edmonton: University of Alberta Press, 1979.

1407. Hin-Smith, Joan. *Three Voices: The Lives of Margaret Laurence, Gabrielle Roy, Frederick Philip Grove.* Toronto: Clarke Irwin, 1975.

1408. Hoy, Helen Elizabeth. "The Portrayal of Women in Recent English-Canadian Fiction." Doctoral dissertation, University of Toronto, 1977.

1409. Innis, Kenneth. "'The History of the Frontier Like a Saga': Parkman, Pratt, and the Jesuit Enterprise." *The Westering Experience in American Literature: Bicentennial Essays.* Eds. Merrill Lewis and L. L. Lee. Bellingham: Bureau for Faculty Research, Western Washington University, 1977, pp. 179-88.

1410. Keith, W. J. "Roderick Haig-Brown." *Canadian Literature* 71 (Winter 1976): 7-20.

1411. Kreisel, Henry. "The Prairie: A State of Mind." *Transactions of the Royal Society of Canada,* 4th ser., 6 (June 1968): 171-80.

1412. Lauriston, Victor. *Arthur Stringer, Son of the North.* Toronto: Ryerson, 1941.

1413. McCourt, Edward. *The Canadian West in Fiction.* Rev. ed. Toronto: Ryerson, 1970.

1414. McLay, Catherine. "Crocus, Saskatchewan: A Country of the Mind." *Journal of Popular*

Culture 14 (Fall 1980): 333–49. W. O. Mitchell.

1415. McLeod, Gordon Duncan. "A Descriptive Bibliography of the Canadian Prairie Novel 1871–1970." Doctoral dissertation, Lakehead University, Ontario, 1974.

1416. McMullen, Lorraine. *Sinclair Ross*. Boston: Twayne, 1979.

1417. ——. "Women in Grove's Novels." *Inscape* 11 (Spring 1974): 77–88.

1418. McMullin, Stanley E. "Grove and the Promised Land." *Canadian Literature* 49 (Summer 1971): 10–19.

1419. Mandel, Eli. "Romance and Realism in Western Canadian Fiction." *Prairie Perspectives 2*. Eds. A. W. Rasporich and H. C. Klassen. Toronto: Holt, Rinehart and Winston, 1973.

1420. Morton, W. L. "Seeing an Unliterary Landscape." *Mosaic* 3 (Spring 1970): 1–10.

1421. New, W. H. *Articulating West: Essays on Purpose and Form in Modern Canadian Literature*. Toronto: New Press, 1972.

1422. ——. "A Feeling of Completion: Aspects of W. O. Mitchell." *Canadian Literature* 17 (Summer 1963): 22–33.

1423. ——. "A Life and Four Landscapes: Frederick John Niven." *Canadian Literature* 32 (Spring 1967): 15–28.

1424. O'Conner, John Joseph William. "The Last Three Steppes: The Canadian West as 'Frontier' in Prairie Literature." Doctoral dissertation, University of Toronto, 1977.

1425. Pacey, Desmond. *Frederick Philip Grove*. Toronto: Ryerson, 1945.

1426. ——, ed. *Frederick Philip Grove*. Toronto: Ryerson, 1970.

1427. Rasky, Frank. *The Taming of the Canadian West*. Toronto: McClelland and Stewart, 1967.

1428. Ricou, Laurence R. "Canadian Prairie Fiction: The Significance of the Landscape." Doctoral dissertation, University of Toronto, 1971.

1429. ——. *Vertical Man/Horizontal World*. Vancouver: University of British Columbia Press, 1973.

1430. Singleton, M. K. "Frederick Niven *Redivivus*: A Scots-Canadian's Pacific Northwest." *Northwest Perspectives: Essays on the Culture of the Pacific Northwest*. Eds. Edwin R. Bingham and Glen A. Love. Seattle: University of Washington Press, 1979, pp. 121–35.

1431. Spettigue, Douglas. *Frederick Philip Grove*. Toronto: Copp Clark, 1969.

1432. Stegner, Wallace. "Letter from Canada: A Son of the West Looks at His Native Region in the Light of Today's Growing Canadian Nationalism." *American West* 11 (January 1974): 28–30.

1433. Stephens, D. G., ed. *Writers of the Prairies*. Vancouver: University of British Columbia Press, 1973.

1434. Stevens, Peter. "Explorer/Settler/Poet." *The Westering Experience in American Literature: Bicentennial Essays.* Eds. Merrill Lewis and L. L. Lee. Bellingham: Bureau for Faculty Research, Western Washington University, 1977, pp. 189-98.

1435. Stich, Klaus Peter. "Immigration and the Canadian West From Propaganda to Fiction." Doctoral dissertation, York University, 1974.

1436. Stobie, Margaret. *Frederick Philip Grove.* New York: Twayne, 1973.

1437. Story, Norah. *The Oxford Companion to Canadian History and Literature.* Toronto: Oxford University Press, 1967.

1438. Surette, P. L. "The Fabular Fiction of Robert Kroetsch." *Canadian Literature* 77 (Summer 1978): 6-19.

1439. Sutherland, Ronald. "Children of the Changing World." *Journal of Canadian Studies* 5 (November 1970): 3-11. W. O. Mitchell.

1440. Tallman, Warren. "Wolf in the Snow: Part One, Four Windows on to Landscapes." *Canadian Literature* 5 (Summer 1960): 7-20.

1441. ——. "Wolf in the Snow: Part Two, The House Repossessed." *Canadian Literature* 6 (Autumn 1960): 41-48.

1442. Thomas, Clara. *The Manawaka World of Margaret Laurence.* Toronto: McClelland and Stewart, 1975.

1443. ——. *Margaret Laurence.* Toronto: McClelland and Stewart, 1969.

1444. Thompson, Eric Callum. "The Prairie Novel in Canada: A Study in Changing Form and Perception." Doctoral dissertation, University of New Brunswick, 1974.

1445. Tiessen, Hildegard E. "A Mighty Inner River: 'Peace' in the Fiction of Rudy Wiebe." *Journal of Canadian Fiction* 2 (Fall 1973): 71-76.

1446. Walden, Keith. "The Symbol and Myth of the Royal Canadian Mounted Police in Some British, American and English Canadian Popular Literature 1873-1973." Doctoral dissertation, Queen's University, Kingston, 1980.

1447. Watt, Frank W. "Western Myth, the World of Ralph Connor." *Canadian Literature* 1 (Summer 1959): 26-36.

1448. Wiebe, Rudy. "A Novelist's Personal Notes on Frederick Philip Grove." *University of Toronto Quarterly* 47 (Spring 1978): 189-99.

1449. ——. "Western Canada Fiction: Past and Future." *Western American Literature* 6 (Spring 1971): 21-30.

1450. Wood, Susan. "God's Doormats: Women in Canadian Prairie Fiction." *Journal of Popular Culture* 14 (Fall 1980): 350-59.

1451. ——. "The Land in Canadian Prose, 1840-1945." Doctoral dissertation, University of Toronto, 1975.

1452. ——. "Ralph Connor and the Tamed West." *The Westering Experience in American Literature: Bicentennial Essays.* Eds. Merrill Lewis and L. L. Lee. Bellingham: Bureau for Faculty Research, Western Washington University, 1977, pp. 199-205.

1453. ——. "Reinventing the Word: Kroetsch's Poetry." *Canadian Literature* 77 (Summer 1978): 28-39.

WORKS ON INDIVIDUAL AUTHORS

EDWARD ABBEY

1454. Benton, Robert M. "Edward Abbey's Anti-Heroes." *The Westering Experience in American Literature: Bicentennial Essays.* Eds. Merrill Lewis and L. L. Lee. Bellingham: Bureau for Faculty Research, Western Washington University, 1977, pp. 172-76.

1455. Erisman, Fred. "A Variant Text of *The Monkey Wrench Gang.*" *Western American Literature* 14 (Fall 1979): 227-28.

1456. Haslam, Gerald. "Introduction," to Edward Abbey, *Fire on the Mountain.* Albuquerque: University of New Mexico Press, 1978.

1457. Herndon, Jerry A. "'Moderate Extremism': Edward Abbey and 'The Moon-Eyed Horse.'" *Western American Literature* 16 (August 1981): 97-103.

1458. Lambert, Neal E. "Introduction," to Edward Abbey, *The Brave Cowboy.* Albuquerque: University of New Mexico Press, 1977.

1459. McCann, Garth. *Edward Abbey.* Western Writers Series, No. 29. Boise, Idaho: Boise State University, 1977.

1460. Pilkington, William T. "Edward Abbey: Southwestern Anarchist." *Western Review* 3 (Winter 1966): 58-62.

1461. ——. "Edward Abbey: Western Philosopher, or How to be a 'Happy Hopi Hippie.'" *Western American Literature* 9 (May 1974): 17-31.

1462. Powell, Lawrence Clark. "A Singular Ranger." *Westways* 66 (March 1974): 32-35, 64-65.

1463. Standiford, Les. "Desert Places: An Exchange with Edward Abbey." *Western Humanities Review* 24 (Autumn 1970): 395-98.

1464. Twining, Edward S. "Edward Abbey, American: Another Radical Conservative." *Denver Quarterly* 12 (Winter 1978): 3-15.

1465. Wylder, Delbert E. "Edward Abbey and the 'Power Elite.'" *Western Review* 6 (Winter 1969): 18-22.

OSCAR ZETA ACOSTA

1466. Smith, Norman D. "Buffaloes and Cockroaches: Acosta's Siege at Aztlán." *Latin American Literary Review* 5 (Spring-Summer 1977): 86-97.

ANDY ADAMS

1467. "Autobiographical Sketch of Andy Adams." *The Junior Book of Authors.* Eds. Stanley J. Kunitz and Howard Haycraft. New York: H. W. Wilson, 1935, pp. 3-4.

1468. Barton, Sandra L. *"Log of a Cowboy* and *In Cold Blood* as Nonfiction Novels." *AFFword: Publication of Arizona Friends of Folklore* 1 (July 1971): 1-6.

1469. Brunvand, Jan H. "The Hat-in-Mud Tale." *The Sunny Slopes of Long Ago.* Texas Folklore Society Publications, 33. Eds. Wilson M. Hudson and Allen Maxwell. Dallas: Southern Methodist University Press, 1966.

1470. ——. "'Sailors' and 'Cowboys' Folklore in Two Popular Classics." *Southern Folklore Quarterly* 29 (December 1965): 266-83.

1471. Capps, Benjamin. "A Critical Look at a Classic Western Novel." *Roundup* 12 (June 1964): 2, 4.

1472. Davidson, Levette J. "The Unpublished Manuscripts of Andy Adams." *Colorado Magazine* 28 (April 1951): 97-107.

1473. Dobie, J. Frank. "Andy Adams, Cowboy Chronicler." *Southwest Review* 11 (January 1926): 92-101.

1474. Graham, Don. "Old and New Cowboy Classics." *Southwest Review* 65 (Summer 1980): 293-303.

1475. Hudson, Wilson M. *Andy Adams: His Life and Writings.* Dallas: Southern Methodist University Press, 1964.

1476. ——. *Andy Adams: Storyteller and Novelist of the Great Plains.* Southwest Writers Series, No. 4. Austin, Tex.: Steck-Vaughn, 1967.

1477. ——, ed. *Why the Chisholm Trail Forks and Other Tales of the Cattle Country.* Austin: University of Texas Press, 1956, pp. xi-xxxi.

1478. Molen, Dayle H. "Andy Adams: Classic Novelist of the Western Cattle Drive." *Montana: The Magazine of Western History* 19 (January 1969): 24-35.

1479. ——. "Andy Adams . . . Log of a Cowboy." *Persimmon Hill* 9 (1979): 48-57.

1480. Quissell, Barbara. "Andy Adams and the Real West." *Western American Literature* 7 (Fall 1972): 211-19.

1481. Taylor, Archer. "Americanisms in *The Log of the Cowboy.*" *Western Folklore* 18 (January 1959): 39-41.

MAX ADELER

See Charles Heber Clark

85

BESS STREETER ALDRICH

1482. Meier, A. Mabel. "Bess Streeter Aldrich: A Literary Portrait." *Nebraska History* 50 (Spring 1969): 67-100.

CHARLES ALEXANDER

1483. Corning, Howard M. "Charles Alexander: Youth of the Oregon Mood." *Oregon Historical Quarterly* 74 (March 1973): 34-70. Includes material on several other Oregon writers of the 1920-1940 period.

HENRY WILSON ALLEN
(Clay Fisher, Will Henry)

1484. Falke, Anne. "The Art of Convention: Images of Women in the Modern Western Novels of Henry Wilson Allen." *North Dakota Quarterly* 42 (Spring 1974): 17-27.
1485. ——. "Clay Fisher or Will Henry? An Author's Choice of Pen Name." *Journal of Popular Culture* 7 (Winter 1973): 692-700.
1486. Needham, Arnold E. "[An Essay Review of three Will Henry books]." *Western American Literature* I (Winter 1967), 297-302.
1487. Rosenberg, Betty. "Introduction," to Will Henry, *From Where the Sun Now Stands.* Boston: Gregg Press, 1978, pp. v-ix.

ALURISTA
See Alberto Urista

RUDOLFO ANAYA

1488. Anaya, Rudolfo A. "The Writer's Landscape: Epiphany in Landscape." *Latin American Literary Review* 5 (Spring-Summer 1977): 98-102.
1489. Cantú, Roberto. "Estructura y sentido de lo onírico en *Bless Me, Ultima*." *Mester* 5 (November 1974): 27-41.
1490. Malpezzi, Frances. "A Study of the Female Protagonist in Frank Waters' *People of the Valley* and Rudolfo Anaya's *Bless Me, Ultima*." *South Dakota Review* 14 (Summer 1976): 102-10.
1491. Mitchell, Carol. "Rudolfo Anaya's *Bless Me, Ultima*: Folk Culture in Literature." *Critique* 22, No. 1 (1980): 55-64.
1492. Rogers, Jane. "The Function of the *La Llorona* Motif in Rudolfo Anaya's *Bless Me, Ultima*." *Latin American Literary Review* 5 (Spring-Summer 1977): 64-69.
1493. Testa, Daniel. "Extensive/Intensive Dimensionality in Anaya's *Bless Me, Ultima*." *Latin American Literary Review* 5 (Spring-Summer 1977): 70-78.
1494. Treviño, Albert D. "*Bless Me, Ultima*: A Critical Interpretation." *De Colores* 3 (1977): 30-33.
1495. Waggoner, Amy. "Tony's Dreams—An Important Dimension in *Bless Me, Ultima*." *Southwestern American Literature* 4 (1974): 74-79.
1496. Wilson, Carter. "'Magical

Strength in the Human Heart':
The Framing of Mortal Confusion in Rudolfo A. Anaya's
Bless Me, Ultima." *Ploughshares* 4 (1978): 190-97.

BROTHER ANTONINUS
See William Everson

JESSE APPLEGATE

1497. Frear, Samuel Thomas. "Jesse Applegate: An Appraisal of an Uncommon Pioneer." Master's thesis, University of Oregon, 1961.

RON ARIAS

1498. Lewis, Marvin A. "On the Road to Tamazunchale." *Revista Chicano-Riqueña* 5 (Fall 1978): 49-52.
1499. Marín, Mariana. "*The Road to Tamazunchale*: Fantasy or Reality." *De Colores* 3 (1977): 34-38.
1500. Martínez, Eliud. "Ron Arias' *The Road to Tamazunchale*: A Chicano Novel of the New Reality." *Latin American Literary Review* 5 (Spring-Summer 1977): 51-63.

GERTRUDE ATHERTON

1501. Cooper, Frederic Taber. *Some American Story Tellers.* New York: Holt, 1911, pp. 115-34.
1502. Forman, Henry James. "A Brilliant California Novelist." *California Historical Society Quar-*

terly 40 (March 1961): 1-10.
1503. Forrey, Carolyn. "Gertrude Atherton and the New Woman." *California Historical Quarterly* 55 (Fall 1976): 194-209.
1504. ——. "Gertrude Atherton and the New Woman." Doctoral dissertation, Yale University, 1971.
1505. McClure, Charlotte S. "A Checklist of the Writings of and About Gertrude Atherton." *American Literary Realism 1870-1910* 9 (Spring 1976): 103-62.
1506. ——. *Gertrude Atherton.* Western Writers Series, No. 23. Boise, Idaho: Boise State University, 1976.
1507. ——. *Gertrude Atherton.* Boston: Twayne, 1979.
1508. ——. "Gertrude Atherton (1857-1948)." *American Literary Realism 1870-1910* 9 (Spring 1976): 95-101.
1509. ——. "Gertrude Atherton's California Woman: From Love Story to Psychological Drama." *Itinerary: Criticism, Essays on California Writers.* Ed. Charles L. Crow. Bowling Green, Ohio: University Press, 1978, pp. 1-9.
1510. McElderry, Bruce R. "Gertrude Atherton and Henry James." *Colby Library Quarterly* 3 (November 1954): 269-72.
1511. Richey, Elinor. "The Flappers Were Her Daughters: The Liberated Literary World of Gertrude Atherton." *American West* 11 (July 1974): 4-10, 60-63.

87

1512. Starr, Kevin. "Gertrude Atherton, Daughter of the Elite." *Americans and the California Dream, 1850-1915.* New York: Oxford University Press, 1973, pp. 345-64.

1513. Underwood, John Curtis. *Literature and Insurgency: Ten Studies in Racial Evolution.* New York: Mitchell Kennerley, 1914, pp. 391-446.

1514. Weir, Sybil. "Gertrude Atherton: The Limits of Feminism in the 1890's." *San Jose Studies* 1 (February 1975): 24-31.

1515. Wheeler, Leslie. "Montana and the Lady Novelist." *Montana: The Magazine of Western History* 27 (Winter 1977): 40-51.

MARY AUSTIN

1516. Austin, Mary. *Earth Horizon: An Autobiography.* Boston: Houghton Mifflin, 1932.

1517. Ballard, Rae Galbraith. "Mary Austin's *Earth Horizon*: The Imperfect Circle." Doctoral dissertation, Claremont Graduate School, 1977.

1518. Berry, J. Wilkes. "Mary Austin: Sibylic Gourmet of the Southwest." *Western Review* 9 (Winter 1972): 3-8.

1519. ———. "Mary Hunter Austin (1868-1934)." *American Literary Realism 1870-1910* 2 (Summer 1969): 125-31.

1520. Doyle, Helen McKnight. *Mary Austin: Woman of Genius.* New York: Gotham House, 1939.

1521. Dubois, Arthur E. "Mary Hunter Austin, 1868-1934." *Southwest Review* 20 (April 1935): 231-64.

1522. Ford, Thomas W. "*The American Rhythm*: Mary Austin's Poetic Principle." *Western American Literature* 5 (Spring 1970): 3-14.

1523. Gaer, Joseph. *Mary Austin, Bibliography and Biographical Data.* Monograph No. 2. Berkeley, Calif.: Library Research Digest, 1934.

1524. Lyday, Jo W. *Mary Austin: The Southwest Works.* Southwest Writers Series, No. 16. Austin, Tex.: Steck-Vaughn, 1968.

1525. ———. *The Works of Mary Austin.* Cassette. Deland, Fla.: Everett/Edwards, 1974.

1526. *Mary Austin: A Memorial.* Ed. Willard Hougland. Santa Fe: Laboratory of Anthropology, 1944.

1527. McClanahan, Muriel H. "Aspects of Southwestern Regionalism in the Prose Work of Mary Hunter Austin." Doctoral dissertation, University of Pittsburgh, 1940.

1528. McClure, Charlotte S. "Mary Hunter Austin." *American Literary Realism 1870-1919* 9 (Summer 1975): 190. Review of dissertations on Austin.

1529. Pearce, T. M. *The Beloved House.* Caldwell, Idaho: Caxton Printers, 1940.

1530. ———. "Mary Austin and the Patterns of New Mexico." *Southwest Review* 22 (January 1937): 140-48.

1531. ——. *Mary Hunter Austin.* New York: Twayne, 1965.

1532. ——, ed. *Literary America, 1903-1934: The Mary Austin Letters.* Westport, Conn.: Greenwood Press, 1979.

1533. Powell, Lawrence Clark. "A Dedication to the Memory of Mary Hunter Austin, 1868-1934." *Arizona and the West* 10 (Spring 1968): 1-4.

1534. ——. "Southwest Classics Reread: A Prophetic Passage." *Westways* 65 (February 1973): 60-65.

1535. Ringler, Donald P. *Mary Austin: Kern County Days.* Bakersfield, Calif: Bear Mountain Books, 1963. The article first appeared in *Southern California Quarterly* 45 (March 1963): 25-63.

1536. Smith, Henry. "The Feel of the Purposeful Earth." *New Mexico Quarterly* I (February 1931): 17-33.

1537. Steffens, Lincoln. "Mary Austin and the Desert: A Portrait." *American Mercury* 72 (June 1911): 244-63.

1538. Thoroughgood, Inez. "Mary Hunter Austin, Interpreter of the Western Scene, 1888-1906." Master's thesis, University of California, Los Angeles, 1950.

1539. Van Doren, Carl. "The American Rhythm: Mary Austin: Discoverer and Prophet." *Century Magazine* 107 (November 1923): 151-56.

1540. Wagenknecht, Edward. "Mary Austin, Sybil." *Cavalcade of the American Novel.* New York: Henry Holt, 1952, pp. 230-35.

1541. Wynn, Dudley. "A Critical Study of the Writings of Mary Hunter Austin, 1868-1934." Doctoral dissertation, New York University, 1940.

1542. ——. "Mary Austin, Woman Alone." *Virginia Quarterly Review* 13 (Spring 1937): 243-56.

1543. Young, Vernon. "Mary Austin and the Earth Performance." *Southwest Review* 35 (Summer 1959): 153-63.

MARGARET JEWETT BAILEY

1544. Duncan, Janice K. "'Ruth Rover'—Vindictive Falsehood or Historical Truth?" *Journal of the West* 12 (April 1973): 240-53.

1545. Nelson, Herbert B. "First True Confession Story Pictures Oregon 'Moral.'" *Oregon Historical Quarterly* 45 (June 1944): 168-76.

1546. ——. *The Literary Impulse in Pioneer Oregon.* Corvallis: Oregon State University Press, 1948, pp. 36-41.

1547. ——. "Ruth Rover's Cup of Sorrow." *Pacific Northwest Quarterly* 50 (July 1959): 91-98.

FREDERIC HOMER BALCH

1548. Ballou, Robert. *Early Klickitat Valley Days.* Goldendale, Wash., 1938, pp. 433-43.

1549. Coon, Delia M. "Frederick [*sic*]

Homer Balch." *Washington Historical* 15 (January 1924): 32-43.

1550. Powers, Alfred. *History of Oregon Literature.* Portland: Metropolitan Press, 1935, pp. 317-32.

1551. Wiley, Leonard. *The Granite Boulder: A Biography of Frederic Homer Balch.* Portland, Oreg.: n.p. 1970.

HUBERT HOWE BANCROFT

1552. Caughey, John. *Hubert Howe Bancroft: Historian of the West.* Berkeley: University of California Press, 1946.

1553. Clark, Harry. *A Venture in History: The Production, Publication, and Sale of the Works of Hubert Howe Bancroft.* Berkeley: University of California Press, 1973.

S. OMAR BARKER

1554. Dewey, Evelyn G. "S. Omar Barker: Man of the Southwest." Master's thesis, Eastern New Mexico University, 1954.

MARY BARNARD

1555. Helle, Anita. "The Odysseys of Mary Barnard." *An Anthology of Northwest Writing: 1900–1950.* Ed. Michael Strelow, et al. Eugene, Oreg.: Northwest Review Books, 1979, pp. 227-32.

WILL CROFT BARNES

1556. White, John I. "Will Croft Barnes: Cowboy, Author, Conservationist." *American West* 16 (March–April 1979): 38-39.

RAYMOND BARRIO

1557. Geuder, Patricia. "Address Systems in the *Plum Plum Pickers.*" *Aztlán* 6 (Fall 1975): 341-46.

1558. Lattin, Vernon. "Paradise and Plums: Appearance and Reality in Barrio's *The Plum Plum Pickers.*" *Critique* 19, No. 1 (1977): 49-57.

PETER S. BEAGLE

1559. Van Becker, David. "Time, Space, and Consciousness in the Fantasy of Peter S. Beagle." *San Jose Studies* 1 (February 1975): 52-61.

ROY BEDICHEK

1560. Bedichek, Roy. "My Father and Then My Mother." *Southwest Review* 52 (1967): 324-42.

1561. Dugger, Ronnie, ed. *Three Men in Texas: Bedichek, Webb, and Dobie.* Austin: University of Texas Press, 1967.

1562. James, Eleanor. *Roy Bedichek.* Southwest Writers Series, No. 32. Austin, Tex.: Steck-Vaughn, 1970.

1563. Owens, William A. *Three*

Friends: Bedichek, Dobie, Webb. Garden City, N.Y.: Doubleday, 1969.

EMERSON BENNETT-SIDNEY MOSS

1564. Mills, Randall V. "Emerson Bennett's Two Oregon Novels." *Oregon Historical Quarterly* 41 (December 1940): 367-81.
1565. Nelson, Herbert B. *The Literary Impulse in Pioneer Oregon.* Corvallis: Oregon State University Press, 1948, pp. 44-51.
1566. Poulsen, Richard C. "Black George, Black Harris, and the Mountain Man Vernacular." *Rendezvous* 8 (Summer 1973): 15-23.
1567. Powers, Alfred. *History of Oregon Literature.* Portland: Metropolitan Press, 1935, pp. 195-203.

THOMAS BERGER

1568. Cleary, Michael. "Finding the Center of the Earth: Satire, History, and Myth in *Little Big Man.*" *Western American Literature* 15 (Fall 1980): 195-221.
1569. Dippie, Brian W. "Jack Crabb and the Sole Survivors of Custer's Last Stand." *Western American Literature* 4 (Fall 1969): 189-202.
1570. Fetrow, Fred M. "The Function of the External Narrator in Thomas Berger's *Little Big Man.*" *Journal of Narrative Technique* 5 (1975): 57-65.
1571. Gurian, Jay. "Style in the Literary Desert: *Little Big Man.*" *Western American Literature* 3 (Winter 1969): 285-96.
1572. Lee, L. L. "American, Western, Picaresque: Thomas Berger's *Little Big Man.*" *South Dakota Review* 4 (Summer 1966): 35-42.
1573. Oliva, Leo E. "Thomas Berger's *Little Big Man* as History." *Western American Literature* 8 (Spring-Summer 1973): 33-54.
1574. Turner, Frederick W., III. "Melville and Thomas Berger: The Novelist as Cultural Anthropologist." *Centennial Review* 13 (Winter 1969): 101-21.
1575. Turner, Joseph William. "The Comic Historical Novel: Some Recent American Experiments." Doctoral dissertation, Emory University, 1976.
1576. Wylder, Delbert E. "Thomas Berger's *Little Big Man* as Literature." *Western American Literature* 3 (Winter 1969): 273-84.

DON BERRY

1577. Love, Glen A. *Don Berry.* Western Writers Series, No. 35. Boise, Idaho: Boise State University, 1978.
1578. Moss, James Davidson. "Use and Abuse of History in the New Western Novel: A Case Study of *Trask.*" Master's thesis, University of Oregon, 1977.

1579. Porter, Kenneth. "Northwest Writer Emerges." *Northwest Review* 3 (Summer 1960): 98-101.

1580. Singer, Barnett. "Toward the Great Northwest Novel." *Research Studies* (Pullman, Wash.) 43 (March 1975): 55-69.

AMBROSE BIERCE

1581. Bahr, H. W. "Ambrose Bierce and Realism." *Southern Quarterly* 1 (July 1963): 309-33.

1582. Fatout, Paul. "Ambrose Bierce (1842-1914)." *American Literary Realism 1870-1910* 1 (Fall 1967): 13-19.

1583. ——. *Ambrose Bierce and the Black Hills.* Norman: University of Oklahoma Press, 1956.

1584. ——. *Ambrose Bierce: The Devil's Lexicographer.* Norman: University of Oklahoma Press, 1951.

1585. Fortenberry, George E., comp. and ed. "Ambrose Bierce (1842-1914?): A Critical Bibliography of Secondary Comment." *American Literary Realism 1870-1910* 4 (Winter 1971): 11-56.

1586. Gaer, Joseph, ed. *Ambrose Gwinett Bierce: Bibliography and Biographical Data.* Berkeley, Calif., 1935; New York: Burt Franklin, 1968.

1587. Goldstein, Jesse Sidney. "Edwin Markham, Ambrose Bierce, and 'The Man with the Hoe.'" *Modern Language Notes* 58 (March 1943): 165-75.

1588. Grattan, C. Hartley. *Bitter Bierce: A Mystery of American Life.* New York: Doubleday, Doran, 1929.

1589. Grenander, M. E. *Ambrose Bierce.* New York: Twayne, 1971.

1590. ——. "Ambrose Bierce, John Camden Hotten, *The Fiend's Delight, and Nuggets and Dust.*" *Huntington Library Quarterly* 28 (August 1965): 353-71.

1591. ——. "Bierce's Turn of the Screw." *Western Humanities Review* 11 (Summer 1957): 257-64.

1592. ——. "The Critical Theories of Ambrose Bierce." Doctoral dissertation, University of Chicago, 1948.

1593. Klein, Marcus. "San Francisco and Her Hateful Ambrose Bierce." *Hudson Review* 7 (August 1954): 392-407.

1594. Loveman, S., ed. *Twenty-one Letters of Ambrose Bierce.* Cleveland: George Kirk, 1922.

1595. McWilliams, Carey. "Ambrose Bierce." *American Mercury* 16 (February 1929): 215-22.

1596. ——. *Ambrose Bierce: A Biography.* New York: A. and C. Boni, 1929; Hampden, Conn.: Archon Books, 1967.

1597. ——. "The Mystery of Ambrose Bierce." *American Mercury* 22 (March 1931): 330-37.

1598. Neale, Walter. *Life of Ambrose Bierce.* New York: Walter Neale, 1929; New York: AMS Press, 1969.

1599. O'Connor, Richard. *Ambrose*

Bierce: A Biography. Boston: Little, Brown, 1967.

1600. Pope, Bertha, ed. *The Letters of Ambrose Bierce.* San Francisco: Book Club of California, 1922; Gordian Press, 1967.

1601. Roth, Russell. "Ambrose Bierce's 'Detestable Creature.'" *Western American Literature* 9 (November 1974): 169-76.

1602. Sheller, Harry L. "The Satire of Ambrose Bierce: Its Objects, Forms, Devices, and Possible Origins." Doctoral dissertation, University of Southern California, 1945.

1603. Starrett, Vincent. *Ambrose Bierce.* Chicago: Walter M. Hill, 1920.

1604. ——. *A Bibliography of the Writings of Ambrose Bierce.* Philadelphia: Centaur Book Shop, 1929.

1605. Stubbs, John C. "Ambrose Bierce's Contributions to *Cosmopolitan*: An Annotated Bibliography." *American Literary Realism 1870-1910* 4 (Winter 1971): 57-59.

1606. Thomas, Jeffrey F. "Ambrose Bierce." *American Literary Realism 1870-1910* 8 (Summer 1975): 198-201. Reviews dissertations on Bierce.

1607. Walker, Dale L. "A Last Laugh for Ambrose Bierce." *American West* 10 (November 1973): 34-39, 63.

1608. Walker, Franklin. *San Francisco's Literary Frontier.* New York: Alfred A. Knopf, 1939.

1609. Wiggins, Robert A. *Ambrose Bierce.* Minneapolis: University of Minnesota Press, 1964.

1610. ——. "Ambrose Bierce: A Romantic in an Age of Realism." *American Literary Realism 1870-1910* 4 (Winter 1971): 1-10.

1611. Woodruff, Stuart C. *The Short Stories of Ambrose Bierce: A Study in Polarity.* Pittsburgh: University of Pittsburgh Press, 1964.

FORRESTER BLAKE

1612. Legris, Maurice. "The Western World of Forrester Blake." *South Dakota Review* 13 (Winter 1975-76): 64-76.

BRUCE BLIVEN

1613. Greb, Gordon. "Seven Million Words Later: An Interview with Bruce Bliven." *San Jose Studies* 2 (May 1976): 62-73.

ROBERT BLY

1614. Alexander, Franklyn. "Robert Bly." *Great Lakes Review* 3 (1976): 66-69. Bibliographical.

1615. Dodd, Wayne. "An Interview with Robert Bly." *Ohio Review* 19 (Fall 1978): 32-48.

1616. Faas, Ekbert. "Robert Bly." *Boundary* 4 (1976): 707-26. Preceded by an interview between Faas and Bly, pp. 677-700.

1617. ——. *Towards a New Poetics: Essays and Interviews.* Santa Barbara, Calif.: Black Sparrow Press, 1978, pp. 199-243.

1618. Friberg, Ingegerd. *Moving Inward: A Study of Robert Bly's Poetry.* Göteborg: Acta University, 1977.

1619. Hertzel, Leo J. "What About Writers in the North?" *South Dakota Review* 5 (Spring 1967): 3-19.

1620. Heyen, William. "Inward to the World: The Poetry of Robert Bly." *Far Point* 3 (1969): 42-50.

1621. Janssens, G. A. M. "The Present State of American Poetry: Robert Bly and James Wright." *English Studies* 51 (April 1970): 112-37.

1622. Justin, Jeffrey Arthur. "Unknown Land Poetry: Walt Whitman, Robert Bly, and Gary Snyder." Doctoral dissertation, University of Michigan, 1973.

1623. Lensing, George S., and Ronald Moran. *Four Poets and the Emotive Imagination: Robert Bly, James Wright, Louis Simpson, and William Stafford.* Baton Rouge: Louisiana State University Press, 1976.

1624. Lockwood, William J. "Robert Bly: The Point Reyes Poems." *Where the West Begins.* Eds. Arthur R. Huseboe and William Geyer. Sioux Falls, S.Dak.: Center for Western Studies Press, 1978, pp. 128-34.

1625. Molesworth, Charles. *The Fierce Embrace: A Study of Contemporary American Poetry.* Columbia: University of Missouri Press, 1979.

1626. ——. "Thrashing in the Depths: The Poetry of Robert Bly." *Rocky Mountain Review* 29 (Autumn 1975): 95-117.

1627. Piccione, Anthony. "Robert Bly and the Deep Image." Doctoral dissertation, Ohio University, 1969.

1628. Sage, Frances Kellogg. "Robert Bly: His Poetry and Literary Criticism." Doctoral dissertation, University of Texas, Austin, 1974.

1629. Steele, Frank. "Three Questions Answered." *Tennessee Poetry Journal* 2 (Winter 1969): 23-28.

MODY C. BOATRIGHT

1630. Speck, Ernest B. *Mody C. Boatright.* Southwest Writers Series. Austin, Tex.: Steck-Vaughn, 1971.

HERBERT EUGENE BOLTON

1631. Bannon, John Francis. *Herbert Eugene Bolton: The Historian and the Man.* Tucson: University of Arizona Press, 1978.

1632. ——, ed. *Bolton and the Spanish Borderlands.* Norman: University of Oklahoma Press, 1964.

1633. Jacobs, Wilbur R., et al. *Turner, Bolton, and Webb: Three Historians of the Frontier.* Seattle: University of Washington Press, 1965, 1979.

1634. Magnaghi, R. M. "Herbert E. Bolton and Sources for American Indian Studies." *Western Historical Quarterly* 6 (January 1975): 33-46.

HAL BORLAND

1635. Barry, Nora Baker. "The Bear's Son Folk Tale in *When the Legends Die* and *House Made of Dawn*." *Western American Literature* 12 (Winter 1978): 275-87.

B. M. BOWER
(Bertha Muzzey Bower Sinclair Cowan)

1636. Bloodworth, William A., Jr. "Mulford and Bower: Myth and History in the Early Western." *Great Plains Quarterly* 1 (Spring 1981): 95-104.
1637. Davison, Stanley R. "*Chip of the Flying U*: The Author Was a Lady." *Montana: The Magazine of Western History* 23 (Spring 1973): 2-15.
1638. Engen, Orrin A. *Writer of the Plains.* Culver City, Calif.: Pontine Press, 1973.
1639. Meyer, Roy W. "B. M. Bower: The Poor Man's Wister." *Journal of Popular Culture* 7 (Winter 1973): 667-79.
1640. Nye, Russel. *The Unembarrassed Muse: The Popular Arts in America.* New York: Dial Press, 1970, pp. 291-92.
1641. West, Gordon. "Remember 'Chip of the Flying U'?" *True West* 20 (September-October 1971): 31.

RICHARD BRADFORD

1642. Etulain, Richard W. "Richard Bradford's *Red Sky at Morning*: New Novel of the South-west." *Western Review* 8 (Spring 1971): 57-62.
1643. King, Scottie. "Richard Bradford—Gray Sky at Morning." *New Mexico Magazine* 58 (February 1980): 48-49.

MAX BRAND
See Frederick Faust

RICHARD BRAUTIGAN

1644. Bales, Kent. "Fishing the Ambivalence, or, A Reading of *Trout Fishing in America*." *Western Humanities Review* 29 (Winter 1975): 29-42.
1645. Hearron, Thomas. "Escape Through Imagination in *Trout Fishing in America*." *Critique* 16 (1974): 25-31.
1646. Hernlund, Patricia. "Author's Intent: *In Watermelon Sugar*." *Critique* 16, No. 1 (1974): 5-17.
1647. Jones, Stephen R. "Richard Brautigan: A Bibliography." *Bulletin of Bibliography* 33 (January 1976): 53-59.
1648. Kern, Robert. "Williams, Brautigan, and the Poetics of Primitivism." *Chicago Review* 27 (Summer 1975): 47-57.
1649. Leavitt, Harvey. "The Regained Paradise of Brautigan's *In Watermelon Sugar*." *Critique* 16, No. 1 (1974): 18-24.
1650. Malley, Terence. *Writers for the Seventies: Richard Brautigan.* New York: Warner Paperback Library, 1972.
1651. Schmitz, Neil. "Richard Brauti-

gan and the Modern Pastoral." *Modern Fiction Studies* 19 (Spring 1973): 109-25.

1652. Vanderwerken, David L. *"Trout Fishing in America* and the American Tradition." *Critique* 16, No. 1 (1974): 32-40.

1653. Wanless, James, and Christine Kolodzie. "Richard Brautigan: A Working Checklist." *Critique* 16, No. 1 (1974): 41-52.

DOROTHY E. BRETT

1654. Brett, Dorothy E. "Autobiography: My Long and Beautiful Journey." *South Dakota Review* 5 (Summer 1967): 11-71.

1655. Manchester, John. "Thoughts on Brett: 1967." *South Dakota Review* 5 (Summer 1967): 3-9.

1656. Morrill, Claire. "Three Women of Taos: Frieda Lawrence, Mabel Luhan, and Dorothy Brett." *South Dakota Review* 2 (Spring 1965): 3-22.

1657. Zytaruk, George J., ed. "Dorothy Brett's Letters to S. S. Kateliansky." *D. H. Lawrence Review* 7 (1974): 240-74.

CAROL RYRIE BRINK

1658. Odland, N. "Carol Ryrie Brink and Caddie Woodlawn." *Elementary English* 45 (1968): 425-28.

FRANK BRINK

1659. Petersen, Lance. "Alaskan Men of Letters: Frank Brink." *Alaska Review* I (Spring 1964): 36-39.

CHARLES FARRAR BROWNE
(Artemus Ward)

1660. Austin, James C. *Artemus Ward.* New York: Twayne, 1964.

1661. ——. "Charles Farrar Browne (1834-1867)." *American Literary Realism 1870-1910* 5 (Spring 1972): 151-65.

1662. Blair, Walter. *Native American Humor.* New York: American Book, 1937.

1663. Fatout, Paul. "Artemus Ward Among the Mormons." *Western Humanities Review* 14 (Spring 1960): 193-99.

1664. Hingston, Edward P. *The Genial Showman.* New York: Harper, 1870.

1665. Jaynes, Bryson L. "Artemus Ward Among the Mormons." *Research Studies of the State College of Washington* 25 (March 1957): 75-84.

1666. Lorch, Fred W. "Mark Twain's 'Artemus Ward' Lecture on the Tour of 1871-1872." *New England Quarterly* 25 (September 1952): 327-43.

1667. McKee, Irving. "Artemus Ward in California and Nevada, 1863-1864." *Pacific Historical Review* 20 (February 1951): 11-23.

1668. Nock, Albert Jay. "Artemus Ward's America." *Atlantic Monthly* 154 (September 1934): 273-81.

1669. Pullen, John J. "Artemus Ward:

The Man Who Made Lincoln Laugh." *Saturday Review* 59 (February 7, 1976): 19-21, 24.

1670. Reed, John Q. "Artemus Ward: A Critical Study." Doctoral dissertation, State University of Iowa, 1955.

1671. Seitz, Don C. *Artemus Ward (Charles Farrar Browne): A Biography and Bibliography.* New York: Harper and Brothers, 1919.

1672. Williams, Stanley T. "Artemus the Delicious." *Virginia Quarterly Review* 28 (Spring 1952): 214-27.

1673. Wright, William. "Artemus Ward in Nevada." *California Illustrated Magazine* 4 (August 1893): 403-5.

J. ROSS BROWNE

1674. Browne, Lina Fergusson. "J. Ross Browne in the Apache Country." *New Mexico Quarterly* 35 (Spring 1965): 5-28.

1675. ———, ed. *J. Ross Browne: His Letters, Journals and Writings.* Albuquerque: University of New Mexico Press, 1969.

1676. Dillon, Richard H. "J. Ross Browne and the Corruptible West." *American West* 2 (Spring 1965): 37-45.

1677. ———. *J. Ross Browne, Confidential Agent in Old California.* Norman: University of Oklahoma Press, 1965.

1678. Powell, Lawrence Clark. "J. Ross Browne's *Adventures in the Apache Country.*" *West-*

ways 63 (October 1971): 18-21, 40-43.

1679. Rock, Francis John. *J. Ross Browne: A Biography.* Washington, D.C.: Catholic University of America, 1929.

1680. Walker, Franklin. *Irreverent Pilgrims: Melville, Browne, and Mark Twain in the Holy Land.* Seattle: University of Washington Press, 1974.

GELETT BURGESS

1681. Backus, Joseph M. "Gelett Burgess: A Biography of the Man Who Wrote 'The Purple Cow.'" Doctoral dissertation, University of California, Berkeley, 1961.

EDGAR RICE BURROUGHS

1682. Morsberger, Robert E. "Introduction," to Edgar Rice Burroughs, *Apache Devil.* Boston: Gregg Press, 1978, pp. v-x.

1683. ———. "Introduction," to Edgar Rice Burroughs, *The Bandit of Hell's Bend.* Boston: Gregg Press, 1979, pp. v-xix.

1684. ———. "Introduction," to Edgar Rice Burroughs, *The Deputy Sheriff of Comanche County.* Boston: Gregg Press, 1979, pp. v-xvii.

1685. ———. "Introduction," to Edgar Rice Burroughs, *The War Chief.* Boston: Gregg Press, 1978, pp. v-xiii.

1686. Topping, Gary. "The Pastoral Ideal in Popular American Literature: Zane Grey and Edgar

Rice Burroughs." *Rendezvous* 12 (Fall 1977): 11-25.

WITTER BYNNER

1687. Colony, Horatio. "Witter Bynner—Poet of Today." *Literary Review* 3 (Spring 1960): 339-61.
1688. Flanner, Hildegarde. "Witter Bynner's Poetry." *University of Kansas City Review* 6 (June 1940): 269-74.
1689. Lindsay, Robert O. *Witter Bynner: A Bibliography.* Albuquerque: University of New Mexico, 1967.
1690. Mearns, Hughes, ed. *Witter Bynner.* New York: Simon and Schuster, 1927.
1691. *The Works of Witter Bynner: Biographical Sketch and Critical Bibliography.* New York: Alfred A. Knopf, 1940.

JAMES M. CAIN

1692. Fine, David M. "James M. Cain and the Los Angeles Novel." *American Studies* 20 (Spring 1979): 25-34.
1693. Reck, Tom S. "J. M. Cain's Los Angeles Novels." *Colorado Quarterly* 22 (Winter 1974): 375-87.

ROBERT CANTWELL

1694. Bowman, John Scott. "The Proletarian Novel in America." Doctoral dissertation, Pennsylvania State College, 1939.
1695. Conroy, Jack. "Robert Cantwell's 'Land of Plenty.'" *Proletarian Writers of the Thirties.* Ed. David Madden. Carbondale: Southern Illinois Press, 1968, pp. 74-84.
1696. Lewis, Merrill. *Robert Cantwell.* Western Writers Series. Boise, Idaho: Boise State University, 1982.
1697. Rideout, Walter B. *The Radical Novel in the United States.* Cambridge, Mass.: Harvard University Press, 1956, pp. 174-78 ff.
1698. Swados, Harvey. "Cantwell Redivivus." *Novel: A Forum on Fiction* 6 (Fall 1972): 92-94.

BENJAMIN CAPPS

1699. Etulain, Richard W. *"The White Man's Road*: An Appreciation." *Southwestern American Literature* 1 (May 1971): 88-92.
1700. Graham, Don. "Old and New Cowboy Classics." *Southwest Review* 65 (Summer 1980): 293-303.
1701. Sonnichsen, C. L. "The New Style Western." *South Dakota Review* 4 (Summer 1966): 22-28.
1702. Speck, Ernest B. *Benjamin Capps.* Western Writers Series, No. 49. Boise, Idaho: Boise State University, 1981.
1703. ——. "The Old West of Benjamin Capps." *Southwestern American Literature* 2 (Winter 1972): 150-52.

SARAH ELIZABETH CARMICHAEL

1704. Murphy, Miriam B. "Sarah Elizabeth Carmichael: Poetic Genius of Pioneer Utah." *Utah Historical Quarterly* 43 (Winter 1975): 52-66.

ROBERT ORMOND CASE

1705. Newton, Dwight B. "Meet Robert Ormond Case." *Roundup* 4 (March 1956): 3-4.

BILL CASEY

1706. Turner, Steve. "Bill Casey: Jottings Before a Journey." *Southwestern American Literature* 1 (May 1971): 80-86.

NEAL CASSADY

1707. Cassady, Carolyn. *Heart Beat: My Life with Jack & Neal.* Berkeley, Calif.: Creative Arts, 1976.
1708. Gifford, Barry, ed. *The Collected Correspondence of Allen Ginsberg and Neal Cassady.* Berkeley, Calif.: Bookpeople, 1977.
1709. Huebel, Harry Russell. "The 'Holy Goof': Neal Cassady and the Post-War American Counter Culture." *Illinois Quarterly* 35 (April 1973): 52-61.

CARLOS CASTANEDA

1710. Brown, Carl R. V. "*Journey to Ixtlan*: Inside the American Indian Oral Tradition." *Arizona Quarterly* 32 (Summer 1976): 138-45.
1711. Olson, Alan M. "From Shaman to Mystic: An Interpretation of the Castaneda Quartet." *Soundings* 61 (Spring 1978): 47-66.

WILLA CATHER

1712. Albertini, Virgil. "Willa Cather's Early Short Stories: A Link to the Agrarian Realists." *Markham Review* 8 (Summer 1979): 69-72.
1713. Arnold, Marilyn. "*One of Ours*: Willa Cather's Losing Battle." *Western American Literature* 13 (Fall 1978): 259-66.
1714. Auchincloss, Louis. *Pioneers and Caretakers: A Study of Nine American Women Novelists.* Minneapolis: University of Minnesota Press, 1965.
1715. Baker, Bruce, II. "Nebraska Regionalism in Selected Works of Willa Cather." *Western American Literature* 3 (Spring 1968): 19-35.
1716. Baum, Bernard. "Willa Cather's Waste Land." *South Atlantic Quarterly* 48 (October 1949): 589-601.
1717. Bennett, Mildred R. *The World of Willa Cather.* New York: Dodd, Mead, 1951; Lincoln: University of Nebraska Press, 1961.
1718. Bloom, Edward A. and Lillian D. "The Genesis of *Death Comes for the Archbishop*." *American Literature* 26 (January 1955): 479-506.

1719. ——. *Willa Cather's Gift of Sympathy.* Carbondale: Southern Illinois University Press, 1962.

1720. ——. "Willa Cather's Novels of the Frontier: A Study in Thematic Symbolism." *American Literature* 21 (March 1949): 71-93.

1721. ——. "Willa Cather's Novels of the Frontier: The Symbolic Function of 'Machine-Made Materialism.'" *University of Toronto Quarterly* 20 (October 1950): 45-60.

1722. Bloom, Lillian D. "On Daring to Look Back with Wharton and Cather." *Novel: A Forum on Fiction* 10 (Winter 1977): 167-78.

1723. Bohlke, L. Brent. "Beginnings: Willa Cather and 'The Clemency of the Court.'" *Prairie Schooner* 48 (Summer 1974): 134-44.

1724. Borgman, Paul. "The Dialectic of Willa Cather's Moral Vision." *Renascence* 27 (Spring 1975): 145-59.

1725. Bradford, Curtis. "Willa Cather's Uncollected Short Stories." *American Literature* 26 (January 1955): 537-51.

1726. Brennan, Joseph X. "Music and Willa Cather." *University Review* 31 (March 1965): 175-83; (June 1965): 257-64.

1727. Brown, E. K. "Homage to Willa Cather." *Yale Review* 36 (September 1946): 77-92.

1728. ——. *Willa Cather: A Critical Biography.* New York: Alfred A. Knopf, 1953. Completed by Leon Edel.

1729. ——. "Willa Cather and the West." *University of Toronto Quarterly* 5 (July 1936): 544-66.

1730. Brown, Marion Marsh, and Ruth Crone. *Willa Cather: The Woman and Her Works.* New York: Charles Scribner's Sons, 1970.

1731. ——. *Only One Point of the Compass: Willa Cather in the Northeast.* Danbury, Conn.: Archer Editions Press, 1980.

1732. Byrne, Kathleen D. "Willa Cather's Pittsburgh Years 1896-1906." *Western Pennsylvania Historical Magazine* 51 (January 1968): 2-15.

1733. ——, and Richard C. Snyder. *Chrysalis: Willa Cather in Pittsburgh.* Pittsburgh: Historical Society of Western Pennsylvania, 1980.

1734. Cassai, Marianne. "Symbolic Techniques in Selected Novels of Willa Cather." Doctoral dissertation, New York University, 1978.

1735. Charles, Sister Peter Damian. "*Death Comes for the Archbishop*: A Novel of Love and Death." *New Mexico Quarterly* 36 (Winter 1966-67): 389-403.

1736. ——. "Love and Death in the Novels of Willa Cather." Doctoral dissertation, University of Notre Dame, 1965.

1737. ——. "*My Ántonia*: A Dark Dimension." *Western American Literature* 2 (Summer 1967): 91-108.

1738. Comeau, Paul. "The Fool Figure in Willa Cather's Fiction." *Western American Literature* 15 (February 1981): 265-78.

1739. Curtin, William M. "Willa Cather and *The Varieties of Religious Experience*." *Renascence* 27 (Spring 1975): 115-23.

1740. ——, ed. *The World and the Parish: Willa Cather's Articles and Reviews, 1893-1902.* 2 vols. Lincoln: University of Nebraska Press, 1970.

1741. Dahl, Curtis. "An American Georgic: Willa Cather's *My Antonia*." *Comparative Literature* 7 (Winter 1955): 43-51.

1742. Daiches, David. *Willa Cather: A Critical Introduction.* Ithaca, N.Y.: Cornell University Press, 1951; New York: Collier Books, 1962.

1743. Dinn, James M. "A Novelist's Miracle: Structure and Myth in *Death Comes for the Archbishop*." *Western American Literature* 7 (Spring 1972): 39-46.

1744. Ditsky, John. "Nature and Character in the Novels of Willa Cather." *Colby Library Quarterly* 10 (September 1974): 391-412.

1745. Feger, Lois. "The Dark Dimension of Willa Cather's *My Antonia*." *English Journal* 59 (September 1970): 774-79.

1746. Ferguson, J. M., Jr. "'Vague Outlines': Willa Cather's Enchanted Bluffs." *Western Review* 7 (Spring 1970): 61-64.

1747. Fetty, Audrey Mae Shelly. "Biblical Allusions in the Fiction of Willa Cather." Doctoral dissertation, University of Nebraska, Lincoln, 1973.

1748. Finestone, Harry. "Willa Cather's Apprenticeship." Doctoral dissertation, University of Chicago, 1953.

1749. Fleming, Patricia Jean. "The Integrated Self: Sexuality and the Double in Willa Cather's Fiction." Doctoral dissertation, Boston University, 1974.

1750. Footman, Robert H. "The Genius of Willa Cather." *American Literature* 10 (May 1938): 123-41.

1751. Forman, H. J. "Willa Cather: A Voice from the Prairie." *Southwest Review* 47 (Summer 1962): 248-58.

1752. Fox, Maynard. "Proponents of Order: Tom Outland and Bishop Latour." *Western American Literature* 4 (Summer 1969): 107-15.

1753. ——. "Symbolic Representation in Willa Cather's *O Pioneers!*" *Western American Literature* 9 (November 1974): 187-96.

1754. Freydberg, Margaret Howe. "Willa Cather: The Light Behind Her Books." *American Scholar* 43 (Spring 1974): 282-87.

1755. Gale, Robert. "Willa Cather and the Usable Past." *Nebraska History* 42 (September 1961): 181-90.

1756. Geismar, Maxwell. "Willa Cather: Lady in the Wilderness." *The Last of the Provincials: The American Novel, 1915-1925.*

Boston: Houghton Mifflin, 1947, pp. 153-220.

1757. Gelfant, Blanch H. "The Forgotten Reaping-Hook: Sex in *My Ántonia.*" *American Literature* 43 (March 1971): 60-82.

1758. Gerber, Philip. *Willa Cather.* Boston: Twayne, 1975.

1759. Giannone, Richard. *Music in Willa Cather's Fiction.* Lincoln: University of Nebraska Press, 1968.

1760. ——. "Willa Cather and the Unfinished Drama of Deliverance." *Prairie Schooner* 52 (Spring 1978): 25-46.

1761. Hamner, Eugenie Lambert. "Affirmations in Willa Cather's *A Lost Lady.*" *Midwest Quarterly* 17 (Spring 1976): 245-51.

1762. Harris, Richard Casey. "Energy and Order in Willa Cather's Novels." Doctoral dissertation, University of North Carolina, Chapel Hill, 1974.

1763. ——. "Renaissance Pastoral Conventions and the Ending of *My Ántonia.*" *Markham Review* 8 (Fall 1978): 8-11.

1764. Helmick, Evelyn Thomas. "The Broken World: Medievalism in *A Lost Lady.*" *Renascence* 28 (Autumn 1975): 39-48.

1765. ——. "The Mysteries of Ántonia." *Midwest Quarterly* 17 (Winter 1976): 173-85.

1766. ——. "Myth in the Works of Willa Cather." *Midcontinent American Studies Journal* 9 (Fall 1968): 63-69.

1767. Hicks, Granville. "The Case Against Willa Cather." *English Journal* 22 (November 1933): 703-10.

1768. Hinz, Evelyn J. "Willa Cather's Technique and the Ideology of Populism." *Western American Literature* 7 (Spring 1972): 47-61.

1769. Hutchinson, Phyllis Martin. "The Writings of Willa Cather: A List of Works by and about Her." *Bulletin of the New York Library* 60 (June 1956): 267-87; (July 1956): 338-56; (August 1956): 378-400.

1770. Jacks, L. V. "Willa Cather and the Southwest." *New Mexico Quarterly* 27 (Spring-Summer 1957): 83-87.

1771. Keeler, Clinton. "Narrative Without Accent: Willa Cather and Puvis de Chavannes." *American Quarterly* 17 (Spring 1965): 119-26.

1772. Krause, Janet Boettcher. "Self-Actualizing Women in Willa Cather's Prairie Novels." Doctoral dissertation, University of Nebraska, Lincoln, 1978.

1773. LaHood, Marvin. "Conrad Richter and Willa Cather: Some Similarities." *Xavier University Studies* 9 (Spring 1970): 33-44.

1774. Lambert, Maude Eugenie. "Theme and Craftsmanship in Willa Cather's Novels." Doctoral dissertation, University of North Carolina, Chapel Hill, 1965.

1775. Lathrop, Jo Anna, comp. *Willa Cather: a Checklist of Her Published Writing.* Lincoln: University of North Carolina, Chapel Hill, 1965.

1776. Lee, Robert Edson. *From East to West*. Urbana: University of Illinois Press, 1965, pp. 112–35.

1777. Lewis, Edith. *Willa Cather Living: A Personal Record*. New York: Alfred A. Knopf, 1953.

1778. McAlpin, Sister Sara. "Enlightening the Commonplace: The Art of Sarah Jewett, Willa Cather and Ruth Suckow." Doctoral dissertation, University of Pennsylvania, 1971.

1779. McCabe, John D., ed. "Special Issue: Willa Cather." *Renascence* 27 (1975).

1780. McClure, Charlotte S. "Willa Cather." *American Literary Realism 1870–1910* 8 (Summer 1975): 209–20. Review of dissertations on Cather.

1781. McFarland, Dorothy Tuck. *Willa Cather*. New York: Frederick Ungar, 1972.

1782. Machen, Meredith R. "Carlyle's Presence in *The Professor's House*." *Western American Literature* 14 (Winter 1980): 273–86.

1783. ——. "Home as Motivation and Metaphor in the Works of Willa Cather." Doctoral dissertation, University of New Mexico, 1979.

1784. McLay, Catherine M. "Religion in the Novels of Willa Cather." *Renascence* 27 (Spring 1975): 125–44.

1785. Martin, Terence. "The Drama of Memory in *My Antonia*." *PMLA* 84 (March 1969): 304–11.

1786. Medoff, Jeslyn. "An Anglo-American Author Creates Anglo-American Villains." *Heritage of Kansas* 12 (Spring 1979): 31–39.

1787. Miller, Bruce E. "The Testing of Willa Cather's Humanism: *A Lost Lady* and Other Cather Novels." *Kansas Quarterly* 5 (Fall 1973): 43–49.

1788. Miller, James E., Jr. "*My Antonia*: A Frontier Drama of Time." *American Quarterly* 10 (Winter 1958): 476–84.

1789. ——. "*My Antonia* and the American Dream." *Prairie Schooner* 48 (Summer 1974): 112–23.

1790. ——. "The Nebraska Encounter: Willa Cather and Wright Morris." *Prairie Schooner* 41 (Summer 1967): 165–67.

1791. Moorhead, Elizabeth. *These Two Were Here: Louise Homer and Willa Cather*. Pittsburgh: University of Pittsburgh Press, 1950.

1792. Moseley, Ann. "The Dual Nature of Art in *The Song of the Lark*." *Western American Literature* 14 (Spring 1979): 19–32.

1793. ——. "The Voyage Perilous: Willa Cather's Mythic Quest." Doctoral dissertation, University of Oklahoma, 1974.

1794. Murphy, John J. "The Art of *Shadows on the Rock*." *Prairie Schooner* 50 (Spring 1976): 37–51.

1795. ——. "'Lucy's Case': An Interpretation of *Lucy Gayheart*." *Markham Review* 9 (Winter 1980): 26–29.

1796. ——. "Willa Cather's Archbishop: A Western and Classical

Perspective." *Western American Literature* 13 (Summer 1978): 141-50.

1797. ——, ed. *Five Essays on Willa Cather: The Merrimack Symposium.* North Andover, Mass.: Merrimack College, 1974.

1798. Murphy, Michael Walter. "The Complex Past in Willa Cather's Novels of the Twenties." Doctoral dissertation, University of Texas, Austin, 1974.

1799. O'Connor, Margaret Anne. "A Guide to the Letters of Willa Cather." *Resources for American Literary Studies* 4 (1974): 145-72.

1800. Parks, B. K. "A Dedication to the Memory of Willa Cather, 1873-1947." *Arizona and the West* 22 (Autumn 1979): 211-14.

1801. Pers, Mona. *Willa Cather's Children.* Uppsala, Sweden: Almquist and Wiksell, 1975.

1802. Piacentino, Edward J. "The Agrarian Mode in Cather's 'Neighbor Rosicky.'" *Markham Review* 8 (Spring 1979): 52-54.

1803. Randall, John H. III. *The Landscape and the Looking Glass: Willa Cather's Search for Value.* Boston: Houghton Mifflin, 1960.

1804. ——. "Willa Cather: The Middle West Revisited." *New Mexico Quarterly* 31 (Spring 1961): 25-36.

1805. Reaver, J. Russell. "Mythic Motivation in Willa Cather's *O Pioneers!.*" *Western Folklore* 27 (January 1968): 19-25.

1806. Reynard, Grant. "Willa Cather's Advice to a Young Artist." *Prairie Schooner* 46 (Spring 1972): 111-24.

1807. Rohrbach, Sister Charlotte. "Willa Cather, An Historian of Western Webster County, Nebraska: An Inquiry." Doctoral dissertation, Saint Louis University, 1976.

1808. Rosowski, Susan J. "The Pattern of Willa Cather's Novels." *Western American Literature* 15 (February 1981): 243-63.

1809. ——. "Willa Cather's *A Lost Lady*: The Paradoxes of Change." *Novel: A Forum on Fiction* 11 (Fall 1977): 51-62.

1810. ——. "Willa Cather's Pioneer Women: A Feminist Interpretation." *Where the West Begins.* Eds. Arthur R. Huseboe and William Geyer. Sioux Falls, S.Dak.: Center for Western Studies Press, 1978, pp. 135-42.

1811. Roulston, Robert. "The Contrapuntal Complexity of Willa Cather's *The Song of the Lark.*" *Midwest Quarterly* 17 (Summer 1976): 350-68.

1812. Schneider, Sister Lucy. "Artistry and Intuition: Willa Cather's 'Land Philosophy.'" *South Dakota Review* 6 (Winter 1968-69): 53-64.

1813. ——. "Cather's 'Land Philosophy' in *Death Comes for the Archbishop.*" *Renascence* 22 (Winter 1970): 78-86.

1814. ——. "Of Land and Light: Willa Cather's *Lucy Gayheart.*"

Kansas Quarterly 5 (Fall 1973):
51-62.

1815. ——. "Willa Cather's Early Stories in Light of Her 'Land Philosophy.'" *Midwest Quarterly* 9 (August 1967): 75-93.

1816. ——. "Willa Cather's 'The Best Years': The Essence of Her 'Land Philosophy.'" *Midwest Quarterly* 15 (Autumn 1973): 61-69.

1817. Schroeter, James Marvin. *Willa Cather and Her Critics.* Ithaca, N.Y.: Cornell University Press, 1967.

1818. Scott, John Charles. "Between Fiction and History: An Exploration into Willa Cather's *Death Comes for the Archbishop.*" Doctoral dissertation, University of New Mexico, 1980.

1819. Seibel, George. "Miss Willa Cather from Nebraska." *New Colophon* 2 (September 1949): 195-208.

1820. Sergeant, Elizabeth Shepley. *Willa Cather: A Memoir.* Philadelphia: Lippincott, 1953; Lincoln: University of Nebraska Press, 1963.

1821. Shelton, Frank W. "The Image of the Rock and the Family in the Novels of Willa Cather." *Markham Review* 6 (Fall 1976): 9-14.

1822. Shively, James R., ed. *Writings from Willa Cather's Campus Years.* Lincoln: University of Nebraska Press, 1950.

1823. Slote, Bernice. "An Appointment with the Future: Willa

Cather." *The Twenties: fiction, poetry, drama.* Ed. Warren French. Deland, Fla.: Everett/Edwards, 1975, pp. 39-49.

1824. ——. "Willa Cather." *Fifteen Modern American Authors.* Ed. Jackson R. Bryer. Durham, N.C.: Duke University Press, 1969, pp. 23-62.

1825. ——. "Willa Cather." *Sixteen Modern American Authors: A Study in Research and Criticism.* Ed. Jackson Bryer. Durham, N.C.: Duke University Press, 1974, pp. 29-73.

1826. ——. "Willa Cather and the Sense of History." *Women, Women Writers, and the West.* Eds. Lawrence L. Lee and Merrill E. Lewis. Troy, N.Y.: Whitston, 1978.

1827. ——. "Willa Cather and the West." *Persimmon Hill* 4 (1975): 48-59.

1828. ——. *Willa Cather: A Pictorial Memoir.* Lincoln: University of Nebraka Press, 1973.

1829. ——. "Willa Cather as a Regional Writer." *Kansas Quarterly* 2 (Spring 1970): 7-15.

1830. ——, ed. *The Kingdom of Art: Willa Cather's First Principles and Critical Statements, 1893-1896.* Lincoln: University of Nebraska Press, 1967.

1831. ——, and Virginia Faulkner, eds. *The Art of Willa Cather.* Lincoln: University of Nebraska Press, 1975.

1832. Stegner, Wallace. "Willa Cather, *My Ántonia.*" *The American Novel from James Fenimore Cooper to William Faulkner.*

Ed. Wallace Stegner. New York: Basic Books, 1965.

1833. ——. "The West Authentic: Willa Cather." *The Sound of Mountain Water.* Garden City, N.Y.: Doubleday, 1969, pp. 237-49.

1834. Stewart, D. H. "Cather's Mortal Comedy." *Queen's Quarterly* 73 (Summer 1966): 244-59.

1835. Stineback, David C. "Willa Cather's Ironic Masterpiece." *Arizona Quarterly* 29 (Winter 1973): 316-30.

1836. Stouck, David. "*O Pioneers!*: Willa Cather and the Epic Imagination." *Prairie Schooner* 46 (Spring 1972): 23-34.

1837. ——. "Perspective as Structure and Theme in *My Ántonia.*" *Texas Studies in Literature and Language* 12 (Summer 1970): 285-94.

1838. ——. "Willa Cather and the Indian Heritage." *Twentieth Century Literature* 22 (December 1976): 433-43.

1839. ——. "Willa Cather and *The Professor's House*: 'Letting Go With the Heart.'" *Western American Literature* 7 (Spring 1972): 13-24.

1840. ——. *Willa Cather's Imagination.* Lincoln: University of Nebraska Press, 1975.

1841. ——. "Willa Cather's Last Four Books." *Novel: A Forum on Fiction* 7 (Fall 1973): 41-53.

1842. ——. *The Works of Willa Cather.* Cassette. Deland, Fla.: Everett/Edwards, 1974.

1843. Stouck, Mary-Ann and David.

"Art and Religion in *Death Comes for the Archbishop.*" *Arizona Quarterly* 29 (Winter 1973): 293-302.

1844. ——. "Hagiographical Style in *Death Comes for the Archbishop.*" *University of Toronto Quarterly* 41 (Summer 1972): 293-307.

1845. Sullivan, Patrick J. "Willa Cather's Southwest." *Western American Literature* 7 (Spring 1972): 25-37.

1846. Thompson, Bernita Lonette Arnold. "Continuity in the Work of Willa Cather." Doctoral dissertation, University of Nebraska, Lincoln, 1974.

1847. Toler, Sister Colette. "Man as Creator of Art and Civilization in the Works of Willa Cather." Doctoral dissertation, University of Notre Dame, 1965.

1848. Van Ghent, Dorothy. *Willa Cather.* Minneapolis: University of Minnesota Press, 1964.

1849. Vigil, Ralph H. "Willa Cather and Historical Reality." *New Mexico Historical Review* 50 (April 1975): 123-38.

1850. Wagenknecht, Edward. "Willa Cather." *Sewanee Review* 37 (April 1929): 221-39.

1851. Walker, Don D. "The Western Humanism of Willa Cather." *Western American Literature* 1 (Summer 1966): 75-90.

1852. Weales, Gerald. "Willa Cather, Girl Reporter." *Southern Review* 8 (July 1972): 681-88.

1853. Wild, Barbara. "'The Thing Not Named' in *The Professor's*

House." Western American Literature 12 (Winter 1978): 263-74.

1854. *Willa Cather: A Pictorial Memoir.* Photographs by Lucia Woods and others; text by Bernice Slote. Lincoln: University of Nebraska Press, 1973.

1855. Wittington, Curtis, Jr. "The 'Burden' of Narration." *Southern Humanities Review* 2 (Spring 1968): 236-45.

1856. Woodress, James. "Willa Cather and History." *Arizona Quarterly* 34 (Autumn 1978): 239-54.

1857. ———. *Willa Cather: Her Life and Art.* New York: Pegasus, 1970.

1858. Yongue, Patricia Lee. "*A Lost Lady*: The End of the First Cycle." *Western American Literature* 7 (Spring 1972): 3-12.

1859. ———. "The Immense Design: A Study of Willa Cather's Creative Process." Doctoral dissertation, University of California, Los Angeles, 1972.

1860. ———. "Search and Research: Willa Cather in Quest of History." *Southwestern American Literature* 5 (1975): 27-39.

1861. ———. "Willa Cather's Aristocrats." *Southern Humanities Review* 14 (Winter 1980): 43-56; (Spring 1980): 111-25.

GEORGE CATLIN

1862. McCracken, Harold. *George Catlin and the Old Frontier.* New York: Dial Press, 1959.

1863. Millichap, Joseph R. *George Catlin.* Western Writers Series, No. 27. Boise, Idaho: Boise State University, 1977.

1864. Ross, Marvin C., ed. *George Catlin.* Norman: University of Oklahoma Press, 1959.

RAYMOND CHANDLER

1865. Kaye, Howard. "Raymond Chandler's Sentimental Novel." *Western American Literature* 10 (August 1975): 135-45.

1866. Speir, Jerry. *Raymond Chandler.* New York: Frederick Ungar, 1981.

J. SMEATON CHASE

1867. Dillon, Richard H. "Prose Poet of the Trail: J. Smeaton Chase." *Book Club of California Quarterly Newsletter* 35 (Spring 1970): 27-36.

PEGGY POND CHURCH

1868. Baker, Gail. "The Art of *The House at Otowi Bridge.*" *New America* 3 (Summer–Fall 1977): 32-36.

BADGER CLARK

1869. Chenoweth, Richard R., ed. "Badger Clark as 'The Prisoner of Camaquey.'" *South Dakota History* 7 (Summer 1977): 271-90.

CHARLES HEBER CLARK
("Max Adeler")

1870. Dussere, David Philip. "A

Critical Biography of Charles Heber Clark ('Max Adeler'): American Journalist and Humorist." Doctoral dissertation, University of Arkansas, 1974.

WALTER VAN TILBURG CLARK

1871. Alt, Jon [Harlan]. *"The City of Trembling Leaves*: Humanity and Eternity." *South Dakota Review* 17 (Winter 1979-80): 8-18.

1872. ——. "Walter Van Tilburg Clark: Humanity and Eternity." Doctoral dissertation, Kansas State University, 1977.

1873. Andersen, Kenneth. "Character Portrayal in *The Ox-Bow Incident*." *Western American Literature* 4 (Winter 1970): 287-98.

1874. ——. "Form in Walter Van Tilburg Clark's *The Ox-Bow Incident*." *Western Review* 6 (Spring 1969): 19-25.

1875. Bates, Barclay W. "Clark's Man for All Seasons: The Achievement of Wholeness in *The Ox-Bow Incident*." *Western American Literature* 3 (Spring 1968): 37-49.

1876. Bluestone, George. *Novels into Film.* Baltimore: The Johns Hopkins Press, 1957, pp. 170-96.

1877. Carpenter, Frederic I. "The West of Walter Van Tilburg Clark." *College English* 13 (February 1952): 243-48.

1878. Cochran, Robert W. "Nature and the Nature of Man in *The Ox-Bow Incident*." *Western*

American Literature 5 (Winter 1971): 253-64.

1879. Cohen, Edward H. "Clark's 'The Portable Phonograph.'" *Explicator* 28 (April 1970): 69.

1880. Cracroft, Richard. "Some Striking Parallels and a Possible Source for *The Ox-Box Incident. . . .*" *Possible Sack* 2 (March 1971): 3-6.

1881. Crain, Mary Beth. "The Ox-Bow Incident Revisited." *Literature/ Film Quarterly* 4 (1976): 240-48.

1882. Deane, Paul. "American Elements in Walter Van Tilburg Clark's *The Track of the Cat*." *Revue des Langues Vivantes* 39 (1973): 39-45.

1883. Eisinger, Chester E. *Fiction of the Forties.* Chicago: University of Chicago Press, 1963, pp. 310-24.

1884. ——. "The Fiction of Walter Van Tilburg Clark: Man and Nature in the West." *Southwest Review* 44 (Summer 1959): 214-26.

1885. Etulain, Richard. "Walter Van Tilburg Clark: A Bibliography." *South Dakota Review* 3 (Autumn 1965): 73-77.

1886. Folsom, James K. *The American Western Novel.* New Haven, Conn.: College and University Press, 1966, pp. 172-76.

1887. Gurian, Jay. "The Unwritten West." *American West* 2 (Winter 1965): 59-63.

1888. Hendricks, George D. "Symbolism in Walter Van Tilburg Clark's *The Track of the Cat*."

Southwestern American Literature 3 (1973): 77-80.

1889. Herrmann, John. "The Death of the Artist as Hero." *South Dakota Review* 4 (Summer 1966): 51-55.

1890. Houghton, Donald E. "The Failure of Speech in *The Ox-Bow Incident.*" *English Journal* 59 (December 1970): 1245-51.

1891. ——. "Man and Animals in 'The Indian Well.'" *Western American Literature* 6 (Fall 1971): 215-18.

1892. Kehl, D. G. "Writing in the Apocalypse: Rhetorical Lessons from Walter Van Tilburg Clark." *College Composition and Communications* 25 (February 1974): 34-41.

1893. Kiefer, Gordon B. "Walter Van Tilburg Clark's Fiction: A Study in Structure." Doctoral dissertation, Texas Tech University, 1979.

1894. Kleis, David John. "The God Becoming: Sensation of the Nuclear in Walter Van Tilburg Clark." Doctoral dissertation, University of Michigan, 1974.

1895. Kuehl, John R. "Walter Van Tilburg Clark: A Bibliography." *Bulletin of Bibliography* 22 (September-December 1956): 18-20.

1896. Lee, L. L. *Walter Van Tilburg Clark.* Western Writers Series, No. 8. Boise, Idaho: Boise State College, 1973.

1897. ——. "Walter Van Tilburg Clark's Ambiguous American Dream." *College English* 26 (February 1965): 382-87.

1898. McCann, Garth. "Patterns of Redemption and the Failure of Irony: *The Ox-Bow Incident* and *The Man Who Killed the Deer.*" *Southwestern American Literature* 4 (1974): 62-67.

1899. Malloy, Jean Norris. "The World of Walter Van Tilburg Clark." Doctoral dissertation, Northwestern University, 1968.

1900. Milton, John R. "The American Novel: The Search for Home, Tradition, and Identity." *Western Humanities Review* 16 (Spring 1962): 169-80.

1901. ——. "Conversation with Walter Van Tilburg Clark." *South Dakota Review* 9 (Spring 1971): 27-38.

1902. ——. *The Novel of the American West.* Lincoln: University of Nebraska Press, 1980, pp. 195-229.

1903. ——. "The Western Attitude: Walter Van Tilburg Clark." *Critique* 2 (Winter 1959): 57-73.

1904. Moore, J. B. "Folklore in *The Track of the Cat.*" *North Carolina Folklore* 12 (December 1964): 30-34.

1905. Peterson, Levi S. "Tragedy and Western American Literature." *Western American Literature* 6 (Winter 1972): 243-49.

1906. Portz, John. "Idea and Symbol in Walter Van Tilburg Clark." *Accent* 17 (Spring 1957): 112-28.

1907. Rogers, Douglas G. "Man and Nature in Clark's *Track of the Cat.*" *South Dakota Review*

12 (Winter 1974-75): 49-55.
1908. Stegner, Wallace. "Walter Clark's Frontier." *Atlantic* 232 (August 1973): 94-98.
1909. Stein, Paul. "Cowboys and Unicorns: The Novels of Walter Van Tilburg Clark." *Western American Literature* 5 (Winter 1971): 265-75.
1910. Swallow, Alan. "The Mavericks." *Critique* 2 (Winter 1959): 74-92.
1911. West, Ray B., Jr. "The Use of Setting in 'The Wind and the Snow of Winter.'" *The Art of Writing Fiction.* New York: Thomas Y. Crowell, 1968, pp. 181-87.
1912. Westbrook, Max. "The Archetypal Ethic of *The Ox-Bow Incident.*" *Western American Literature* 1 (Summer 1966): 105-18.
1913. ——. "Internal Debate as Discipline: Clark's *The Watchful Gods.*" *Western American Literature* 1 (Fall 1966): 153-65.
1914. ——. *Walter Van Tilburg Clark.* New York: Twayne, 1969.
1915. ——. *The Works of Walter Van Tilburg Clark.* Cassette. Deland, Fla.: Everett/Edwards, 1974.
1916. Wilner, Herbert. "Walter Van Tilburg Clark." *Western Review* 20 (Winter 1956): 103-22.
1917. Young, Vernon. "An American Dream and Its Parody." *Arizona Quarterly* 6 (Summer 1950): 112-23.
1918. ——. "Gods Without Heroes: The Tentative Myth of Van Tilburg Clark." *Arizona Quarterly* 7 (Summer 1951): 110-19.

WILLIAM CLARK
(Lewis and Clark)
See Meriwether Lewis

SAMUEL CLEMENS
(Mark Twain)
1919. Anderson, Frederick, ed. *Mark Twain: The Critical Heritage.* New York: Barnes and Noble, 1971.
1920. Baender, Paul. "The 'Jumping Frog' as a Comedian's First Virtue." *Modern Philology* 60 (February 1963): 192-200.
1921. Baldanza, Frank. *Mark Twain: An Introduction and Interpretation.* New York: Barnes and Noble, 1961.
1922. Beidler, Philip D. "Realistic Style and the Problem of Context in *The Innocents Abroad* and *Roughing It.*" *American Literature* 52 (March 1980): 33-49.
1923. Bellamy, Gladys Carmen. *Mark Twain as a Literary Artist.* Norman: University of Oklahoma Press, 1950.
1924. Benson, Ivan. *Mark Twain's Western Years.* Stanford, Calif.: Stanford University Press, 1938.
1925. Blair, Walter. *Mark Twain and Huck Finn.* Berkeley: University of California Press, 1960.
1926. ——. "Mark Twain's Other Masterpiece: 'Jim Baker's Blue-Jay Yarn.'" *Studies in American*

Humor 1 (January 1975): 132–47.

1927. Blues, Thomas. *Mark Twain and the Community.* Lexington: University Press of Kentucky, 1970.

1928. Branch, Edgar M. "A Chronological Bibliography of the Writings of Samuel Clemens to June 8, 1867." *American Literature* 18 (May 1946): 109–59.

1929. ——. *The Literary Apprenticeship of Mark Twain.* Urbana: University of Illinois Press, 1950.

1930. ——. "Mark Twain Reports the Races in Sacramento." *Huntington Library Quarterly* 32 (Fall 1969): 179–86.

1931. ——. "'My Voice Is Still for Setchell': A Background Study of 'Jim Smiley and His Jumping Frog.'" *PMLA* 82 (December 1967): 591–601.

1932. ——, ed. *Clemens of the "Call": Mark Twain in San Francisco.* Berkeley: University of California Press, 1969.

1933. Brashear, Minnie M. *Mark Twain, Son of Missouri.* Chapel Hill: University of North Carolina Press, 1934.

1934. Bray, Robert. "Mark Twain Biography: Entering a New Phase." *Midwest Quarterly* 15 (Spring 1974): 286–301.

1935. Brooks, Van Wyck. *The Ordeal of Mark Twain.* Rev. ed. New York: E. P. Dutton, 1933.

1936. Budd, Louis J. *Mark Twain: Social Philosopher.* Bloomington: Indiana University Press, 1962.

1937. ——, ed. "A Listing of and Selection from Newspaper and Magazine Interviews with Samuel L. Clemens, 1874–1910." *American Literary Realism 1870–1910* 10 (Winter 1977): ix–xii, 1–100.

1938. Burnet, R. A. "Mark Twain in the Northwest–1895." *Pacific Northwest Quarterly* 42 (July 1951): 187–202.

1939. Camp, James E., and X. J. Kennedy, eds. *Mark Twain's Frontier: A Textbook of Primary Source Materials for Student Research and Writing.* New York: Holt, Rinehart, Winston, 1963.

1940. Canby, Henry Seidel. *Turn West, Turn East.* Boston: Houghton Mifflin, 1951.

1941. Cardwell, Guy A. "Samuel Clemens' Magical Pseudonym." *New England Quarterly* 48 (June 1975): 175–93.

1942. Carstensen, Vernon. "The West Mark Twain Did Not See." *Pacific Northwest Quarterly* 55 (October 1964): 170–76.

1943. Carter, Paul J., Jr. "The Influence of the Nevada Frontier on Mark Twain." *Western Humanities Review* 13 (Winter 1959): 61–70.

1944. Clark, Harry Hayden. "Mark Twain." *Eight American Authors.* Ed. Floyd Stovall. New York: Modern Language Association, 1956; New York: W. W. Norton, 1963.

1945. Clemens, Samuel L. *Roughing It.* Ed. with intro. and notes, Franklin R. Rogers. Berkeley:

University of California Press, 1972.

1946. Covici, Pascal, Jr. *Mark Twain's Humor: The Image of a World.* Dallas: Southern Methodist University Press, 1962.

1947. Cox, James M. *Mark Twain: The Fate of Humor.* Princeton, N.J.: Princeton University Press, 1966.

1948. Cracroft, Richard H. "Distorting Polygamy for Fun and Profit: Artemas [*sic*] Ward and Mark Twain Among the Mormons." *BYU Studies* 14 (Winter 1974): 272-88.

1949. ——. "The Gentle Blasphemer: Mark Twain, Holy Scripture, and the Book of Mormon." *BYU Studies* 11 (Winter 1971): 119-40.

1950. Cunliffe, Marcus. "American Humor and the Rise of the West: Mark Twain." *The Literature of the United States.* London: Penguin Books, 1954, pp. 151-69.

1951. Delaney, Paul. "You Can't Go Back to the Raft Ag'in Huck Honey!: Mark Twain's Western Sequel to *Huckleberry Finn.*" *Western American Literature* 11 (November 1976): 215-29.

1952. Dennis, Larry R. "Mark Twain and the Dark Angel." *Midwest Quarterly* 8 (January 1967): 181-97.

1953. DeVoto, Bernard. *Mark Twain at Work.* Cambridge, Mass.: Harvard University Press, 1942.

1954. ——. *Mark Twain's America.* Boston: Little, Brown, 1932.

1955. Ducey, Cathryn Annette. "The Development of a Frontier Thesis: Mark Twain, Domingo Faustino Sarmiento, and Frederick Jackson Turner." Doctoral dissertation, University of Hawaii, 1975.

1956. Duckett, Margaret. *Mark Twain and Bret Harte.* Norman: University of Oklahoma Press, 1964.

1957. Fatout, Paul. *Mark Twain in Virginia City.* Bloomington: Indiana University Press, 1964.

1958. ——, ed. *Mark Twain Speaking.* Iowa City: University of Iowa Press, 1976.

1959. Fender, Stephen. "'The Prodigal in a Far Country Chawing of Husks': Mark Twain's Search for a Style in the West." *Modern Language Review* 71 (October 1976): 737-56.

1960. Ferguson, DeLancey. *Mark Twain: Man and Legend.* Indianapolis: Bobbs-Merrill, 1943.

1961. Foner, Philip S. *Mark Twain: Social Critic.* New York: International Publishers, 1958.

1962. Fried, Martin B. "The Composition, Sources, and Popularity of Mark Twain's *Roughing It.*" Doctoral dissertation, University of Chicago, 1951.

1963. Fuller, Daniel J. "Mark Twain and Hamlin Garland: Contrarieties in Regionalism." *Mark Twain Journal* 17 (Winter 1973/74): 14-18.

1964. Gale, Robert L. *Plots and Characters in the Works of Mark Twain.* 2 vols. Hamden, Conn.: Archon, 1973.

1965. Geismar, Maxwell. *Mark Twain:*

An American Prophet. Boston: Houghton Mifflin, 1970.

1966. Gernes, Sonia Grace. "The Relationship of Storyteller to Community in the Tales of the Southwest Humorists, Mark Twain and William Faulkner." Doctoral dissertation, University of Washington, 1975.

1967. Gibson, William M. *The Art of Mark Twain.* New York: Oxford University Press, 1976.

1968. Goudie, Andrea. "'What Fools These Mortals Be!': A Puckish Interpretation of Mark Twain's Narrative Stance." *Kansas Quarterly* 5 (Fall 1973): 19-31.

1969. Gribben, Alan. "Removing Mark Twain's Mask: A Decade of Criticism and Scholarship." *ESQ: A Journal of the American Renaissance* 26 (1980): 100-108, 149-71.

1970. Hays, John Q. "Mark Twain's Rebellion Against God: Origins." *Southwestern American Literature* 3 (1973): 27-38.

1971. Hill, Hamlin. "Mark Twain and His Enemies." *Southern Review* 4 (Spring 1968): 520-29.

1972. ——. *Mark Twain: God's Fool.* New York: Harper and Row, 1973.

1973. ——. "Who Killed Mark Twain?" *American Literary Realism 1870-1910* 7 (Spring 1974): 119-24.

1974. Howell, Elmo. "Mark Twain's Arkansas." *Arkansas Historical Quarterly* 29 (August 1970): 195-208.

1975. Howells, William Dean. *My Mark Twain.* New York: Harper, 1910.

1976. Hudson, Ruth. "A Literary 'Area of Freedom' between Irving and Twain." *Western Humanities Review* 13 (Winter 1959): 46-60.

1977. James, G. W. "Mark Twain and the Pacific Coast." *Pacific Monthly* 24 (1910): 115-32.

1978. Johnson, Merle. *A Bibliography of the Works of Mark Twain.* Rev. ed. New York: Harper, 1935.

1979. Kaplan, Justin. *Mr. Clemens and Mark Twain: A Biography.* New York: Simon and Schuster, 1966.

1980. Krause, S. J. "The Art and Satire of Twain's 'Jumping Frog' Story." *American Quarterly* 16 (Winter 1964): 562-76.

1981. ——. "Cooper's Literary Offenses: Mark Twain in Wonderland." *New England Quarterly* 38 (September 1965): 291-311.

1982. ——. "Steinbeck and Mark Twain." *Steinbeck Newsletter* 6 (Fall 1973): 104-11.

1983. Kuperman, David Arnold. "Travels and Travelers in the Writing of Mark Twain." Doctoral dissertation, Indiana University, 1975.

1984. Leary, Lewis. *Mark Twain.* Minneapolis: University of Minnesota Press, 1960.

1985. Lee, Robert Edson. *From West To East.* Urbana: University of Illinois Press, 1966, pp. 82-111.

1986. Levy, Alfred J. "The Dramatic Integrity of Huck Finn." *Ball State University Forum* 20 (Spring 1979): 28-37.

1987. Long, E. Hudson. *Mark Twain Handbook.* New York: Hendricks House, 1957.

1988. Loomis, C. Grant. "Dan De Quille's Mark Twain." *Pacific Historical Review* 15 (September 1946): 336-47.

1989. Lorch, Fred W. "Mark Twain's Lecture from *Roughing It.*" *American Literature* 22 (November 1950): 290-307.

1990. ——. *The Trouble Begins at Eight.* Ames: Iowa State University Press, 1968.

1991. Lynn, Kenneth S. "Huck and Jim." *Yale Review* 17 (Spring 1958): 421-31.

1992. ——. *Mark Twain and Southwestern Humor.* Boston: Little, Brown, 1959.

1993. Mack, Effie Mona. *Mark Twain in Nevada.* New York: Charles Scribner's Sons, 1947.

1994. McKee, John DeWitt. "*Roughing It* as Retrospective Reporting." *Western American Literature* 5 (Summer 1970): 113-19.

1995. McMahan, Elizabeth. "Mark Twain's Criticisms of His America." *Illinois Quarterly* 39 (Winter 1976): 5-17.

1996. Macnaughton, William R. *Mark Twain's Last Years as a Writer.* Columbia: University of Missouri Press, 1979.

1997. Marks, Barry A. "The Huck Finn Swindle." *Western American Literature* 14 (Summer 1979): 115-32.

1998. Marx, Leo. "Mr. Eliot, Mr. Trilling, and Huckleberry Finn." *American Scholar* 22 (August 1953): 423-40.

1999. ——. "The Pilot and the Passenger: Landscape Conventions and the Style of *Huckleberry Finn.*" *American Literature* 28 (May 1956): 129-46.

2000. Meyer, Harold. "Mark Twain on the Comstock." *Southwest Review* 12 (April 1927): 197-207.

2001. Mobley, Lawrence E. "Mark Twain and the Golden Era." *Bibliographical Society of America, Papers* 58 (1964): 8-23.

2002. Nibbelink, Harman. "Mark Twain and the Mormons." *Mark Twain Journal* 17 (Winter 1973/74): 1-5.

2003. Paine, Albert Bigelow. *Mark Twain: A Biography.* 3 vols. New York: Harper, 1912.

2004. Pettit, Arthur G. "Mark Twain and His Times: A Bicentennial Appreciation." *South Atlantic Quarterly* 76 (Spring 1977): 133-46.

2005. ——. "Mark Twain's Attitude Toward The Negro in the West, 1861-1867." *Western Historical Quarterly* 1 (January 1970): 51-62.

2006. Reed, J. Q. "Mark Twain: West Coast Journalist." *Midwest Journal* 1 (Winter 1960): 141-61.

2007. Robinson, Forrest G. "'Seeing the Elephant': Some Perspectives on Mark Twain's *Roughing*

It." American Studies 21 (Fall 1980): 43-64.

2008. Robinson, William Hedges, Jr. "Mark Twain: Senatorial Secretary." *American West* 10 (January 1973): 16-17, 60-62.

2009. Rogers, Franklin R. "The Road to Reality: Burlesque Travel Literature and Mark Twain's *Roughing It." Bulletin of the New York Public Library* 67 (March 1963): 155-68.

2010. ——, ed. *The Pattern for Mark Twain's Roughing It.* Berkeley: University of California Press, 1961.

2011. Rodgers, Paul C., Jr. "Artemus Ward and Mark Twain's 'Jumping Frog.'" *Nineteenth-Century Fiction* 28 (December 1973): 273-86.

2012. Rowlette, Robert. "'Mark Twain on Artemus Ward': Twain's Literary Debt to Ward." *American Literary Realism 1870-1910* 6 (Winter 1973): 13-25.

2013. Ryan, Pat M., Jr. "Mark Twain: Frontier Theatre Critic." *Arizona Quarterly* 16 (August 1960): 197-209.

2014. Schmitz, Neil. "The Paradox of Liberation in *Huckleberry Finn." Texas Studies in Literature and Language* 13 (Spring 1971): 125-36.

2015. Sloane, David E. E. *Mark Twain as a Literary Comedian.* Baton Rouge: Louisiana State University Press, 1979.

2016. Smith, Henry Nash. *Democracy and the Novel: Popular Resistance to Classic American Writers.* New York: Oxford University Press, 1978.

2017. ——. *Mark Twain: The Development of a Writer.* Cambridge, Mass: Harvard University Press, 1962.

2018. ——, and Frederick Anderson, eds. *Mark Twain of the Enterprise.* Berkeley: University of California Press, 1957.

2019. ——, and William M. Gibson, eds. *Mark Twain-Howells Letters.* 2 vols. Cambridge, Mass.: Harvard University Press, 1960.

2020. Solomon, Andrew. "Jim and Huck: Magnificent Misfits." *Mark Twain Journal* 16 (Winter 1972): 17-24.

2021. Solomon, Roger B. *Mark Twain and the Image of History.* New Haven, Conn.: Yale University Press, 1961.

2022. Stone, Albert E., Jr. *The Innocent Eye: Childhood in Mark Twain's Imagination.* New Haven, Conn.: Yale University Press, 1961.

2023. Taper, Bernard, ed. *Mark Twain's San Francisco.* New York: McGraw-Hill, 1963.

2024. Taylor, J. Golden. "Introduction to 'The Celebrated Jumping Frog of Calaveras County.'" *American West* 2 (Fall 1965): 73-76.

2025. Tenney, Thomas Asa. *Mark Twain: A Reference Guide.* Boston: G. K. Hall, 1977.

2026. ——. "Mark Twain: A Reference Guide First Annual Supplement." *American Literary Realism 1870-1910* 10 (Autumn 1977): 327-412.

2027. ——. "Mark Twain: A Reference

Guide: Second Annual Supplement." *American Literary Realism 1870-1910* 11 (Autumn 1978): 158-218.

2028. Towers, Tom H. "'Hateful Reality': The Failure of the Territory in *Roughing It.*" *Western American Literature* 9 (May 1974): 3-15.

2029. ———. "'I Never Thought We Might Want to Come Back': Strategies of Transcendence in *Tom Sawyer.*" *Modern Fiction Studies* 21 (Winter 1975/76): 509-20.

2030. Vorpahl, B. M. "'Very Much Like A Fire-Cracker': Owen Wister on Mark Twain." *Western American Literature* 6 (Summer 1971): 83-98.

2031. Wagenknecht, Edward. *Mark Twain: The Man and His Work.* Rev. ed. Norman: University of Oklahoma Press, 1961.

2032. Warren, Robert Penn. "Mark Twain." *Southern Review* 8 (July 1972): 459-92.

2033. Watkins, T. H. "Mark Twain and His Mississippi." *American West* 10 (November 1973): 12-19.

2034. Wecter, Dixon. "Mark Twain and the West." *Huntington Library Quarterly* 8 (August 1945): 359-77.

2035. ———. *Sam Clemens of Hannibal.* Ed. Elizabeth Wecter. Boston: Houghton Mifflin, 1952.

2036. West, Ray B., Jr. "Mark Twain's Idyl of Frontier America." *University of Kansas City Review* 15 (1948): 92-104.

2037. Wexman, Virginia. "The Role of Structure in *Tom Sawyer* and *Huckleberry Finn.*" *American Literary Realism 1870-1910* 6 (Winter 1973): 1-11.

2038. Wiggins, Robert A. *Mark Twain: Jackleg Novelist.* Seattle: University of Washington Press, 1964.

2039. Wister, Owen. "In Homage to Mark Twain." *Harper's Magazine* 171 (October 1935): 547-66.

2040. Ziff, Larzer. "Authorship and Craft: The Example of Mark Twain." *Southern Review* 12 (Spring 1976): 246-60.

JAMES CLYMAN

2041. Walker, Don D. "James Clyman's 'Narrative': Its Significance in the Literature of the Fur Trade." *Possible Sack* 4 (May 1973): 1-8.

2042. Zochert, Donald. "'A View of the Sublime Awful': The Language of a Pioneer." *Western American Literature* 6 (Winter 1972): 251-57.

WALT COBURN

2043. Porter, Willard H. "Walt Coburn: Word Wrangler of the Old West." *Persimmon Hill* 8 (1978): 58-65.

WILLIAM T. COGGESHALL

2044. Andrews, William D. "William T. Coggeshall: 'Booster' of Western Literature." *Ohio History* 81 (Summer 1972): 210-20.

WILL LEVINGTON COMFORT

2045. Powell, Lawrence Clark. "Southwest Classics Reread: Massacre and Vengeance in Apacheria." *Westways* 64 (May 1972): 55-59.

INA COOLBRITH

2046. Graham, Ina Agnes. "My Aunt, Ina Coolbrith." *Pacific Historian* 17 (Fall 1973): 12-19.
2047. Hubbard, George U. "Ina Coolbrith's Friendship with John Greenleaf Whittier." *New England Quarterly* 45 (1972): 109-18.
2048. Hurst, Lannie. "Ina Coolbrith: Forgotten As Poet . . . Remembered As Librarian." *PNLA Quarterly* 41 (Summer 1977): 4-11.
2049. Morrow, Patrick D. "Power Behind the Throne: Ina Coolbrith and the Politics of Submission." *Kate Chopin Newsletter* 2 (Spring 1976): 13-18.
2050. Rhodelhamel, Josephine DeWitt, and Raymund Francis Wood. *Ina Coolbrith: Librarian and Laureate of California.* Provo, Utah: Brigham University Press, 1973.
2051. Wood, Raymund F. "Librarian and Laureate: Ina Coolbrith of California." *Markham Review* 5 (1976): 35-39.

DANE COOLIDGE

2052. Ulph, Owen. "Dane Coolidge: An Introduction to the Work of a Now Obscure Western Writer and Photographer." *American West* 14 (November-December 1977): 32-47.

JAMES FENIMORE COOPER

2053. Axelrad, Allan M. "History and Utopia: A Study of the World View of James Fenimore Cooper." Doctoral dissertation, University of Pennsylvania, 1974.
2054. Baym, Nina. "The Women of Cooper's Leatherstocking Tales." *American Quarterly* 23 (December 1971): 696-709.
2055. Beard, James Franklin. "Cooper and the Revolutionary Mythos." *Early American Literature* 11 (Spring 1976): 84-104.
2056. ——. "James Fenimore Cooper." *Fifteen American Authors Before 1900: Bibliographic Essays on Research and Criticism.* Eds. Robert A. Rees and Earl N. Harbert. Madison: University of Wisconsin Press, 1971, pp. 63-96.
2057. ——, ed. *The Letters and Journals of James Fenimore Cooper.* 6 vols. Cambridge, Mass.: Harvard University Press, 1960-.
2058. Bewley, Marius. *The Eccentric Design.* New York: Columbia University Press, 1959, pp. 47-100.
2059. ——. "The Cage and the Prairie: Two Notes on Symbolism." *Hudson Review* 10 (Autumn 1957): 403-14.
2060. Bier, Jesse. "Lapsarians on *The Prairie*: Cooper's Novel." *Texas Studies in Literature and Language* 4 (Spring 1962): 49-57.

2061. Boynton, Henry W. *James Feni-more Cooper.* New York: Appleton-Century, 1931.

2062. Burkhardt, Peggy Craven. "Feni-more Cooper's Literary Defenders." Doctoral dissertation, University of Iowa, 1971.

2063. Butler, Michael D. "Narrative Structure and Historical Process in *The Last of the Mohicans.*" *American Literature* 48 (May 1976): 117-39.

2064. Chase, Richard. *The American Novel and Its Tradition.* Garden City, N.Y.: Doubleday, 1957, pp. 52-65.

2065. Clavel, Marcel. *Fenimore Cooper and His Critics.* Aix-en-Provence: Imprimerie Universitaire de Provence, 1938.

2066. Cunningham, Mary, ed. *James Fenimore Cooper: A Re-Appraisal.* Cooperstown, N.Y.: New York State Historical Association, 1954.

2067. Dekker, George. *James Fenimore Cooper: The Novelist.* London: Routledge and Kegan Paul, 1967.

2068. Flanagan, John T. "The Authenticity of Cooper's *The Prairie.*" *Modern Language Quarterly* 2 (March 1941): 99-104.

2069. Frederick, John T. "Cooper's Eloquent Indians." *PMLA* 71 (1956): 1004-17.

2070. Fussell, Edwin. *Frontier: American Literature and the American West.* Princeton, N.J.: Princeton University Press, 1965, pp. 27-68.

2071. Gerlach, John. "James Fenimore Cooper and the Kingdom of God." *Illinois Quarterly* 35 (April 1973): 32-50.

2072. Gilbert, Susan Hull. "James Fenimore Cooper: The Historical Novel and the Critics." Doctoral dissertation, University of North Carolina, Chapel Hill, 1974.

2073. Gladsky, Thomas S. "James Fenimore Cooper and the Genteel Hero of Romance." Doctoral dissertation, University of North Carolina, Greensboro, 1975.

2074. Grossman, James. *James Fenimore Cooper.* New York: William Sloane, 1949.

2075. House, Kay Seymour. *Cooper's Americans.* Columbus: Ohio State University Press, 1965.

2076. Jones, Howard Mumford. *The Frontier in American Fiction.* Jerusalem, 1926, pp. 26-50.

2077. Kaul, A. N. *The American Vision: Actual and Ideal in Nineteenth-Century Fiction.* New Haven, Conn.: Yale University Press, 1963, pp. 84-138.

2078. Kelly, William Patrick, III. "The Leatherstocking Tales: Fiction and the American Historical Experience." Doctoral dissertation, Indiana University, 1977.

2079. Lawrence, D. H. *Studies in Classic American Literature.* New York: Thomas Seltzer, 1923, pp. 50-92.

2080. Lewis, Merrill. "Lost-and Found-in the Wilderness: The Desert Metaphor in Cooper's *The Prairie.*" *Western American*

118

Literature 5 (Fall 1970): 195–204.

2081. Lounsbury, Thomas R. *James Fenimore Cooper.* Boston: Houghton Mifflin, 1882.

2082. Martin, Terence. "Beginnings and Endings in the Leatherstocking Tales." *Nineteenth-Century Fiction* 33 (June 1978): 69–87.

2083. ———. "Surviving on the Frontier: The Doubled Consciousness of Natty Bumppo." *South Atlantic Quarterly* 75 (Autumn 1976): 447–59.

2084. May, Judith Stinson. "Family and Aggression in the Leatherstocking Series." Doctoral dissertation, University of Illinois, Urbana-Champaign, 1976.

2085. Meyer, William Claus. "The Development of Myth in the Leatherstocking Tales of James Fennimore Cooper." Doctoral dissertation, Ball State University, 1972.

2086. Mikkelsen, Hubert Aage. "James Fenimore Cooper's Fiction: Theory and Practice." Doctoral dissertation, St. John's University, 1976.

2087. Mills, Gordon. "The Symbolic Wilderness: James Fenimore Cooper and Jack London." *Nineteenth-Century Fiction* 13 (March 1959): 329–40.

2088. Movalli, Charles Joseph. "Pride and Prejudice: James Fenimore Cooper's Frontier Fiction and His Social Criticism." Doctoral dissertation, University of Connecticut, 1972.

2089. Muszynska-Wallace, E. Soteris.

"The Sources of *The Prairie.*" *American Literature* 21 (May 1949): 191–200.

2090. Nelson, Carl. "Cooper's Verbal Faction: The Hierarchy of Rhetoric, Voice, and Silence in *The Prairie.*" *West Virginia University Philological Papers* 24 (1977): 37–47.

2091. Nevius, Blake. *Cooper's Landscapes: An Essay on the Picturesque Vision.* Berkeley: University of California Press, 1976.

2092. Noble, David W. "Cooper, Leatherstocking and the Death of the American Adam." *American Quarterly* 16 (Fall 1964): 419–31.

2093. Øverland, Örm. *The Making and Meaning of an American Classic: James Fenimore Cooper's "The Prairie."* New York: Humanities Press, 1973.

2094. Paine, Gregory. "The Indians of *The Leatherstocking Tales.*" *Studies in Philology* 23 (1926): 16–39.

2095. Pearce, Roy Harvey. "The Leatherstocking Tales Re-examined." *South Atlantic Quarterly* 46 (October 1947): 524–36.

2096. Peck, H. Daniel. *A World by Itself: The Pastoral Moment in Cooper's Fiction.* New Haven, Conn.: Yale University Press, 1977.

2097. Poulsen, Richard C. "Fenimore Cooper and the Exploration of the Great West." *Heritage of Kansas* 10 (Spring 1977): 15–24.

2098. Pound, Louise. "The Dialect of

Cooper's Leatherstocking." *American Speech* 2 (1927): 479-88.

2099. Railton, Stephen. *Fenimore Cooper: A Study of His Life and Imagination.* Princeton, N.J.: Princeton University Press, 1978.

2100. Ringe, Donald A. *James Fenimore Cooper.* New York: Twayne, 1962.

2101. ——. "Man and Nature in Cooper's *The Prairie.*" *Nineteenth-Century Fiction* 15 (March 1961): 313-23.

2102. ——. *The Pictorial Mode: Space and Time in the Art of Bryant, Irving and Cooper.* Lexington: University Press of Kentucky, 1972.

2103. Ross, John F. *The Social Criticism of Fenimore Cooper.* Berkeley: University of California Press, 1933.

2104. Ross, Morton L. "Cooper's *The Pioneers* and the Ethnographic Impulse." *American Studies* 16 (Autumn 1975): 49-65.

2105. Rucker, Mary E. "Natural, Tribal and Civil Law in Cooper's *The Prairie.*" *Western American Literature* 12 (November 1977): 215-22.

2106. Russell, Jason A. "Cooper: Interpreter of the Real and Historical Indian." *Journal of American History* 23 (1930): 41-71.

2107. Sequeira, Isaac. "The Frontier Attack on Cooper, 1850-1900." *Indian Journal of American Studies* 8 (1978): 25-35.

2108. Sheppard, Keith S. "Natty Bumppo: Cooper's Americanized Adam." Doctoral dissertation, Wayne State University, 1973.

2109. Shulenberger, Arvid. *Cooper's Theory of Fiction: His Prefaces and Their Relation to His Novels.* University of Kansas Humanities Studies, No. 32. Lawrence: University of Kansas Press, 1955.

2110. Smith, Henry Nash. "Consciousness and Social Order: The Theme of Transcendence in the Leatherstocking Tales." *Western American Literature* 5 (Fall 1970): 177-94.

2111. ——. "Introduction" to James Fenimore Cooper, *The Prairie.* New York: Holt, Rinehart and Winston, 1950, pp. v-xxii.

2112. ——. *Virgin Land: The American West as Symbol and Myth.* Cambridge, Mass.: Harvard University Press, 1950.

2113. Snook, Donald Gene. "Leadership and Order in the Border Novels of James Fenimore Cooper." Doctoral dissertation, University of North Carolina, Chapel Hill, 1974.

2114. Spiller, Robert E. *Fenimore Cooper: Critic of His Times.* New York: Minton, Balch, 1931.

2115. ——. *James Fenimore Cooper.* Minneapolis: University of Minnesota Press, 1965.

2116. ——, and Philip C. Blackburn. *A Descriptive Bibliography of the Writings of James Fenimore Cooper.* New York: R. R. Bowker, 1934.

2117. Stein, W. B. *"The Prairie*: A Scenario of the Wise Old Man." *Bucknell Review* 19 (Spring 1971): 15-36.

2118. Steinberg, Alan L. "James Fenimore Cooper: The Sentimental Frontier." *South Dakota Review* 15 (Spring 1977): 94-108.

2119. Steinbrink, Jeffrey Carl. "Attitudes Toward History and Uses of the Past in Cooper, Hawthorne, Mark Twain and Fitzgerald." Doctoral dissertation, University of North Carolina, Chapel Hill, 1974.

2120. Twain, Mark. "Fenimore Cooper's Literary Offenses." *North American Review* 156 (1895): 1-12.

2121. Van Antwerp, Richard Fenn. "The Design of Cooper's Fiction." Doctoral dissertation, University of Pittsburgh, 1975.

2122. Vance, William L. "'Man and Beast': The Meaning of Cooper's *The Prairie." PMLA* 89 (1974): 323-31.

2123. Vlach, Gordon R. "Fenimore Cooper's Leatherstocking as Folk Hero." *New York Folklore Quarterly* 27 (December 1971): 323-38.

2124. Walker, Warren S. "Buckskin West: Leatherstocking at High Noon." *New York Folklore Quarterly* 24 (June 1968): 88-102.

2125. ——. *James Fenimore Cooper: An Introduction and Interpretation.* New York: Barnes and Noble, 1962.

2126. ——. *Plots and Characters in the Fiction of James Fenimore Cooper.* Hamden, Conn.: Shoe String Press, 1978.

2127. Waples, Dorothy. *The Whig Myth of James Fenimore Cooper.* New Haven, Conn.: Yale University Press, 1938.

2128. Wasserstrom, William. "Cooper, Freud and the Origins of Culture." *American Imago* 17 (Winter 1960): 423-37.

2129. Williams, James Gary. "James Fenimore Cooper and Christianity: A Study of the Religious Novels." Doctoral dissertation, Cornell University, 1973.

2130. Wilson, Jennie Lee. "The Heroes of James Fenimore Cooper." Doctoral dissertation, University of Kansas, 1975.

2131. Yasuna, Edward Carl. "The Power of the Lord in the Howling Wilderness: The Achievement of Thomas Cole and James Fenimore Cooper." Doctoral dissertation, Ohio State University, 1976.

2132. Zoellner, Robert H. "Conceptual Ambivalence in Cooper's Leatherstocking." *American Literature* 31 (January 1960): 397-420.

PAUL COREY

2133. McCown, Robert A. "Paul Corey's Mantz Trilogy." *Books at Iowa* 17 (November 1972): 15-19, 23-26. On the manuscripts of an Iowa farm novelist.

EDWIN CORLE

2134. Beidler, Peter G. *Fig Tree John: An Indian in Fact and Fiction.* Tucson: University of Arizona Press, 1977.

2135. Corser, Cristin D. "The Indian as Symbol of Transcendent Spirituality in Oliver La Farge, Frank Waters, and Edwin Corle." Master's thesis, Brigham Young University, 1973.

GREGORY CORSO

2136. Cook, Bruce. *The Beat Generation.* New York: Charles Scribner's Sons, 1971.

2137. Dullea, Gerard J. "Ginsburg and Corso: Image and Imagination." *Thoth* 2 (Winter 1971): 17–27.

2138. Howard, Richard. *Alone With America: Essays in the Art of Poetry in the United States.* New York: Atheneum, 1969, pp. 57–64.

2139. Wilson, Robert. *A Bibliography of Works by Gregory Corso.* New York: Phoenix Book Shop, 1966.

STEPHEN CRANE

2140. Beebe, Maurice, and Thomas A. Gullason. "Criticism of Stephen Crane: A Selected Checklist with an Index to Studies of Separate Works." *Modern Fiction Studies* 5 (Autumn 1959): 282–91.

2141. Beer, Thomas. *Stephen Crane: A Study in American Letters.* New York: Knopf, 1923.

2142. Bergon, Frank. *Stephen Crane's Artistry.* New York: Columbia University Press, 1975.

2143. ——, ed. *The Western Writings of Stephen Crane.* New York: New American Library, 1979.

2144. Bernard, Kenneth. "'The Bride Comes to Yellow Sky': History as Elegy." *English Record* 17 (April 1967): 17–20.

2145. Berryman, John. *Stephen Crane.* New York: William Sloane, 1950.

2146. Burns, Shannon, and James A. Levernier. "Androgyny in Stephen Crane's 'The Bride Comes to Yellow Sky.'" *Research Studies* 45 (1977): 236–43.

2147. Cady, Edwin H. *Stephen Crane.* New York: Twayne, 1962.

2148. Cather, Willa. "When I Knew Stephen Crane." *Prairie Schooner* 23 (Fall 1949): 231–36.

2149. Cook, Robert G. "Stephen Crane's 'The Bride Comes to Yellow Sky.'" *Studies in Short Fiction* 2 (Summer 1965): 368–69.

2150. Cox, James Trammell. "Stephen Crane as Symbolic Naturalist: An Analysis of 'The Blue Hotel.'" *Modern Fiction Studies* 3 (Summer 1957): 147–58.

2151. Deamer, Robert Glen. "Remarks on the Western Stance of Stephen Crane." *Western American Literature* 15 (Summer 1980): 123–41.

2152. ——. "Stephen Crane and Western Myth." *Western American Literature* 7 (Summer 1972): 11–23.

2153. Dean, James L. "The Wests of Howells and Crane." *American Literary Realism 1870-1910* 10 (Summer 1977): 254-66.

2154. Garland, Hamlin. "Stephen Crane as I Knew Him." *Yale Review* 3 (April 1914): 494-506.

2155. Gibson, Donald. "'The Blue Hotel' and the Ideal of Human Courage." *Texas Studies in Language and Literature* 6 (Autumn 1964): 388-97.

2156. ——. *The Fiction of Stephen Crane.* Carbondale: Southern Illinois Press, 1968.

2157. Gullason, Thomas A. "The Permanence of Stephen Crane." *Studies in the Novel* 10 (Spring 1978): 86-95.

2158. Hudspeth, Robert N., ed. "The Thoth Annual Bibliography of Stephen Crane Scholarship." *Thoth* 4 (1963): 30-58 ff.

2159. James, Overton Philip. "The 'Game' in 'The Bride Comes to Yellow Sky.'" *Xavier University Studies* 4 (March 1965): 3-11.

2160. Katz, Joseph. *The Merrill Checklist of Stephen Crane.* Columbus, Ohio: Charles E. Merrill, 1969.

2161. ——, ed. *Stephen Crane in the West and Mexico.* Kent, Ohio: Kent State University Press, 1971.

2162. ——, ed. *Stephen Crane: The Blue Hotel.* Merrill Literary Casebook Series. Columbus, Ohio: Charles E. Merrill, 1970.

2163. Kinnamon, Jon M. "Henry James, the Bartender in Stephen Crane's 'The Blue Hotel.'" *Arizona Quarterly* 30 (Summer 1974): 160-66.

2164. MacLean, H. N. "The Two Worlds of 'The Blue Hotel.'" *Modern Fiction Studies* 5 (Autumn 1959): 260-70.

2165. Marovitz, Sanford E. "Scratchy the Demon in 'The Bride Comes to Yellow Sky.'" *Tennessee Studies in English* 16 (1971): 137-40.

2166. Monteiro, George. "Society and Nature in Stephen Crane's 'The Men in the Storm.'" *Prairie Schooner* 45 (Spring 1971): 13-17.

2167. ——. "Stephen Crane's 'The Bride Comes to Yellow Sky.'" *Approaches to the Short Story.* Eds. Neil Isaacs and Louis Leiter. San Francisco: Chandler, 1963, pp. 221-38.

2168. ——. "Stephen Crane's 'Yellow Sky' Sequel." *Arizona Quarterly* 30 (Summer 1974): 119-26.

2169. Peredes, Raymund A. "Stephen Crane and The Mexican." *Western American Literature* 6 (Spring 1971): 31-38.

2170. Pizer, Donald. "Stephen Crane: A Review of Scholarship and Criticism Since 1969." *Studies in the Novel* 10 (Spring 1978): 120-45.

2171. Robertson, Jamie. "Stephen Crane, Eastern Outsider in the West and Mexico." *Western American Literature* 13 (Fall 1978): 243-57.

2172. Satterwhite, Joseph N. "Stephen Crane's 'The Blue Hotel': The Failure of Understanding."

Modern Fiction Studies 2 (Winter 1956-57): 238-41.

2173. Slote, Bernice. "Stephen Crane & Willa Cather." *Serif* 6 (December 1969): 3-15.

2174. ——. "Stephen Crane in Nebraska." *Prairie Schooner* 43 (Summer 1969): 192-99.

2175. Solomon, Eric. *Stephen Crane: From Parody to Realism.* Cambridge, Mass.: Harvard University Press, 1967.

2176. Stallman, R. W. *Stephen Crane: A Biography.* New York: George Braziller, 1968.

2177. ——. *Stephen Crane: A Critical Bibliography.* Ames: Iowa State University Press, 1972.

2178. Sutton, Walter. "Pity and Fear in 'The Blue Hotel.'" *American Quarterly* 4 (Spring 1952): 73-78.

2179. Tibbetts, A. M. "Stephen Crane's 'The Bride Comes to Yellow Sky.'" *English Journal* 54 (April 1965): 314-16.

2180. Van Der Beets, Richard. "Character as Structure: Ironic Parallel and Transformation in 'The Blue Hotel.'" *Studies in Short Fiction* 5 (Spring 1968): 294-95.

2181. Vanouse, Donald. "Popular Culture in the Writings of Stephen Crane." *Journal of Popular Culture* 10 (Fall 1976): 424-30.

2182. Vorpahl, Ben M. "Murder by the Minute: Old and New in 'The Bride Comes to Yellow Sky.'" *Nineteenth-Century Fiction* 26 (September 1971): 196-218.

2183. Wertheim, Stanley. "Stephen Crane." *Hawthorne, Melville, Stephen Crane: A Critical Bibliography.* Eds. Theodore L. Gross and Stanley Wertheim. New York: Free Press, 1971, pp. 203-301.

2184. West, Ray B., Jr. "The Use of Action in 'The Bride Comes to Yellow Sky.'" *The Art of Writing Fiction.* New York: Thomas Y. Crowell, 1968, pp. 134-40.

2185. Wolford, Chester, L. "The Eagle and the Crow: High Tragedy and Epic in 'The Blue Hotel.'" *Prairie Schooner* 51 (Fall 1977): 260-74.

2186. Williams, Ames W., and Vincent Starrett. *Stephen Crane: A Bibliography.* Glendale, Calif.: John Valentine, 1948.

J. W. CRAWFORD

2187. Nolan, Paul T. "Captain Jack Crawford: Gold Searcher Turned Playwright." *Alaska Review* 1 (Spring 1964): 41-47.

2188. ——. "J. W. Crawford: Poet-Scout of the Black Hills." *South Dakota Review* 2 (Spring 1965): 40-47.

2189. ——. "J. W. Crawford's *The Dregs*: A New Mexico Pioneer in the Short Drama." *New Mexico Quarterly* 33 (Winter 1963-64): 388-403.

HOMER CROY

2190. O'Dell, Charles A. "Homer Croy, Maryville Writer: The First Forty Years 1883-1923."

Northwest Missouri State University Studies 33 (August 1972): 3-59.

EUGENE CUNNINGHAM

2191. Pike, Donald G. "Eugene Cunningham: Realism and the Action Novel." *Western American Literature* 7 (Fall 1972): 224-29.

2192. Price, Carol. "The Novels of Eugene Cunningham: A Southwestern Perspective." *Southwest Heritage* 10 (Fall/Winter 1980-81).

J. V. CUNNINGHAM

2193. Kaye, Frances W. "The West as Desolation: J. V. Cunningham's *To What Strangers, What Welcome.*" *Southern Review* 11 (Autumn 1975): 820-24.

2194. Stall, Lindon. "The Trivial, Vulgar, and Exalted: The Poems of J. V. Cunningham." *Southern Review* 9 (October 1973): 1044-48.

2195. Stein, Robert A. "The Collected Poems and Epigrams of J. V. Cunningham." *Western Humanities Review* 27 (Winter 1973): 1-12.

DAN CUSHMAN

2196. Beidler, Peter G. "The Popularity of Dan Cushman's *Stay Away, Joe* Among American Indians." *Arizona Quarterly* 33 (Autumn 1977): 216-40.

ROLLIN MALLORY DAGGETT

2197. Weisenburger, Francis Phelps. *Idol of the West: The Fabulous Career of Rollin Mallory Daggett.* Syracuse, N.Y.: Syracuse University Press, 1965.

RICHARD HENRY DANA

2198. Allison, James. "Journal of a Voyage from Boston to the Coast of California by Richard Henry Dana, Jr." *American Neptune* 12 (July 1952): 177-86.

2199. Gale, Robert L. *Richard Henry Dana.* New York: Twayne, 1969.

2200. Hart, James David. "Richard Henry Dana, Jr." Doctoral dissertation, Harvard University, 1936.

2201. Hill, Douglas B., Jr. "Richard Henry Dana, Jr. and *Two Years Before the Mast.*" *Criticism* 9 (Fall 1967): 312-25.

2202. Lucid, Robert Francis. "The Composition, Reception, Reputation and Influence of *Two Years Before the Mast.*" Doctoral dissertation, University of Chicago, 1958.

2203. ———, ed. *The Journal of Richard Henry Dana, Jr.* 3 vols. Cambridge, Mass.: Belknap Press, 1968.

H. L. DAVIS

2204. Armstrong, George M. "H. L. Davis's *Beulah Land*: A Revisionist's Novel of Westering."

125

The Westering Experience in American Literature: Bicentennial Essays. Eds. Merrill Lewis and L. L. Lee. Bellingham: Bureau for Faculty Research, Western Washington University, 1977, pp. 144-53.

2205. ———. "An Unworn and Edged Tool: H. L. Davis's Last Word on the West, 'The Kettle of Fire.'" Northwest Perspectives: Essays on the Culture of the Pacific Northwest. Eds. Edwin R. Bingham and Glen A. Love. Seattle: University of Washington Press, 1979, pp. 169-85.

2206. Bain, Robert. H. L. Davis. Western Writers Series, No. 11. Boise, Idaho: Boise State University, 1974.

2207. Brunvand, Jan Harold. "Honey in the Horn and 'Acres of Clams': The Regional Fiction of H. L. Davis." Western American Literature 2 (Summer 1967): 135-45.

2208. Bryant, Paul T. H. L. Davis. Boston: Twayne, 1978. Includes a complete bibliography.

2209. ———. "H. L. Davis: Viable Uses for the Past." Western American Literature 3 (Spring 1968): 3-18.

2210. Clare, Warren L. "'Posers, Parasites, and Pismires': Status Rerum, by James Stevens and H. L. Davis." Pacific Northwest Quarterly 61 (January 1970): 22-30.

2211. Corning, Howard M. "The Prose and the Poetry of It." Oregon Historical Quarterly 74 (September 1973): 244-67. On Oregon writers of the twentieth century, especially H. L. Davis.

2212. Etulain, Richard W. "H. L. Davis: A Bibliographical Addendum." Western American Literature 5 (Summer 1970): 129-35.

2213. Greiner, Francis F. "Voice of the West: Harold L. Davis." Oregon Historical Quarterly 66 (September 1965): 240-48.

2214. Gurian, Jay. "The Unwritten West." American West 2 (Winter 1965): 59-63.

2215. Hegbloom, Kirk. "Theme and Folklore in H. L. Davis' Winds of Morning." Master's thesis, University of Idaho, 1967.

2216. Hitt, Helen. "History in Pacific Northwest Novels Written Since 1920." Oregon Historical Quarterly 51 (September 1950): 180-206.

2217. Hodgins, Francis E., Jr. "The Literary Emancipation of a Region." Doctoral dissertation, Michigan State University, 1957, pp. 457-84.

2218. Hutchens, John K. "H. L. Davis, Novelist: His West Lives On." New York Times Book Review, 25 April 1961, pp. 23, 37.

2219. Jenkins, Eli Seth. "H. L. Davis: A Critical Study." Doctoral dissertation, University of Southern California, 1960.

2220. Jones, Phillip L. "The West of H. L. Davis." South Dakota Review 6 (Winter 1968-69): 72-84.

2221. Kellogg, George. "H. L. Davis, 1896-1960: A Bibliography."

Texas Studies in Language and Literature 5 (Summer 1963): 294-303.

2222. Kohler, Dayton. "H. L. Davis: Writer in the West." *College English* 14 (December 1952): 133-40. Also in *English Journal* 41 (December 1952): 519-26.

2223. Lauber, John. "A Western Classic: H. L. Davis' *Honey in the Horn.*" *Western Humanities Review* 16 (Winter 1962): 85-86.

2224. Lorentz, Pare. "H. L. Davis: Portrait of the West." Honor's thesis, Harvard College, 1959.

2225. Mencken, H. L. "Editorial Notes." *American Mercury* 19 (April 1930): xxvi, xxviii.

2226. Potts, James T. "H. L. Davis' View: Reclaiming and Recovering the Land." *Oregon Historical Quarterly* 82 (Summer 1981): 117-51.

2227. ———. "The West of H. L. Davis." Doctoral dissertation, University of Arizona, 1977.

2228. Ridgeway, Ann N., ed. *The Selected Letters of Robinson Jeffers.* Baltimore: The Johns Hopkins Press, 1968, pp. 122-26, 177, 190.

2229. Sandburg, Carl. "Something About H. L. Davis." *Rocky Mountain Herald* 90 (April 1, 1950): 1-2.

2230. Stevens, James. "'Bunk-Shanty Ballads and Tales': The Annual Society Address." *Oregon Historical Quarterly* 50 (December 1949): 235-42.

2231. ———. "The Northwest Takes to Poesy." *American Mercury* 16 (January 1929): 64-70.

ROBERT DAY

2232. Cansler, Loman D. "Last of the Big Cattle Drives." *Heritage of Kansas* 9 (Fall 1976): 10-19.

WILLIAM DECKER

2233. Etulain, Richard. "Recent Western Fiction." *Journal of the West* 8 (October 1969): 656-58.

GEORGE H. DERBY
(John Phoenix)

2234. Delano, Alonzo. "Reminiscences of John Phoenix, Esq. the Veritable Squibob." *Hesperian* (March 1862): 30-34.

2235. Stewart, George R. *John Phoenix, Esq., The Veritable Squibob: A Life of Captain George H. Derby, USA.* New York: Henry Holt, 1937; New York: Da Capo Press, 1969.

2236. Thompson, Mrs. Launt. "A Forgotten American Humorist." *United Service Magazine* (October 1902): 343-61.

CABEZA DE VACA

2237. Pilkington, William T. "The Journey of Cabeza de Vaca: An American Prototype." *South Dakota Review* 6 (Spring 1968): 73-82.

BERNARD DE VOTO

2238. Arthur, Anthony. "The Prince as Frog: John C. Fremont and *Year of Decision: 1846.*" *The Westering Experience in American Literature: Bicentennial Essays.* Eds. Merrill Lewis and L. L. Lee. Bellingham: Bureau for Faculty Research, Western Washington University, 1977, pp. 129-34.

2239. Bowen, Catherine Drinker, et al. *Four Portraits and One Subject: Bernard DeVoto.* Boston: Houghton Mifflin, 1963.

2240. Boyling, Mary Ellen F. "'No Mind Is Ever of One Piece . . .': Bernard DeVoto's Literary Correspondence." Doctoral dissertation, Stanford University, 1973.

2241. Cousins, Norman. "The Controversial Mr. DeVoto." *Saturday Review/World* 6 (April 1974): 5-7. Essay review of Stegner's biography of DeVoto.

2242. Jones, Alfred Haworth. "The Persistence of the Progressive Mind: The Case of Bernard DeVoto." *American Studies* 12 (Spring 1971): 37-48.

2243. Lee, Robert Edson. *From West to East.* Urbana: University of Illinois Press, 1966, pp. 136-52.

2244. ——. "The Work of Bernard DeVoto, Introduction and Annotated Check List." Doctoral dissertation, State University of Iowa, 1957.

2245. Lemons, William Everett, Jr. "Western Historical Perspectives of DeVoto, Webb, Dobie, and Hyde." Doctoral dissertation, University of Minnesota, 1973.

2246. Mattingly, Garrett. *Bernard DeVoto, A Preliminary Appraisal.* Boston: Little, Brown, 1938.

2247. Pruessing, Peter Skiles. "Manifest Destiny and 'The Literary Fallacy': The Paradox of Bernard DeVoto's Treatment of Westward Expansion." Master's thesis, Iowa State University, 1968.

2248. Rawls, James J. "Bernard DeVoto and the Art of Popular History." *Pacific Historian* 25 (Spring 1981): 46-51.

2249. Sawey, Orlan. *Bernard DeVoto.* New York: Twayne, 1969.

2250. ——. "Bernard DeVoto's Western Novels." *Western American Literature* 2 (Fall 1967): 171-82.

2251. Smith, Gregory. "Nonmember Geographers: Bernard DeVoto and His Biographer, Wallace Stegner." *Professional Geographer* 28 (May 1976).

2252. Stegner, Wallace. "DeVoto's Western Adventures." *American West* 10 (November 1973): 20-27.

2253. ——. "Historian by Serendipity." *American Heritage* 24 (August 1973): 28-32.

2254. ——. *The Sound of Mountain Water.* Garden City, N.Y.: Doubleday, 1969, pp. 202-22; New York: E. P. Dutton, 1980, pp. 250-75.

2255. ——. *The Uneasy Chair: A Biography of Bernard DeVoto.*

Garden City, N.Y.: Doubleday, 1974.

2256. ——, ed. *The Letters of Bernard DeVoto*. Garden City, N.Y.: Doubleday, 1975.

2257. W[alker], D[on] D. "The Dogmas of DeVoto." *Possible Sack* 2 (August 1971): 6-8; 3 (November 1971): 1-7; (February 1972): 1-4; (March 1972): 14-18.

AL DEWLEN

2258. Merren, John. "Character and Theme in the Amarillo Novels of Al Dewlen." *Western Review* 6 (Spring 1969): 3-9.

JOAN DIDION

2259. Brady, H. Jennifer. "Points West, Then and Now: The Fiction of Joan Didion." *Contemporary Fiction* 20 (Autumn 1979): 452-70.

2260. Chabot, C. Barry. "Joan Didion's *Play It As It Lays* and the Vacuity of the 'Here and Now.'" *Critique* 21, No. 3 (1980): 53-60.

2261. Geherin, David J. "Nothingness and Beyond: Joan Didion's *Play It As It Lays*." *Critique* 16, No. 1 (1974): 64-78.

2262. Henderson, Katherine Usher. *Joan Didion*. New York: Frederick Ungar, 1981.

2263. Jacobs, Fred Rue. *Joan Didion: Bibliography*. Keene, Calif.: Loop, 1977.

2264. Mallon, Thomas. "The Limits of History in the Novels of Joan Didion." *Critique* 21, No. 3 (1980): 43-52.

2265. Stineback, David C. "On the Limits of Fiction." *Midwest Quarterly* 14 (Summer 1973): 339-48.

2266. Winchell, Mark Royden. *Joan Didion*. Boston: Twayne, 1980.

MAYNARD DIXON

2267. Starr, Kevin. "Painterly Poet, Poetic Painter: The Dual Art of Maynard Dixon." *California Historical Quarterly* 56 (Winter 1977-78): 290-309.

J. FRANK DOBIE

2268. Abernethy, Francis Edward. *J. Frank Dobie*. Southwest Writers Series, No. 1. Austin, Tex.: Steck-Vaughn, 1967.

2269. Alsmeyer, Henry Louis, Jr. "J. Frank Dobie's Attitude Towards Physical Nature." Doctoral dissertation, Texas A & M University, 1973.

2270. Bode, Winston. *A Portrait of Pancho: The Life of a Great Texan, J. Frank Dobie*. Austin, Tex.: Pemberton Press, 1965.

2271. Campbell, Jeff H. "Pancho at College—Toga or Sombrero?" *Southwestern American Literature* 1 (September 1971): 149-55.

2272. Dobie, Bertha. "Dobie's Sunday Pieces." *Southwest Review* 50 (Spring 1965): 114-19.

2273. Dykes, Jeff. "A Dedication to the Memory of James Frank Dobie, 1888-1964." *Arizona and the West* 8 (Autumn 1966): 203-6.

2274. Hogue, Alexandre. "A Portrait of Pancho Dobie." *Southwest Review* 50 (Spring 1965): 101-13.

2275. McVicker, Mary Louise. *The Writings of J. Frank Dobie: A Bibliography.* Lawton, Okla.: Museum of the Great Plains, 1968.

2276. Peterson, Vernon. "J. Frank Dobie as 'The Father of Song.'" *South Dakota Review* 13 (Summer 1975): 73-81.

2277. Pilkington, Tom. *The Works of J. Frank Dobie.* Cassette. Deland, Fla.: Everett/Edwards, 1974.

2278. Tinkle, Lon. *An American Original: The Life of J. Frank Dobie.* Boston: Little, Brown, 1978.

2279. Turner, Martha Anne. "Was Frank Dobie a Throwback to Mark Twain?" *Western Review* 5 (Winter 1968): 3-12.

2280. White, Victor. "Paisano and a Chair." *Southwest Review* 56 (Spring 1971): 188-96.

2281. Yarborough, Ralph W. *Frank Dobie: Man and Friend.* Washington, D.C.: Potomac Corral of the Westerners, 1967.

E. L. DOCTOROW

2282. Arnold, Marilyn. "History As Fate in E. L. Doctorow's Tale of a Western Town." *South Dakota Review* 18 (Spring 1980): 53-63.

2283. Emblidge, David. "Marching Backward into the Future." *Southwest Review* 62 (Autumn 1977): 397-409.

IGNATIUS DONNELLY

2284. Anderson, David D. *Ignatius Donnelly.* Boston: Twayne, 1980.

2285. Axelrad, Allan M. "Ideology and Utopia in the Works of Ignatius Donnelly." *American Studies* 12 (Fall 1971): 47-65.

2286. Baker, J. Wayne. "Populist Themes in the Fiction of Ignatius Donnelly." *American Studies* 14 (Fall 1973): 65-83.

2287. Bovee, John R. "Ignatius Donnelly as a Man of Letters." Doctoral dissertation, Washington State University, 1968.

2288. Patterson, John. "From Yoeman to Beast: Images of Blackness in *Caesar's Column.*" *American Studies* 12 (Fall 1971): 21-31.

2289. Ridge, Martin. *Ignatius Donnelly: The Portrait of a Politician.* Chicago: University of Chicago Press, 1962.

2290. Wright, David E. "The Art and Vision of Ignatius Donnelly." Doctoral dissertation, Michigan State University, 1974.

ED DORN

2291. Alpert, Barry. "Ed Dorn: An Interview." *Vort* 1 (Fall 1972): 2-20.

2292. Butterick, George F. "Ed Dorn:

A Checklist." *Athanor* (Winter 1973).

2293. Davidson, Michael. "To Eliminate the Draw: Edward Dorn's *Slinger." American Literature* 53 (November 1981): 443-64.

2294. Dresman, Paul C. "Between Here and Formerly: A Study of History in the Work of Edward Dorn." Doctoral dissertation, University of California, San Diego, 1980.

2295. Lockwood, William J. "Ed Dorn's Mystique of the Real: His Poems for North America." *Contemporary Literature* 19 (Winter 1978): 58-79.

2296. Okada, Roy K. "An Interview with Edward Dorn." *Contemporary Literature* 15 (Summer 1974): 297-314.

2297. Paul, Sherman. *The Lost America of Love: Rereading Robert Creeley, Edward Dorn, and Robert Duncan.* Baton Rouge: Louisiana State University Press, 1981.

2298. Wesling, Donald. "A Bibliography on Edward Dorn for America." *Parnassus* 5 (Spring-Summer 1977): 142-60.

J. HYATT DOWNING

2299. Wadden, Anthony T. "J. Hyatt Downing: The Chronicle of an Era." *Books at Iowa* (April 1968): 11-23.

2300. ———. "Late to the Harvest: The Fiction of J. Hyatt Downing." *Western American Literature* 6 (Fall 1971): 203-14.

GLENN WARD DRESBACH

2301. Ford, Edsel. "Glenn Ward Dresbach: The New Mexico Years, 1915-1920." *New Mexico Quarterly* 34 (Spring 1964): 78-96.

NORMAN DUBIE

2302. Fay, Julie, and David Wojahn. "Norman Dubie; Dark Spiralling Figures: An Interview." *American Poetry Review* 7 (July/August 1978): 7-11.

ROBERT DUNCAN

2303. Cooley, Dennis. "Keeping the Green: the Vegetation of Renewal in Robert Duncan's Poetry." Doctoral dissertation, University of Rochester, 1972.

2304. Davidson, Robert M. "Disorders of the Net: The Poetry of Robert Duncan." Doctoral dissertation, State University of New York, Buffalo, 1973.

2305. Paul, Sherman. *The Lost America of Love: Rereading Robert Creeley, Edward Dorn, and Robert Duncan.* Baton Rouge: Louisiana State University Press, 1981.

2306. Weber, Robert C. "Roots of Language: The Major Poetry of Robert Duncan." Doctoral dissertation, University of Wisconsin, 1973.

ABIGAIL SCOTT DUNIWAY

2307. Capell, Letita Lee. "A Biography

of Abigail Scott Duniway." Master's thesis, University of Oregon, 1934.

2308. Moynihan, Ruth Barnes." Abigail Scott Duniway of Oregon: Woman and Suffragist of the American Frontier." 2 vols. Doctoral dissertation, Yale University, 1979.

2309. Ross, Nancy Wilson. *Westward the Women*. New York: Alfred A. Knopf, 1945, pp. 137-54.

JOHN C. DUVAL

2310. Anderson, John Q. *John C. Duval: First Texas Man of Letters*. Southwest Writers Series, No. 2. Austin, Tex.: Steck-Vaughn, 1967.

2311. Dobie, J. Frank. *John C. Duval, First Texas Man of Letters: His Life and Some of His Unpublished Writings*. Dallas: Southern Methodist University Press, 1939.

EVA EMERY DYE

2312. Ellingsen, Melva G. "Eva and Clio; or, the Muse Meets Its Mistress." *Call Number* 19 (Fall 1957): 17-22.

2313. Powers, Alfred. *History of Oregon Literature*. Portland: Metropolitan Press, 1935, pp. 404-14.

2314. Taber, Ronald W. "Sacagawea and the Suffragettes: An Interpretation of a Myth." *Pacific Northwest Quarterly* 58 (January 1967): 7-13.

WILLIAM EASTLAKE

2315. Angell, Richard C. "Eastlake: At Home and Abroad." *New Mexico Quarterly* 34 (Summer 1964): 204-9.

2316. Graham, Don. "William Eastlake's First Novel: An Account of the Making of *Go in Beauty*." *Western American Literature* 16 (Spring 1981): 27-37.

2317. Haslam, Gerald. *William Eastlake*. Southwest Writers Series, No. 36. Austin, Tex.: Steck-Vaughn, 1970.

2318. ——. "William Eastlake: Portrait of the Artist as Shaman." *Western Review* 8 (Spring 1971): 2-13.

2319. McCaffery, Larry. "Absurdity and Oppositions in William Eastlake's Southwestern Novels." *Critique* 19, No. 2 (1977): 62-76.

2320. Milton, John R. "The Land as Form in Frank Waters and William Eastlake." *Kansas Quarterly* 2 (Spring 1970): 104-9.

2321. Woolf, Douglas. "One of the Truly Good Men." *Evergreen Review* 2 (Spring 1959): 194-96.

2322. Wylder, Delbert E. "The Novels of William Eastlake." *New Mexico Quarterly* 34 (Summer 1964): 188-203.

CHARLES ALEXANDER EASTMAN

2323. Copeland, Marion W. *Charles Alexander Eastman (Ohiyesa)*. Western Writers Series, No. 33.

Boise, Idaho: Boise State University, 1978.

2324. Miller, David Reed. "Charles Alexander Eastman: One Man's Journey." Master's thesis, University of North Dakota, 1975.

2325. O'Brien, Lynne Woods. *Plains Indian Auobiographies.* Western Writers Series, No. 10. Boise, Idaho: Boise State College, 1973.

2326. Stensland, Anna Lee. "Charles Alexander Eastman: Sioux Storyteller and Historian." *American Indian Quarterly* 3 (Autumn 1977): 199-208.

2327. Wilson, Raymond. "Charles Alexander Eastman (Ohiyesa), Santee Sioux." Doctoral dissertation, University of New Mexico, 1977.

ELAINE GOODALE EASTMAN

2328. Graber, Kay, ed. *The Memoirs of Elaine Goodale Eastman, 1885-91.* Lincoln: University of Nebraska Press, 1978.

EDWARD EGGLESTON

2329. Johannsen, Robert W. "Literature and History: The Early Novels of Edward Eggleston." *Indiana Magazine of History* 48 (March 1952): 37-54.

2330. Randel, William Pierce. *Edward Eggleston.* Gloucester, Mass.: Peter Smith, 1962.

2331. ——. "Edward Eggleston (1837-1902)." *American Literary Realism 1870-1910* 1 (Fall 1967): 36-38.

2332. ——. "Edward Eggleston's Minnesota Fiction." *Minnesota History* 33 (Spring 1953): 189-93.

2333. Roth, John D. "Down East and Southwestern Humor in the Western Novels of Edward Eggleston." Doctoral dissertation, University of Alabama, 1971.

LOREN EISELEY

2334. Carlisle, E. Fred. "The Poetic Achievement of Loren Eiseley." *Prairie Schooner* 51 (Summer 1977): 111-29.

2335. Kassebaum, L. Harvey. "To Survive Our Century: The Narrative Voice of Loren Eiseley: An Essay in Appreciation." Doctoral dissertation, Indiana University of Pennsylvania, 1979.

2336. Schwartz, James M. "The "Immense Journey" of An Artist: The Literary Technique and Style of Loren Eiseley." Doctoral dissertation, Ohio State University, 1977.

2337. ——. "Loren Eiseley: The Scientist as Literary Artist." *Georgia Review* 31 (Winter 1977): 855-71.

ANNE ELLIS

2338. Matlack, Anne. "The Spirit of Anne Ellis." *Colorado Quarterly* 4 (1955-56): 61-72.

RALPH ELLISON

2339. Bucco, Martin. "Ellison's Invisible West." *Western American Literature* 10 (November 1975): 237–38.

LOULA GRACE ERDMAN

2340. Nelson, Jane. "Introduction" to Loula Grace Erdman, *The Years of the Locust.* Boston: Gregg Press, 1979, pp. v–xiii.

2341. Sewell, Ernestine. "An Interview with Loula Grace Erdman." *Southwestern American Literature* 2 (Spring 1972): 33–41.

2342. ———. *Loula Grace Erdman.* Southwest Writers Series, No. 33. Austin, Tex.: Steck-Vaughn, 1970.

HELEN EUSTIS

2243. Burns, Stuart L. "St. Petersburg Re-Visited: Helen Eustis and Mark Twain." *Western American Literature* 5 (Summer 1970): 99–112.

MAX EVANS

2344. Milton, John R., ed. "Interview: Max Evans." *South Dakota Review* 5 (Summer 1967): 77–87.

2345. ———. *Three West: Conversations with Vardis Fisher, Max Evans, Michael Straight.* Vermillion, S.D.: Dakota Press, 1970.

2346. Sonnichsen, C. L. "The New Style Western." *South Dakota Review* 4 (Summer 1966): 22–28.

WILLIAM EVERSON
(Brother Antoninus)

2347. Bartlett, Lee, ed. *Benchmark and Blaze: The Emergence of William Everson.* Metuchen, N.J.: Scarecrow Press, 1979.

2348. Cargas, H. J. "An Interview with Brother Antoninus." *Renascence* 18 (Spring 1966): 137–45.

2349. Dill, Vicky Schreiber. "The Books of William Everson." *Books of Iowa* 28 (1978): 9–24.

2350. McDonnell, T. P. "Poet from the West: Evenings with Brother Antoninus." *Commonweal* 78 (March 29, 1963): 13–14.

2351. Rizzo, Fred F. "A Study of the Poetry of William Everson." Doctoral dissertation, University of Oklahoma, 1966.

2352. Stafford, William E., ed. *The Achievement of Brother Antoninus: A Comprehensive Selection of His Poems With a Critical Introduction.* Glenview, Ill.: Scott, Foresman, 1967.

FREDERICK FAUST
(Max Brand)

2353. Bloodworth, William A., Jr. "Max Brand's West." *Western American Literature* 16 (Fall 1981): 177–91.

2354. Chapman, Edgar L. "The Image of the Indian in Max Brand's Pulp Western Novels." *Heritage of Kansas* 11 (Spring 1978): 16–45.

2355. Easton, Robert. *Max Brand: The Big "Westerner."* Norman: University of Oklahoma Press, 1970.

2356. Nachbar, Jack. "Introduction" to Max Brand, *The Untamed.* Boston: Gregg Press, 1978, pp. v-xii.

2357. Reynolds, Quentin. *The Fiction Factory.* New York: Random House, 1955.

2358. Richardson, Darrell C., ed. and comp. *Max Brand: The Man and His Work.* Los Angeles: Fantasy, 1952.

2359. Schoolcraft, John, ed. *The Notebooks and Poems of "Max Brand."* New York: Dodd, Mead, 1957.

FEIKE FEIKEMA
(See Frederick Feikema Manfred)

EDNA FERBER

2360. Brenni, Vito J., and Betty Lee Spencer. "Edna Ferber: A Selected Bibliography." *Bulletin of Bibliography* 22 (September-December 1958): 152-56.

2361. Gilbert, Julie Goldsmith. *Ferber: A Biography.* Garden City, N.Y.: Doubleday, 1978.

2362. Overton, Grant. "Edna Ferber." *The Women Who Make Our Novels.* New York: Dodd, Mead, 1928, pp. 126-38.

2263. Plante, Patricia R. "Mark Twain, Edna Ferber and the Mississippi." *Mark Twain Journal* 13 (Winter 1965-66): 8-10.

2264. Shaughnessy, Mary Rose. *Women and Success in American Society in the Works of Edna Ferber.* New York: Gordon, 1976.

ERNA FERGUSSON

2365. Powell, Lawrence C. "Erna Fergusson and *Dancing Gods.*" *Westways* 63 (March 1971): 13-17, 62.

2366. Remley, David A. *Erna Fergusson.* Southwest Writers Series, No. 24. Austin, Tex.: Steck-Vaughn, 1969.

HARVEY FERGUSSON

2367. Baldwin, Charles C. "Harvey Fergusson." *The Men Who Make Our Novels.* New York: Dodd, Mead, 1924, pp. 154-65.

2368. Cohen, Saul. *Harvey Fergusson: A Checklist.* Los Angeles: University of California at Los Angeles Library, 1965. Best published bibliography of Fergusson's works.

2369. Fergusson, Erna. *New Mexico: A Pageant of Three Peoples.* New York: Knopf, 1951.

2370. Folsom, James K. *Harvey Fergusson.* Southwest Writers Series, No. 20. Austin, Tex.: Steck-Vaughn, 1969.

2371. McGinity, Sue Simmons. "Harvey Fergusson's Use of Animal Imagery in Characterizing Spanish-American Women." *Western Review* 8 (Winter 1971): 46-50.

2372. Milton, John R. "Conversation with Harvey Fergusson." *South Dakota Review* 9 (Spring 1971): 39-45.

2373. ——. *The Novel of the American West.* Lincoln: University of Nebraska Press, 1980, pp. 230-63.

2374. "Modern Man and Harvey Fergusson—A Symposium." *New Mexico Quarterly* 6 (May 1936): 123-35.

2375. Pearson, Lorene. "Harvey Fergusson and the Crossroads." *New Mexico Quarterly* 21 (Autumn 1951): 334-55.

2376. Pilkington, William T. *Harvey Fergusson.* Boston: Twayne, 1975.

2377. ———. "The Southwestern Novels of Harvey Fergusson." *New Mexico Quarterly* 35 (Winter 1965-66): 330-43.

2378. Powell, Lawrence Clark. "Southwest Classics Reread: *Wolf Song.*" *Westways* 64 (January 1972): 22-24, 41, 58-59. Reprinted in *Southwest Classics*, Los Angeles: Ward Ritchie Press, 1974.

2379. Robinson, Cecil. "Legend of Destiny: The American Southwest in the Novels of Harvey Fergusson." *American West* 4 (November 1967): 16-18, 67-68.

2380. ———. *With the Ears of Strangers: The Mexican in American Literature.* Tucson: University of Arizona Press, 1963; rev. ed. *Mexico and the Hispanic Southwest in American Literature.* Tucson: University of Arizona Press, 1977.

2381. Thrift, Bonnie B. R. "Harvey Fergusson's Use of Southwest History and Customs in His Novels." Master's thesis, University of Texas, 1940.

LAWRENCE FERLINGHETTI

2382. Butler, J. A. "Ferlinghetti: Dirty Old Man?" *Renascence* 18 (Spring 1966): 115-23.

2383. Cherkovski, Neeli. *Ferlinghetti: A Biography.* Garden City, N.Y.: Doubleday, 1979.

2384. Cook, Bruce. *The Beat Generation.* New York: Charles Scribners, 1971.

2385. Ianni, L. A. "Lawrence Ferlinghetti's Fourth Person Singular and the Theory of Relativity." *Wisconsin Studies in Contemporary Literature* 8 (Summer 1967): 392-406.

2386. Lin, Maurice Yaofu. "Children of Adam: Ginsberg, Ferlinghetti and Snyder in the Emerson-Whitman Tradition." Doctoral dissertation, University of Minnsota, 1973.

2387. Skau, Michael. "Toward Underivative Creation: Lawrence Ferlinghetti's *Her.*" *Critique* 19, No. 3 (1978): 40-46.

THOMAS HORNSBY FERRIL

2388. Effinger, Cecil. "Music in the Poems of Thomas Hornsby Ferril." *Colorado Quarterly* 3 (Summer 1954): 59-66.

2389. Firebaugh, Joseph J. "Pioneer in the Parlor Car: Thomas Hornsby Ferril." *Prairie Schooner* 21 (Spring 1947): 69-85.

2390. Hollister, Marian E. "A Critical Analysis of Thomas Hornsby Ferril." Master's thesis, Colorado College, 1950.

2391. Richards, Robert F. "Literature and Politics." *Colorado Quarterly* 19 (Summer 1970): 97–106.

2392. ——. "The Long Dimension of Ferril's Poetry." *Colorado Quarterly* 3 (Summer 1954): 22–38.

2393. ——. "The Poetry of Thomas Hornsby Ferril." Doctoral dissertation, Columbia University, 1961.

2394. ——. "Thomas Hornsby Ferril: A Biographical Sketch." *Western American Literature* 9 (November 1974): 205–14.

2395. ——. "Thomas Hornsby Ferril and the Problems of the Poet in the West." *Kansas Quarterly* 2 (Spring 1970): 110–16.

2396. Roe, Margie M. "Thomas Hornsby Ferril, Poet and Critic of the Rocky Mountain Region." Master's thesis, Southern Methodist University, 1966.

2397. Scherting, Jack. "An Approach to the Western Poetry of Thomas Hornsby Ferril." *Western American Literature* 7 (Fall 1972): 179–90.

2398. ——. *The Works of Thomas Hornsby Ferril.* Cassette. Deland, Fla.: Everett/Edwards, 1974.

2399. Trusky, A. Thomas. *Thomas Hornsby Ferril.* Western Writers Series, No. 6. Boise, Idaho: Boise State College, 1973.

LESLIE FIEDLER

2400. Bellman, S. I. "The American Artist as European Frontiersman: Leslie Fiedler's *The Second Stone.*" *Critique* 6 (Winter 1963): 131–43.

2401. ——. "The Frontiers of Leslie Fiedler." *Southwest Review* 48 (Winter 1963): 86–89.

2402. Bluefarb, Sam. "Pictures of the Anti-Stereotype: Leslie Fiedler's Triptych, The Last Jew in America." *College Language Association Journal* 18 (1975): 412–21.

2403. Feinstein, Herbert. "Contemporary American Fiction: Harvey Swados and Leslie Fiedler." *Wisconsin Studies in Contemporary Literature* 2 (Winter 1961): 79–98.

2404. Larson, Charles R. "Leslie Fiedler: The Critic and the Myth, the Critic as Myth." *Literary Review* 14 (Winter 1970–71): 133–43.

2405. Schultz, Max F. *Radical Sophistication: Studies in Comtemporary Jewish-American Novelists.* Athens: Ohio University Press, 1969, pp. 154–72.

EUGENE FIELD

2406. Conrow, Robert. *Field Days.* New York: Charles Scribner's Sons, 1974.

2407. Smith, Duane A. "Eugene Field: Political Satirist." *Colorado Quarterly* 22 (1974): 495–508.

CLAY FISHER
See Henry Wilson Allen

VARDIS FISHER

2408. *American Book Collector* 14 (September 1963): 7-39. Special Fisher number.

2409. Arrington, Leonard J., and Jon Haupt. "The Mormon Heritage of Vardis Fisher." *Brigham Young University Studies* 18 (Fall 1977): 27-47.

2410. Bishop, John Peale. "The Strange Case of Vardis Fisher." *The Collected Essays of John Peale Bishop.* New York: Charles Scribner's Sons, 1948, pp. 56-65.

2411. ———. "The Strange Case of Vardis Fisher." *Southern Review* 3 (Autumn 1937): 348-59.

2412. Chatterton, Wayne. *Vardis Fisher: The Frontier and Regional Works.* Western Writers Series, No. 1. Boise, Idaho: Boise State College, 1972.

2413. Crandall, Allen. *Fisher of the Antelope Hills.* Manhattan, Kans.: Crandall Press, 1949.

2414. Davis, David Brion. "'Children of God': A Historian's Evaluation." *Western Humanities Review* 8 (Winter 1953): 49-56.

2415. Day, George F. *The Uses of History in the Novels of Vardis Fisher.* New York: Revisionist Press, 1976.

2416. Etulain, Richard W. [*sic*]. "The New Western Novel." *Idaho Yesterdays* 15 (Winter 1972): 12-17.

2417. Fisher, Vardis. "The Western Writer and the Eastern Establishment." *Western American Literature* 1 (Winter 1967): 244-59.

2418. Flora, Joseph M. "The Early Power of Vardis Fisher." *American Book Collector* 14 (September 1963): 15-19.

2419. ———. *Vardis Fisher.* New York: Twayne, 1965.

2420. ———. "Vardis Fisher and the Mormons." *Dialogue* 4 (Autumn 1969): 48-55.

2421. ———. "Vardis Fisher and James Branch Cabell: An Essay on Influence and Reputation." *Cabellian* 2 (Autumn 1969): 12-16.

2422. ———. "Vardis Fisher and Wallace Stegner: Teacher and Student." *Western American Literature* 5 (Summer 1970): 121-28.

2423. ———. "Westering and Woman: A Thematic Study of Kesey's *One Flew Over the Cuckoo's Nest* and Fisher's *Mountain Man.*" *Heritage of Kansas* 10 (Spring 1977): 3-14.

2424. Grover, Dorys C. *A Solitary Voice: Vardis Fisher, A Collection of Essays.* New York: Revisionist Press, 1973.

2425. ———. "A Study of the Poetry of Vardis Fisher." Doctoral dissertation, Washington State University, 1970.

2426. ———. "Vardis Fisher: The Antelope People Sonnets." *Texas Quarterly* 17 (Spring 1974): 97-106.

2427. ———. *The Works of Vardis Fisher.* Cassette. Deland, Fla.: Everett/Edwards, 1974.

2428. Hanks, Ida Mae. "Antelope, Idaho, in the Novels of Vardis Fisher." Master's thesis, University of Idaho, 1942.

2429. Hunsaker, Kenneth B. "The Twentieth Century Mormon Novel." Doctoral dissertation, Pennsylvania State University, 1968.

2430. Kellogg, George. "Vardis Fisher: A Bibliography." *Western American Literature* 5 (Spring 1970): 45-64.

2431. Long, Louise. "Children of God." *Southwest Review* 25 (October 1939): 102-8.

2432. McAllister, Mick. "You Can't Go Home: Jeremiah Johnson and the Wilderness." *Western American Literature* 13 (Spring 1978): 35-49.

2433. Meldrum, Barbara. "Vardis Fisher's Antelope People: Pursuing an Elusive Dream." *Northwest Perspectives: Essays on the Culture of the Pacific Northwest.* Eds. Edwin R. Bingham and Glen A. Love. Seattle: University of Washington Press, 1979, pp. 153-66.

2434. Milton, John R. *The Novel of the American West.* Lincoln: University of Nebraska Press, 1980, pp. 117-59.

2435. ——. "The Primitive World of Vardis Fisher: The Idaho Novels." *Midwest Quarterly* 17 (Summer 1976): 369-84.

2436. ——. *Three West: Conversations with Vardis Fisher, Max Evans, Michael Straight.* Vermillion, S.Dak.: Dakota Press, 1970.

2437. ——. "The Western Novel: Sources and Forms." *Chicago Review* 16 (Summer 1963): 74-100.

2438. Morton, Beatrice K. "An Early Stage of Fisher's Journey to the East, *Passions Spin the Plot.*" *South Dakota Review* 18 (Spring 1980): 43-52.

2439. Parkinson, Linda F. L. "Wider Than Mormonism: Vardis Fisher's Prophets and His Vision of Man." Master's thesis, University of Idaho, 1965.

2440. Rein, David. *Vardis Fisher: Challenge to Evasion.* Chicago: Black Cat Press, Normandie House, 1937.

2441. Snell, George. *Shapers of American Fiction.* New York: E. P. Dutton, 1943, pp. 276-88.

2442. Taber, Ronald W. "Sacajawea and the Suffragettes: An Interpretation of a Myth." *Pacific Northwest Quarterly* 58 (January 1967): 7-13.

2443. ——. "Vardis Fisher and the *Idaho Guide*: Preserving Culture for the New Deal." *Pacific Northwest Quarterly* 59 (April 1968): 68-76.

2444. ——. "Vardis Fisher: March 31, 1895-July 9, 1968." *Idaho Yesterdays* 12 (Fall 1968): 2-8.

2445. ——. "Vardis Fisher: New Directions for the Historical Novel." *Western American Literature* 1 (Winter 1967): 285-96.

2446. Thomas, Alfred Krupp. "The Epic of Evolution, Its Etiology and Art: A Study of Vardis Fisher's *Testament of*

Man." Doctoral dissertation, Pennsylvania State University, 1967.

F. SCOTT FITZGERALD

2447. Gross, Barry. "Back West: Time and Place in *The Great Gatsby.*" *Western American Literature* 8 (Spring-Summer 1973): 3-13.
2448. Reiter, Joan Govan. "F. Scott Fitzgerald: Hollywood as Literary Material." Doctoral dissertation, Northwestern University, 1972.

JOHN GOULD FLETCHER

2449. Aldrich, Ann R. "Regionalism in the Writings of John Gould Fletcher." Doctoral dissertation, University of Arkansas, 1975.
2450. Douglass, Thomas E. "The Correspondence of John Gould Fletcher: A Catalogue." Doctoral dissertation, University of Arkansas, 1965. A guide to the correspondence at the University of Arkansas.
2451. Morton, Bruce. *John Gould Fletcher: A Bibliography.* Kent, Ohio: Kent State University Press, 1979.
2452. Stephens, Edna Buell. *John Gould Fletcher.* New York: Twayne, 1967.

TIMOTHY FLINT

2453. Flint, Timothy. *Recollections of the Last Ten Years.* Boston, 1826; New York: Alfred A. Knopf, 1932.
2454. Folsom, James K. *Timothy Flint.* New York: Twayne, 1965.
2455. Hamilton, John A. "Timothy Flint's 'Lost Novel.'" *American Literature* 22 (March 1950): 54-56.
2456. Kirkpatrick, John Ervin. *Timothy Flint.* Cleveland: Arthur H. Clark, 1911.
2457. Lee, Robert Edson. *From West to East.* Urbana: University of Illinois Press, 1966, pp. 39-54.
2458. Lombard, C. "Timothy Flint: Early American Disciple of French Romanticism." *Revue de Littérature Comparée* 36 (April-June 1962): 276-82.
2459. Morris, Robert L. "Three Arkansas Travelers." *Arkansas Historical Quarterly* 4 (Autumn 1945): 215-30.
2460. Seelye, John D. "Timothy Flint's 'Wicked River' and *The Confidence Man.*" *PMLA* 78 (March 1963): 75-79.
2461. Stimson, Frederick S. "'Francis Berrian': Hispanic Influence on American Romanticism." *Hispanica* 42 (December 1959): 511-16.
2462. Turner, Arlin. "James K. Paulding and Timothy Flint." *Mississippi Valley Historical Review* 34 (June 1947): 105-11.
2463. Vorpahl, Ben Merchant. "The Eden Theme and Three Novels by Timothy Flint." *Studies in Romanticism* 10 (Spring 1971): 105-29.

2464. Walker, Lennie Merle. "Picturesque New Mexico Revealed in Novel as Early as 1826." *New Mexico Historical Review* 13 (July 1938): 325-28.

ROBERT FLYNN

2465. Etulain, Richard. "Recent Western Fiction." *Journal of the West* 8 (October 1969): 656-58.

MARY HALLOCK FOOTE

2466. Armitage, Shelley. "Mary Haddock [*sic*] Foote." *Southwest Heritage* 9 (Winter 1979-80): 2-7.

2467. Benn, Mary Lou. "Mary Hallock Foote: Early Leadville Writer." *Colorado Magazine* 33 (April 1956): 93-103.

2468. ——. "Mary Hallock Foote in Idaho." *University of Wyoming Publications* 20 (July 1956): 157-78.

2469. ——. "Mary Hallock Foote: Pioneer Woman Novelist." Master's thesis, University of Wyoming, 1965.

2470. Cragg, Barbara. "Mary Hallock Foote's Images of the Old West." *Landscape* 24 (Winter 1980): 42-47.

2471. Etulain, Richard W. "Mary Hallock Foote: A Checklist." *Western American Literature* 10 (May 1975): 59-65.

2472. ——. "Mary Hallock Foote (1847-1938)." *American Literary Realism 1870-1910* 5 (Spring 1972): 145-50.

2473. Foote, Arthur B. "Memoir of Arthur DeWint Foote." *Transactions of the American Society of Civil Engineers* 99 (1934): 1449-52.

2474. Johnson, Lee Ann. *Mary Hallock Foote.* Boston: Twayne, 1980.

2475. Maguire, James H. *Mary Hallock Foote.* Western Writers Series, No. 2. Boise, Idaho: Boise State College, 1972.

2476. Paul, Rodman W. "When Culture Came to Boise: Mary Hallock Foote in Idaho." *Idaho Yesterdays* 20 (Summer 1976): 2-12.

2477. ——, ed. *A Victorian Gentlewoman in the Far West: The Reminiscences of Mary Hallock Foote.* San Marino, Calif.: Huntington Library, 1972.

2478. Taft, Robert. *Artists and Illustrators of the Old West: 1850-1900.* New York: Charles Scribner's Sons, 1953, pp. 172-75, 345-47.

GEORGE C. FRASER

2479. Jett, Stephen C. "The Journals of George C. Fraser '93: Early Twentieth-Century Travels in the South and Southwest." *Princeton University Library Chronicle* 35 (1974): 290-308.

WAYNE GARD

2480. Adams, Ramon F. *Wayne Gard: Historian of the West.* Southwest Writers Series, No. 31. Austin, Tex.: Steck-Vaughn, 1970.

HAMLIN GARLAND

2481. Ahnebrink, Lars. *The Beginnings of Naturalism in American Fiction, 1891-1903.* Upsala, 1950, pp. 63-89; New York: Russell & Russell, 1961.

2482. Alsen, Eberhard. "Hamlin Garland's First Novel: *A Spoil of Office.*" *Western American Literature* 4 (Summer 1969): 91-105.

2483. Arvidson, Lloyd A. "A Bibliography of the Published Writings of Hamlin Garland." Master's thesis, University of Southern California, 1952.

2484. ——, ed. *Centennial Tributes and a Checklist of the Hamlin Garland Papers in the University of Southern California Library.* Los Angeles: University of Southern California Library, 1962.

2485. Bryer, Jackson R., and Eugene Harding. "Hamlin Garland (1860-1940): A Bibliography of Secondary Comment." *American Literary Realism 1870-1910* 3 (Fall 1970): 290-387.

2486. ——. *Hamlin Garland and the Critics: An Annotated Bibliography.* Troy, N.Y.: Whitston, 1973.

2487. ——. "Hamlin Garland: Reviews and Notices of His Work." *American Literary Realism 1870-1910* 4 (Spring 1971): 102-56.

2488. Carter, Joseph L. "Hamlin Garland and the Western Myth." Doctoral dissertation, Kent State University, 1973.

2489. ——. "Hamlin Garland's Liberated Women." *American Literary Realism 1870-1910* 6 (Summer 1973): 255-58.

2490. Culbert, Gary Allen. "Hamlin Garland's Image of Woman: An Allegiance to Ideality." Doctoral dissertation, University of Wisconsin, Madison, 1974.

2491. Davis, Jack L. "Hamlin Garland's Indians and the Quality of Civilized Life." *Where the West Begins.* Eds. Arthur R. Huseboe and William Geyer. Sioux Falls, S.Dak.: Center for Western Studies Press, 1978, pp. 51-62.

2492. Duffey, Bernard. "Hamlin Garland's 'Decline' from Realism." *American Literature* 25 (March 1953): 69-74.

2493. Evans, T. Jeff. "The Return Motif as a Function of Realism in *Main-Travelled Roads.*" *Kansas Quarterly* 5 (Fall 1973): 33-40.

2494. Fite, Gilbert. "Hamlin Garland and the Farmers' Frontier." *Heritage of Kansas* 10 (Summer 1977): 3-9.

2495. Fleeger, Wayne Robert. "Garland's Middle Period: Romantic Fiction, 1898-1916." Doctoral dissertation, Drake University, 1977.

2496. French, Warren. "What Shall We Do About Hamlin Garland?" *American Literary Realism 1870-1910* 3 (Fall 1970): 283-89.

2497. Fujii, Gertrude Sugioka. "The Veritism of Hamlin Garland."

Doctoral dissertation, University of Southern California, 1970.

2498. Garland, Hamlin. "The West in Literature." *Arena* 6 (1892): 669-76.

2499. Gish, Robert F. "Desertion and Rescue on the Dakota Plains: Hamlin Garland in the Land of the Straddle-Bug." *South Dakota Review* 16 (Autumn 1978): 30-45.

2500. ——. *Hamlin Garland: The Far West.* Western Writers Series, No. 24. Boise, Idaho: Boise State University, 1976.

2501. ——. "Hamlin Garland's Dakota: History and Story." *South Dakota History* 9 (Summer 1979): 193-209.

2502. ——. "Hamlin Garland's Northwest Travels: 'Camp' Westering." *The Westering Experience in American Literature: Bicentennial Essays.* Eds. Merrill Lewis and L. L. Lee. Bellingham: Bureau for Faculty Research, Western Washington University, 1977, pp. 94-105.

2503. Gronewold, Benjamin F. "The Social Criticism of Hamlin Garland." Doctoral dissertation, New York University, 1943.

2504. Harris, Elbert L. "Hamlin Garland's Use of the American Scene in His Fiction." Doctoral dissertation, University of Pennsylvania, 1959.

2505. Harrison, Stanley R. "Hamlin Garland and the Double Vision of Naturalism." *Studies in Short Fiction* 6 (Fall 1969): 548-56.

2506. Harver, Hyla Hope. "The Influence of Scientific Theories of Expression on Garland's *Main Travelled Roads.*" Doctoral dissertation, University of Tulsa, 1973.

2507. Higgins, J. E. "A Man from the Middle Borders: Hamlin Garland's Diaries." *Wisconsin Magazine of History* 46 (Summer 1963): 295-302.

2508. Hill, Eldon C. "A Biographical Study of Hamlin Garland from 1860 to 1895." Doctoral dissertation, Ohio State University, 1940.

2509. Hiscoe, David W. "Feeding and Consuming in Garland's *Main-Travelled Roads.*" *Western American Literature* 15 (May 1980): 3-15.

2510. Holloway, Jean. *Hamlin Garland: A Biography.* Austin: University of Texas Press, 1960.

2511. Holsinger, Paul M. "Hamlin Garland's Colorado." *Colorado Magazine* 44 (Winter 1967): 1-10.

2512. Houston, Neal B. "A Dedication to . . . Hamlin Garland: 1860-1940." *Arizona and the West* 11 (Autumn 1969): 209-12.

2513. Kaye, Frances W. "Hamlin Garland: A Closer Look at the Later Fiction." *North Dakota Quarterly* 43 (1976): 45-56.

2514. ——. "Hamlin Garland and Frederick Philip Grove: Self-Conscious Chronicles of the Pioneers." *Canadian Review of American Studies* 10 (Spring 1979): 31-39.

143

2515. Koerner, James D. "Comment on 'Hamlin Garland's "Decline" from Realism.'" *American Literature* 26 (November 1954): 427-32.

2516. Larkin, Sharon. "The Warning of the American Agrarian Myth: Garland and the Garden." *Heritage of Kansas* 9 (Spring 1976): 19-27.

2517. Littlefield, Daniel F., Jr., and Lonnie E. Underhill. "The Emerging New West in Hamlin Garland's Fiction, 1910-1916." *Markham Review* 9 (Winter 1980): 35-40.

2518. McCullough, Joseph B. *Hamlin Garland.* Boston: Twayne, 1978.

2519. ——. "Hamlin Garland's Quarrel with *The Dial.*" *American Literary Realism 1870-1910* 9 (Winter 1976): 77-80.

2520. ——. "Hamlin Garland's Letters to James Whitcomb Riley." *American Literary Realism 1870-1910* 9 (Summer 1976): 249-60.

2521. Mane, Robert. *Hamlin Garland: L'Homme et L'oeuvre (1860-1940).* Paris: Didier, 1968.

2522. Martinec, Barbara. "Hamlin Garland's Revisions of *Main-Travelled Roads.*" *American Literary Realism 1870-1910* 5 (Spring 1972): 167-72.

2523. Meyer, Roy W. "Hamlin Garland and the American Indian." *Western American Literature* 2 (Summer 1967): 109-25.

2524. Miller, Charles T. "Hamlin Garland's Retreat from Realism." *Western American Literature* 1 (Summer 1966): 119-29.

2525. Morgan, H. Wayne. *American Writers in Rebellion: From Mark Twain to Dreiser.* New York: Hill and Wang, 1965.

2526. Neumann, Edwin J. "Hamlin Garland and the Mountain West." Doctoral dissertation, Northwestern University, 1951.

2527. Pilkington, John. "Fuller, Garland, Taft, and the Art of the West." *Publications in Language and Literature* 8 (Fall 1972, supplement): 39-56.

2528. Pizer, Donald. "Hamlin Garland (1860-1940)." *American Literary Realism 1870-1910* 1 (Fall 1967): 45-51.

2529. ——. "Hamlin Garland: A Bibliography of Newspaper and Periodical Publications (1885-1895)." *Bulletin of Bibliography* 22 (January-April 1957): 41-44.

2530. ——. "Hamlin Garland's *A Son of the Middle Border*: An Appreciation." *South Atlantic Quarterly* 65 (Autumn 1966): 448-59.

2531. ——. "Hamlin Garland's *A Son of the Middle Border*: Autobiography as Art." *Essays in American and English Literature Presented to Bruce Robert McElderry, Jr.* Ed. Max F. Schultz, et al. Athens: Ohio University Press, 1967, pp. 76-107.

2532. ——. *Hamlin Garland's Early Work and Career.* Berkeley: University of California Press, 1960.

2533. ——, ed. *Hamlin Garland's Diaries*. San Marino, Calif.: Huntington Library, 1968.

2534. Reamer, Owen J. "Garland and the Indians." *New Mexico Quarterly* 34 (Autumn 1964): 257-80.

2535. ——. "Hamlin Garland: Literary Pioneer and Typical American." Doctoral dissertation, University of Texas, 1951.

2536. Saum, Lewis O. "Hamlin Garland and Reform." *South Dakota Review* 10 (Winter 1972-73): 36-62.

2537. Savage, George Howard. "'Synthetic Evolution' and the American West: The Influence of Herbert Spencer on the Later Novels of Hamlin Garland." Doctoral dissertation, University of Tulsa, 1974.

2538. Silet, Charles L. P. *Henry Blake Fuller and Hamlin Garland—A Reference Guide*. Boston: G. K. Hall, 1977.

2539. ——, and Robert E. Welch. "Further Additions to *Hamlin Garland and the Critics*." *American Literary Realism 1870-1910* 9 (Summer 1976): 268-75.

2540. Simpson, Claude M., Jr. "Hamlin Garland's Decline." *Southwest Review* 26 (Winter 1941): 223-34.

2541. Stronks, James. "A Supplement to Bryer & Harding's *Hamlin Garland and the Critics/An Annotated Bibliography*." *American Literary Realism 1870-1910* 9 (Summer 1976): 261-67.

2542. ——. "Supplements to the Standard Bibliographies of Crane, Dreiser, Frederick, Fuller, Garland, London, and Norris." *American Literary Realism 1870-1910* 11 (Spring 1978): 124-33.

2543. Taylor, Walter F. *The Economic Novel in America*. Chapel Hill: University of North Carolina Press, 1942, pp. 148-83.

2544. Underhill, Lonnie E., and Daniel F. Littlefield, Jr. "Hamlin Garland and the Navajos." *Journal of Arizona History* 13 (Winter 1972): 275-85.

2545. ——, eds. *Hamlin Garland's Observations on the American Indian 1895-1905*. Tucson: University of Arizona Press, 1976.

2346. Vogelbaum, Alexandra Doris van Ophuijsen. "The New Heroines: The Emergence of Sexuality in the Treatment of the American Fictional Heroine, 1890-1900." Doctoral dissertation, Tulane University, 1978.

2547. Wagner, William D. "The Short Stories of Hamlin Garland." Doctoral dissertation, Bowling Green State University, 1972.

2548. Walcutt, Charles Child. *American Literary Naturalism, A Divided Stream*. Minneapolis: University of Minnesota Press, 1956, pp. 53-65 and passim.

2549. Whitford, Kathryn. "Crusader Without a Cause: An Examination of Hamlin Garland's Middle Border." *Midcontinent American Studies*

Journal 6 (Spring 1965): 61-72.

2550. ———. "Patterns of Observation: A Study of Hamlin Garland's Middle Border Landscape." *Transactions of the Wisconsin Academy of Science, Arts, and Letters* 50 (1961): 331-38.

HECTOR LEWIS GARRARD
(Lewis H. Garrard)

2551. Bewley, Marius. "*Wah-To-Yah and the Taos Trail*: A Minor Classic." *Masks and Mirrors*. New York: Atheneum, 1970, pp. 221-25.

2552. Bieber, Ralph P. "Editor's Introduction." *Wah-to-Yah, and the Taos Trail* by Lewis Hector Garrard. Glendale, Calif.: Arthur H. Clark, 1938.

2553. Foster, Edward Halsey. *Josiah Gregg and Lewis H. Garrard*. Western Writers Series, No. 28. Boise, Idaho: Boise State University, 1977.

2554. Guthrie, A. B., Jr. "Introduction." *Wah-To-Yah and the Taos Trail*. Norman: University of Oklahoma Press, 1955, pp. ix-xvi.

2555. Meyer, Roy W. "New Light on Lewis Garrard." *Western Historical Quarterly* 6 (July 1975): 261-78.

2556. Powell, Lawrence Clark. "Southwest Classics Reread: Two for the Santa Fe Trail." *Westways* 64 (October 1972): 56-59, 73-74.

FREDERICH GERSTÄCKER

2557. Bukey, E. B. "Frederick Gerstaecker and Arkansas." *Arkansas Historical Quarterly* 31 (Spring 1972): 3-14.

2558. Kolb, Alfred. "Friedrich Gerstäcker and the American Dream." *Modern Language Studies* 5 (1975): 103-8.

2559. ———. "Friedrich Gerstäcker and the American Frontier." Doctoral dissertation, Syracuse University, 1966.

2560. ———. "Gerstäcker's America." *Thoth* 7 (Winter 1966): 12-21.

2561. Steeves, Harrison R. "The First of the Westerns." *Southwest Review* 53 (Winter 1968): 74-84.

BREWSTER GHISELIN

2562. Raine, Kathleen. "Country of the Minotaur." *Sewanee Review* 79 (1971): 288-92.

2563. Smith, Dave. "The Poetry of Brewster Ghiselin." *Western Humanities Review* 35 (Summer 1981): 162-65.

ARCHER B. GILFILLAN

2564. McLean, Austin J. "A Herder's Life in South Dakota: The Cipher Diary of Archer B. Gilfillan." *Where The West Begins*. Ed. Arthur R. Huseboe and William Geyer. Sioux Falls, S.Dak.: Center for Western Studies Press, 1978, pp. 63-71.

ALLEN GINSBERG

2565. Ball, Gordon, ed. *Allen Verbatim.* New York: McGraw-Hill, 1974.

2566. Bett, Carolyn E. "The Poetry of Allen Ginsberg." Master's thesis, University of Toronto, 1967.

2567. Cook, Bruce. *The Beat Generation.* New York: Charles Scribner's Sons, 1971.

2568. Dowden, George, comp. *A Bibliography of Works by Allen Ginsberg.* San Francisco: City Lights Books, 1971.

2569. Eckman, Frederick. "Neither Tame nor Fleecy." *Poetry* 90 (September 1957): 386-97.

2570. Ehrlich, J. W. *Howl of the Censor.* San Carlos, Calif., 1961.

2571. Ginsberg, Allen. *Journals: Early Fifties–Early Sixties.* New York: Grove Press, 1977.

2572. Golffing, Francis, and Barbara Gibbs. "The Public Voice: Remarks on Poetry Today," *Commentary* 28 (July 1959): 63-69.

2573. Hahn, Stephen. "The Prophetic Voice of Allen Ginsberg." *Prospects: An Annual of American Cultural Studies.* Vol. 2. Ed. Jack Salzman. New York: Burt Franklin, 1976, pp. 527-67.

2574. Kramer, Jane. *Allen Ginsberg in America.* New York: Random House, 1968.

2575. Kraus, Michelle P. *Allen Ginsberg: An Annotated Bibliography.* Metuchen, N.J.: Scarecrow, 1980.

2576. Menkin, E. Z. "Allen Ginsberg: A Bibliographical and Biographical Sketch." *Thoth* 8 (Winter 1967): 35-40.

2577. Merrill, Thomas F. *Allen Ginsberg.* New York: Twayne, 1969.

2578. Molesworth, Charles. *The Fierce Embrace: A Study of Contemporary American Poetry.* Columbia: University of Missouri Press, 1979.

2579. Penglase, John Dols. "Allen Ginsberg: The Flowering Vision of the Heart." Doctoral dissertation, University of Wisconsin, Milwaukee, 1975.

2580. Rosenthal, M. L. *The New Poetry.* New York: Macmillan, 1967.

2581. Rumaker, Michael. "Allen Ginsberg's *Howl.*" *Black Mountain Review* 7 (Autumn 1957): 228-37.

2582. Trilling, Diana. "The Other Night at Columbia." *Partisan Review* 26 (Spring 1959): 214-30.

2583. Tytell, John. *Naked Angels: The Lives and Literature of the Beat Generation.* New York: McGraw-Hill, 1976.

FRED GIPSON

2584. Henderson, Sam H. *Fred Gipson.* Southwest Writers Series, No. 10. Austin, Tex.: Steck-Vaughn, 1967.

2585. Polk, Stella Gipson. "My

Brother—Fred Gipson." *True West* 21 (July-August 1974): 16-18.

FREDERICK GLIDDEN
(Luke Short)

2586. Gale, Robert L. *Luke Short.* Boston: Twayne, 1981.
2587. Nye, Russel B. *The Unembarrassed Muse: The Popular Arts in America.* New York: Dial Press, 1970.
2588. Olsen, T. V. "Luke Short, Writer's Writer." *Roundup* 21 (March 1973): 10-11, 13.
2589. Short, Luke. "Ernest Haycox: An Appreciation." *Call Number* 25 (Fall 1963-Spring 1964): 2-3.
2590. Thomas, Phillip D. "The Paperback West of Luke Short." *Journal of Popular Culture* 7 (Winter 1973): 701-8.

CAROLINE GORDON

2591. Rodenberger, M. Lou. "Folk Narrative in Caroline Gordon's Frontier Fiction." *Heritage of Kansas* 10 (Summer 1977): 32-40.

WILLIAM GOYEN

2592. Duncan, Erika. "Come a Spiritual Healer: A Profile of William Goyen." *Book Forum* 3 (1977): 296-303. Includes a bibliography.
2593. Gossett, Louise Y. "The Voices of Distance: William Goyen." *Violence in Recent Southern*

Fiction. Durham, N.C.: Duke University Press, 1965, pp. 131-45.
2594. Grimm, Clyde L., Jr. "William Goyen: A Bibliographic Chronicle." *Bulletin of Bibliography* 35 (July-September 1978): 123-31.
2595. Paul, Jay S. "'Marvelous Reciprocity': The Fiction of William Goyen." *Critique* 19, no. 2 (1977): 77-92.
2596. Phillips, Robert. "The Art of Fiction, LXIII." *Paris Review* 68 (Winter 1976): 58-100.
2597. ——. "The Romance of Prophecy: Goyen's *In a Farther Country.*" *Southwest Review* 56 (Summer 1971): 213-20.
2598. ——. "Secret and Symbol: Entrances to Goyen's *House of Breath.*" *Southwest Review* 59 (Summer 1974): 248-53.
2599. ——. *William Goyen.* Boston: Twayne, 1979.
2600. Stern, Daniel. "On William Goyen's *The House of Breath.*" *Rediscoveries.* Ed. David Madden. New York: Crown, 1971, pp. 256-69.

JOHN GRAVES

2601. Bradford, M. E. "Arden up the Brazos: John Graves and the Uses of Pastoral." *Southern Review* 8 (October 1972): 949-55. An essay review.
2602. ——. "In Keeping with the Way: John Graves's *Hard Scrabble.*" *Southwest Review* 60 (Spring 1975): 190-95.

148

JOSIAH GREGG

2603. Foster, Edward Halsey. *Josiah Gregg and Lewis H. Garrard.* Western Writers Series, No. 28. Boise, Idaho: Boise State University, 1977.

2604. Gregg, Josiah. *Diary and Letters.* 2 vols. Ed. Maurice Garland Fulton. Norman: University of Oklahoma Press, 1941-44.

2605. Horgan, Paul. *Josiah Gregg and His Vision of the Early Far West.* New York: Farrar Straus and Giroux, 1979.

2606. ——. "The Prairies Revisited: A Re-estimation of Josiah Gregg." *Southwest Review* 26 (Winter 1941): 145-66.

2607. Lee, John Thomas. "The Authorship of Gregg's *Commerce of the Prairies.*" *Mississippi Valley Historical Review* 16 (March 1930): 451-66.

2608. Powell, Lawrence C. "Josiah Gregg's *Commerce of the Prairies.*" *Westways* 63 (May 1971): 14-17, 68-70.

2609. Twitchell, Ralph Emerson. *Dr. Josiah Gregg: Historian of the Santa Fe Trail.* Santa Fe: Santa Fe New Mexican, 1924.

ZANE GREY

2610. Ball, Lee, Jr. "Zane Grey's Novels as History: A Review Essay." *Red River Valley Historical Review* I (Winter 1974).

2611. Bauer, Erwin A. "Ohio's Writer of the Purple Sage," in Zane Grey, *Blue Feather and Other Stories.* New York: Harper and Brothers, 1961, pp. 229-34.

2612. Cawelti, John G. *Adventure, Mystery, and Romance: Formula Stories as Art and Popular Culture.* Chicago: University of Chicago Press, 1976, pp. 215-30.

2613. Etulain, Richard W. "A Dedication to . . . Zane Grey 1872-1939." *Arizona and the West* 12 (Autumn 1970): 217-20.

2614. Gentles, Ruth G. *The Zane Grey Omnibus.* New York: Harper and Brothers, 1943.

2615. Goble, Danney. "'The Days That Were No More': A Look at Zane Grey's West." *Journal of Arizona History* 14 (Spring 1973): 63-75.

2616. ——. "Zane Grey's West: An Intellectual Reaction." Master's thesis, University of Oklahoma, 1969.

2617. Grey, Zane. "Breaking Through: The Story of My Own Life." *American Magazine* 97 (July 1924): 11-13 ff.

2618. Gruber, Frank. *Zane Grey: A Biography.* New York: World, 1970.

2619. Jackson, Carlton. *Zane Grey.* New York: Twayne, 1973.

2620. Karr, Jean. *Zane Grey: Man of the West.* New York: Greenberg, 1949.

2621. Patrick, A. "Getting into Six Figures: Zane Grey." *Bookman* 60 (December 1924): 424-29.

2622. Powell, L. C. "Books Determine." *Wilson Library Bulletin*

30 (September 1955): 62-65.

2623. ———. "Southwest Classics Reread: Writer of the Purple Sage." *Westways* 64 (August 1972): 50-55, 69.

2624. Ronald, Ann. *Zane Grey.* Western Writers Series No. 17. Boise, Idaho: Boise State University, 1975.

2625. Schneider, Norris F. *Zane Grey.* ... Zanesville, Ohio: n.p., 1967.

2626. Scott, Kenneth W. *"The Heritage of the Desert*: Zane Grey Discovers the West." *Markham Review* 2 (February 1970): 10-15.

2627. ———. *Zane Grey. Born to West: A Reference Guide.* Boston: G. K. Hall, 1979.

2628. Stott, Graham St. John. "Zane Grey and James Simpson Emmett." *Brigham Young University Studies* 18 (Summer 1978): 491-503.

2629. Topping, Gary. "The Pastoral Ideal in Popular American Literature: Zane Grey and Edgar Rice Burroughs." *Rendezvous* 12 (Fall 1977): 11-25.

2630. ———. "Zane Grey: A Literary Reassessment." *Western American Literature* 13 (Spring 1978): 51-64.

2631. ———. "Zane Grey in Zion: An Examination of His Supposed Anti-Mormonism." *Brigham Young University Studies* 18 (Summer 1978): 483-90.

2632. ———. "Zane Grey's West." *Journal of Popular Culture* 7 (Winter 1973): 681-89.

2633. ———. "Zane Grey's West: Essays in Intellectual History and Criticism." Doctoral dissertation, University of Utah, 1977.

2634. Walle, Alf Howard, III. "The Frontier Hero: A Static Figure in an Evolving World." Doctoral dissertation, State University of New York, Buffalo, 1976.

2635. Wheeler, Joseph Lawrence. "Zane Grey's Impact on American Life and Letters: A Study in the Popular Novel." Doctoral dissertation, George Peabody College for Teachers, 1975.

2636. Whipple, T. K. "American Sagas." *Study Out the Land.* Berkeley: University of California Press, 1943, pp. 19-29.

2637. Wilson, Daniel J. "Nature in Western Popular Literature from the Dime Novel to Zane Grey." *North Dakota Quarterly* 44 (Spring 1976): 41-50.

2638. *Zane Grey, The Man and His Works.* New York: Harper & Brothers, 1928. A collection of essays about Grey.

JOHN HOWARD GRIFFIN

2639. Campbell, Jeff H. *John Howard Griffin.* Southwest Writers Series, No. 35. Austin, Tex.: Steck-Vaughn, 1970.

2640. Geismar, Maxwell. "John Howard Griffin: The Devil in Texas." *American Moderns.* New York: Hill and Wang, 1958, pp. 251-65.

2641. McDonnell, Thomas P. "John Howard Griffin: An Interview." *Ramparts* 1 (January 1963): 6-16.

A. B. GUTHRIE, JR.

2642. Allred, Jared Rulon. "A. B. Guthrie, Jr.: The Artist in the Wilderness." Doctoral dissertation, University of Utah, 1972-73.

2643. ——. "The Magical West of A. B. Guthrie." *Possible Sack* 4 (April 1973): 1-5.

2644. Arpin, Roger C. "A. B. Guthrie's *The Big Sky*: The Reshaping of a Myth." *Publications of the Arkansas Philological Association* 3 (1977): 1-5.

2645. Astro, Richard. "*The Big Sky* and the Limits of Wilderness Fiction." *Western American Literature* 9 (August 1974): 105-14.

2646. Coon, Gilbert D. "A. B. Guthrie, Jr.'s Tetralogy: An American Synthesis." *North Dakota Quarterly* 44 (Spring 1976): 73-80.

2647. ——. "A Study of A. B. Guthrie, Jr., and His Tetralogy." Doctoral dissertation, Washington State University, 1972.

2648. Cracroft, Richard H. "*The Big Sky*: A. B. Guthrie's Use of Historical Sources." *Western American Literature* 6 (Fall 1971): 163-76.

2649. Erisman, Fred. "The Education of Jason Beard: A. B. Guthrie's Western Suspense Stories." *Clues* 1 (1980): 126-31.

2650. ——. "Introduction" to A. B. Guthrie, Jr., *These Thousand Hills.* Boston: Gregg Press, 1979, pp. v-xii.

2651. ——. "Western Fiction as an Ecological Parable." *Environmental Review* 2 (Spring 1978): 15-23.

2652. Etulain, Richard W. "A. B. Guthrie: A Bibliography." *Western American Literature* 4 (Summer 1969): 133-38.

2653. ——. "Introduction" to A. B. Guthrie, Jr., *The Big It and Other Stories.* Boston: Gregg Press, 1980, pp. v-x.

2654. Falk, Armand. "The Riddle of Experience." Master's thesis, University of Montana, 1965.

2655. Folsom, James K. *The American Western Novel.* New Haven, Conn.: College and University Press, 1966, pp. 64-76.

2656. Ford, Thomas W. *A. B. Guthrie, Jr.* Southwest Writers Series, No. 15. Austin, Tex.: Steck-Vaughn, 1968.

2657. ——. *A. B. Guthrie, Jr.* Boston: Twayne, 1981.

2658. Guthrie, A. B., Jr. *The Blue Hen's Chick.* New York: McGraw-Hill, 1965.

2659. Hairston, Joe B. "Community in the West." *South Dakota Review* 11 (Spring 1973): 17-26.

2660. Hodgins, Francis E., Jr. "The Literary Emancipation of a Region. . . ." Doctoral dissertation, Michigan State University, 1957, pp. 485-517.

2661. Hood, Charles E. "Hard Work and Tough Dreaming: A Biography of A. B. Guthrie, Jr." Master's thesis, University of Montana, 1969.

2662. ——. "The Man and the Book:

Guthrie's *The Big Sky*." *Montana Journalism Review* 14 (1971): 6-15.

2663. Kite, Merilyn. "A. B. Guthrie, Jr.: A Critical Evaluation of His Works." Master's thesis, University of Wyoming, 1965.

2664. Kohler, Dayton. "A. B. Guthrie, Jr. and the West." *College English* 12 (February 1951): 249-56. Also in *English Journal* 40 (February 1951): 65-72.

2665. Lansaw, Paul. "The Big Skywriter." *Westways* 65 (July 1973): 24-26, 75.

2666. Milton, John R. *The Novel of the American West*. Lincoln: University of Nebraska Press, 1980, pp. 160-94.

2667. Mitchell, Mildred. "The Women in A. B. Guthrie's Novels." Master's thesis, Southwest Texas State College, 1965.

2668. Putnam, Jackson K. "Down to Earth: A. B. Guthrie's Quest for Moral and Historical Truth." *Essays on Western History. . . .* Grand Forks: University of North Dakota Press, 1970, pp. 51-61.

2669. Ray, Charles Eugene. "An Interdisciplinary Study Based on Four Selected Novels by A. B. Guthrie, Jr." Doctoral dissertation, Middle Tennessee State University, 1974.

2670. Stegner, Wallace. "Foreword." Sentry Edition of *The Big Sky*. Boston: Houghton Mifflin, 1965.

2671. Stephan, Peter M. "Fact, Interpretation, and Theme in the Historical Novels of A. B. Guthrie, Jr." Master's thesis, North Texas State University, 1968.

2672. Stewart, Donald C. "A. B. Guthrie's Vanishing Paradise: An Essay on Historical Fiction." *Journal of the West* 15 (July 1976): 83-96.

2673. ———. "The Functions of Bird and Sky Imagery in A. B. Guthrie's *The Big Sky*." *Critique* 19 (1977): 53-61.

2674. Stineback, David C. "On History and Its Consequences: A. B. Guthrie's *These Thousand Hills*." *Western American Literature* 6 (Fall 1971): 177-89.

2675. W[alker], D[on] D. "The Indian in Him: A Note on the Conception of Evil in A. B. Guthrie's First Novel." *Possible Sack* 2 (May 1971): 11-13.

2676. ———. "The Mountain Man as Literary Hero." *Western American Literature* 1 (Spring 1966): 15-25.

2677. ———. "The Primitivistic and the Historical in Guthrie's Fiction." *Possible Sack* 2 (June 1971): 1-5.

2678. Williams, John. "The 'Western': Definition of the Myth." *Nation* 193 (November 18, 1961): 401-6.

2679. Young, Vernon. "An American Dream and Its Parody." *Arizona Quarterly* 6 (Summer 1950): 112-23.

JOHN HAINES

2680. Allen, Carolyn J. "Death and Dreams in John Haines' *Writers News.*" *Alaska Review* 4 (Fall-Winter 1969): 28-36.
2681. Wilson, James R. "Relentless Self-Scrutiny: The Poetry of John Haines." *Alaska Review* 4 (Fall-Winter 1969): 16-27.

J. EVETTS HALEY

2682. Bradford, M. E. "The Care and Keeping of Memory: J. Evetts Haley and Plutarchian Biography." *Southwestern American Literature* 3 (1973): 69-76.
2683. Robinson, Chandler A. *J. Evetts Haley: Cowman-Historian.* El Paso, Tex.: Carl Hertzog, 1967.

DICK WICK HALL

2684. Boyer, Mary G., ed. "Dick Wick Hall." *Arizona in Literature.* Glendale, Calif.: Arthur H. Clark, 1935, pp. 495-511.
2685. Mitten, Irma Catherine. "The Life and Literary Career of Dick Wick Hall, Arizona Humorist." Master's thesis, University of Southern California, 1940.
2686. Myers, Samuel L. "Dick Wick Hall: Humorist with a Serious Purpose." *Journal of Arizona History* 11 (Winter 1970): 255-78.
2687. Nutt, Francis Dorothy. *Dick Wick Hall: Stories From the Salome Sun by Arizona's Most Famous Humorist.* Flagstaff, Ariz.: Northland Press, 1968.

HAZEL HALL

2688. Matthews, Eleanor H. "Hazel Hall." *An Anthology of Northwest Writing: 1900-1950.* Ed. Michael Strelow, et al. Eugene, Oreg.: Northwest Review Books, 1979, pp. 98-103.

JAMES HALL

2689. Donald, David. "The Autobiography of James Hall, Western Literary Pioneer." *Ohio State Archaeological and Historical Quarterly* 56 (1947): 295-304.
2690. Flanagan, John T. *James Hall, Literary Pioneer of the Ohio Valley.* Minneapolis: University of Minnesota Press, 1941.
2691. Lee, Robert Edson. *From West to East.* Urbana: University of Illinois Press, 1966, pp. 54-57.
2692. Randall, Randolph C. *James Hall, Spokesman of the New West.* Columbus: Ohio State University Press, 1964.
2693. Todd, Edgeley W. "The Authorship of 'The Missouri Trapper.'" *Missouri Historical Society Bulletin* 15 (April 1959): 194-200.
2694. ——. "James Hall and the Hugh Glass Legend." *American Quarterly* 7 (Winter 1955): 362-70.

DONALD HAMILTON

2695. Erisman, Fred. "Western Motifs in the Thrillers of Donald Hamilton." *Western American Literature* 10 (February 1976): 283-92.

DASHIELL HAMMETT

2696. Meador, Roy. "Dash: An Account of the Thin Man from San Francisco." *Air California* (December 1978): 59-62, 66-67.
2697. Ruehlmann, William. *Saint with a Gun.* New York: New York University Press, 1974.
2698. Whitley, John S. "Stirring Things Up: Dashiell Hammett's Continental Op." *Journal of American Studies* 14 (December 1980).

BRET HARTE

2699. Barnett, Linda D. "Bret Harte: An Annotated Bibliography of Secondary Comment." *American Literary Realism 1870-1910,* Part 1 (1865-1904), 5 (Summer 1972): 189-320; Part 2 (1905-1971), 5 (Fall 1972): 331-484.
2700. ——. *Bret Harte: A Reference Guide.* Boston: G. K. Hall, 1980.
2701. ——. "The Critics of Bret Harte: An Annotated Bibliography." Doctoral dissertation, University of Southern California, 1972.

2702. Beisman, Emmeline B. "The Prospector and the Pioneer: A Key to the Selected Short Stories of Bret Harte." Doctoral dissertation, University of New Mexico, 1975.
2703. Boggan, J. R. "The Regeneration of 'Roaring Camp.'" *Nineteenth-Century Fiction* 22 (December 1967): 271-80.
2704. Booth, Bradford A. "Unpublished Letters of Bret Harte." *American Literature* 16 (May 1944): 131-42.
2705. Boynton, Henry W. *Bret Harte.* New York: McLure, Phillips, 1903.
2706. Brady, Duer S. "A New Look at Bret Harte and the *Overland Monthly.*" Doctoral dissertation, University of Arkansas, 1962.
2707. Brown, Allen B. "The Christ Motif in 'The Luck of Roaring Camp.'" *Papers of the Michigan Academy of Sciences, Art, and Letters* 56 (1961): 629-33.
2708. Buckland, Roscoe. "Jack Hamlin: Bret Harte's Romantic Rogue." *Western American Literature* 8 (Fall 1973): 111-22.
2709. Duckett, Margaret. "The 'Crusade' of a Nineteenth-Century Liberal." *Tennessee Studies in Literature* 4 (1959): 109-20.
2710. ——. "Bret Harte and the Indians of Northern California." *Huntington Library Quarterly* 18 (November 1954): 59-83.
2711. ——. "Bret Harte's Portrayal

of Half-Breeds." *American Literature* 25 (May 1953): 193-212.

2712. ——. *Mark Twain and Bret Harte.* Norman: University of Oklahoma Press, 1964.

2713. ——. "Plain Language from Bret Harte." *Nineteenth Century Fiction* 11 (March 1957): 241-60.

2714. Erskine, John. "Bret Harte." *Leading American Novelists.* New York: Henry Holt, 1910, pp. 325-69.

2715. Gaer, Joseph, ed. *Bret Harte: Bibliography and Biographical Data.* California Literary Research Monograph, No. 10, 1935; New York: Burt Franklin, 1968.

2716. Gardner, Joseph H. "Bret Harte and Dickensian Mode in America." *Canadian Review of American Studies* 2 (Fall 1971): 89-101.

2717. Glover, Donald E. "The Later Career of Bret Harte: 1880-1902." Doctoral dissertation, University of Virginia, 1965.

2718. ——. "A Reconsideration of Bret Harte's Later Work." *Western American Literature* 8 (Fall 1973): 143-51.

2719. Harrison, Joseph B., ed. *Bret Harte: Respresentative Selections.* New York: American Book, 1941.

2720. Harte, Bret. *The Letters of Bret Harte.* Ed. Geoffrey Bret Harte. Boston: Houghton Mifflin, 1926.

2721. Harte, John Bret. "A Dedication to the Memory of Francis Bret Harte, 1836-1902." *Arizona and the West* 18 (Spring 1976): 1-4.

2722. Hazard, Lucy L. "Eden to Eldorado." *University of California Chronicle* 35 (January 1933): 107-21.

2723. Kuhlman, Susan. *Knave, Fool, and Genius: The Confidence Man as He Appears in Nineteenth-Century American Fiction.* Chapel Hill: University of North Carolina Press, 1973.

2724. May, Charles E. "Bret Harte's 'Tennessee's Partner': The Reader Euchred." *South Dakota Review* 15 (Spring 1977): 109-17.

2725. May, Ernest. "Bret Harte and the *Overland Monthly*." *American Literature* 22 (November 1950): 260-71.

2726. ——. "*The Overland Monthly* under Bret Harte." Master's thesis, University of California, Los Angeles, 1949.

2727. Merwin, Henry C. "Bret Harte's Heroines." *Atlantic Monthly* 102 (September 1908): 297-307.

2728. ——. *The Life of Bret Harte.* Boston: Houghton Mifflin, 1911.

2729. Morrow, Patrick. *Bret Harte.* Western Writers Series, No. 5. Boise, Idaho: Boise State College, 1972.

2730. ——. "Bret Harte (1836-1902)." *American Literary Realism 1870-1910* 3 (Spring 1970): 167-77.

2731. ——. "Bret Harte and the Perils of Pop Poetry." *Journal of Popular Culture* 13 (Spring 1980): 476-82.

2732. ——. *Bret Harte: Literary Critic.* Bowling Green, Ohio: Bowling Green State University Popular Press, 1979.

2733. ——. "Bret Harte, Popular Fiction, and the Local Color Movement." *Western American Literature* 8 (Fall 1973): 123-31.

2734. ——. "The Predicament of Bret Harte." *American Literary Realism 1870-1910* 5 (Summer 1972): 181-88.

2735. ——. *The Works of Bret Harte.* Cassette. Deland, Fla.: Everett/Edwards, 1974.

2736. Murphy, Brenda, and George Monteiro. "The Unpublished Letters of Bret Harte to John Hay." *American Literary Realism 1870-1910* 12 (Spring 1979): 77-110.

2737. O'Brien, Dominic Vincent. "Bret Harte: A Survey of the Criticism of His Work." Doctoral dissertation, University of Pennsylvania, 1968.

2738. O'Connor, Richard. *Bret Harte: A Biography.* Boston: Little, Brown, 1966.

2739. Oliver, Egbert S. "The Pig-Tailed China Boys Out West." *Western Humanities Review* 12 (Spring 1958): 159-78.

2740. *Overland Monthly* [Special Bret Harte Number] 40 (September 1902).

2741. Pattee, Fred Lewis. "Bret Harte." *The Development of the American Short Story.* New York: Harper & Brothers, 1923, pp. 220-44 passim.

2742. ——. "Bret Harte." *A History of American Literature Since 1870.* New York: Century, 1915, pp. 65-82.

2743. Scheick, William J. "William Dean Howells to Bret Harte: A Missing Letter." *American Literary Realism 1870-1910* 9 (Summer 1976): 276-79.

2744. Schroeder, Fred E. H. "The Development of the Super-Ego on the American Frontier." *Soundings* 57 (Summer 1974): 189-205.

2745. Stegner, Wallace. "The West Synthetic: Bret Harte." *The Sound of Mountain Water.* Garden City, N.Y.: Doubleday, 1969, pp. 23-36.

2746. Stewart, George R., Jr. "A Bibliography of the Writings of Bret Harte in the Magazines and Newspapers of California, 1857-1871." *University of California Publications in English* 3 (September 30, 1933): 119-70. Reprint. Norwood, Pa.: Norwood Editions, 1977.

2747. ——. *Bret Harte: Argonaut and Exile.* Boston: Houghton Mifflin, 1931; Port Washington, N.Y.: Kennikat Press, 1968.

2748. ——. "The Bret Harte Legend." *University of California Chronicle* 30 (July 1928): 338-50.

2749. ——. "Bret Harte on the Frontier." *Southwest Review* 11 (April 1926): 265-73.

2750. Thomas, Jeffrey F. "Bret Harte." *American Literary*

Realism 1870-1910 8 (1975): 266-70. Analysis of dissertations on Harte.

2751. ——. "Bret Harte and the Power of Sex." *Western American Literature* 8 (Fall 1973): 91-109.

2752. Timpe, Eugene F. "Bret Harte's German Public." *Jahrbuch für Amerikastudien* 10 (1965): 215-20.

2753. Walterhouse, Roger R. *Bret Harte, Joaquin Miller, and the Western Local Color Story: A Study in the Origins of Popular Fiction.* Chicago: Private Edition, University of Chicago Libraries, 1939.

WALTER HAVIGHURST

2754. Jones, Joel M. "To Feel the Heartland's Pulse: The Writing of Walter Havighurst." *Kansas Quarterly* 2 (Spring 1970): 88-96.

JOHN HAY

2755. Clymer, Kenton J. "John Hay and Mark Twain." *Missouri Historical Review* 67 (April 1973): 397-406.

2756. Gale, Robert L. *John Hay.* Boston: Twayne, 1978.

2757. Sloane, David E. "John Hay (1838-1905)." *American Literary Realism 1870-1910* 3 (Spring 1970): 178-88.

2758. Thayer, William Roscoe. *The Life and Letters of John Hay.* 2 vols. Boston: Houghton Mifflin, 1915.

2759. Thurman, Kelley. *John Hay as a Man of Letters.* Reseda, Calif.: Mojave, 1974.

ERNEST HAYCOX

2760. DeVoto, Bernard. "Phaëthon on Gunsmoke Trail." *Harpers* 209 (December 1954): 10-11, 14, 16.

2761. "Ernest Haycox Memorial Number." *Call Number* 25 (1963-64): 1-31.

2762. Etulain, Richard W. "Ernest Haycox: The Historical Western, 1937-43." *South Dakota Review* 5 (Spring 1967): 35-54.

2763. ——. "Ernest Haycox: Popular Novelist of the Pacific Northwest." *Northwest Perspectives: Essays on the Culture of the Pacific Northwest.* Eds. Edwin R. Bingham and Glen A. Love. Seattle: University of Washington Press, 1979, pp. 137-50.

2764. ——. "The Literary Career of a Western Writer: Ernest Haycox 1899-1950." Doctoral dissertation, University of Oregon, 1966.

2765. Fargo, James. "The Western and Ernest Haycox." *Prairie Schooner* 26 (Summer 1952): 177-84.

2766. Garfield, Brian. "Ernest Haycox: A Study in Style." *Roundup* 21 (February 1973): 1-3, 5.

2767. Haycox, Ernest, Jr. "Introduction" to Ernest Haycox, *Bugles in the Afternoon.* New York: Gregg Press, 1978, pp. v-xi.
2768. Haycox, Jill Marie. "Introduction" to Ernest Haycox, *The Border Trumpet.* Boston: Gregg Press, 1978, pp. v-viii.
2769. ——. "Introduction" to Ernest Haycox, *Canyon Passage.* Boston: Gregg Press, 1979, pp. v-ix.
2770. ——. "Introduction" to Ernest Haycox, *The Earthbreakers.* Boston: Gregg Press, 1979, pp. v-ix.
2771. Nesbitt, John D. "A New Look at Two Popular Western Classics." *South Dakota Review* 18 (Spring 1980): 30-42. Deals with *Bugles in the Afternoon.*
2772. Newton, D. B. "After Haycox: Whither Go We?" *Roundup* 21 (November 1973): 4-8.
2773. ——. "The Legend of Ernest Haycox." *Roundup* 21 (October 1973): 8-11.
2774. "A Special Ernest Haycox Anniversary Issue." *Roundup* 21 (October 1973). Contains three brief essays on Haycox and a short bibliography of his works.

ERNEST HEMINGWAY

2775. Durham, Philip. "Ernest Hemingway's Grace Under Pressure: The Western Code." *Pacific Historical Review* 45 (August 1976): 425-32.
2776. Johnston, Kenneth G. "Hemingway's 'Wine of Wyoming': Disappointment in America." *Western American Literature* 9 (November 1974): 159-67.
2777. Winslow, Richard. "'A Good Country': Hemingway at the L Bar T Ranch, Wyoming." *Fitz-Gerald/Hemingway Annual 1975.* Englewood, Colo.: Microcard Editions, 1975, pp. 259-72.

ALICE CORBIN HENDERSON

2778. Bynner, Witter, and Oliver La Farge, eds. "Alice Corbin: An Appreciation." *New Mexico Quarterly Review* 19 (Spring 1949): 34-79. Includes several essays by friends of Alice Corbin Henderson.
2779. Pearce, T. M. *Alice Corbin Henderson.* Southwest Writers Series, No. 21. Austin, Tex.: Steck-Vaughn, 1969.

O. HENRY
See William Sydney Porter

WILL HENRY
See Henry Wilson Allen

ELLA HIGGINSON

2780. Reynolds, Helen Louise. "Ella Higginson: Northwest Author." Master's thesis, University of Washington, 1941.
2781. Vore, Elizabeth. "Ella Higginson, A Successful Pacific Coast Writer," *Overland* 33 (May 1899): 434-36.

EDWIN B. HILL

2782. Myers, John Myers. "A Checklist of Items Published by the Private Press of Edwin B. Hill." *American Book Collector* 18 (October 1967): 22-27.

RUTH BEEBE HILL

2783. Medicine, Bea. *"Hanta Yo*: A New Phenomenon." *Indian Historian* 12 (Summer 1979): 2-5.

TONY HILLERMAN

2784. Strenski, Ellen, and Robley Evans. "Ritual and Murder in Tony Hillerman's Indian Detective Novels." *Western American Literature* 16 (Fall 1981): 205-16.

EDWARD HOAGLAND

2785. Fontana, Ernest L. "The Territory of the Past in Hoagland's *Notes from the Century Before." Western American Literature* 9 (May 1974): 45-51.

PAUL HORGAN

2786. Biebel, Charles D. "Paul Horgan's Early Albuquerque: Notes on a Southwest City in Transition." *New Mexico Humanities Review* 3 (Summer 1980): 35-45. Illustrated.
2787. Carter, Alfred. "On the Fiction of Paul Horgan." *New Mexico Quarterly* 7 (August 1937): 207-16.
2788. Cooper, Guy L. "Paul Horgan: American Synthesis." Doctoral dissertation, University of Arkansas, 1971.
2789. Day, James M. *Paul Horgan.* Southwest Writers Series, No. 8. Austin, Tex.: Steck-Vaughn, 1967.
2790. Donchak, Stella Cassano. "Paul Horgan: Craftsman and Literary Artist." Doctoral dissertation, Case Western Reserve University, 1970.
2791. Gish, Robert F. "Albuquerque as Recurrent Frontier in Paul Horgan's *The Common Heart." New Mexico Humanities Review* 3 (Summer 1980): 23-33.
2792. Kraft, James. "About Paul Horgan's *Things as They Are." Canadian Review of American Studies* 2 (Spring 1971): 48-52.
2793. ——. "No Quarter Given: An Essay on Paul Horgan." *Southwestern Historical Quarterly* 80 (July 1976): 1-32.
2794. Lindenau, Judith W. "Paul Horgan's *Mountain Standard Time." South Dakota Review* 1 (May 1964): 57-64.
2795. McConnell, Richard M. M., and Susan A. Frey. "Paul Horgan: A Bibliography." *Western American Literature* 6 (Summer 1971): 137-50.
2796. ——. *Paul Horgan's Humble Powers: A Bibliography.* Washington, D.C.: Information Resources Press, 1971.

159

2797. Powell, Lawrence D. "Letter from the Southwest." *Westways* 67 (January 1975): 22-26.

2798. Reeve, Frank Durer. "A Letter to Clio." *New Mexico Historical Review* 31 (April 1956): 102-32.

EMERSON HOUGH

2799. Downey, Linda K. "Woman on the Trail: Hough's *North of 36.*" *Western American Literature* 14 (Fall 1979): 217-20.

2800. Gaston, Edwin W., Jr. *The Early Novel of the Southwest.* Albuquerque: University of New Mexico Press, 1961.

2801. Grahame, Pauline. "A Novelist of the Unsung." *Palimpsest* 11 (February 1930): 67-77.

2802. Gray, Richard H. "A Dedication to the Memory of Emerson Hough, 1857-1923." *Arizona and the West* 17 (Spring 1975): 1-4.

2803. Grover, Dorys C. "Emerson Hough and J. Frank Dobie." *Southwestern American Literature* 5 (1975): 100-110.

2804. ——. "W. H. D. Koerner and Emerson Hough: A Western Collaboration." *Montana: The Magazine of Western History* 29 (April 1979): 2-15.

2805. Henry, Stuart. *Conquering Our Great American Plains: A Historical Development.* New York: E. P. Dutton, 1930.

2806. Hutchinson, W. H. *A Bar Cross Man: The Life and Writings of Eugene Manlove Rhodes.* Norman: University of Oklahoma Press, 1956.

2807. ——. "Grassfire on the Great Plains." *Southwest Review* 41 (Spring 1956): 181-85.

2808. Johnson, Carole McCoole. "Emerson Hough and the American West: A Biographical and Critical Study." Doctoral dissertation, University of Texas, Austin, 1975.

2809. ——. "Emerson Hough's American West." *Books at Iowa* 21 (November 1974): 26-42.

2810. ——. "Emerson Hough's *The Story of the Outlaw*: A Critique and a Judgment." *Arizona and the West* 17 (Winter 1975): 309-26.

2811. Miller, John H. "Emerson Hough: Merry Christmas. Sued You Today." *Indiana University Bookman* 8 (March 1967): 23-35.

2812. Stone, Lee Alexander. *Emerson Hough: His Place in American Letters.* Chicago: n.p., 1925.

2813. Wylder, Delbert E. *Emerson Hough.* Southwest Writers Series, No. 19. Austin, Tex.: Steck-Vaughn, 1969.

2814. ——. *Emerson Hough.* Boston: Twayne, 1981.

2815. ——. "Emerson Hough and the Popular Novel." *Southwestern American Literature* 2 (Fall 1972): 83-89.

2816. ——. "Emerson Hough as Conservationist and Muckraker." *Western American Literature* 11 (August 1977): 93-109.

2817. ——. "Emerson Hough's *Heart's Desire.*" *Western American Literature* 1 (Spring 1966): 44-54.

ROBERT ERWIN HOWARD

2818. Lord, Glenn. *The Last Celt: A Bio-Bibliography of Robert Erwin Howard.* West Kingston, R.I.: Donald M. Grant, 1976.
2819. Schweitzer, Darrell. *Conan's World and Robert E. Howard.* Popular Writers of Today. San Bernadino, Calif.: Borgo, 1978.
2820. Walker, Dale L. "Pulp King of the Post Oaks." *Western American Literature* 11 (February 1977): 349-52.

EDGAR WATSON HOWE

2821. Albertini, Virgil. "Edgar Watson Howe and *The Story of a Country Town.*" *Northwest Missouri State University Studies* 35 (February 1975): 19-29.
2822. Bucco, Martin. *E. W. Howe.* Western Writers Series, No. 26. Boise, Idaho: Boise State University, 1977.
2823. Brune, Ruth E. "The Early Life of Edgar Watson Howe." Doctoral dissertation, University of Colorado, 1949.
2824. Cosgrove, Robert William. "Joseph Kirkland and Edgar Watson Howe: A Reappraisal of Their Fiction With Emphasis on Their Realism." Doctoral dissertation, Purdue University, 1974.
2825. Dick, Everett. "Ed Howe, a Notable Figure on the Sod-House Frontier." *Nebraska History Magazine* 18 (April-June 1937): 138-43.
2826. Eichelberger, Clayton L. "EWH: Critical Bibliography of Secondary Comment." *American Literary Realism 1870-1910* 2 (Spring 1969): 1-49.
2827. ——. "Edgar Watson Howe and Joseph Kirkland: More Critical Comment." *American Literary Realism 1870-1910* 4 (Summer 1971): 279-90.
2828. Howe, E. W. *Plain People.* New York: Dodd, Mead, 1929.
2829. Mayer, Charles W. "Realizing 'A Whole Order of Things': E. W. Howe's *The Story of a Country Town.*" *Western American Literature* 11 (May 1976): 23-36.
2830. Pickett, Calder M. *Ed Howe: Country Town Philosopher.* Lawrence: University Press of Kansas, 1968.
2831. ——. "Edgar Watson Howe and the Kansas Scene." *Kansas Quarterly* 2 (Spring 1970): 39-45.
2832. ——. "Edgar Watson Howe: Legend and Truth." *American Literary Realism 1870-1910* 2 (Spring 1969): 70-73.
2833. Powers, Richard. "Tradition in E. W. Howe's *The Story of a Country Town.*" *Midcontinent American Studies Journal* 9 (Fall 1968): 51-62.
2834. Ropp, Philip H. "Edgar Watson

Howe." Doctoral dissertation, University of Virginia, 1949.

2835. Sackett, S. J. *E. W. Howe.* New York: Twayne, 1972.

2836. Schorer, C. E. "Growing Up with the Country." *Midwest Journal* 6 (Fall 1954): 12-26.

2837. Simpson, Claude, M. "Introduction" to E. W. Howe's, *The Story of a Country Town.* Cambridge, Mass.: Harvard University Press, 1961, pp. vii-xxxi.

2838. Stronks, James B. "William Dean Howells, Ed Howe, and *The Story of a Country Town.*" *American Literature* 29 (January 1958): 473-78.

2839. Ward, John William. "Afterword" to E. W. Howe, *The Story of a Country Town.* New York: Signet, 1964, pp. 299-309.

2840. Woodhouse, William Lloyd. "The Writings and Philosophy of E. W. Howe." Master's thesis, University of Kansas, 1941.

WILLIAM DEAN HOWELLS

2841. Dean, James L. "The Wests of Howells and Crane." *American Literary Realism 1870-1910* 10 (Summer 1977): 254-66.

LOIS PHILLIPS HUDSON

2842. Peters, E. Roxanne. "'. . . And Ridiculous to be from North Dakota': An Analysis of the Work and Literary Reputation of Lois Phillips Hudson." Master's thesis, University of North Dakota, 1974.

2843. ——. "Lois Phillips Hudson: Reaper of the Dust." *North Dakota Quarterly* 44 (Autumn 1976): 18-29.

RICHARD HUGO

2844. Allen, Michael. "'Because Poems Are People': An Interview with Richard Hugo." *Ohio Review* 19 (Winter 1978): 74-90.

2845. ——. "'Only the eternal nothing of space': Richard Hugo's West." *Western American Literature* 15 (May 1980): 25-35.

2846. Bell, Vereen M. "We Are Called Human." *Parnassus* 6 (Spring-Summer 1978): 143-50.

2847. Dillon, David. "Gains Made in Isolation: An Interview with Richard Hugo." *Southwest Review* 62 (Spring 1977): 101-15.

2848. Garber, Frederick. "Fat Man at the Margin: The Poetry of Richard Hugo." *Iowa Review* 3 (1972): 58-67. Followed by Hugo's comments, pp. 67-76.

2849. ——. "Large Man in the Mountains: The Recent Work of Richard Hugo." *Western American Literature* 10 (November 1975): 205-18.

2850. Howard, Richard. "Richard Hugo." *Alone With America: Essays on the Art of Poetry in the United States Since 1950.* New York: Atheneum, 1969, pp. 232-46.

2851. Hugo, Richard. "The Real West Marginal Way." *American Poets in 1976.* Ed. William

Heyen. Indianapolis: Bobbs-Merrill, 1976, pp. 108-27.

2852. ——. *The Triggering Town: Lectures and Essays on Poetry and Writing.* New York: W. W. Norton, [1979].

2853. Lockwood, William J. "Richard Hugo's Return to the Pacific Northwest: Early and Recent Poems." *The Westering Experience in American Literature: Bicentennial Essays.* Eds. Merrill Lewis and L. L. Lee. Bellingham: Bureau for Faculty Research, Western Washington University, 1977, pp. 161-71.

2854. "Special Richard Hugo Issue." *Slackwater Review* (Lewiston, Idaho, 1978): 7-195. An important issue containing new poems, several interpretive articles, and a brief bibliography, pp. 179-87.

2855. "The Third Time the World Happens: A Dialogue on Writing Between Richard Hugo and William Stafford." *Northwest Review* 13 (March 1974): 26-47.

WILLIAM HUMPHREY

2856. Boatright, James. "William Humphrey (1924-)." *A Bibliographical Guide to the Study of Southern Literature.* Ed. Louis D. Rubin, Jr. Baton Rouge: Louisiana State University Press, 1969, pp. 224-25.

2857. Hoffman, Frederick J. *The Art of Southern Fiction.* Carbondale: Southern Illinois University Press, 1967, pp. 103-6.

2858. Lee, James W. *William Humphrey.* Southwest Writers Series, No. 7. Austin, Tex.: Steck-Vaughn, 1967.

2859. Rubin, Louis D., Jr. *The Curious Death of the Novel.* Baton Rouge: Louisiana State University Press, 1967, pp. 263-65 ff.

LUIS INCLÁN

2860. Paredes, Americo. "Luis Inclán: First of the Cowboy Writers." *American Quarterly* 12 (Spring 1960): 55-70.

WILLIAM INGE

2861. Armato, Philip M. "The Bum as Scapegoat in William Inge's *Picnic.*" *Western American Literature* 10 (February 1976): 273-82.

2862. Barrett, Charles M. "William Inge: The Mid-Century Playwright." Master's thesis, University of North Carolina, Chapel Hill, 1957.

2863. Herron, Ima Honaker. "Our Vanishing Towns: Modern Broadway Versions." *Southwest Review* 51 (Summer 1966): 209-20.

2864. Manley, Francis. "William Inge: A Bibliography." *American Book Collector* 16 (1965): 13-21.

2865. Miller, Jordan Y. "William Inge: Last of the Realists?" *Kansas Quarterly* 2 (Spring 1970): 17-26.

163

2866. Mitchell, Marilyn. "The Teacher as Outsider in the Works of William Inge." *Midwest Quarterly* 17 (Summer 1976): 385-93.

2867. Shuman, R. Baird. *William Inge.* New York: Twayne, 1965.

2868. Voss, Ralph Frederick. "The Art of William Inge." Doctoral dissertation, University of Texas, Austin, 1975.

2869. Weales, Gerald. *American Drama Since World War II.* New York: Harcourt, Brace and World, 1962.

WASHINGTON IRVING

2870. Beach, Leonard B. "American Literature Re-Examined: Washington Irving, the Artist in a Changing World." *University of Kansas City Review* 14 (1948): 259-66.

2871. Clark, William Bedford. "How the West Won: Irving's Comic Inversion of the Westering Myth in *A Tour on the Prairies.*" *American Literature* 50 (November 1978): 335-47.

2872. Cracroft, Richard H. "The American West of Washington Irving." Doctoral dissertation, University of Wisconsin, 1970.

2873. ——. *Washington Irving: The Western Works.* Western Writers Series, No. 14. Boise, Idaho: Boise State University, 1974.

2874. Dervin, James Allen. "Washington Irving Tours the Frontier: A New Yorker Sees and Shapes the Raw Materials of Frontier Life." Doctoral dissertation, University of North Carolina, Chapel Hill, 1974.

2875. Dula, Martha. "Audience Response to *A Tour on the Prairies* in 1835." *Western American Literature* 8 (Spring-Summer 1973): 68-74.

2876. Franklin, Wayne. "The Misadventures of Irving's Bonneville: Trapping and Being Trapped in the Rocky Mountains." *The Westering Experience in American Literature: Bicentennial Essays.* Eds. Merrill Lewis and L. L. Lee. Bellingham: Bureau for Faculty Research, Western Washington University, 1977, pp. 122-28.

2877. Gardner, J. H. "One Hundred Years Ago in the Region of Tulsa," *Chronicles of Oklahoma* 11 (June 1933): 765-85.

2878. Hudson, Ruth. "A Literary 'Area of Freedom' Between Irving and Twain." *Western Humanities Review* 13 (Winter 1959): 46-60.

2879. Irving, Pierre M. *The Life and Letters of Washington Irving.* 4 vols. New York: Putnam, 1862-64.

2880. Irving, Washington. *A Tour of the Prairies.* Ed. with intro., John Francis McDermott. Norman: University of Oklahoma Press, 1956.

2881. ——. *The Western Journals of Washington Irving.* Ed. and annotated, John Francis McDermott. Norman: University of Oklahoma Press, 1944.

2882. Jacobs, John Tobias. "The Western Journey: Exploration, Education and Autobiography in Irving, Parkman, and Thoreau." Doctoral dissertation, University of Notre Dame, 1976.

2883. Keiser, Albert. *The Indian in American Literature.* New York: Oxford University Press, 1933, pp. 52-64.

2884. Kime, Wayne R. "The Completeness of Washington Irving's *A Tour on the Prairies.*" *Western American Literature* 8 (Spring-Summer 1973): 55-65.

2885. ——. "Washington Irving and Frontier Speech." *American Speech* 42 (February 1967): 5-18.

2886. ——. "Washington Irving's *Astoria*: A Critical Study." Doctoral dissertation, University of Delaware, 1968.

2887. ——. "Washington Irving's Revision of the *Tonquin* Episode in *Astoria.*" *Western American Literature* 4 (Spring 1969): 51-59.

2888. Lee, Robert Edson. *From West to East.* Urbana: University of Illinois Press, 1966, pp. 58-69.

2889. Lyon, Thomas J. "Washington Irving's Wilderness." *Western American Literature* 1 (Fall 1966): 167-74.

2890. McDermott, John Francis. "Washington Irving and the Journal of Captain Bonneville." *Mississippi Valley Historical Review* 43 (December 1956): 459-67.

2891. Martin, Terence. "Rip, Ichabod, and the American Imagination." *American Literature* 31 (May 1959): 137-49.

2892. Myers, Andrew B. "Washington Irving, Fur Trade Chronicler: An Analysis of *Astoria* with Notes for a Corrected Edition." Doctoral dissertation, Columbia University, 1964.

2893. Pochmann, Henry A. "Washington Irving." *Fifteen American Authors Before 1900: Bibliographic Essays on Research and Criticism.* Eds. Robert A Rees and Earl N. Harbert. Madison: University of Wisconsin Press, 1971, pp. 245-61.

2894. Russell, Jason A. "Irving: Recorder of Indian Life." *Journal of American History* 25 (1931): 185-95.

2895. Rust, Richard D. "Irving Rediscovers the Frontier." *American Transcendental Quarterly* 18 (Spring 1973): 40-44.

2896. Scheick, William J. "Frontier Robin Hood: Wilderness, Civilization and the Half-Breed in Irving's *A Tour on the Prairies.*" *Southwestern American Literature* 4 (1974): 14-21.

2897. Short, Julee. "Irving's Eden: Oklahoma, 1832." *Journal of the West* 10 (October 1971): 700-712.

2898. Spaulding, George F., ed. *On the Western Tour with Washington Irving: The Journal and Letters of Count de Pourtales.* Trans. Seymour Feiler. Norman: University of Oklahoma Press, 1968.

165

2899. Spaulding, Kenneth A. "A Note on *Astoria*: Irving's Use of the Robert Stuart Manuscript." *American Literature* 22 (May 1950): 150-57.

2900. Springer, Haskell. *Washington Irving: A Reference Guide.* Boston: G. K. Hall, 1976.

2901. Terrell, Dahlia Jewel. "A Textual Study of Washington Irving's *A Tour on the Prairies.*" Doctoral dissertation, University of Texas, 1966.

2902. Thoburn, Joseph B. "Centennial of the Tour on the Prairies by Washington Irving (1832-1932)." *Chronicles of Oklahoma* 10 (September 1932): 426-33.

2903. Todd, Edgeley W. "Washington Irving Discovers the Frontier." *Western Humanities Review* 11 (Winter 1957): 29-39.

2904. Von Frank, Albert James. "Frontier Consciousness in American Literature." Doctoral dissertation, University of Missouri, Columbia, 1976.

2905. Wagenknecht, Edward. *Washington Irving: Moderation Displayed.* New York: Oxford University Press, 1962.

2906. Williams, Stanley T. *Life of Washington Irving.* 2 vols. New York: Oxford University Press, 1935.

2907. ——, and Barbara D. Simpson, eds. *Washington Irving on the Prairie, or, A Narrative of a Tour of the Southwest in the Year 1832.* New York: American Book, 1937.

2908. ——, and Mary A. Edge. *A Bibliography of the Writings of Washington Irving: A Check List.* New York: Oxford University Press, 1936.

HELEN HUNT JACKSON

2909. Banning, Evelyn I. *Helen Hunt Jackson.* New York: Vanguard Press, 1973.

2910. Byers, John R., Jr. "Helen Hunt Jackson (1830-1885)." *American Literary Realism 1870-1910* 2 (Summer 1969): 143-48.

2911. ——. "The Indian Matter of Helen Hunt Jackson's *Ramona*: From Fact to Fiction." *American Indian Quarterly* 11 (Winter 1975-76): 331-46.

2912. —— and Elizabeth S. "Helen Hunt Jackson (1830-1885): A Critical Bibliography of Secondary Comment." *American Literary Realism 1870-1910* 6 (Summer 1973): 197-241.

2913. Kime, Wayne R. "Helen Hunt Jackson." *American Literary Realism 1870-1910* 8 (1975): 291-92. Review of dissertations about Jackson.

2914. McConnell, Virginia. "'H.H.,' Colorado and the Indian Problem." *Journal of the West* 12 (April 1973): 272-80.

2915. Marsden, Michael T. "A Dedication to the Memory of Helen Hunt Jackson, 1830-1885." *Arizona and the West* 21 (Summer 1979): 109-12.

2916. Martin, Minerva L. "Helen Hunt Jackson, in Relation to Her

Time." Doctoral dissertation, University of Louisiana, 1940.

2917. Nevins, Allan. "Helen Hunt Jackson, Sentimentalist vs. Realist." *American Scholar* 10 (Summer 1941): 269-85.

2918. Odell, Ruth. *Helen Hunt Jackson.* New York: D. Appleton-Century, 1939.

2919. Pound, Louise. "Biographical Accuracy and 'H. H.'" *American Literature* 2 (January 1931): 418-21.

WILL JAMES

2920. Amaral, Anthony. "A Dedication to the Memory of Will James, 1892-1942." *Arizona and the West* 10 (Autumn 1968): 206-10.

2921. ——. *Will James: The Gild Edged Cowboy.* Los Angeles: Westernlore Press, 1969; rev. ed. *Will James: The Last Cowboy Legend.* Reno: University of Nevada Press, 1980.

2922. Meinzer, Helen Abbott. "Will James: A Study of His Life and Work in the Light of the New Emphasis on Regionalism." Master's thesis, University of Idaho, 1947.

MITCHELL F. JAYNE

2923. Lawson, Lewis A. "Old Fish Hawk: From Stereotype to Archetype." *American Indian Quarterly* 3 (Winter 1977-78): 321-33.

ROBINSON JEFFERS

2924. Adamic, Louis. *Robinson Jeffers, a Portrait.* Seattle: University of Washington Book Store, 1929.

2925. Adams, John H. "The Poetry of Robinson Jeffers: Reinterpretation and Reevaluation." Doctoral dissertation, Denver University, 1967.

2926. Alberts, S. S. *A Bibliography of the Works of Robinson Jeffers.* New York: Random House, 1933; New York: Burt Franklin, 1968.

2927. Alexander, John R. "Conflict in the Narrative Poetry of Robinson Jeffers." *Sewanee Review* 80 (Winter 1972): 85-99.

2928. Allred, Jerry. "Robinson Jeffers and the Problem of Western Violence." *Possible Sack* 3 (October 1972): 6-13.

2929. Antoninus, Brother. *Robinson Jeffers: Fragments of an Older Fury.* Berkeley, Calif.: Oyez, 1968.

2930. Beach, J. W. *The Concept of Nature in Nineteenth-Century English Poetry.* New York: Macmillan, 1936, pp. 522-46.

2931. Beilke, Marlan. *Shining Clarity: Man and God in the Works of Robinson Jeffers.* Amador City, Calif.: Quintessence Publications, 1977.

2932. Bennett, Melba B. *Robinson Jeffers and the Sea.* San Francisco: Belber, Lilenthal, 1936.

2933. ——. *The Stone Mason of Tor*

167

House: The Life and Work of Robinson Jeffers. [Menlo Park, Calif.] : Ward Ritchie Press, 1966.

2934. Boyers, Robert. "A Sovereign Voice: The Poetry of Robinson Jeffers." *Sewanee Review* 78 (July-September 1969): 487-507.

2935. Brophy, Robert. *California State University, Long Beach Library: Robinson Jeffers Collection.* Long Beach, Calif., 1975. Twenty-five-page checklist; includes description of manuscripts for 24 unpublished poems.

2936. ——. "Jeffers Theses and Dissertations: A Summary Listing." *Robinson Jeffers Newsletter* 45 (June 1976): 8-10.

2937. ——. "Landscape as Genesis and Analogue in Jeffers' Narratives." *Robinson Jeffers Newsletter* 29 (August 1971): 11-16.

2938. ——. "The Prose of Robinson Jeffers: An Annotated Checklist." *Robinson Jeffers Newsletter* 46 (September 1976): 14-36.

2939. ——. "The Ritual Ending of 'Roan Stallion.'" *Robinson Jeffers Newsletter* 34 (February 1973): 11-15.

2940. ——. *Robinson Jeffers.* Western Writers Series, No. 19. Boise: Boise State University, 1975.

2941. ——. *Robinson Jeffers: Myth, Ritual and Symbol in His Narrative Poems.* Cleveland: Case Western Reserve University Press, 1973; 2d ed. Ham-

den, Conn.: Archon Press, 1976.

2942. ——. "'Tamar,' 'The Cenci' and Incest." *American Literature* 42 (May 1970): 241-44.

2943. ——. *The Works of Robinson Jeffers.* Cassette. Deland, Fla.: Everett/Edwards, 1975.

2944. ——, and John Ahouse. *A Ward Ritchie Checklist: Works by and about Robinson Jeffers.* Long Beach, Calif., 1979.

2945. Carpenter, Frederic I. "Death Comes for Robinson Jeffers." *University Review* 7 (December 1940): 97-105.

2946. ——. "The Inhumanism of Robinson Jeffers." *Western American Literature* 16 (Spring 1981): 19-25.

2947. ——. "'Post Mortem': 'The Poet is Dead.'" *Western American Literature* 12 (May 1977): 3-10.

2948. ——. *Robinson Jeffers.* New York: Twayne, 1962.

2949. ——. "Robinson Jeffers and the Torches of Violence." *The Twenties: Poetry and Prose.* Deland, Fla.: Everett/Edwards, 1966.

2950. ——. "Robinson Jeffers Today: Beyond Good and Beneath Evil." *American Literature* 49 (March 1977): 88-96.

2951. ——. "The Values of Robinson Jeffers." *American Literature* 11 (January 1940): 353-66.

2952. Cestre, Charles. "Robinson Jeffers." *Revue Ango-Américane* 4 (1927): 489-502.

2953. Chatfield, Hale. "Robinson Jeffers: His Philosophy and His

Major Themes." *Laurel Review* 6 (1966): 56-71.

2954. Clark, Walter Van Tilburg. "A Study in Robinson Jeffers." Master's thesis, University of Vermont, 1934.

2955. Coffin, Arthur B. *Robinson Jeffers*. Madison: University of Wisconsin Press, 1971.

2956. Commanger, Henry Steele. "The Cult of the Irrational." *The American Mind*. New Haven, Conn.: Yale University Press, 1950, pp. 120-40.

2957. Davis, Harold L. "Jeffers Denies Us Twice." *Poetry* 31 (1928): 274-79.

2958. De Casseres, Benjamin. "Robinson Jeffers: Tragic Terror." *Bookman* 66 (November 1927): 262-66.

2959. DeMott, Robert. "Robinson Jeffers' 'Tamar.'" *The Twenties: fiction, poetry, drama*. Ed. Warren French. Deland, Fla.: Everett/Edwards, 1975, pp. 405-25.

2960. Deutsch, Babette. "A Look at the Worst." *Poetry in Our Time*. New York: Holt, 1952, pp. 1-27.

2961. Gierasch, Walter. "Robinson Jeffers." *English Journal* [College edition] 28 (April 1939): 284-95.

2962. Gilbert, Rudolph. *Shine, Perishing Republic: Robinson Jeffers and the Tragic Sense in Modern Poetry*. Boston: Bruce Humphries, 1936.

2963. Greenan, Edith. *Of Una Jeffers*. Los Angeles: Ward Ritchie Press, 1939.

2964. Harmsen, Tyrus. "Robinson Jeffers: Student at Occidental College." *Robinson Jeffers Newsletter* 50 (March 1978): 21-27.

2965. Hotchkiss, William. *Jeffers: The Sivaistic Vision*. Auburn, Calif.: Blue Oak Press, 1975.

2966. Jerome, Judson. "Poetry: How and Why the Language of Robinson Jeffers." *Revista de Lettras* 1 (1969): 99-105.

2967. Johnson, William Savage. "The 'Savior' in the Poetry of Robinson Jeffers." *American Literature* 15 (May 1943): 159-68.

2968. Kafka, Robb. "Robinson Jeffers' Published Writings, 1903-1911." *Robinson Jeffers Newsletter* 53 (June 1979): 47-68.

2969. Keller, Karl. "California, Yankees, and the Death of God: The Allegory in Jeffers' *Roan Stallion*." *Texas Studies in Literature and Language* 12 (Spring 1970): 111-20.

2970. ——. "Jeffers' Pace." *Robinson Jeffers Newsletter* 32 (July 1972): 7-17.

2971. Kiley, George B. "Robinson Jeffers: The Short Poems." Doctoral dissertation, University of Pittsburgh, 1957.

2972. Le Master, J. R. "Lorca, Jeffers, and the Myth of Tamar." *New Laurel Review* 1 (1971): 44-51.

2973. Lyon, Horace. *Jeffers Country: The Seed Plots of Robinson Jeffers' Poetry*. San Francisco: Scrimshaw, 1971. Photographs by Horace Lyon; poem excerpts and original preface by Robinson Jeffers.

2974. Macdonald, Dwight. "Robinson Jeffers." *Miscellany* 1 (July 1930): 1-10; (September 1930): 1-24.

2975. McGinty, Brian. "The View from Hawk's Tower: Poet Robinson Jeffers and the Rugged Coast That Shaped Him." *American West* 10 (November 1973): 4-9.

2976. Messer, Richard. "Jeffers' Inhumanism: A Vision of the Self." *Itinerary: Criticism, Essays on California Writers.* Ed. Charles L. Crow. Bowling Green, Ohio: University Press, 1978, pp. 11-19.

2977. Miura, Tokuhiro. "Poetics of Robinson Jeffers: Disclaimer of Modernism." *Bungaku-bu Kigo* (Hosei University, Japan) 23 (1977): 1-29.

2978. Monjian, Mercedes C. *Robinson Jeffers: A Study in Inhumanism.* Pittsburgh: University of Pittsburgh Press, 1958.

2979. Morris, Lawrence S. "Robinson Jeffers: The Tragedy of a Modern Mystic." *New Republic* 54 (May 16, 1928): 386-90.

2980. Moss, Sidney P. "Robinson Jeffers: A Defense." *American Book Collector* 10 (September 1959): 8-14.

2981. Nickerson, Edward A. "The Holy Light in Jeffers' Poetry." *Robinson Jeffers Newsletter* 47 (December 1976): 19-28.

2982. ———. "The Return to Rhyme." *Robinson Jeffers Newsletter* 39 (July 1974): 12-21.

2983. ———. "Robinson Jeffers and the Paeon." *Western American Literature* 10 (November 1975): 189-93.

2984. ———. "Robinson Jeffers: Apocalypse and His 'Inevitable Place.'" *Western American Literature* 11 (August 1977): 111-22.

2985. ———. "Robinson Jeffers, Poet of Apocalypse." Doctoral dissertation, State University of New York, Albany, 1973.

2986. Nolte, William H. *The Merrill Guide to Robinson Jeffers.* Columbus, Ohio: Charles E. Merrill, 1970.

2987. ———. "Robinson Jeffers, An Uncanny Prophet." *Alternative: An American Spectator* 10 (May 1976): 11-15.

2988. ———. "Robinson Jeffers as Didactic Poet." *Virginia Quarterly Review* 42 (Spring 1966): 257-71.

2989. ———. "Robinson Jeffers Redivivus." *Georgia Review* 33 (Summer 1978): 429-34.

2990. ———. *Rock and Hawk: Robinson Jeffers and the Romantic Agony.* Athens: University of Georgia Press, 1979.

2991. Nuwer, Henry. "Jeffer's Influence upon Walter Van Tilburg Clark." *Robinson Jeffers Newsletter* 44 (March 1976): 11-17.

2992. Parker, Jean Louise. "Robinson Jeffers: A Study of the Phenomena of Human Consciousness." Doctoral dissertation,

Pennsylvania State University, 1970.

2993. Powell, Lawrence Clark. "The Double Marriage of Robinson Jeffers." *Southwest Review* 41 (Summer 1956): 278-82.

2994. ——. *Robinson Jeffers: The Man and His Work.* Pasadena, Calif.: San Pasqual Press, 1940.

2995. Redinger, Ellsworth L. "The Poetic Dramas of Robinson Jeffers." Doctoral dissertation, University of Southern California, 1971.

2996. Ridgeway, Ann N., ed. *The Selected Letters of Robinson Jeffers, 1897-1962.* Baltimore: Johns Hopkins Press, 1968.

2997. Ritchie, Ward. *I Remember Robinson Jeffers.* Los Angeles: Zamorano Club, 1978.

2998. ——. *Some Recollections on Robinson Jeffers.* Laguna Beach, Calif.: Laguna Verde, 1977.

2999. *Robinson Jeffers: A Checklist.* San Francisco: Gleeson Library Associates, 1967.

3000. *Robinson Jeffers Newsletter.* Edited by Melba B. Bennett (nos. 1-22) and Robert J. Brophy (nos. 23-). Los Angeles: Robinson Jeffers Committee, Occidental College, 1962-.

3001. Rogers, Covington. "A Checklist of Robinson Jeffers' Poetical Writings Since 1934." *Robinson Jeffers Newsletter* 48 (March 1977): 11-24.

3002. ——, and John Meador. *The Robinson Jeffers Collection at the University of Houston.*

University of Houston, 1975. A 32-page checklist. First technical description of 16 works by Jeffers, supplementing Alberts's *Bibliography*, 1933.

3003. Schwartz, Delmore. "The Enigma of Robinson Jeffers: I. Sources of Violence." *Poetry* 55 (October 1939): 30-38.

3004. Scott, Robert I. "The Ends of Tragedy: Robinson Jeffers' Satires on Human Importance." *Canadian Review of American Studies* 10 (Fall 1979): 231-41.

3005. ——. "Poet as Prophet: Jeffers' Unpublished Poems About World War II." *North American Review* (Spring 1978): 82-86.

3006. ——. "Robinson Jeffers' Tragedies as Rediscoveries of the World." *Rocky Mountain Review* 29 (Autumn 1975): 147-65.

3007. ——. "Scholarly Materials: Poetry Manuscripts, University of Texas." *Robinson Jeffers Newsletter* 45 (June 1976): 13-16.

3008. Sessions, George. "Spinoza and Jeffers on Man in Nature." *Inquiry* 20 (1977): 481-528.

3009. Shebl, James. *In This Wild Water: Suppressed Poems of Robinson Jeffers.* Pasadena, Calif.: Ward Ritchie, 1976.

3010. Shiglas, Jerry Ashburn. "The Divided Mind of Robinson Jeffers." Doctoral dissertation, Duke University, 1972.

3011. Short, R. W. "The Tower Beyond Tragedy." *Southern*

171

Review 7 (Summer 1941): 132-44.

3012. Smith, Alfred. *The Flight of the Hawk.* San Francisco: Sunset Press, 1979.

3013. Squires, Radcliffe. "Robinson Jeffers: The Anatomy of Violence." *Modern American Poetry: Essays in Criticism.* Ed. Guy Owens. Deland, Fla.: Everett/Edwards, 1975.

3014. ——. *The Loyalties of Robinson Jeffers.* Ann Arbor: University of Michigan Press, 1956.

3015. Starr, Kevin. "Robinson Jeffers and the Integrity of Nature." *Sierra Club Bulletin* 62 (May 1977): 36-40.

3016. Stephens, George D. "The Narrative and Dramatic Poetry of Robinson Jeffers." Doctoral dissertation, University of Southern California, 1953.

3017. Sterling, George. *Robinson Jeffers, the Man and the Artist.* New York: Boni and Liveright, 1926.

3018. Taylor, Frajan. "The Enigma of Robinson Jeffers: II The Hawk and the Stone." *Poetry* 55 (October 1939): 39-46.

3019. Turlish, Molly S. "Story Patterns from Greek and Biblical Sources in the Poetry of Robinson Jeffers." Doctoral dissertation, University of Michigan, 1971.

3020. Van Dam, Danis. "Greek Shadows on the Monterey Coast: Environment in Robinson Jeffers' Poetry." *Robinson Jeffers Newsletter* 40 (November 1974): 9-17.

3021. Vardamis, Alex A. *The Critical Reputation of Robinson Jeffers: A Bibliographical Study.* Hamden, Conn.: Archon Books, 1972.

3022. Vaughn, Eric. "'Dear Judas': Time and the Dramatic Structure of the Dream." *Robinson Jeffers Newsletter* 51 (July 1978): 7-22.

2023. Waggoner, Hyatt Howe. *The Heel of Elohim: Science and Values in Modern Poetry.* Norman: University of Oklahoma Press, 1950, pp. 105-32.

3024. ——. "Science and the Poetry of Robinson Jeffers." *American Literature* 10 (November 1938): 275-88.

3025. Warren, R. P. "Jeffers on the Age." *Poetry* 49 (February 1937): 278-82.

3026. Watts, Harold H. "Multivalence in Robinson Jeffers." *College English* 3 (November 1941): 109-20.

3027. ——. "Robinson Jeffers and Eating the Serpent." *Sewanee Review* 49 (January 1941): 39-55.

3028. Weedin, Everett K., Jr. "Robinson Jeffers: The Achievement of His Narrative Verse." Doctoral dissertation, Cornell University, 1967.

3029. White, Kenneth. *The Coast Opposite Humanity: An Essay on the Poetry of Robinson Jeffers.* Dyfed, England: Unicorn, 1975.

3030. White, William. "Robinson Jeffers: A Checklist, 1959-1965." *Serif* 3 (June 1966): 36-39.

3031. Wilder, Amos. "The Nihilism of Mr. Robinson Jeffers." *Spiritual Aspects of the New Poetry.* New York: Harper and Brothers, 1940, pp. 141-52.
3032. Winters, Yvor. "Robinson Jeffers." *Poetry* 35 (February 1930): 279-86.
3033. Woodbridge, H. C. "A Bibliographical Note on Jeffers." *American Book Collector* 10 (September 1959): 15-18.
3034. Young, Vernon. "Such Counsels He Gave to Us: Jeffers Revisited." *Parnassus* 6 (Fall/Winter 1977): 178-97.

DOROTHY M. JOHNSON

3035. Alter, Judy. *Dorothy Johnson.* Western Writers Series, No. 44. Boise, Idaho: Boise State University, 1980.
3036. ——. "Introduction" to Dorothy Johnson, *Indian Country.* Boston: Gregg Press, 1979.
3037. Arthur, Anthony. "Introduction" to Dorothy Johnson, *The Hanging Tree.* Boston: Gregg Press, 1980.
3038. James, Elizabeth. "A Thematic Analysis of Dorothy Johnson's Fiction." Master's thesis, Colorado State University, 1971.
3039. Mathews, Sue, and James W. Healey. "The Winning of the Western Fiction Market: An Interview with Dorothy M. Johnson." *Prairie Schooner* 52 (Summer 1978): 158-67.
3040. Schaefer, Jack. "Introduction" to Dorothy Johnson, *Indian Country.* New York: Ballantine, 1953.
3041. Smith, Stephen. "The Years and The Wind and The Rain: A Biography of Dorothy M. Johnson." Master's thesis, University of Montana, 1969.

ELMER KELTON

3042. Clayton, Lawrence. "The End of the West Motif in the Work of Edward Abbey, Jane Kramer, and Elmer Kelton." *RE: Artes Liberales* 6 (Fall 1979): 11-18.
3043. Grover, Dorys C. "Elmer Kelton and the Popular Western Novel." *Southwest Heritage* 8 (Summer 1978): 8-19.
3044. Lee, Billy C. "Elmer Kelton: A PQ Interview." *Paperback Quarterly* 1 (Summer 1978): 16-30.

JACK KEROUAC

3045. Allen, Eliot D. "That Was No Lady–That Was Jack Kerouac's Girl." *Essays in Modern American Literature.* Ed. Richard E. Langford. Deland, Fla.: Stetson University Press, 1963, pp. 97-102.
3046. Askew, Melvin W. "Quests, Cars, and Kerouac." *University of Kansas City Review* 28 (Spring 1962): 231-40.
3047. Ball, Vernon Francis. "Of Glory Obscur'd: Beatific Vision in the Narrative of Jack Kerouac." Doctoral dissertation, Ball State University, 1976.

3048. Berrigan, Ted, et al. "The Art of Fiction XLI: Jack Kerouac." *Paris Review* 43 (Summer 1968): 60-105. An important interview.

3049. Cassady, Carolyn. *Heart Beat: My Life with Jack & Neal.* Berkeley, Calif.: Creative Arts, 1976.

3050. Charters, Ann. *A Bibliography of Work by Jack Kerouac.* New York: Phoenix Book Shop, 1967; rev. ed. 1975.

3051. ——. *Kerouac: A Biography.* San Francisco: Straight Arrow Books, 1973.

3052. Cook, Bruce. *The Beat Generation.* New York: Charles Scribner's Sons, 1971.

3053. Dardess, George. "The Delicate Dynamics of Friendship: A Reconsideration of Kerouac's *On The Road.*" *American Literature* 46 (May 1974): 200-206.

3054. ——. "The Logic of Spontaneity: A Reconsideration of Kerouac's 'Spontaneous Prose Method.'" *Boundary* 2 (1975): 729-43.

3055. Donaldson, Scott, ed. *Jack Kerouac, On the Road: Text and Criticism.* New York: Penguin Books, 1979. Contains text, criticism, and bibliography.

3056. Duffey, Bernard. "The Three Worlds of Jack Kerouac." *Recent American Fiction.* Ed. Joseph J. Waldmeir. Boston: Houghton Mifflin, 1963, pp. 175-84.

3057. Feied, Frederick. *No Pie in the Sky: The Hobo as American Cultural Hero in the Works of Jack London, John Dos Passos, and Jack Kerouac.* New York: Citadel, 1964.

3058. Frohock, W. M. "Jack Kerouac and the Beats." *Strangers to This Ground.* Dallas: Southern Methodist University Press, 1961, pp. 132-47.

3059. Gelfant, Blanche H. "Jack Kerouac." *Contemporary Literature* 15 (Summer 1974): 415-22.

3060. Gifford, Barry. *Krouac's Town.* Santa Barbara, Calif.: Capra Press, 1973; Berkeley, Calif.: Creative Arts, 1977.

3061. ——, and Lawrence Lee. *Jack's Book: An Oral Biography of Jack Kerouac.* New York: St. Martin's Press, 1978.

3062. Hart, John E. "Future Hero in Paradise: Kerouac's *The Dharma Bums.*" *Critique* 14 (1973): 52-62.

3063. Hipkiss, Roberta. *Jack Kerouac: Prophet of the New Romanticism.* Lawrence: Regents Press of Kansas, 1976.

3064. Huebel, Harry Russell. *Jack Kerouac.* Western Writers Series, No. 39. Boise, Idaho: Boise State University, 1979.

3065. Hull, Keith N. "A Dharma Bum Goes West to Meet the East." *Western American Literature* 11 (February 1977): 321-29.

3066. Hunt, Tim. *Kerouac's Crooked Road: Development of a Fiction.* Hamden, Conn.: Archon, 1980.

3067. "Jack Kerouac and Neal

Cassady." *Transatlantic Review* 33-34 (Winter 1969-1970): 115-25.

3068. Jarvis, Charles D. *Visions of Kerouac: The Life of Jack Kerouac.* 2d ed. Lowell, Mass.: Ithaca Press, 1974.

3069. Jones, Granville. "Jack Kerouac and the American Conscience." *Lectures on Modern Novelists.* Carnegie Series in English, No. 7. Pittsburgh: Carnegie Tech, 1963, pp. 25-39.

3070. Leer, Norman. "Three American Novels and Contemporary Society." *Wisconsin Studies in Contemporary Literature* 3 (Fall 1962): 67-86.

3071. Le Pellec, Yves. "Jack Kerouac and the American Critics—A Selected Bibliography." *Caliban* 10 (1973): 77-92.

3072. McNally, Dennis. *Desolate Angel: Jack Kerouac, The Beat Generation, and America.* New York: Random House, 1979.

3073. Milewski, Robert J. *Jack Kerouac: An Annotated Bibliography of Secondary Sources, 1944-1979.* Metuchen, N.J.: Scarecrow, 1980.

3074. Nisonger, Thomas Evans. "Jack Kerouac: A Bibliography of Biographical and Critical Material, 1950-1979." *Bulletin of Bibliography* 37 (January/ March 1980): 23-32.

3075. Øverland, Örm. "West and Back Again." *Jack Kerouac, On the Road: Text and Citicism.* Ed. Scott Donaldson. New York: Penguin Books, 1979, pp. 451-64.

3076. Primeau, Ronald. "'The Endless Poem': Jack Kerouac's Midwest." *Great Lakes Review* 2 (Winter 1976): 19-26.

3077. Rubin, Louis D. "Two Gentlemen of San Francisco: Notes on Kerouac and Responsibility." *Western Review* 23 (Spring 1959): 278-83.

3078. Tallman, Warren. "Kerouac's Sound." *Tamarack Review* 11 (Spring 1959): 58-74.

3079. Tytell, John. *Naked Angels: The Lives and Literature of Beat Generation.* New York: McGraw-Hill, 1976.

3080. Vopat, Carole Gottlieb. "Jack Kerouac's *On the Road*: A Re-evaluation." *Midwest Quarterly* 14 (July 1973): 385-407.

3081. Webb, Howard W., Jr. "The Singular Worlds of Jack Kerouac." *Contemporary American Novelists.* Ed. Harry T. Moore. Carbondale: Southern Illinois University Press, 1964, pp. 120-33.

3082. Williams, Bruce Keith. "The Shrouded Traveller on the Road: Death and the Work of Jack Kerouac." Doctoral dissertation, Claremont Graduate School, 1977.

KEN KESEY

3083. Barsness, John A. "Ken Kesey: The Hero in Modern Dress." *Bulletin of the Rocky Mountain Language Association* 23 (March 1969): 27-33.

3084. Beidler, Peter G., and John W. Hunt, eds. "Perspectives on a

Cuckoo's Nest: A Symposium on Ken Kesey." *Lex et Scientia: International Journal of Law & Science* 13 (1977). Special issue devoted to Kesey's novel.

3085. Billingsley, Ronald G. "The Artistry of Ken Kesey: A Study of *One Flew Over the Cuckoo's Nest* and of *Sometimes a Great Notion.*" Doctoral dissertation, University of Oregon, 1971.

3086. Blessing, Richard. "The Moving Target: Ken Kesey's Evolving Hero." *Journal of Popular Culture* 4 (Winter 1971): 615-27.

3087. Busby, Mark. "Eugene Manlove Rhodes: Ken Kesey Passed by Here." *Western American Literature* 15 (Summer 1980): 83-92.

3088. Carnes, Bruce. *Ken Kesey.* Western Writers Series No. 12. Boise, Idaho: Boise State University, 1974.

3089. Cowley, Malcolm. "Ken Kesey at Stanford." *Kesey.* Ed. Michael Strelow, et al. Eugene, Oreg.: Northwest Review Books, 1977, pp. 1-4.

3090. Dunnivant, James. "Ken Kesey and the Fictive Image of the Western Male in Contemporary American Fiction." Master's thesis, Sonoma State College, 1973.

3091. Fiedler, Leslie. *The Return of the Vanishing American.* New York: Stein and Day, 1965, pp. 159-87.

3092. Flora, Joseph M. "Westering and Woman: A Thematic Study of

Kesey's *One Flew Over the Cuckoo's Nest* and *Fisher's Mountain Man.*" *Heritage of Kansas* 10 (Spring 1977): 3-14.

3093. Forrey, Robert. "Ken Kesey's Psychopathic Savior: A Rejoinder." *Modern Fiction Studies* 21 (Summer 1975): 222-30.

3094. Foster, John Wilson. "Hustling to Some Purpose: Kesey's *One Flew Over the Cuckoo's Nest.*" *Western American Literature* 9 (August 1974): 115-29.

3095. Hauck, Richard B. "The Comic Christ and the Modern Reader." *College English* 31 (February 1970): 498-506.

3096. Hill, Richard Allen. "The Law of Ken Kesey." Doctoral dissertation, Emory University, 1976.

3097. Hoge, James O. "Psychedelic Stimulation and the Creative Imagination: The Case of Ken Kesey." *Southern Humanities Review* 6 (1972): 381-91.

3098. Kesey, Ken. *Kesey's Garage Sale.* New York: Viking Press, 1973. A jumbled collection of essays, cartoons, and useful biographical material.

3099. ——. "Letters from Mexico." *The Single Voice: An Anthology of Contemporary Fiction.* Ed. Jerome Charyn. London: Collier-Macmillan, 1969, pp. 417-26. Includes "An Introductory Note" by Ed McClanahan, pp. 414-17.

3100. Knapp, James F. "Tangled in the Language of the Past:

Ken Kesey and Cultural Revolution." *Midwest Quarterly* 19 (1978): 398-412.

3101. Krassner, Paul. "An Impolite Interview with Ken Kesey." *Realist* 90 (May-June 1971): 1, 46-53.

3102. Kunz, Don R. "Mechanistic and Totemistic Symbolization in Kesey's *One Flew Over the Cuckoo's Nest.*" *Studies in American Fiction* 3 (Spring 1975): 65-82.

3103. Leeds, Barry H. "Theme and Technique in *One Flew Over the Cuckoo's Nest.*" *Connecticut Review* 7 (April 1974): 35-50.

3104. Lish, Gordon, ed. "What the Hell You Looking in Here For, Daisy Mae: An Interview with Ken Kesey." *Genesis West* 2 (Fall 1963): 17-29.

3105. Malin, Irving. "Ken Kesey: *One Flew Over the Cuckoo's Nest.*" *Critique* 5, No. 2 (1962): 81-84.

3106. Marsden, James Douglas. "Modern Echoes of Transcendentalism: Kesey, Snyder, and Other Counter Cultural Authors." Doctoral dissertation, Brown University, 1977.

3107. Martin, Terence. "*One Flew Over the Cuckoo's Nest* and the High Cost of Living." *Modern Fiction Studies* 19 (Spring 1973): 43-55.

3108. Maxwell, Richard. "The Abdication of Masculinity in *One Flew Over the Cuckoo's Nest.*" *Twenty-Seven to One.* Ed. Bradford B. Broughton. Og-densburg, N.Y.: Ryan Press, 1970, pp. 203-11.

3109. Olderman, Raymond M. *Beyond the Waste Land: A Study of the American Novel in the Nineteen-Sixties.* New Haven, Conn.: Yale University Press, 1972.

3110. Pearson, Carol. "The Cowboy Saint and the Indian Poet: The Comic Hero in Kesey's *One Flew Over the Cuckoo's Nest.*" *Studies in American Humor* 1 (1974): 91-98.

3111. Pinsker, Sanford. "The Graying of Black Humor." *Studies in the 20th Century* 9 (Spring 1972): 15-33.

3112. Pratt, John Clark. "On Editing Kesey: Confessions of a Straight Man." *Kesey.* Ed. Michael Strelow, et al. Eugene, Oreg.: Northwest Review Books, 1977, pp. 5-16.

3113. ——, ed. *One Flew Over the Cuckoo's Nest: Text and Criticism.* New York: Viking Press, 1973. Includes text, nearly a dozen critical essays, and other useful information.

3114. Schopf, William. "Blindfolded and Backwards: Promethean and Bemushroomed Heroism in *One Flew Over the Cuckoo's Nest* and *Catch-22.*" *Bulletin of the Rocky Mountain Modern Language Association* 3 (Fall 1972): 89-97.

3115. Sherman, W. D. "The Novels of Ken Kesey." *Journal of American Studies* 5 (August 1971): 185-96.

3116. Sherwood, Terry G. "*One Flew

Over the Cuckoo's Nest and the Comic Strip." *Critique* 13 (No. 1): 96-109.

3117. Singer, Barnett. "Outsider Versus Insider: Malamud's and Kesey's Pacific Northwest." *South Dakota Review* 13 (Winter 1975-76): 127-44.

3118. Stein, Howard F. "The Cuckoo's Nest, the Banality of Evil and the Psychopath as Hero." *Journal of American Culture* 2 (Winter 1980): 635-45.

3119. Strelow, Michael, et al. *Kesey.* Eugene, Oreg.: Northwest Review Books, 1977.

3120. Sullivan, Ruth. "Big Mama, Big Papa, and Little Sons in Ken Kesey's *One Flew Over the Cuckoo's Nest.*" *Literature and Psychology* 25, No. 1 (1975): 34-44.

3121. Sutherland, Janet. "A Defense of Ken Kesey's *One Flew Over the Cuckoo's Nest.*" *English Journal* 61 (January 1972): 28-36.

3122. Tanner, Stephen L. "Salvation through Laughter: Ken Kesey and the Cuckoo's Nest." *Southwest Review* 58 (Spring 1973): 125-37.

3123. Tanner, Tony. *City of Words: American Fiction 1950-1970.* New York: Harper and Row, 1971.

3124. ——. "Edge City: Ken Kesey and His Pranksters." *London Magazine* 9 (December 1969): 5-24.

3125. Waldmeir, Joseph J. "Two Novelists of the Absurd: Heller and Kesey." *Wisconsin Studies in Contemporary Literature* 5 (Autumn 1964): 192-204.

3126. Weixlmann, Joseph. "Ken Kesey: A Bibliography." *Western American Literature* 10 (November 1975): 219-31.

3127. Widmer, Kingsley. "*One Flew Over the Cuckoo's Nest.*" *Twentieth Century American Novel.* Cassette. Deland, Fla.: Everett/Edwards, 1970.

3128. Witke, Charles. "Pastoral Convention in Vergil and Kesey." *Pacific Coast Philology* 1 (April 1966): 20-24.

3129. Wolfe, Tom. *The Electric Kool-Aid Acid Test.* New York: Farrar, Straus and Giroux, 1968.

3130. Zashin, Elliot M. "Political Theorist and Demiurge: The Rise and Fall of Ken Kesey." *Centennial Review* 17 (Spring 1973): 199-213.

CHARLES KING

3131. Burton, Wilfred C. "The Novels of Charles King, 1844-1933." Doctoral dissertation, New York University, 1962.

3132. Peterson, Clell T. "Charles King: Soldier and Novelist." *American Book Collector* 16 (December 1965): 9-12.

3133. Sackett, S. J. "Captain Charles King, U.S.A." *Midwest Quarterly* 3 (October 1961): 69-80.

CLARENCE KING

3134. Crosby, Harry. "So Deep a Trail:

A Biography of Clarence King."
Doctoral dissertation, Stanford
University, 1953.

3135. Dickason, David H. "Clarence
King's First Western Journey."
Huntington Library Quarterly
7 (November 1943): 71-87.

3136. ——. "Henry Adams and Clarence King: The Record of a
Friendship." *New England
Quarterly* 17 (June 1944):
229-54.

3137. Hoebzema, Loren. "The Literary Landscape of Clarence
King's *Mountaineering in the
Sierra Nevada.*" *Exploration* 4
(1977): 17-23.

3138. Long, Barbara N. Messner. "An
Edition of *Mountaineering in
the Sierra Nevada* by Clarence
King." Doctoral dissertation,
University of Pennsylvania,
1973.

3139. Shebl, James M. *King, of the
Mountains.* Pacific Center for
Western Historical Studies,
Monograph No. 5. Stockton,
Calif.: University of the Pacific, 1974.

3140. Thomas, Jeffrey F. "Clarence
King." *American Literary Realism 1870-1910* 8 (Autumn
1975): 294-95. Comments on
dissertations written about
King.

3141. Wild, Peter. *Clarence King.*
Western Writers Series, No. 48.
Boise, Idaho: Boise State University, 1981.

3142. Wilkins, Thurman. *Clarence
King: A Biography.* New York:
Macmillan, 1958.

3143. Wilson, Richard B. "American

Vision and Landscape: The
Western Images of Clarence
King and Timothy O'Sullivan." Doctoral dissertation,
University of New Mexico,
1979.

RUDYARD KIPLING

3144. Espey, David B. "Kipling's Colorado Hero." *South Dakota Review* 13 (Summer 1975): 82-90.

JOSEPH KIRKLAND

3145. Flanagan, John T. "Joseph Kirkland, Pioneer Realist." *American Literature* 11 (November
1939): 273-84.

3146. Henson, Clyde E. "Joseph Kirkland (1830-1894)." *American
Literary Realism 1870-1910* 1
(Fall 1967): 67-70.

3147. ——. "Joseph Kirkland's Influence on Hamlin Garland."
American Literature 23 (January 1952): 458-63.

3148. ——. *Joseph Kirkland.* New
York: Twayne, 1962.

3149. Holaday, Clayton A. "Joseph
Kirkland: Biography and Criticism." Doctoral dissertation,
Indiana University, 1950.

3150. Lease, Benjamin. "Realism and
Joseph Kirkland's *Zury.*"
American Literature 23 (January 1952): 464-66.

CAROLYN KIZER

3151. Chappell, Fred. "'I'm in the Racket': Carolyn Kizer's Poetry."

St. *Andrew's Review* 1 (Fall-Winter 1971): 13-16.

3152. Howard, Richard. *Alone with America: Essays on the Art of Poetry in the United States Since 1950.* New York: Atheneum, 1969, pp. 272-80.

3153. ——. "Carolyn Kizer." *Tri-Quarterly* 7 (Fall 1966): 109-17.

KYŌ KOIKE

3154. Zabilski, Carol. "Dr. Kyō Koike, 1878-1947: Physician, Poet, Photographer." *Pacific Northwest Quarterly* 68 (April 1977): 73-79.

HERBERT KRAUSE

3155. Huseboe, Arthur R. and William Geyer. "Herbert Krause and the Western Experience." *Where the West Begins.* Eds. Arthur R. Huseboe and William Geyer. Sioux Falls, S.Dak.: Center for Western Studies Press, 1978, pp. 5-12.

3156. Janssen, Judith M. "'Black Frost in Summer': Central Themes in the Novels of Herbert Krause." *South Dakota Review* 5 (Spring 1967): 55-65.

3157. Paulson, Kristoffer F. "Ole Rǒlvaag, Herbert Krause, and the Frontier Thesis of Frederick Jackson Turner." *Where the West Begins.* Eds. Arthur R. Huseboe and William Geyer. Sioux Falls, S.Dak.: Center for

Western Studies Press, 1978, pp. 24-33.

3158. Steensma, Robert C. "'Our Comings and Goings': Herbert Krause's *Wind Without Rain.*" *Where the West Begins.* Eds. Arthur R. Huseboe and William Geyer. Sioux Falls, S.Dak.: Center for Western Studies Press, 1978, pp. 13-23.

JOSEPH WOOD KRUTCH

3159. Holtz, William. "Homage to Joseph Wood Krutch: Tragedy and the Ecological Imperative." *American Scholar* 43 (Spring 1974): 267-79.

3160. Lehman, Anthony L. "Joseph Wood Krutch." *Quarterly Newsletter of the Book Club of California* 37 (Summer 1972): 51-63.

3161. Margolis, John D. *Joseph Wood Krutch: A Writer's Life.* Knoxville: University of Tennessee Press, 1980.

3162. Pavich, Paul N. "Joseph Wood Krutch: Persistent Champion of Man and Nature." *Western American Literature* 13 (Summer 1978): 151-58.

3163. Powell, Lawrence C. "Joseph Wood Krutch's *The Desert Year.*" *Westways* 63 (June 1971): 14-17, 66-67.

PETER B. KYNE

3164. Bode, Carl. "Cappy Ricks and the Monk in the Garden." *PMLA* 64 (March 1949): 59-69.

OLIVER LAFARGE

3165. Allen, Charles. "The Fiction of Oliver LaFarge." *Arizona Quarterly* 1 (Winter 1945): 74-81.

3166. Brokaw, Zoanne S. "Oliver La-Farge: His Fictional Navajo." Master's thesis, University of Arizona, 1965.

3167. Bunker, Robert. "Oliver La-Farge: The Search for Self." *New Mexico Quarterly* 20 (Summer 1950): 211-24.

3168. Byrd, Charles Lively. "A Descriptive Bibliography of the Oliver LaFarge Collection at the University of Texas." Doctoral dissertation, University of Texas, Austin, 1974.

3169. Gillis, Everett A. *Oliver LaFarge.* Southwest Writers Series, No. 9. Austin, Tex.: Steck-Vaughn, 1967.

3170. McHenry, Carol S. "Tradition: Ballast in Transition: A Literary Biography of Oliver La-Farge." Master's thesis, University of New Mexico, 1966.

3171. McNickle, D'Arcy. *Indian Man: A Life of Oliver LaFarge.* Bloomington: Indiana University Press, 1971.

3172. Mansfield-Kelley, Deane. "Oliver LaFarge and the Indian Woman in American Literature." Doctoral dissertation, University of Texas, Austin, 1979.

3173. Pearce, T. M. *Oliver LaFarge.* New York: Twayne, 1972.

3174. Powell, Lawrence C. "Oliver LaFarge's *Laughing Boy.*" *Westways* 63 (December 1973): 22-24, 50-52.

3175. Scott, Winfield Townley. "Introduction" to Oliver LaFarge, *The Man with the Calabash Pipe.* Boston: Houghton Mifflin, 1968, pp. xi-xxi.

LOUIS L'AMOUR

3176. Bulow, Ernest L. "Still Tall in the Saddle: Louis L'Amour's Classic Western Hero." *Possible Sack* 3 (June-July 1972): 1-8.

3177. Gonzalez, Arturo F. "Louis L'Amour: Writing High in the Bestseller Saddle." *Writer's Digest* 60 (December 1980): 22-29.

3178. Hinds, Harold E., Jr. "Mexican and Mexican-American Images in the Western Novels of Louis L'Amour." *Latin American Literary Review* 5 (Spring-Summer 1977): 129-41.

3179. Jarrod, Keith. "Introduction" to Louis L'Amour, *Crossfire Trail.* Boston: Gregg Press, 1980, pp. v-x.

3180. Klaschus, Candace. "The Frontier Novels of Louis L'Amour." Master's thesis, San Francisco State University, 1978.

3181. Laing, Wesley. "Introduction" to Louis L'Amour, *Kilkenny.* Boston: Gregg Press, 1980, pp. v-x.

3182. Lee, Wayne C. "Introduction" to Louis L'Amour, *Utah Blaine.* Boston: Gregg Press, 1980, pp. v-ix.

3183. McMillan, Scott R. "Introduction" to Louis L'Amour, *Showdown at Yellow Butte.*

Boston: Gregg Press, 1980, pp. v-x.

3184. Marsden, Michael T. "A Conversation with Louis L'Amour." *Journal of American Culture* 2 (Winter 1980): 646-58.

3185. ——. "The Concept of Family in the Fiction of Louis L'Amour." *North Dakota Quarterly* 46 (Summer 1978): 12-21.

3186. ——. "Introduction" to Louis L'Amour, *Hondo*. Boston: Gregg Press, 1978, pp. v-x.

3187. ——. "The Popular Western Novel as a Cultural Artifact." *Arizona and the West* 20 (Autumn 1978): 203-14.

3188. Nesbitt, John D. "Change of Purpose in the Novels of Louis L'Amour." *Western American Literature* 13 (Spring 1978): 65-81.

3189. ——. "A New Look at Two Popular Western Classics." *South Dakota Review* 18 (Spring 1980): 30-42. Discusses *Hondo*.

3190. Walker, Don D. "Notes on the Popular Western." *Possible Sack* 3 (November 1971): 11-13.

JOHN S. LANGRISCHE

3191. Cochran, Alice C. "John S. Langrische and the Theatre of the Mining Frontier." Master's thesis, Southern Methodist University, 1969.

CLINTON F. LARSON

3192. "A Conversation with Clinton

F. Larson." *Dialogue* 4 (Autumn 1969): 74-80.

D. H. LAWRENCE

3193. Foster, Joseph. *D. H. Lawrence in Taos*. Albuquerque: University of New Mexico Press, 1971.

3194. Halperin, Irving. "Unity in *St. Mawr*." *South Dakota Review* 4 (Summer 1966): 58-60.

3195. Merrild, Knud. *With D. H. Lawrence in New Mexico: A Memoir of D. H. Lawrence*. New York: Barnes and Noble, 1965.

3196. Smith, Bob L. "D. H. Lawrence's *St. Mawr*: Transposition of a Myth." *Arizona Quarterly* 24 (Autumn 1968): 197-208.

3197. Waters, Frank. "Quetzalcoatl Versus D. H. Lawrence's *Plumed Serpent*." *Western American Literature* 3 (Summer 1968): 103-13.

TOM LEA

3198. Antone, Evan H. "Tom Lea: A Study of His Life and Work." Doctoral dissertation, University of California, Los Angeles, 1971.

3199. Bennett, Patrick. "Wells of Sight and Sound: An Interview with Tom Lea." *Southwest Review* 65 (Spring 1980): 113-27.

3200. Braddy, Haldeen. "Artist Illustrators of the Southwest: H. D. Bugbee, Tom Lea and Jose Cisneros." *Western Review* 1 (Fall 1964): 37-41.

3201. Bromfield, Louis. "Triumphs in

the Arena." *Saturday Review of Literature* 32 (April 23, 1949): 10-12.

3202. Dykes, Jeff C. "Tentative Bibliographic Check Lists of Western Illustrators." *American Book Collector* 15 (April 1965): 25-32.

3203. Lovelace, Lisabeth. "Tom Lea Bibliography." *Texas Library Journal* 47 (1971): 217.

3204. Rodenberger, Lou. "Tom Lea, Artist and Novelist: Interpreter of Southwest Border Life." *Southwest Heritage* (Summer 1980).

3205. Sattelmeyer, Robert. "Introduction" to Tom Lea, *The Wonderful Country*. Boston: Gregg Press, 1979, pp. v-xii.

3206. West, John O. *Tom Lea, Artist in Two Mediums*. Southwest Writers Series, No. 5. Austin, Tex.: Steck-Vaughn, 1967.

ALAN LEMAY

3207. Calder, Jenni. *There Must Be a Lone Ranger: The American West in Film and in Reality*. New York: Taplinger, 1974.

3208. Etulain, Richard W. "Introduction" to Alan LeMay, *The Searchers*. Boston: Gregg Press, 1978, pp. v-ix.

3209. Graham, Don. "Introduction" to Alan LeMay, *The Unforgiven*. Boston: Gregg Press, 1978, pp. v-viii.

ALFRED HENRY LEWIS

3210. Boyer, M. G., ed. *Arizona in Literature*. Glendale, Calif.: Arthur H. Clark, 1934.

3211. Filler, Louis. "The West Belongs to All of Us." *Old Wolfville: Chapters from the Fiction of Alfred Henry Lewis*. Yellow Springs, Ohio: Antioch Press, 1968, pp. vii-xii.

3212. ——. "Wolfville." *New Mexico Quarterly Review* 13 (Spring 1943): 35-47.

3213. Herron, Ima Honaker. *The Small Town in American Literature*. Durham, N.C.: Duke University Press, 1939, pp. 280-82.

3214. Humphries, Rolfe. "Introduction" to *Wolfville Yarns of Alfred Henry Lewis*. [Kent, Ohio]: Kent State University Press, 1968, pp. v-xviii.

3215. Manzo, Flournoy D. "Alfred Henry Lewis: Western Storyteller." *Arizona and the West* 10 (Spring 1968): 5-24.

3216. ——. "Alfred Henry Lewis: Western Story Teller." Master's thesis, Texas Western College, 1966.

3217. Mehl, R. F. "Jack London, Alfred Henry Lewis, and Primitive Woman." *Jack London Newsletter* 6 (May-August 1973): 66-70.

3218. Ravitz, Abe C. *Alfred Henry Lewis*. Western Writers Series, No. 32. Boise, Idaho: Boise State University, 1978.

3219. Turner, Tressa. "The Life and Works of Alfred Henry Lewis." Master's thesis, University of Texas, 1936.

JAMES FRANKLIN LEWIS

3220. Lund, Mary Graham. "James Franklin Lewis, Transhumanist." *University Review* 33 (June 1967): 307-12.

JANET LEWIS

3221. Crow, Charles L. *Janet Lewis.* Western Writers Series, No. 41. Boise, Idaho: Boise State University, 1980.

3222. Davie, Donald. "The Historical Novels of Janet Lewis." *Southern Review* 2, N. S. (Winter 1966): 40-60.

3223. Hofheins, Roger, and Dan Tooker. "A Conversation with Janet Lewis." *Southern Review* 10 (April 1974): 329-41.

3224. Inglis, Fred. "The Novels of Janet Lewis." *Critique* 7, No. 2 (1965): 47-64.

3225. Killoh, Ellen. "Patriarchal Women: A Study of Three Novels by Janet Lewis." *Southern Review* 10 (April 1974): 342-64.

3226. Swallow, Alan. "The Mavericks." *Critique* 2 (Winter 1959): 77-79.

MERIWETHER LEWIS
(Lewis and Clark)

3227. Bakeless, John E. *Lewis and Clark: Partners in Discovery.* New York: William Morrow, 1947.

3228. Bewley, Marius. "The Heroic and the Romantic West." *Masks and Mirrors.* New York:

Atheneum, 1970, pp. 213-20.

3229. Criswell, Elijah H. *Lewis and Clark: Linguistic Pioneers.* Columbia: University of Missouri Press, 1940.

3230. DeVoto, Bernard, ed. *The Journals of Lewis and Clark.* Boston: Houghton Mifflin, 1953.

3231. Dillon, Richard. *Meriwether Lewis: A Biography.* New York: Coward-McCann, 1965.

3232. Jackson, Donald, ed. *Letters of the Lewis and Clark Expedition with Related Documents, 1783-1854.* Urbana: University of Illinois Press, 1962.

3233. Lee, Robert Edson. *From West to East.* Urbana: University of Illinois Press, 1966, pp. 11-38.

3234. Nichols, William. "Lewis and Clark Probe the Heart of Darkness." *American Scholar* 49 (Winter 1979-80): 94-101.

3235. Steffen, Jerome O. *William Clark: Jeffersonian Man on the Frontier.* Norman: University of Oklahoma Press, 1977.

3236. Stevenson, Elizabeth. "Meriwether and I." *Virginia Quarterly Review* 43 (Autumn 1967): 580-91.

3237. Thwaites, Reuben Gold, ed. *Original Journals of the Lewis and Clark Expedition, 1804-1806.* 8 vols. New York: Dodd, Mead, 1904-1905.

SINCLAIR LEWIS

3238. Austin, Allen. "An Interview with Sinclair Lewis." *University of Kansas City Review* 24 (March 1958): 199-210.

3239. Baker, Joseph E. "Sinclair Lewis, Plato, and the Regional Escape." *English Journal* [college edition] 28 (June 1939): 460-72.

3240. Barry, James D. *"Dodsworth*: Sinclair Lewis's Novel of Character." *Ball State University Forum* 10 (Spring 1969): 8-14.

3241. Beck, Warren. "How Good Is Sinclair Lewis?" *College English* 9 (January 1948): 173-80.

3242. Brown, Daniel R. "Lewis's Satire—A Negative Emphasis." *Renascence* 18 (Winter 1966): 63-72.

3243. Bucco, Martin. "The Serialized Novels of Sinclair Lewis." *Western American Literature* 4 (Spring 1969): 29-37.

3244. Carpenter, Frederic I. "Sinclair Lewis and the Fortress of Reality." *College English* 16 (April 1955): 416-23.

3245. Conroy, Stephen S. "Sinclair Lewis's Sociological Imagination." *American Literature* 42 (November 1972): 348-62.

3246. Couch, William, Jr. "Sinclair Lewis: Crisis in the American Dream." *CLA Journal* 7 (March 1964): 224-34.

3247. Derleth, August. "Three Literary Men: A Memoir of Sinclair Lewis, Sherwood Anderson, and Edgar Lee Masters." *Arts in Society* (Winter 1959): 11-46.

3248. DeVoto, Bernard. *The Literary Fallacy.* Boston: Little, Brown, 1944, pp. 95-123.

3249. Dooley, D. J. *The Art of Sinclair Lewis.* Lincoln: University of Nebraska Press, 1967.

3250. Douglas, George H. *"Main Street* After Fifty Years." *Prairie Schooner* 44 (Winter 1970-71): 338-48.

3251. Fife, Jim L. "Two Views of the American West." *Western American Literature* 1 (Spring 1966): 34-43.

3252. Flanagan, John T. "A Long Way to Gopher Prairie: Sinclair Lewis's Apprenticeship." *Southwest Review* 32 (Autumn 1947): 403-13.

3253. ———. "The Minnesota Backgrounds of Sinclair Lewis's Fiction." *Minnesota History* 37 (March 1960): 1-13.

3254. Fleming, Robert E. with Esther. *Sinclair Lewis: A Reference Guide.* Boston: G. K. Hall, 1980.

3255. *From Main Street to Stockholm: Letters of Sinclair Lewis, 1919-1930.* Ed. with intro. Harrison Smith. New York: Harcourt, Brace, 1952.

3256. Geismar, Maxwell. *The Last of the Provincials: The American Novel, 1915-1925.* Boston: Houghton Mifflin, 1947, pp. 69-150.

3257. Grebstein, Sheldon Norman. *Sinclair Lewis.* New York: Twayne, 1962.

3258. ———. "Sinclair Lewis and the Nobel Prize." *Western Humanities Review* 13 (Spring 1959): 163-71.

3259. ——. Sinclair Lewis' Minnesota Boyhood." *Minnesota History* 34 (Autumn 1954): 85-89.

3260. Griffin, Robert J., ed. *Twentieth Century Interpretations of "Arrowsmith": A Collection of Critical Essays.* Englewood Cliffs, N.J.: Prentice-Hall, 1968.

3261. Hartwick, Harry. "The Village Virus." *The Foreground of American Fiction.* New York: American Book, 1934, pp. 250-81.

3262. Hilfer, Anthony Channell. *The Revolt from the Village.* Chapel Hill: University of North Carolina Press, 1969, pp. 158-92.

3263. Horton, T. D. "Sinclair Lewis: The Symbol of an Era." *North American Review* 248 (Winter 1939): 374-93.

3264. Lewis, Grace Hegger. *With Love from Gracie.* New York: Harcourt, Brace, 1955.

3265. Lewis, Robert W. "*Babbitt* and the Dream of Romance." *North Dakota Quarterly* 40 (Winter 1972): 7-14.

3266. Light, Martin. "H. G. Wells and Sinclair Lewis: Friendship, Literary Influence, and Letters." *English Fiction in Transition (1880-1920)* 5 (1962): 1-20.

3267. ——. "Lewis' Finicky Girls and Faithful Workers." *University Review* 30 (Winter 1963): 151-59.

3268. ——. *The Quixotic Vision of Sinclair Lewis.* West Lafayette, Ind.: Purdue University Press, 1975.

3269. ——, ed. *Studies in Babbitt.* Columbus, Ohio: Charles E. Merrill, 1971.

3270. Love, Glen A. "New Pioneering on the Prairies: Nature, Progress, and the Individual in the Novels of Sinclair Lewis." *American Quarterly* 25 (December 1973): 558-77.

3271. Lundquist, James. *The Merrill Checklist of Sinclair Lewis.* Columbus: Charles E. Merrill Publishing Company, 1970.

3272. ——. *The Merrill Guide to Sinclair Lewis.* Columbus: Charles E. Merrill Publishing Company, 1970.

3273. ——. *Sinclair Lewis.* Modern Literature Monographs. New York: Frederick Ungar, 1973.

3274. ——, ed. *Sinclair Lewis Newsletter.* St. Cloud State College [Minnesota] , 1969-.

3275. Manfred, Frederick F. "Sinclair Lewis: A Portrait." *American Scholar* 23 (Spring 1954): 162-84.

3276. O'Connor, Richard. *Sinclair Lewis.* American Writers Series. New York: McGraw-Hill, 1971.

3277. Petrullo, Helen B. "*Babbitt* as Situational Satire." *Kansas Quarterly* 1 (Summer 1969): 89-97.

3278. ——. "*Main Street, Cass Timberlane* and Determinism." *South Dakota Review* 7 (Winter 1969-70): 30-42.

3279. Rosenberg, Charles E. "Martin Arrowsmith: The Scientist as Hero." *American Quarterly* 15 (Fall 1963): 447-58.

3280. Schorer, Mark. *Sinclair Lewis.* University of Minnesota

Pamphlets on American Writers. Minneapolis: University of Minnesota, 1963.

3281. ——. *Sinclair Lewis: An American Life.* New York: McGraw-Hill, 1961.

3282. ——, ed. *Sinclair Lewis: A Collection of Critical Essays.* Englewood Cliffs, N.J.: Prentice-Hall, 1962.

3283. Sheean, Vincent. *Dorothy and Red.* Boston: Houghton Mifflin, 1963.

3284. ——. "The Tangled Romance of Sinclair Lewis and Dorothy Thompson." *Harper's* 227 (October 1963): 121-72.

3285. Simon, Tobin. "The Short Stories of Sinclair Lewis." Doctoral dissertation, New York University, 1972.

3286. *South Dakota Review* 7 (Winter 1969-70): 3-78. Special issue on Lewis.

3287. Thompson, Dorothy. "The Boy and Man from Sauk Centre." *Atlantic* 206 (November 1960): 39-48.

3288. Wagenaar, Dick. "The Knight and the Pioneer: Europe and America in the Fiction of Sinclair Lewis." *American Literature* 50 (May 1978): 230-49.

FRANK B. LINDERMAN

3289. Merriam, H. G. "The Life and Work of Frank B. Linderman." *Montana Adventure: The Recollections of Frank B. Linderman.* Lincoln: University of Nebraska Press, 1968, pp. 199-214.

3290. ——. "Sign-Talker with Straight Tongue: Frank Bird Linderman." *Montana: Magazine of Western History* 12 (Summer 1962): 2-20.

3291. Smith, Jean P. "Frank B. Linderman: Sign Talker." *Frontier* 11 (November 1930): 59 ff.

3292. Van de Water, F. F. "The Work of Frank B. Linderman." *Frontier and Midland* 19 (Spring 1939): 148-52.

3293. White, C. "Bibliography of the Writings of Frank Bird Linderman." *Frontier and Midland* 19 (Spring 1939): 147-48.

VACHEL LINDSAY

3294. Avery, Emmett L. "Vachel Lindsay in Spokane." *Pacific Spectator* 3 (1949): 338-53.

3295. ——. "Vachel Lindsay: Spokane Journalist." *Research Studies of the State College of Washington* 25 (March 1957): 101-10.

3296. ——. "Vachel Lindsay's 'Poem Games' in Spokane." *Research Studies of Washington State University* 30 (Summer 1962): 109-14.

3297. Gilliland, Marshall A. "Vachel Lindsay: Poet and Newspaper Columnist in Spokane, 1924-1929." Doctoral dissertation, Washington State University, 1968.

3298. Hallwas, John E. "Poetry and Prophecy: Vachel Lindsay's 'The Jazz Age.'" *Illinois Quarterly* 40 (Fall 1977): 30-37.

3299. Massa, Ann. *Vachel Lindsay:*

Fieldworker for the American Dream. Bloomington: Indiana University Press, 1970.

3300. Ruggles, Eleanor. *The West-Going Heart: A Life of Vachel Lindsay*. New York: W. W. Norton, 1959.

3301. Taylor, Marjorie Anne. "The Folk Imagination of Vachel Lindsay." Doctoral dissertation, Wayne State University, 1976.

3302. Trombly, A. E. "Listeners and Readers: The Unforgetting of Vachel Lindsay." *Southwest Review* 47 (August 1962): 294-302.

JOHN A. LOMAX

3303. Clayton, Lawrence Ray. "John A. Lomax's *Cowboy Songs and Other Frontier Ballads*: A Critical Study." Doctoral dissertation, Texas Tech University, 1974.

3304. Gillis, Everett A., Jack D. Wages, Lawrence R. Clayton. "John A. Lomax and the Songs of the West." *Southwestern American Literature* 5 (1975): 14-21.

JACK LONDON

3305. Barltrop, Robert. *Jack London: The Man, the Writer, the Rebel*. London: Pluto Press, 1976.

3306. Baskett, Sam S. "A Brace for London Criticism: An Essay Review." *Modern Fiction Studies* 22 (Spring 1976): 101-6.

3307. ——. "Jack London on the Oakland Waterfront." *American Literature* 27 (November 1955): 363-71.

3308. ——. "Jack London's Heart of Darkness." *American Quarterly* 10 (Spring 1958): 66-77.

3309. ——. "*Martin Eden*: Jack London's Poem of the Mind." *Modern Fiction Studies* 22 (Spring 1976): 23-36.

3310. Bennett, Kenneth I. "Jack London: The Quest for an Ethic." Doctoral dissertation, Kent State University, 1977.

3311. Benoit, Raymond. "Jack London's *The Call of the Wild*." *American Quarterly* 20 (Summer 1968): 246-48.

3312. Bowen, James K. "Jack London's 'To Build a Fire': Epistemology and the White Wilderness." *Western American Literature* 5 (Winter 1971): 287-89.

3313. Buske, Frank E. "The Wilderness, the Frontier, and the Literature of Alaska to 1914: John Muir, Jack London, and Rex Beach." Doctoral dissertation, University of California, Davis, 1976.

3314. Collins, Billy Gene. "The Frontier in the Stories of Jack London." Doctoral dissertation, Kansas State University, 1970.

3315. Dodson, Mary Kay. "Naturalism in the Works of Jack London." *Jack London Newsletter* 4 (September-December 1971): 130-39.

3316. Drizari, Nelo. "Jack London and the 'Impossible Dream.'"

Pacific Historian 21 (Spring 1977): 36-46.

3317. Ellis, James. "A Reading of *The Sea Wolf*." *Western American Literature* 2 (Summer 1967): 127-34.

3318. Erbentraut, Edwin B. "The Intellectual Undertow in *Martin Eden*." *Jack London Newsletter* 3 (January-April 1970): 12-24.

3319. Etulain, Richard W. "The Lives of Jack London." *Western American Literature* 11 (Summer 1976): 149-64.

3320. ———. *The Works of Jack London.* Cassette. Deland, Fla.: Everett/Edwards, 1976.

3321. ———, ed. *Jack London on the Road: The Tramp Diary and Other Hobo Writings.* Logan: Utah State University Press, 1979.

3322. Findley, Sue. "Naturalism in 'To Build a Fire.'" *Jack London Newsletter* 2 (May-August 1969): 45-48.

3323. Fleming, Becky London. "Memories of My Father, Jack London." *Pacific Historian* 18 (Fall 1974): 5-10.

3324. Foner, Philip S. *Jack London: American Rebel.* New York: Citadel, 1947, 1964.

3325. Fracchia, Charles A. "Jack London's Personal Wilderness." *Sierra Club Bulletin* 63 (June 1978): 47-50.

3326. Geismar, Maxwell. *Rebels and Ancestors: The American Novel, 1890-1915.* Boston: Houghton Mifflin, 1953, pp. 139-216.

3327. Gower, Ronald A. "The Creative Conflict: Struggle and Escape in Jack London's Fiction." *Jack London Newsletter* 4 (May-August 1971): 77-114.

3328. Graham, Don. "Jack London's Tale Told by a High-Grade Feeb." *Studies in Short Fiction* 15 (Fall 1978): 429-33.

3329. Gurian, Jay. "The Romantic Necessity in Literary Naturalism: Jack London." *American Literature* 38 (March 1966): 112-20.

3330. Hamilton, David Mike. "Some Chin-Chin and Tea—Jack London in Japan." *Pacific Historian* 23 (Summer 1979): 19-25.

3331. Harpham, Geoffrey. "Jack London and the Tradition of Superman Socialism." *American Studies* 16 (Spring 1975): 23-33.

3332. Haydock, James. "Jack London: A Bibliography of Criticism." *Bulletin of Bibliography* 23 (May-August 1960): 42-46.

3333. Hendricks, King. *Jack London: Master Craftsman of the Short Story.* Logan: Utah State University, 1966.

3334. ———, and Irving Shepard, eds. *Letters from Jack London, Containing an Unpublished Correspondence between London and Sinclair Lewis.* New York: Odyssey, 1965.

3335. Hensley, Dennis E. "Jack London Speaks About Writing." *Jack London Newsletter* 10 (January-April 1977): 43-47.

189

3336. ———. "Jack London's Use of Maritime History in *The Sea Wolf.*" *Pacific Historian* 23 (Summer 1979): 1-8.

3337. Jennings, Ann S. "London's Code of the Northland." *Alaska Review* 1 (Fall 1964): 43-48.

3338. Kardell, Margaret M. "Jack London's *The Acorn-Planter.*" *Pacific Historian* 21 (Summer 1977): 189-95.

3339. Kingman, Russ. *A Pictorial Life of Jack London.* New York: Crown, 1979.

3340. Koenig, Jacqueline. "Irving Stone's Jack London." *Pacific Historian* 22 (Fall 1978): 246-49.

3341. Labor, Earle. "From 'All Gold Canyon' to *The Acorn-Planter*: Jack London's Agrarian Vision." *Western American Literature* 11 (Summer 1976): 83-101.

3342. ———. *Jack London.* New York: Twayne, 1974.

3343. ———. "Jack London, 1876-1976: A Centennial Recognition." *Modern Fiction Studies* 22 (Spring 1976): 3-7.

3344. ———. "Jack London's 'Planchette': The Road Never Taken." *Pacific Historian* 21 (Summer 1977): 138-46.

3345. ———. "Jack London's Symbolic Wilderness: Four Versions." *Nineteenth-Century Fiction* 17 (Summer 1962): 149-61.

3346. Lachtman, Howard. "All That Glitters: Jack London's *Gold.*" *Jack London Newsletter* 5 (September-December 1972): 172-78.

3347. ———. "Criticism of Jack London: A Selected Checklist." *Modern Fiction Studies* 22 (Spring 1976): 107-26.

3348. ———. "Four Horses, A Wife and A Valet: Up The California Coast With Jack London." *Pacific Historian* 21 (Summer 1977): 103-34.

3349. ———. "Jack and George: Notes on a Literary Friendship." *Pacific Historian* 22 (Summer 1978): 27-42. George Sterling.

3350. ———. "Man and Superwoman in Jack London's 'The Kanaka Surf.'" *Western American Literature* 7 (Summer 1972): 101-10.

3351. ———. "On the Delta Water: Jack London in Old Stockton." *Pacific Historian* 23 (Summer 1979): 9-18.

3352. ———. "Revisiting Jack London's Valley of the Moon." *Pacific Historian* 24 (Summer 1980): 141-56.

3353. ———. "The Wide World of Jack London." Doctoral dissertation, University of the Pacific, 1974.

3354. London, Charmian. *The Book of Jack London.* 2 vols. New York: Century, 1921.

3355. London, Jack. *Jack London Reports: War Correspondence, Sports Articles, and Miscellaneous Writings.* Eds. King Hendricks and Irving Shepard. Garden City, N.Y.: Doubleday, 1970.

3356. ———. *No Mentor But Myself: A Collection of Articles, Essays, Reviews and Letters on*

Writing and Writers. Ed. Dale L. Walker. Port Washington, N.Y.: Kennikat Press, 1979.

3357. London, Joan. *Jack London and His Times: An Unconventional Biography*. New York: Doubleday, Doran, 1939; Seattle: University of Washington, 1968.

3358. Lynn, Kenneth S. *The Dream of Success*. Boston: Little, Brown, 1955, pp. 75-118.

3359. McClintock, James I. "Jack London's Use of Carl Jung's Psychology of the Unconscious." *American Literature* 62 (November 1970): 336-47.

3360. ——. *White Logic: Jack London's Short Stories*. Grand Rapids, Mich.: Wolf House Books, 1975.

3361. McMillan, Marilyn Johnson. "Jack London's Reputation as a Novelist: An Annotated Bibliography." Master's thesis, Sacramento State College, 1967.

3362. Mann, John S. "The Theme of the Double in *The Call of the Wild*." *Markham Review* 8 (Fall 1978): 1-5.

3363. Mehl, R. F. "Jack London, Alfred Henry Lewis, and Primitive Woman." *Jack London Newsletter* 6 (May-August 1973): 66-70.

3364. Mills, Gordon. "Jack London's Quest for Salvation." *American Quarterly* 7 (Spring 1955): 3-14.

3365. ——. "The Symbolic Wilderness: James Fenimore Cooper and Jack London." *Nineteenth-Century Fiction* 13 (March 1959): 329-40.

3366. ——. "The Transformation of Material in a Mimetic Fiction." *Modern Fiction Studies* 22 (Spring 1976): 9-22.

3367. Nichol, John. "The Role of 'Local Color' in Jack London's Alaska Wilderness Tales." *Western Review* 6 (Winter 1969): 51-56.

3368. Noto, Sal. "Homage to Jack London: The House of Happy Walls." *Pacific Historian* 22 (Summer 1978): [Jack London Insert], 1-11.

3369. ——. "Jack London as Social Critic." *Jack London Newsletter* 4 (September-December 1971): 145-50.

3370. O'Connor, Richard. *Jack London: A Biography*. Boston: Little, Brown, 1964.

3371. Ownbey, Ray Wilson, ed. *Jack London: Essays in Criticism*. Santa Barbara, Calif., and Salt Lake City: Peregrine Smith, 1978.

3372. Pankake, Jon Allan. "The Broken Myths of Jack London: Civilization, Nature, and the Self in the Major Works." Doctoral dissertation, University of Minnesota, 1975.

3373. ——. "Jack London's Wild Man: The Broken Myths of *Before Adam*." *Modern Fiction Studies* 22 (Spring 1976): 37-50.

3374. Pearsall, Robert Brainard. "Elizabeth Barrett Meets Wolf Larsen." *Western American Literature* 4 (Spring 1969): 3-13.

3375. Peterson, Clell T. "Jack London's Sonoma Novels." *American Book Collector* 9 (October 1958): 15-20.

3376. ——. "The Theme of Jack London's 'To Build a Fire.'" *American Book Collector* 17 (November 1966): 15-18.

3377. Price, Starling. "Jack London's America." Doctoral dissertation, University of Minnesota, 1970.

3378. Rather, Lois. *Jack London, 1905.* Oakland, Calif.: Rather Press, 1974.

3379. Rothberg, Abraham. "Old Stock: Jack London and His Valley of the Moon." *Southwest Review* 62 (Autumn 1977): 361-68.

3380. Sherman, Joan R. *Jack London: A Reference Guide.* Boston: G. K. Hall, 1977. The starting place for research on London.

3381. Shivers, Alfred S. "Jack London: Author in Search of a Biographer." *American Book Collector* 12 (March 1962): 25-27.

3382. ——. "Jack London: Not a Suicide." *Dalhousie Review* 49 (Spring 1969): 43-57.

3383. ——. "The Romantic in Jack London: Far Away from Frozen Places." *Alaskan Review* 1 (Winter 1963): 38-47.

3384. Silet, Charles L. P. "Upton Sinclair to Jack London: A Literary Friendship." *Jack London Newsletter* 5 (May-August 1972): 49-76.

3385. Sinclair, Andrew. *Jack: A Biography of Jack London.* New York: Harper and Row, 1977.

3386. ——. "Jack London: The Man Who Invented Himself." *American Heritage* 28 (August 1977): 99-107.

3387. Skipp, Frances E. "Jack London." *American Literary Realism 1870-1910* 8 (Autumn 1975): 299-306. Summarizes and evaluates doctoral dissertations on London.

3388. Spinner, Jonathan S. "A Syllabus for the 20th Century: Jack London's *The Call of the Wild.*" *Jack London Newsletter* 7 (May-August 1974): 73-78.

3389. Stasz, Clarice. "Androgyny in the Novels of Jack London." *Western American Literature* 11 (Summer 1976): 121-33.

3390. ——. "The Social Construction of Biography: The Case of Jack London." *Modern Fiction Studies* 22 (Spring 1976): 51-72.

3391. Stone, Irving. *Sailor on Horseback: The Biography of Jack London.* Boston: Houghton Mifflin, 1938; reprinted in *Irving Stone's Jack London,* Garden City, N.Y.: Doubleday, 1977, pp. 9-305.

3392. Teich, Nathaniel. "Marxist Dialectics in Content, Form, Point of View: Structures in Jack London's *The Iron Heel.*" *Modern Fiction Studies* 22 (Spring 1976): 85-100.

3393. Tierney, William. "Jack London's California Ranch Novels." *Pacific Historian* 21 (Summer 1977): 147-58.

3394. Van Der Beets, Richard. "Nietzsche of the North: Heredity and Race in London's *The Son of the Wolf.*" *Western American Literature* 2 (Fall 1967): 229-33.

3395. Walcutt, Charles Child. *American Literary Naturalism, A Divided Stream.* Minneapolis: University of Minnesota Press, 1956, pp. 87-113.

3396. ——. *Jack London.* Minneapolis: University of Minnesota Press, 1966.

3397. Walker, Dale L. *The Alien Worlds of Jack London.* Wolf House Books Monograph Number One. Grand Rapids, Mich.: Wolf House Books, 1973. Deals with London's fantasy fiction.

3398. ——. "Jack London (1876-1916)." *American Literary Realism 1870-1910* 1 (Fall 1967): 71-78.

3399. ——, and James E. Sisson. *The Fiction of Jack London: A Chronological Bibliography.* El Paso: Texas Western Press, 1972.

3400. Walker, Franklin. "Ideas and Action in Jack London's Fiction." *Essays on American Literature in Honor of Jay Hubell.* Ed. Clarence Gohdes. Durham, N.C.: Duke University Press, 1967.

3401. ——. *Jack London and the Klondike.* San Marino, Calif.: Huntington Library, 1966.

3402. ——. "Jack London, *Martin Eden.*" *The American Novel from James Fenimore Cooper to William Faulkner.* Ed. Wallace Stegner. New York: Basic Books, 1965.

3403. ——. "Jack London's Use of Sinclair Lewis Plots, Together with a Printing of Three of the Plots." *Huntington Library Quarterly* 17 (November 1953): 59-74.

3404. Ward, Susan Eileen. "Ideas into Fiction: Popular Rhetoric in the Fiction of Jack London." Doctoral dissertation, University of Connecticut, 1975.

3405. ——. "Jack London's Women: Civilization vs The Frontier." *Jack London Newsletter* 9 (May/August 1976): 81-85.

3406. Warner, Richard H. "A Contemporary Sketch of Jack London." *American Literature* 38 (November 1966): 376-80.

3407. Whitfield, Stephen J. "American Writing as a Wildlife Preserve: Jack London and Norman Mailer." *Southern Quarterly* 15 (January 1977): 135-48.

3408. Wilcox, Earl J. "Jack London and the Tradition of American Literary Naturalism." Doctoral dissertation, Vanderbilt University, 1966.

3409. ——. "Jack London's Naturalism: The Example of *The Call of the Wild.*" *Jack London Newsletter* 2 (September-December 1969): 91-101.

3410. ——. "'The Kipling of the Klondike': Naturalism in London's Early Fiction." *Jack London Newsletter* 6 (January-April 1973): 1-12.

3411. ——. "Le Milieu, Le Moment, La Race: Literary Naturalism in Jack London's *White Fang.*" *Jack London Newsletter* 3 (May-August 1970): 42-55.

3412. Willson, Carolyn Johnston. "Jack London's Socialism." Doctoral dissertation, University of California, Berkeley, 1976.

3413. ———. "London Album: A California Legend at Work and Play." *California Historical Quarterly* 15 (Fall 1976): 218-45.

3414. ———. "'Rattling the Bones': Jack London, Socialist Evangelist." *Western American Literature* 11 (Summer 1976): 135-48.

3415. Winslow, Cedric Reimers. "The Crisis of Liberalism in the Novels of Theodore Dreiser, Frank Norris, and Jack London." 3 vols. Doctoral dissertation, New York University, 1977.

3416. Woodbridge, Hensley C. "Jack London: A Bibliography (A Supplement)." *American Book Collector* 17 (November 1966): 32-35.

3417. ———. "Jack London's Current Reputation Abroad." *Pacific Historian* 21 (Summer 1977): 166-77.

3418. ———, ed. *Jack London Newsletter.* Carbondale: Southern Illinois University Library, 1967-.

3419. ———, John London, and George H. Tweney, comps. *Jack London: A Bibliography.* Georgetown, Calif.: Talisman Press, 1966; enl. ed. Millwood, N.Y.: Kraus, 1973.

3420. Yoder, Jon A. "Jack London as Wolf Barleycorn." *Western American Literature* 11 (Summer 1976): 103-19.

HANIEL LONG

3421. Almon, Bert. "Woman as Interpreter: Haniel Long's *Malinche.*" *Southwest Review* 59 (Summer 1974): 221-39.

3422. Burlingame, Robert. "Haniel Long: His Seasons." *Southwest Review* 65 (Winter 1981): 21-38.

3423. Powell, Lawrence Clark. "Haniel Long and *Interlinear to Cabeza De Vaca.*" *Westways* 63 (April 1971): 26-29, 78.

3424. Sarton, May. "The Leopard Land: Haniel and Alice Long's Santa Fe." *Southwest Review* 57 (1972): 1-14.

MILTON LOTT

3425. Remley, David. "Introduction" to Milton Lott, *The Last Hunt.* Boston: Gregg Press, 1979, pp. v-xv.

MABEL DODGE LUHAN

3426. Brett, Dorothy E. "Autobiography: My Long and Beautiful Journey." *South Dakota Review* 5 (Summer 1967): 11-71.

3427. Morrill, Claire. "Three Women of Taos: Frieda Lawrence, Mabel Luhan, and Dorothy Brett." *South Dakota Review* 2 (Spring 1965): 3-22.

3428. Rudnick, Lois. "Mable Dodge

Luhan and Robinson Jeffers." *Robinson Jeffers Newsletter* 49 (June 1977): 21--49.

3429. ——. "The Unexpurgated Self: A Critical Biography of Mabel Dodge Luhan." Doctoral dissertation, Brown University, 1977.

CHARLES FLETCHER LUMMIS

3430. Bingham, Edwin R. *Charles F. Lummis: Editor of the Southwest.* San Marino, Calif.: Huntington Library, 1955.

3431. Fiske, Turbesé Lummis, and Keith Lummis. *Charles F. Lummis: The Man and His West.* Norman: University of Oklahoma Press, 1975.

3432. Fleming, Robert E. *Charles F. Lummis.* Western Writers Series, No. 50. Boise, Idaho: Boise State University, 1981.

3433. Gordon, Dudley C. "Charles Fletcher Lummis, Cultural Pioneer of the Southwest." *Arizona and the West* 1 (Winter 1959): 305-16.

3434. ——. *Charles F. Lummis: Crusader in Corduroy.* Los Angeles: Cultural Assets Press, 1972.

3435. ——. "Charles F. Lummis: Pioneer American Folklorist." *Western Folklore* 28 (July 1969): 175-81.

3436. Newmark, Marco. "Charles Fletcher Lummis." *Historical Society of Southern California Quarterly* 32 (March 1950): 45-60.

3437. Powell, Lawrence Clark. "California Classics Reread: Charles Fletcher Lummis and *The Land of Sunshine.*" *Westways* 62 (January 1970): 20-23, 35.

3438. ——. "Song of the Southwest." *Westways* 64 (May 1973): 44-47, 82-87.

3439. Simmons, Marc. *Two Southwesterners: Charles Lummis and Amado Chaves.* Cerillos, N.Mex.: San Marcos Press, 1968.

GILES LUTZ

3440. Etulain, Richard. "Recent Western Fiction." *Journal of the West* 8 (October 1969): 656-58.

HARRIS MERTON LYON

3441. Lyon, Zoe. "Harris Merton Lyon: Early American Realist." *Studies in Short Fiction* 5 (Summer 1968): 368-77.

MARGARET HILL MCCARTER

3442. Carl, Sister M. Hildalita. "Kansas History as Seen in the Works of Margaret Hill McCarter." Master's thesis, Creighton University, 1937.

MICHAEL MCCLURE

3443. Clements, Marshall. *A Catalog of Works by Michael McClure.* New York: Phoenix Book Shop, 1965.

3444. Lynch, Michael. "A Broad Silk

Banner." *Parnassus* 4 (Spring-Summer 1976): 156-65.

WILMA ELIZABETH MCDANIEL

3445. Haslam, Gerald. "'Gravy Says A Lot': The Poetry of Wilma Elizabeth McDaniel." *Western American Literature* 13 (Summer 1978): 159-64.

ROSS MACDONALD

3446. Pry, Elmer. "Ross Macdonald's Violent California: Imagery Patterns in *The Underground Man*." *Western American Literature* 9 (November 1974): 197-203.

3447. Speir, Jerry. *Ross Macdonald*. New York: Frederick Ungar, 1978.

3448. Wolfe, Peter. *Dreamers Who Live Their Dreams: The World of Ross Macdonald's Novels*. Bowling Green, Ohio: Bowling Green University Popular Press, 1976.

THOMAS MCGRATH

3449. Engel, Bernard F. "Thomas McGrath's Dakota." *Midwestern Miscellany* 4 (1976): 3-7.

3450. McGrath, Thomas. "McGrath on McGrath." *Epoch* 22 (1973): 207-19.

3451. Smeall, Joseph F. S. "Thomas McGrath: A Review Essay." *North Dakota Quarterly* 40 (Winter 1972): 29-38.

3452. Stern, Frederick C. "'The Delegate for Poetry': McGrath as

Communist Poet." *Where the West Begins*. Eds. Arthur R. Huseboe and William Geyer. Sioux Falls, S.Dak.: Center for Western Studies Press, 1978, pp. 119-27.

THOMAS MCGUANE

3453. Carter, Albert Howard, III. "McGuane's First Three Novels: Games, Fun, Nemesis." *Critique* 17, No. 1 (1975): 91-104.

3454. McCaffery, Larry. "Thomas McGuane: A Bibliography, 1969-1978." *Bulletin of Bibliography* 35 (October-December 1978): 169-71.

3455. Welch, Dennis M. "Death and Fun in the Novels of Thomas McGuane." *University of Windsor Review* 14 (1978): 14-20.

MARY MACLANE

3456. Wheeler, Leslie. "Montana's Shocking 'Lit'ry Lady.'" *Montana: The Magazine of Western History* 27 (Summer 1977): 20-33.

NORMAN MACLEOD

3457. Trusky, A. Thomas. "Norman Wicklund MacLeod, Poet from the West." *Prairie Schooner* 50 (Fall 1976): 257-68.

3458. Wald, Alan. "Tethered to the Past: The Poetry of Norman MacLeod." *Minnesota Review* 11 (1978): 107-11.

LARRY MCMURTRY

3459. Ahearn, Kerry. "Morte D'Urban: The Texas Novels of Larry McMurtry." *Texas Quarterly* 19 (Autumn 1976): 109-29.

3460. Allen, Elizabeth. "Leaving Cheyenne: The Evolution of the Cowboy in Larry McMurtry's Fiction." Master's thesis, Southwest Texas State University, 1975.

3461. Busby, Mark. "Damn the Saddle on the Wall: Anti-Myth in Larry McMurtry's *Horseman, Pass By*." *New Mexico Humanities Review* 3 (Summer 1980): 5-10.

3462. Crooks, Alan. "Larry McMurtry —A Writer in Transition: An Essay-Review." *Western American Literature* 7 (Summer 1972): 151-55.

3463. Davis, Kenneth W. "The Themes of Initiation in the Work of Larry McMurtry and Tom Mayer." *Arlington Quarterly* 2 (Winter 1969-1970): 29-43.

3464. Degenfelder, E. Pauline. "McMurtry and the Movies: *Hud* and *The Last Picture Show*." *Western Humanities Review* 29 (Winter 1975): 81-91.

3465. Dubose, Thomas. "*The Last Picture Show*: Theme." *RE: Artes Liberales* 3 (1977): 43-45.

3466. England, D. Gene. "Rites of Passage in Larry McMurtry's *The Last Picture Show*." *Heritage of Kansas* 12 (Winter 1979): 37-48.

3467. Folsom, James K. "*Shane* and *Hud*: Two Stories in Search of a Medium." *Western Humanities Review* 24 (Autumn 1970): 359-72.

3468. Giles, James R. "Larry McMurtry's *Leaving Cheyenne* and the Novels of John Rechy: Four Trips Along 'the Mythical Pecos.'" *Forum* 10 (Summer-Fall 1972): 34-40.

3469. Granzow, Barbara. "The Western Writer: A Study of Larry McMurtry's *All My Friends Are Going To Be Strangers*." *Southwestern American Literature* 4 (1974): 37-52.

3470. Landess, Thomas. *Larry McMurtry*. Southwest Writers Series, No. 23. Austin, Tex.: Steck-Vaughn, 1969.

3471. Neinstein, Raymond L. *The Ghost Country: A Study of the Novels of Larry McMurtry*. Berkeley, Calif.: Creative Arts, 1976.

3472. Peavy, Charles D. "Coming of Age in Texas: The Novels of Larry McMurtry." *Western American Literature* 4 (Fall 1969): 171-88.

3473. ——. *Larry McMurtry*. Boston: Twayne, 1977.

3474. ——. "A Larry McMurtry Bibliography." *Western American Literature* 3 (Fall 1968): 235-48.

3475. ——. "Larry McMurtry and Black Humor: A Note on *The Last Picture Show*." *Western American Literature* 2 (Fall 1969): 223-27.

3476. Phillips, Billie. "McMurtry's Women: 'Eros [Libido, Caritas, and Philia] in [and out of] Archer County.'" *Southwestern American Literature* 4 (1974): 29-36.

3477. Phillips, Raymond C., Jr. "The Ranch as Place and Symbol in the Novels of Larry McMurtry." *South Dakota Review* 13 (Summer 1975): 27-47.

3478. Pilkington, William T. "The Dirt Farmer and the Cowboy: Notes on Two Texas Essayists." *RE: Arts and Letters* 3 (Fall 1969): 42-54.

3479. ——. "The Recent Southwestern Novel." *Southwestern American Literature* 1 (January 1971): 12-15.

3480. Schmidt, Dorey, ed. *Larry McMurtry: Unredeemed Dreams.* Edinburg, Tex.: Pan American University, 1978. A useful collection of essays, including a selective bibliography and an interview with McMurtry.

3481. Sniffen, Jimmie Clifton." The Emergence of Woman in the Novels of Larry McMurtry." Master's thesis, Stephen F. Austin State University, 1972.

3482. Sonnichsen, C. L. "The New Style Western." *South Dakota Review* 4 (Summer 1966): 22-28.

3483. Stout, Janis P. "Journeying as a Metaphor for Cultural Loss in the Novels of Larry McMurtry." *Western American Literature* 11 (May 1976): 37-50.

3484. Summerlin, Tim. "Larry McMurtry and the Persistent Frontier." *Southwestern American Literature* 4 (1974): 22-28.

3485. Tovar, Inez Hernandez. "The Quest Theme in the Fiction of Larry McMurtry." Master's thesis, University of Houston, 1972.

CHARLES L. MCNICHOLS

3486. Berner, Robert L. "Charles L. McNichols and *Crazy Weather*: A Reconsideration." *Western American Literature* 6 (Spring 1971): 39-51.

D'ARCY MCNICKLE

3487. Larson, Charles R. *American Indian Fiction.* Albuquerque: University of New Mexico Press, 1978, pp. 68-78.

NORMAN MAILER

3488. Evans, Timothy. "Boiling the Archetypal Pot: Norman Mailer's American Dream." *Southwest Review* 60 (Spring 1975): 159-70.

3489. Witt, Grace. "The Bad Man as Hipster: Norman Mailer's Use of Frontier Metaphor." *Western American Literature* 4 (Fall 1969): 202-17.

BERNARD MALAMUD

3490. Astro, Richard. "In the Heart of the Valley: Bernard Malamud's *A New Life.*" *Bernard Malamud: A Collection of Critical Essays.* Eds. Leslie A.

Field and Joyce W. Field. Englewood Cliffs, N.J.: Prentice-Hall, 1975, pp. 143-55.

3491. Barsness, John A. "*A New Life*: The Frontier Myth in Perspective." *Western American Literature* 3 (Winter 1969): 297-302.

3492. Fiedler, Leslie A. "Malamud's Travesty Western." *Novel: A Forum on Fiction* 10 (Spring 1977): 212-19.

3493. Hollander, John. "To Find the Westward Path." *Partisan Review* 29 (Winter 1962): 137-39.

3494. Kosofsky, Rita Nathalie. *Bernard Malamud: An Annotated Checklist*. Kent, Ohio: Kent State University Press, 1969.

3495. Richman, Sidney. *Bernard Malamud*. New York: Twayne, 1966, pp. 78-97.

3496. Schulz, Max F. "Malamud's *A New Life*: The New Wasteland of the Fifties." *Western Review* 6 (Summer 1969): 37-44.

3497. Singer, Barnett. "Outsider Versus Insider: Malamud's and Kesey's Pacific Northwest." *South Dakota Review* 13 (Winter 1975-76): 127-44.

3498. Solotaroff, Theodore. "Bernard Malamud's Fiction: The Old Life and the New." *Commentary* 30 (March 1962): 197-204.

3499. Witherington, Paul. "Malamud's Allusive Design in *A New Life*." *Western American Literature* 10 (August 1975): 114-23.

JAMES C. MALIN

3500. Bell, Robert G. "James C. Malin and the Grasslands of North America." *Agricultural History* 46 (July 1972): 414-24.

3501. Bogue, Allan G. "The Heirs of James C. Malin: A Grasslands Historiography." *Great Plains Quarterly* I (Spring 1981): 105-31.

3502. LeDuc, Thomas H. "An Ecological Interpretation of Grasslands History: The Work of James C. Malin as Historian and as Critic of Historians." *Nebraska History* 31 (September 1950): 226-33.

FREDERICK FEIKEMA MANFRED

3503. Arthur, Anthony. "Manfred, Neihardt, and Hugh Glass: Variations on an American Epic." *Where the West Begins*. Eds. Arthur R. Huseboe and William Geyer. Sioux Falls, S.Dak.: Center for Western Studies Press, 1978, pp. 99-109.

3504. Austin, James C. "Legend, Myth and Symbol in Frederick Manfred's *Lord Grizzly*." *Critique* 6 (Winter 1963-64): 122-30.

3505. Bebeau, Don. "A Search for Voice: A Sense of Place in *The Golden Bowl*." *South Dakota Review* 7 (Winter 1969-70): 79-86.

3506. Byrd, Forrest Mickey. "Prologomenon to Frederick Manfred." Doctoral dissertation,

University of Nebraska, Lincoln, 1975.

3507. Flora, Joseph. *Frederick Manfred*. Western Writers Series, No. 13. Boise, Idaho: Boise State University, 1974.

3508. ——. "Siouxland Panorama: Frederick Manfred's *Green Earth*." *Midwestern Miscellany* 7 (1979): 56-63.

3509. Husboe, Arthur R. "Manfred's *Conquering Horse* and Parkman's *The Oregon Trail*." *College of Arts and Sciences Report* (Vermillion, S.Dak.) 9 (Spring 1961): 21-24.

3510. Kellogg, George. "Frederick Manfred: A Bibliography." *Twentieth Century Literature* 11 (April 1965): 30-35.

3511. ——. *Frederick Manfred: A Bibliography*. Denver: Alan Swallow, 1965. Reprints above item.

3512. Lee, James W. "An Interview in Minnesota with Frederick Manfred." *Studies in the Novel* 5 (Fall 1973): 358-82.

3513. McCord, Nancy Nelson. "Manfred's Elof Lofblom." *Western American Literature* 16 (Summer 1981): 125-34.

3514. Michael, Larry A. "Literary Allusions in the Fiction of Frederick Manfred." Master's thesis, University of South Dakota, 1965.

3515. Milton, John R. "Frederick Feikema Manfred." *Western Review* 22 (Spring 1958): 181-98.

3516. ——. "Interview [with] Frederick Manfred." *Fiction* 9 (1976): 16-19, 61.

3517. ——. "Interview with Frederick Manfred." *South Dakota Review* 7 (Winter 1969-70): 110-30.

3518. ——. "*Lord Grizzly*: Rhythm, Form and Meaning in the Western Novel." *Western American Literature* 1 (Spring 1966): 6-14.

3519. ——. *The Novel of the American West*. Lincoln: University of Nebraska Press, 1980, pp. 160-94.

3520. ——. "Voice from Siouxland: Frederick Feikema Manfred." *College English* 19 (December 1957): 104-11.

3521. ——, ed. *Conversations with Frederick Manfred*. Salt Lake City: University of Utah Press, 1974.

3522. Moen, Ole O. "The Voice of the Siouxland: Man and Nature in Frederick Manfred's Writing." Doctoral dissertation, University of Minnesota, 1978.

3523. Oppewall, Peter. "Manfred and Calvin College." *Where the West Begins*. Eds. Arthur R. Huseboe and William Geyer. Sioux Falls, S.Dak.: Center for Western Studies Press, 1978, pp. 86-98.

3524. Peet, Howard. "Evolution of a Man Named Fred." Master's thesis, Moorhead State College, 1965.

3525. Roth, Russell. "The Inception of a Saga: Frederick Manfred's 'Buckskin Man.'" *South Dakota Review* 7 (Winter 1969-70): 87-99.

3526. *South Dakota Review* 7 (Winter

1969-70). Special issue on Manfred.

3527. Spies, George H. "John Steinbeck's *The Grapes of Wrath* and Frederick Manfred's *The Golden Bowl*: A Comparative Study." Doctoral dissertation, Ball State University, 1973.

3528. Swallow, Alan. "The Mavericks." *Critique* 2 (Winter 1959): 88-92.

3529. Ter Matt, Cornelius John. "Three Novelists and a Community: A Study of American Novelists with Dutch Calvinist Origins." Doctoral dissertation, University of Michigan, 1963.

3530. "West of the Mississippi: An Interview with Frederick Manfred." *Critique* 2 (Winter 1959): 35-56.

3531. Westbrook, Max. "Introduction" to Frederick Manfred, *This Is the Year*. Boston: Gregg Press, 1979, pp. v-vii. Includes Manfred's revisions of the novel.

3532. ———. "*Riders of Judgment*: An Exercise in Ontological Criticism." *Western American Literature* 12 (May 1977): 41-51.

3533. Wright, Robert C. *Frederick Manfred*. Boston: Twayne, 1979.

3534. ———. "The Myth of the Isolated Self in Manfred's Siouxland Novels." *Where the West Begins*. Eds. Arthur R. Huseboe and William Geyer. Sioux Falls, S.Dak.: Center for Western Studies Press, 1978, pp. 110-18.

3435. Wylder, Delbert E. "Frederick Manfred: The Quest of an Independent Writer." *Books at Iowa* 31 (November 1979): 16-31.

3536. ———. "Manfred's Indian Novel." *South Dakota Review* 7 (Winter 1969-70): 100-109.

EDWIN MARKHAM

3537. Arlt, G. O. "Poet Laureate: Edwin Markham." *Historical Society of Southern California Quarterly* 34 (September 1952): 199-212.

3538. Chase, Don M. "Edwin Markham California Prophet." *Pacific Historian* 20 (Summer 1976): 167-76.

3539. Clemens, Cyril, et al. "Edwin Markham Number." *Mark Twain Quarterly* 4 (Spring 1941): 1-20.

3540. Farley, Marie Breniman. "Memories of Edwin Markham." *Pacific Historian* 15 (Winter 1971): 30-32.

3541. Filler, Louis. "Edwin Markham, Poetry and What Have You." *Antioch Review* 23 (Winter 1963-64): 447-59.

3542. ———. *The Unknown Edwin Markham: His Mystery and Its Significance*. Yellow Springs, Ohio: Antioch Press, 1966.

3543. Goldstein, Jessie S. "Edwin Markham, Ambrose Bierce, and 'The Man with the Hoe.'" *Modern Language Notes* 58 (March 1943): 165-75.

3544. ———. "Escapade of a Poet." *Pacific Historical Review* 13 (September 1944): 303-13.

201

3545. ——. "Life of Edwin Markham." Doctoral dissertation, New York University, 1945.

3546. ——. "Two Literary Radicals: Garland and Markham in Chicago, 1893." *American Literature* 17 (May 1945): 152-60.

3547. Grose, G. R. "Edwin Markham: Poet of the Social Conscience." *Personalist* 17 (April 1936): 149-56.

3548. Haaland, C. Carlyle. "The Mystique of Markham's California: The Culmination of the Millenial Motif in America." *Markham Review* 4 (February 1975): 89-95.

3549. Slade, Joseph W. " 'Putting You in the Papers': Ambrose Bierce's Letters to Edwin Markham." *Prospects: An Annual Journal of American Cultural Studies.* Vol. I. Ed. Jack Salzman. New York: Burt Franklin, 1975, pp. 335-68.

3550. Synnestvedt, Sigfried T. "Bread, Beauty, and Brotherhood: The Ethical Consciousness of Edwin Markham." Doctoral dissertation, University of Pennsylvania, 1959.

ALICE MARRIOTT

3551. Kohler, Turner S. *Alice Marriott.* Southwest Writers Series, No. 27. Austin, Tex.: Steck-Vaughn, 1969.

3552. ——. "Alice Marriott: The Anthropologist as Artist." *Southwestern American Literature* 1 (May 1971): 72-79.

FRANCIS S. MARRYAT

3553. LeRoy, Bruce. "Frank Marryat, *Mountains and Molehills.*" *Book Club of California Quarterly News-Letter* 38 (Summer 1973): 51-62.

JOHN JOSEPH MATHEWS

3554. Larson, Charles R. *American Indian Fiction.* Albuquerque: University of New Mexico Press, 1978, pp. 34-37, 55-65.

3555. Oaks, Priscilla. "Introduction" to John Joseph Mathews, *Sundown.* Boston: Gregg Press, 1978, pp. v-xi.

TOM MAYER

3556. Davis, Kenneth W. "The Theme of Initiation in the Works of Larry McMurtry and Tom Mayer." *Arlington Quarterly* 2 (Winter 1969-70): 29-43.

RITA MENDOZA

3557. Lewis, Marvin A. "Rita Mendoza: Chicana Poetess." *Latin American Literary Review* 5 (Spring-Summer 1977): 79-85.

OSCAR MICHEAUX

3558. Hebert, Janis. "Oscar Micheaux: A Black Pioneer." *South Dakota Review* 11 (Winter 1973-74): 62-69.

3559. Day, A. Grove. *James Michener.* 2d ed. Boston: Twayne, 1977. Contains a section on *Centennial.*

3560. Kings, John. *In Search of "Centennial": A Journey with James A. Michener.* New York: Random House, 1978.

3561. Michener, James. *About 'Centennial': Some Notes on the Novel.* New York: Random House [?], 1974.

GEORGE MILBURN

3562. Disbrow, Jimmie L. "The Local-Color Artistry of George Milburn." Doctoral dissertation, Oklahoma State University, 1972.

3563. Downs, Alexis. "George Milburn: Ozark Folklore in Oklahoma Fiction." *Chronicles of Oklahoma* 55 (Fall 1977): 309-23.

3564. Herron, Ima Honaker. *The Small Town in American Literature.* Durham, N.C.: Duke University Press, 1939.

3565. Rackleff, Julia. "Folk Speech in the Short Stories and Novels of George Milburn." Master's thesis, University of Tulsa, 1949.

3566. Turner, Steven. *George Milburn.* Southwest Writers Series, No. 28. Austin, Tex.: Steck-Vaughn, 1970.

3567. Allen, Merritt P. *Joaquin Miller: Frontier Poet.* New York: Harper and Brothers, 1932.

3568. Beebe, Beatrice B., ed. "Letters of Joaquin Miller." *Frontier* 12 (1932): 121-24, 223-28, 344-47.

3569. Brendemuhl, Gabriella C. "Joaquin Miller's Indebtedness to Byron in Connection with His Early Narrative Poems." Doctoral dissertation, University of Chicago, 1921.

3570. Buchanan, L. E. "Joaquin Miller in the Passing of the Old West." *Research Studies of Washington State University* 32 (1964): 326-33.

3571. Duckett, Margaret. "Carlyle, 'Columbus,' and Joaquin Miller." *Philological Quarterly* 35 (1956): 443-47.

3572. Dunbar, John Raine. "Joaquin Miller: Sedition and Civil War." *Pacific Historical Review* 19 (February 1950): 31-36.

3573. Dykes, Mattie M. "Joaquin Miller: A Biographical Study." Doctoral dissertation, University of Chicago, 1922.

3574. Frost, O. W. *Joaquin Miller.* New York: Twayne, 1967.

3575. Haight, Mary M. "Joaquin Miller in Oregon, 1852-54 and 1857-70." Doctoral dissertation, University of Washington, 1936.

3576. Lawson, Benjamin S. *Joaquin Miller.* Western Writers Series, No. 43. Boise, Idaho: Boise

State University, 1980.

3577. ——. "Joaquin Miller in England." *South Dakota Review* 12 (Winter 1974-75): 89-101.

3578. Longtin, Ray C. *Three Writers of the Far West: A Reference Guide.* Boston: G. K. Hall, 1980.

3579. Marberry, M. Marion. *Splendid Poseur: Joaquin Miller—American Poet.* New York: Thomas Y. Crowell, 1953.

3580. Miller, Juanita. *My Father, C. H. Joaquin Miller, Poet.* Oakland, Calif.: Tooley-Towne, [1941].

3581. Peterson, Martin Severin. *Joaquin Miller: Literary Frontiersman.* Palo Alto, Calif.: Stanford University Press, 1937.

3582. Powers, Alfred. *History of Oregon Literature.* Portland: Metropolitan Press, 1935.

3583. Reade, Frank R. "Cincinnatus Hiner Miller: A Critical Biography." Doctoral dissertation, University of Virginia, 1926.

3584. Richards, John S., ed. *Joaquin Miller: His California Diary.* Seattle: F. McCaffrey, 1936.

3585. Rosenus, A. H. "Joaquin Miller and His 'Shadow.'" *Western American Literature* 10 (May 1976): 51-59.

3586. ——, ed. *Selected Writings of Joaquin Miller.* Eugene, Oreg.: Urion Press, 1977.

3587. Sherman, Stuart P., ed. *The Poetical Works of Joaquin Miller.* New York: G. P. Putnam, 1923.

3588. Thompson, H. C. "Reminiscences of Joaquin Miller and Canyon City." *Oregon Histori-*cal Quarterly 45 (December 1944): 326-36.

3589. Wagner, Harr. *Joaquin Miller and His Other Self.* San Francisco: Harr Wagner, 1929.

3590. Walker, Franklin. *San Francisco's Literary Frontier.* New York: Alfred A. Knopf, 1939.

3591. Walterhouse, Roger R. "Bret Harte, Joaquin Miller, and the Western Local Color Story." Doctoral dissertation, University of Chicago, 1936.

ENOS MILLS

3592. Abbott, Carl. "'To Arouse Interest in the Outdoors': The Literary Career of Enos Mills." *Montana: The Magazine of Western History* 31 (April 1981): 2-15.

3593. Wild, Peter. *Enos Mills.* Western Writers Series, No. 36. Boise, Idaho: Boise State University, 1979.

JOHN R. MILTON

3594. Pavich, Paul N. "Myth and Paramyth in John R. Milton's *Notes to a Bald Buffalo.*" *Where the West Begins.* Eds. Arthur R. Huseboe and William Geyer. Sioux Falls, S.Dak.: Center for Western Studies Press, 1978, pp. 80-85.

3595. Sanford, Geraldine. "Mountain Climbing with Milton." *Dakota Arts Quarterly* (Fall 1979): 4-7.

3596. ——. "To Pay A Little Blood: Pursuit of the Vision in *Notes* to a Bald Buffalo." *Heritage of Kansas* 11 (Winter 1978): 28-34.

VILHELM MOBERG

3597. Robb, Kenneth A. "A Swedish Emigrant in the Land of Oranges." *Itinerary: Criticism, Essays on California Writers.* Ed. Charles L. Crow. Bowling Green, Ohio: University Press, 1978, pp. 79-87.

N. SCOTT MOMADAY

3598. Barry, Nora Baker. "The Bear's Son Folk Tale in *When the Legends Die* and *House Made of Dawn.*" *Western American Literature* 12 (Winter 1978): 275-87.

3599. Berner, Robert L. "N. Scott Momaday: Beyond Rainy Mountain." *American Indian Culture and Research Journal* 3 (1979): 57-67.

3600. Billingsley, R. G. "*House Made of Dawn*: Momaday's Treatise on the Word." *Southwestern American Literature* 5 (1975): 81-87.

3601. Bloodworth, William. "Neihardt, Momaday, and the Art of Indian Autobiography." *Where the West Begins.* Eds. Arthur R. Huseboe and William Geyer. Sioux Falls, S.Dak.: Center for Western Studies Press, 1978, pp. 152-60.

3602. Davis, Jack L. "Language and Consciousness in *House Made of Dawn.*" *New America* 3

(Summer-Fall 1977): 56-59.

3603. ——. "The Whorf Hypothesis and Native American Literature." *South Dakota Review* 14 (Summer 1976): 59-72.

3604. Dickinson-Brown, Roger. "The Art and Importance of N. Scott Momaday." *Southern Review* 14 (January 1978): 30-45.

3605. Dillingham, Peter. "The Literature of the American Indian." *English Journal* 62 (January 1973): 37-41.

3606. Evers, Lawrence J. "Words and Place: A Reading of *House Made of Dawn.*" *Western American Literature* 11 (February 1977): 297-320.

3607. Hyde, Mary Marra. "The Works of N. Scott Momaday: An Organic Bridge Between Delusion and Understanding." Master's thesis, Brigham Young University, 1974.

3608. Hylton, Marion Willard. "On a Trail of Pollen: Momaday's *House Made of Dawn.*" *Critique* 14 No. 2 (1972): 60-69.

3609. Kerr, Blaine. "The Novel as Sacred Text: N. Scott Momaday's Myth-making Ethic." *Southwest Review* 63 (Spring 1978): 172-79.

3610. Kousaleos, Peter G. "A Study of the Language, Structure, and Symbolism in Jean Toomer's *Cane* and N. Scott Momaday's *House Made of Dawn.*" Doctoral dissertation, Ohio University, 1973.

3611. Larson, Charles R. *American Indian Fiction.* Albuquerque:

205

University of New Mexico Press, 1978, pp. 78-95, 165-72.

3612. McAllister, H. S. "Be a Man, Be a Woman: Androgyny in *House Made of Dawn.*" *American Indian Quarterly* 11 (Spring 1975): 14-22.

3613. ——. "Incarnate Grace and the Paths of Salvation in *House Made of Dawn.*" *South Dakota Review* 12 (Winter 1974-75): 115-25.

3614. ——. "The Topology of Remembrance in *The Way to Rainy Mountain.*" *Denver Quarterly* 12 (Winter 1978): 19-31.

3615. Mason, Kenneth D. "Beautyway: The Poetry of N. Scott Momaday." *South Dakota Review* 18 (Summer 1980): 61-83.

3616. Nelson, Margaret Faye. "Ethnic Identity in the Prose Works of N. Scott Momaday." Doctoral dissertation, Oklahoma State University, 1979.

3617. Nicholas, Charles A. *"The Way to Rainy Mountain*: N. Scott Momaday's Hard Journey Back." *South Dakota Review* 13 (Winter 1975-76): 149-58.

3618. Oleson, Carole. "The Remembered Earth: Momaday's *House Made of Dawn.*" *South Dakota Review* 11 (Spring 1973): 59-78.

3619. Roemer, Kenneth M. "Survey Courses, Indian Literature, and *The Way to Rainy Mountain.*" *College English* 37 (February 1976): 619-24.

3620. Smith, Marie. "Rainy Mountain, Legends and Students." *Arizona English Bulletin* 13 (April 1971): 41-44.

3621. Trimble, Martha Scott. *N. Scott Momaday.* Western Writers Series No. 9. Boise, Idaho: Boise State College, 1973.

3622. Trimmer, Joseph F. "Native Americans and the America Mix: N. Scott Momaday's *House Made of Dawn.*" *Indiana Social Studies Quarterly* 28 (1975): 75-91.

3623. Velie, Alan R. "Cain and Abel in N. Scott Momaday's *House Made of Dawn.*" *Journal of the West* 17 (April 1978): 55-62.

3624. Watkins, Floyd C. *In Time and Place: Some Origins of American Fiction.* Athens: University of Georgia Press, 1977, pp. 133-71. On *House Made of Dawn.*

3625. Winters, Yvor. *Forms of Discovery.* Chicago: Alan Swallow, 1967, pp. 279-84.

3626. Woodward, Charles Lowell. "The Concept of the Creative Word in the Writings of N. Scott Momaday." Doctoral dissertation, University of Oklahoma, 1975.

3627. Zachrau, Thekla. "N. Scott Momaday: Towards an Indian Identity." *American Indian Culture and Research Journal* 3 (1979): 39-56.

WRIGHT MORRIS

3628. Albers, Randall K. "The Female Transformation: The Role of

Women in Two Novels by Wright Morris." *Prairie Schooner* 53 (Summer 1979): 95–115.

3629. Baumbach, Jonathan. "Wake Before Bomb: *Ceremony in Lone Tree.*" *Critique* 4 (Winter 1961–62): 56–71.

3630. Bleufarb [*sic*], Sam. "Point of View: An Interview with Wright Morris." *Accent* 19 (Winter 1959): 34–46.

3631. Booth, Wayne C. "The Shaping of Prophecy: Craft and Idea in the Novels of Wright Morris." *American Scholar* 31 (Autumn 1962): 608–26.

3632. ——. "The Two Worlds in the Fiction of Wright Morris." *Sewanee Review* 65 (Summer 1957): 375–99.

3633. Brenner, Jack. "Wright Morris's West: Fallout from a Pioneer Past." *Denver Quarterly* 10 (Winter 1976): 63–75.

3634. Burns, Leslie Edward. "A Psychological Reading of Wright Morris' Early Novels." Doctoral dissertation, New York University, 1978.

3635. Carpenter, Frederic I. "Wright Morris and the Territory Ahead." *College English* 21 (December 1959): 147–56.

3636. Cohn, Jack Rice. "Wright Morris: The Design of the Midwestern Fiction." Doctoral dissertation, University of California, Berkeley, 1970.

3637. Crump, G. B. *The Novels of Wright Morris: A Critical Interpretation.* Lincoln: University of Nebraska Press, 1978.

3638. ——. "Wright Morris's *One Day*: The Bad News on the Hour." *Midamerica* 3 (1976): 77–91.

3639. Dymond, Richard Bruce. "The Impoverished Self: A Study of Selected Fiction of Wright Morris." Doctoral dissertation, University of Rochester, 1973.

3640. Eisinger, Chester E. *Fiction of the Forties.* Chicago: University of Chicago Press, 1963, pp. 328–41.

3641. Flanagan, John T. "The Fiction of Wright Morris." *Studia Germanica Gandensia* 3 (1961): 209–31.

3642. Garrett, George. "Morris The Magician: A Look at *In Orbit.*" *Hollins Critic* 4 (June 1967): 1–12.

3643. Guettinger, Roger J. "The Problem with Jigsaw Puzzles: Form in the Fiction of Wright Morris." *Texas Quarterly* 11 (Spring 1968): 209–20.

3644. Hafer, Jack. "Setting and Theme in Wright Morris's *Ceremony in Lone Tree.*" *Heritage of Kansas* 10 (Summer 1977): 10–20.

3645. Harper, Robert D. "Wright Morris's *Ceremony in Lone Tree*: A Picture of Life in Middle America." *Western America Literature* 11 (November 1976): 199–213.

3646. Hicks, Granville, ed. "Introduction." *Wright Morris: A Reader.* New York: Harper and Row, 1970.

3647. ——. "Wright Morris." *Literary Horizons: A Quarter Century of American Fiction.* New

York: New York University Press, 1970, pp. 7-47.

3648. Howard, Leon. *Wright Morris.* Minneapolis: University of Minnesota Press, 1968.

3649. Hunt, John W., Jr. "The Journey Back: The Early Novels of Wright Morris." *Critique* 5 (Spring-Summer 1962): 41-60.

3650. Klein, Marcus. *After Alienation.* New York: World, 1964, pp. 196-246.

3651. Knoll, Robert E. *Conversations with Wright Morris.* Lincoln: University of Nebraska Press, 1977. A significant collection of essays, interviews, and bibliographical listings.

3652. Linden, Stanton J., and David Madden. "A Wright Morris Bibliography." *Critique* 4 (Winter 1961-62): 77-87.

3653. Machann, Ginny Brown. "*Ceremony at Lone Tree* and *Badlands*: The Starkweather Case and the Nebraska Plains." *Prairie Schooner* 53 (Summer 1979): 165-72.

3654. Madden, David. "The Great Plains in the Novels of Wright Morris." *Critique* 4 (Winter 1961-62): 5-23.

3655. ——. "The Hero and the Witness in Wright Morris' Field of Vision." *Prairie Schooner* 34 (Fall 1960): 263-78.

3656. ——. "Morris' *Cannibals*, Cain's *Serenade*: The Dynamics of Style and Technique." *Journal of Popular Culture* 8 (Summer 1974): 59-70.

3657. ——. *Wright Morris.* New York: Twayne, 1964.

3658. ——. "Wright Morris' *In Orbit*: An Unbroken Series of Poetic Gestures." *Critique* 10 (Fall 1968): 102-19.

3659. ——, et al. "Wright Morris Issue." *Critique* 4 (Winter 1961-62): 5-87.

3660. Miller, James E., Jr. "The Nebraska Encounter: Willa Cather and Wright Morris." *Prairie Schooner* 41 (Summer 1967): 165-67.

3661. Miller, Ralph N. "The Fiction of Wright Morris: The Sense of Ending." *MidAmerica* 3 (1976): 56-76.

3662. Morris, Wright. *The Territory Ahead.* New York: Harcourt, Brace, 1958.

3663. Neinstein, Raymond L. "Wright Morris: The Metaphysics of Home." *Prairie Schooner* 53 (Summer 1979): 121-54.

3664. Nelson, Carolyn W. "The Spiritual Quest in the Works of Wright Morris." Doctoral dissertation, University of Chicago, 1966.

3665. Nemanic, Gerald. "A Ripening Eye: Wright Morris and the Field of Vision." *MidAmerica* 1 (1974): 120-31.

3666. ——, and Harry White. "GLR/ Interview: Wright Morris." *Great Lakes Review* 1 (1975): 1-29.

3667. Rook, Constance Merriam. "Character in the Early Fiction of Wright Morris." Doctoral dissertation. University of North Carolina, Chapel Hill, 1973.

3668. Shetty, M. Nalini [V.] "The Fiction of Wright Morris." Doctoral dissertation, University of Pittsburgh, 1967.

3669. ——. "Of Human Bondage: Captivity in Time and Hero in the Fiction of Wright Morris." *Indian Response to American Literature.* Ed. C. D. Narasimhaiah. New Delhi: United States Educational Foundation in India, 1967, pp. 191-207.

3670. ——. "Wright Morris and the Territory Ahead." *Indian Essays in American Literature.* Bombay: Popular Prakashan, 1969, pp. 71-83.

3671. Trachtenberg, Alan. "The Craft of Vision." *Critique* 4 (Winter 1961-62): 41-55.

3672. Tucker, Martin. "The Landscape of Wright Morris." *Lock Haven Review* 7 (1965): 43-51.

3673. Waldeland, Lynne. "The Deep Sleep: The Fifties in the Novels of Wright Morris." *Silhouettes on the Shade: Images of the 50's Reexamined.* Muncie, Ind.: Ball State University, 1973, pp. 25-43.

3674. ——. "Wright Morris: His Theory and Practice of the Craft of Fiction." Doctoral dissertation, Purdue University, 1970.

3675. Waterman, Arthur E. "The Novels of Wright Morris: An Escape from Nostalgia." *Critique* 4 (Winter 1961-62): 24-40.

3676. ——. "Wright Morris' *One Day*: The Novel of Revelation." *Furman Studies* 15 (May 1968): 29-36.

3677. Westdal, Lincoln Wesley. "Consciousness in the Novels of Wright Morris." Doctoral dissertation, University of Nevada, Reno, 1976.

3678. Wilson, J. C. "Wright Morris and the Search for the 'Still Point.'" *Prairie Schooner* 49 (Summer 1975): 154-63.

JOHN MUIR

3679. Badé, William F. *The Life and Letters of John Muir.* Boston: Houghton Mifflin, 1924.

3680. Cohen, Michael P. "John Muir's Public Voice." *Western American Literature* 10 (November 1975): 177-87.

3681. Colby, William E., ed. *Studies in the Sierra.* San Francisco: Sierra Club, 1950.

3682. Cosbey, Robert C. "John Muir." Doctoral dissertation, Ohio State University, 1949.

3683. Fleck, Richard F. "John Muir's Evolving Attitudes Toward Native American Cultures." *American Indian Quarterly* 4 (February 1978): 19-31.

3684. Foerster, Norman. "Muir." *Nature in American Literature.* New York: Russell and Russell, 1958.

3685. Hadley, Edith. "John Muir's Views of Nature and Their Consequences." Doctoral dissertation, University of Wisconsin, 1956.

3686. Lyon, Thomas J. *John Muir.* Western Writers Series, No. 3. Boise, Idaho: Boise State College, 1972.

3687. Merritt, J. I. "Turning Point: John Muir in the Sierra, 1871." *American West* 16 (July/August 1979): 4-15, 62-63.

3688. Nash, Roderick. *Wilderness and the American Mind*. Rev. ed. New Haven: Yale University Press, 1973, pp. 122-40, 158-68.

3689. Simonson, Harold P. "The Tempered Romanticism of John Muir." *Western American Literature* 13 (Fall 1978): 227-41.

3690. Smith, Herbert F. *John Muir*. New York: Twayne, 1965.

3691. Teale, Edwin May, ed. *The Wilderness World of John Muir*. Boston: Houghton Mifflin, 1954.

3692. Weber, Daniel B. "John Muir: The Function of Wilderness in an Industrial Society." Doctoral dissertation, University of Minnesota, 1964.

3693. Wolfe, Linnie Marsh. *Son of the Wilderness: The Life of John Muir*. Boston: Houghton Mifflin, 1954.

3694. ——, ed. *John of the Mountains: The Unpublished Journals of John Muir*. Boston: Houghton Mifflin, 1938.

CLARENCE MULFORD

3695. Alderman, Taylor. "*The Great Gatsby* and *Hopalong Cassidy*." *Fitzgerald/Hemingway Annual 1975*. Englewood, Colo.: Microcard Editions Books, 1975, pp. 83-87.

3696. Bloodworth, William A., Jr. "Mulford and Bower: Myth and History in the Early Western." *Great Plains Quarterly* 1 (Spring 1981): 95-104.

3697. Durham, Philip. "Jay Gatsby and Hopalong Cassidy." *Themes and Directions in American Literature: Essays in Honor of Leon Howard*. Eds. Ray B. Browne and Donald Pizer. Purdue University Studies. Lafayette, Ind.: Purdue University Press, 1969, pp. 163-70.

3698. Jensen, Oliver. "Hopalong Hits the Jackpot." *Life* 28 (June 12, 1950): 63-68, 70.

3699. Perham, Joseph A. "Reflections on Hopalong Cassidy: A Study of Clarence E. Mulford." Master's thesis, University of Maine, 1966.

AMADO JESUS MURO
See Chester Seltzer

JOHN G. NEIHARDT

3700. Adkins, Nelson F. "A Study of John G. Neihardt's 'Song of Three Friends.'" *American Speech* 3 (April 1928): 276-90.

3701. Aly, Lucile F. *John G. Neihardt: A Critical Biography*. Amsterdam: Rodopi, 1977.

3702. ——. "John G. Neihardt and Rhetorical Poetry." *Rhetoric of the People*. Amsterdam: Rodopi, 1974, pp. 139-335.

3703. ——. "John G. Neihardt and the American Epic." *Western*

American Literature 13 (Winter 1979): 309-25.

3704. ——. "John G. Neihardt as Speaker and Reader." Doctoral dissertation, University of Missouri, 1959.

3705. ——. "Poetry and History in Neihardt's *Cycle of the West*." *Western American Literature* 16 (Spring 1981): 3-18.

3706. ——. "The Word-Sender: John G. Neihardt and His Audiences." *Quarterly Journal of Speech* 43 (April 1957): 151-54.

3707. Arthur, Anthony. "Manfred, Neihardt, and Hugh Glass: Variations on an American Epic." *Where the West Begins.* Eds. Arthur R. Huseboe and William Geyer. Sioux Falls, S.Dak.: Center for Western Studies Press, 1978, pp. 99-109.

3708. Black, W. E. "Ethic and Metaphysic: A Study of John G. Neihardt." *Western American Literature* 2 (Fall 1967): 205-12.

3709. Bloodworth, William. "Neihardt, Momaday, and the Art of Indian Autobiography." *Where the West Begins.* Eds. Arthur R. Huseboe and William Geyer. Sioux Falls, S.Dak.: Center for Western Studies Press, 1978, pp. 152-60.

3710. DeLowry, Linda Diane. "Dynamic Patterns: A Thematic Study of the Works of John G. Neihardt." Doctoral dissertation, University of Pittsburgh, 1975.

3711. Flanagan, John T. "John G. Neihardt, Chronicler of the West." *Arizona Quarterly* 21 (Spring 1965): 7-20.

3712. Grant, George Paul. "The Poetic Development of John G. Neihardt." Doctoral dissertation, University of Pittsburgh, 1958.

3713. House, Julian T. *John G. Neihardt, Man and Poet.* Wayne, Nebr.: F. H. Jones and Son, 1920.

3714. Kay, Arthur Murray. "The Epic Intent and the American Dream: The Westering Theme in Modern American Narrative Poetry." Doctoral dissertation, Columbia University, 1961, pp. 158-84.

3715. Lee, Fred L. "John G. Neihardt: The Man and His Western Writings: The Bancroft Years, 1900-1921." *Trail Guide* 17 (September–December 1973): 3-35.

3716. Lemons, William Everett. "John G. Neihardt's Conception of the Plains Indian." Master's thesis, University of Colorado, 1950.

3717. McCluskey, Sally. "*Black Elk Speaks*: and So Does John Neihardt." *Western American Literature* 6 (Winter 1972): 231-42.

3718. ——. "Image and Idea in the Poetry of John G. Neihardt." Doctoral dissertation, Northern Illinois University, 1974.

3719. Milton, John R. *The Works of John G. Neihardt.* Cassette.

Deland, Fla.: Everett/Edwards, 1974.

3720. Neihardt, John G. *All Is But a Beginning: Youth Remembered–1881-1901.* New York: Harcourt Brace Jovanovich, 1972.

3721. ——. *Patterns and Coincidences: A Sequel to "All Is But a Beginning."* Columbia: University of Missouri Press, 1978.

3722. Richards, John Thomas. "John G. Neihardt as Critic and Reviewer." Doctoral dissertation, University of Missouri, Columbia, 1976.

3723. ——. *Luminous Sanity: Literary Criticism Written by John G. Neihardt.* Cape Girardeau, Mo.: Concordia Publishing House, 1973.

3724. Rothwell, Kenneth S. "In Search of a Western Epic: Neihardt, Sandburg and Jaffe as Regionalists and 'Astoriadists.'" *Kansas Quarterly* 2 (Spring 1970): 53-63.

3725. Slote, Bernice D. "Neihardt: Nebraska's Poet Laureate." *Prairie Schooner* 41 (Summer 1967): 178-81.

3726. Todd, Edgeley W. "The Frontier Epic: Frank Norris and John G. Neihardt." *Western Humanities Review* 13 (Winter 1959): 40-45.

3727. Wahlstrom, Billie Joyce. "Transforming Fact: The Poetics of History in John G. Neihardt's *Cycle of the West.*" Doctoral dissertation, University of Michigan, 1975.

3728. Whitney, Blair. *John G. Neihardt.* Boston: Twayne, 1976.

JOHN NICHOLS

3729. Blessing, Richard A. "For Pookie, With Love and Good Riddance: John Nichols' *The Sterile Cuckoo.*" *Journal of Popular Culture* 7 (Summer 1973): 124-35.

3730. Márquez, Antonio. "An Interview with John Nichols." *New America* 3 (Spring 1979): 28-33.

CHARLES NORRIS

3731. Goldsmith, Arnold L. "Charles and Frank Norris." *Western American Literature* 2 (Spring 1967): 30-49.

FRANK NORRIS

3732. Ahnebrink, Lars. *The Beginnings of Naturalism in American Fiction.* Upsala: Upsala University Press, 1950.

3733. Bauer, Walter John, Jr. "The Man-Woman Relationship in the Novels of Frank Norris." Doctoral dissertation, New York University, 1973.

3734. Beller, Hilliard Irwin. "Value and Antimonies in the Novels of Frank Norris." Doctoral dissertation, New York University, 1970.

3735. Bernstein, Suzy Jahss. "The Novels of Frank Norris: An Analysis of Their Structure."

Doctoral dissertation, Columbia University, 1970.

3736. Bixler, Paul H. "Frank Norris's Literary Reputation." *American Literature* 6 (May 1934): 109-21.

3737. Chase, Richard. *The American Novel and Its Tradition.* Garden City, N.Y.: Doubleday, 1957, pp. 185-204.

3738. Cooperman, Stanley. "Frank Norris and the Werewolf of Guilt." *Modern Language Quarterly* 20 (September (1959): 252-58.

3739. Crisler, Jessee Shattuck. "A Critical and Textual Study of Frank Norris's *McTeague*." Doctoral dissertation, University of South Carolina, 1973.

3740. ——, and Joseph R. McElrath, Jr. *Frank Norris: A Reference Guide.* Boston: G. K. Hall, 1974.

3741. Crow, Charles L. "The Real Vanamee and His Influence on Frank Norris' *The Octopus*." *Western American Literature* 9 (August 1974): 131-39.

3742. Davison, Richard Allan. "Frank Norris' *The Octopus*: Some Observations on Vanamee, Shelgrim and St. Paul." *Literature and Ideas in America.* Ed. Robert Falk. Columbus: Ohio University Press, 1976, pp. 182-203.

3743. ——, ed. *The Merrill Studies in The Octopus.* Columbus, Ohio: Charles E. Merrill, 1969.

3744. Dillingham, William B. "Frank Norris." *Fifteen American Authors Before 1900: Bibliographic Essays on Research and Criticism.* Eds. Robert A. Rees and Earl N. Harbert. Madison: University of Wisconsin Press, 1971, pp. 307-32.

3745. ——. "Frank Norris and the Genteel Tradition." *Tennessee Studies in Literature* 5 (1960): 15-24.

3746. ——. *Frank Norris: Instinct and Art.* Lincoln: University of Nebraska Press, 1969; Boston: Houghton Mifflin, 1969.

3747. Folsom, James K. "Social Darwinism or Social Protest? The 'Philosophy' of *The Octopus*." *Modern Fiction Studies* 7 (Winter 1962-63): 393-400.

3748. French, Warren. *Frank Norris.* New York: Twayne, 1962.

3749. ——. "Frank Norris (1870-1902)." *American Literary Realism 1870-1910* 1 (Fall 1967): 84-89.

3750. Frohock, W. M. *Frank Norris.* Minneapolis: University of Minnesota Press, 1969.

3751. Gaer, Joseph, ed. *Frank Norris: Bibliography and Biographical Data.* Monograph, No. 3. Berkeley: California Literary Research Project, 1934.

3752. Gardner, Joseph H. "Dickens, Romance, and *McTeague*: A Study in Mutual Interpretation." *Essays in Literature* 1 (Spring 1974): 69-82.

3753. Geismar, Maxwell. *Rebels and Ancestors: The American Novel, 1890-1915.* Boston: Houghton Mifflin, 1953, pp. 3-66.

213

3754. Ginanni, Francis Ralph. "Impressionistic Techniques in the Novels of Frank Norris." Doctoral dissertation, Auburn University, 1970.

3755. Goldman, Suzy Bernstein. "*McTeague*: The Imagistic Network." *Western American Literature* 7 (Summer 1972): 83-99.

3756. Goldsmith, Arnold L. "Charles and Frank Norris." *Western American Literature* 2 (Spring 1967): 30-49.

3757. ———. "The Development of Frank Norris's Philosophy." *Studies in Honor of John Wilcox.* Eds. A. Dayle Wallace and Woodburn O. Ross. Detroit: Wayne State University Press, 1958, pp. 175-94.

3758. Graham, D. B. "Art in *McTeague*." *Studies in American Fiction* 3 (Autumn 1975): 143-55.

3759. ———. *The Fiction of Frank Norris—The Aesthetic Context.* Columbia: University of Missouri Press, 1978.

3760. ———. "Frank Norris and Les Jeunes: Architectural Criticism and Aesthetic Values." *American Literary Realism 1870-1910* 11 (Autumn 1978): 235-48.

3761. ———. "Studio Art in *The Octopus*." *American Literature* 44 (January 1973): 657-66.

3762. ———, ed. *Critical Essays on Frank Norris.* Boston: G. K. Hall, 1980.

3763. Hart, James D., ed. *A Novelist in the Making.* Cambridge, Mass.: Harvard University Press, 1970.

3764. Hill, John S. *Checklist of Frank Norris.* Columbus: Charles E. Merrill Publishing, 1970.

3765. Hoffmann, Charles G. "Norris and the Responsibility of the Novelist." *South Atlantic Quarterly* 54 (October 1955): 508-15.

3766. Johnson, George W. "Frank Norris and Romance." *American Literature* 33 (March 1961): 52-63.

3767. ———. "The Frontier Behind Frank Norris' *McTeague*." *Huntington Library Quarterly* 26 (November 1962): 91-104.

3768. Kaplan, Charles. "Norris's Use of Sources in *The Pit*." *American Literature* 25 (March 1953): 75-84.

3769. Katz, Joseph. "The Elusive Criticism Syndicated by Frank Norris." *Proof* 3 (1973): 221-51.

3770. ———. "Eroticism in American Literary Realism." *Studies in American Fiction* 5 (Spring 1977): 35-50.

3771. ———. "The Shorter Publications of Frank Norris: A Checklist." *Proof* 3 (1973): 155-220.

3772. Kwiat, Joseph J. "Frank Norris: The Novelist as Social Critic and Literary Theorist." *Arizona Quarterly* 18 (Winter 1962): 319-28.

3773. ———. "The Social Responsibilities of the American Painter and Writer: Robert Henri and

John Sloan; Frank Norris and Theodore Dreiser." *Centennial Review* 21 (Winter 1977): 19-35.

3774. Lohf, Kenneth A., and Eugene P. Sheehy. *Frank Norris: A Bibliography.* Los Gatos, Calif.: Talisman Press, 1959.

3775. Love, Glen A. "Frank Norris's Western Metropolitans." *Western American Literature* 10 (May 1976): 3-22.

3776. Lundy, Robert D. "The Making of *McTeague* and *The Octopus.*" Doctoral dissertation, University of California, 1956.

3777. Lynn, Kenneth S. *The Dream of Success.* Boston: Little, Brown, 1955, pp. 158-207.

3778. McElrath, Joseph R., Jr. "Allegory in Frank Norris's *Blix:* Its Relevance to *Vandover.*" *Markham Review* 8 (Winter 1979): 25-27.

3779. ——. "The Comedy of Frank Norris's *McTeague.*" *Studies in American Humor* 2 (October 1975): 88-95.

3780. ——. "A Critical Edition of Frank Norris's *Moran of the Lady Letty: A Story of Adventure off the California Coast.*" Doctoral dissertation, University of South Carolina, 1973.

3781. ——. "The Erratic Design of Frank Norris's *Moran of the Lady Letty.*" *American Literary Realism 1870-1910* 10 (Spring 1977): 114-24.

3782. ——. "Frank Norris." *American Literary Realism 1870-1910* 8 (Autumn 1975): 307-19. Reviews dissertations on Norris.

3783. ——. "Frank Norris: A Bibliographical Essay." *American Literary Realism 1870-1910* 11 (Autumn 1978): 219-34.

3784. ——. "Frank Norris: Early Posthumous Responses." *American Literary Realism 1870-1910* 12 (Spring 1979): 1-76.

3785. ——. "Frank Norris's *Vandover and the Brute*: Narrative Technique and the Socio-Critical Viewpoint." *Studies in American Fiction* 4 (Spring 1976): 27-43.

3786. Marchand, Ernest. *Frank Norris: A Study.* Stanford, Calif.: Stanford University Press, 1942.

3887. Messenger, Christian. "Frank Norris and the College Sportsman." *American Literary Realism 1870-1910* 12 (Autumn 1979): 288-94.

3788. Meyer, George W. "A New Interpretation of *The Octopus.*" *College English* 4 (March 1943): 351-59.

3789. Micklus, Robert. "Ambivalent Warriors in *The Octopus.*" *Western American Literature* 16 (Summer 1981): 115-23.

3790. Miller, Edwin Haviland. "The Art of Frank Norris in *McTeague.*" *Markham Review* 8 (Summer 1979): 61-66.

3791. Morgan, H. Wayne. *American Writers in Rebellion: From Mark Twain to Dreiser.* New York: Hill and Wang, 1965.

3792. Morsberger, Robert E. "The Inconsistent *Octopus.*" *Western American Literature* 16 (Summer 1981): 105-13.

215

3793. Murthy, S. S. "Frank Norris and Scott Fitzgerald: Some Parallels in Their Thoughts and Art." Doctoral dissertation, University of Utah, 1976.

3794. Musick, Gerald Donald. "Frank Norris's Character Types." Doctoral dissertation, University of Wisconsin, 1973.

3795. Pizer, Donald. "Another Look at *The Octopus.*" *Nineteenth-Century Fiction* 10 (December 1955): 217-24.

3796. ——. "The Concept of Nature in Frank Norris' *The Octopus.*" *American Quarterly* 14 (Spring 1962): 73-80.

3797. ——. "Evolutionary Ethical Dualism in Frank Norris' *Vandover and the Brute* and *McTeague.*" *PMLA* 76 (December 1961): 552-60.

3798. ——. "Frank Norris' Definition of Naturalism." *Modern Fiction Studies* 8 (Winter 1962-63): 408-10.

3799. ——. "The Masculine-Feminine Ethic in Frank Norris' Popular Novels." *Texas Studies in Language and Literature* 6 (Spring 1964): 84-91.

3800. ——. "Nineteenth-Century American Naturalism: An Essay in Definition." *Bucknell Review* 13 (December 1965): 1-18.

3801. ——. *The Novels of Frank Norris.* Bloomington: Indiana University Press, 1966.

3802. ——. "Synthetic Criticism and Frank Norris: Or, Mr. Marx, Mr. Taylor, and *The Octopus.*" *American Literature* 34 (January 1963): 532-41.

3803. ——, ed. *The Literary Criticism of Frank Norris.* Austin: University of Texas Press, 1964.

3804. Poncet, Andre. *Frank Norris (1870-1902).* Paris: University of Paris, 1977.

3805. Reninger, H. Williard. "Norris Explains *The Octopus*: A Correlation of His Theory and Practice." *American Literature* 12 (May 1940): 218-27.

3806. Schneider, Robert W. *Five Novelists of the Progressive Era.* New York: Columbia University Press, 1965.

3807. ——. "Frank Norris: The Naturalist as Victorian." *Midcontinent American Studies Journal* 3 (Spring 1962): 13-27.

3808. Taylor, Walter Fuller. *The Economic Novel in America.* Chapel Hill: University of North Carolina Press, 1942, pp. 282-306.

3809. Vance, William L. "Romance in *The Octopus.*" *Genre* 3 (June 1970): 111-36.

3810. Vogelbaum, Alexandra Doris van Ophuijsen. "The New Heroines: The Emergence of Sexuality in the Treatment of the American Fictional Heroine, 1890-1900." Doctoral dissertation, Tulane University, 1978.

3811. Walcutt, Charles Child. *American Literary Naturalism: A Divided Stream.* Minneapolis: University of Minnesota Press, 1956, pp. 114-56.

3812. ——. "Frank Norris and the Search for Form." *University* of Kansas City Review 14 (Winter 1947): 126-36.

3813. ——. "Frank Norris on Realism and Naturalism." *American Literature* 13 (March 1941): 61-63.

3814. ——. "The Naturalism of *Vandover and the Brute*." *Forms of Modern Fiction*. Ed. William Van O'Connor. Minneapolis: University of Minnesota Press, 1948, pp. 154-68.

3815. Walker, Don D. "The Western Naturalism of Frank Norris." *Western American Literature* 2 (Spring 1967): 14-29.

3816. Walker, Franklin. "Four Additional Frank Norris Letters." *Book Club of California Quarterly News-Letter* 40 (Winter 1974): 3-8.

3817. ——. *Frank Norris: A Biography*. New York: Doubleday, Doran, 1932; London: Russell & Russell, 1963.

3818. ——, ed. *The Letters of Frank Norris*. San Francisco: Book Club of California, 1956.

3819. Winslow, Cedric Reimers. "The Crisis of Liberalism in the Novels of Theodore Dreiser, Frank Norris, and Jack London." 3 vols. Doctoral dissertation, New York University, 1977.

EDGAR WILSON NYE
(Bill Nye)

3820. Bakerville, Barnet. "19th Century Burlesque of Oratory." *American Quarterly* 20 (Winter 1968): 726-43.

3821. Blair, Walter. "The Background of Bill Nye in American Humor." Doctoral dissertation, University of Chicago, 1931.

3822. Chaplin, W. E. "Bill Nye." *Frontier* 11 (1931): 223-26.

3823. Davidson, Levette J. "Bill Nye and *The Denver Tribune*." *Colorado Magazine* 4 (January 1928): 13-18.

3824. Eitel, Edmund H. "Letters of Riley and Bill Nye." *Harpers Monthly Magazine* 138 (March 1919): 473-84.

3825. Hasley, Louis. "The Durable Humor of Bill Nye." *Mark Twain Journal* 15 (Winter 1970-71): 7-19.

3826. ——, ed. *The Best of Bill Nye's Humor*. New Haven, Conn.: College and University Press, 1972.

3827. Heestand, Diane Elissa. "The Writing of Bill Nye in Laramie." Master's thesis, University of Wyoming, 1968.

3828. Kesterson, David B. *Bill Nye: The Western Writings*. Western Writers Series, No. 22. Boise, Idaho: Boise State University, 1976.

3829. Lanier, Doris. "Bill Nye in the South." *Annals of Wyoming* 46 (Fall 1974): 253-62.

3830. Larson, T. A. "Laramie's Bill Nye." *1952 Brand Book*. Denver: Denver Westerners, 1953, pp. 35-56.

3831. ——, ed. *Bill Nye's Western Humor*. Lincoln: University of Nebraska Press, 1968.

3832. Lindsey, Ethel Leona. "Edgar Wilson Nye and American

Humor." Master's thesis, University of Wyoming, 1929.

3833. Nye, Frank Wilson, ed. *Bill Nye: His Own Life.* New York: Century, 1926.

3834. Rush, Nixon Orwin, ed. *Letters of Edgar Wilson Nye.* Laramie: University of Wyoming Library, 1950.

3835. Schwartz, Thomas. "Edgar Wilson (Bill) Nye." *American Literary Realism 1870-1910* 8 (Autumn 1975): 320. Comments on dissertations written about Nye.

JOHN OKADA

3836. Inada, Lawson Fusao. "The Vision of America in John Okada's *No-No Boy.*" *Proceedings of the Comparative Literature Symposium* (Lubbock, Tex.) 9 (1978): 275-87.

TILLIE OLSEN

3837. Burkom, Selma, and Margaret Williams. "De-Riddling Tillie Olsen's Writings." *San Jose Studies* 2 (February 1976): 65-83.

3838. Rose, Ellen Cronan. "Lemning: Or Why Tillie Writes." *Hollins Critic* 13 (1976): 1-13.

SIGURD OLSON

3839. Hertzel, Leo J. "What About Writers in the North?" *South Dakota Review* 5 (Spring 1967): 3-19.

D. J. O'MALLEY

3840. White, John I. "'Kid' O'Malley: Montana's Cowboy Poet." *Montana Magazine of History* 17 (July 1967): 60-73.

SIMON ORTIZ

3841. Gingerich, Willard. "The Old Voices of Acoma: Simon Ortiz's Mythic Indigenism." *Southwest Review* 64 (Winter 1979): 18-30.

JOHN MILTON OSKISON

3842. Larson, Charles R. *American Indian Fiction.* Albuquerque: University of New Mexico Press, 1978, pp. 34-37, 46-55.

3843. Strickland, Arney L. "John Milton Oskison: A Writer of the Transitional Period of the Oklahoma Indian Territory." *Southwestern American Literature* 2 (Winter 1972): 125-34.

WAYNE D. OVERHOLSER

3844. Marsden, Michael T. "The Taming of Civilization in the Western Fiction of Wayne D. Overholser." *Kansas Quarterly* 10 (Fall 1978): 105-11.

WILLIAM A. OWENS

3845. Owens, William A. "Writing A Novel—Problem and Solution." *Southwest Review* 40 (Summer 1955): 254-61.

3846. Pilkington, William T. *William A. Owens.* Southwest Writers Series, No. 17. Austin, Tex.: Steck-Vaughn, 1968.

FRANCIS PARKMAN

3847. Beaver, Harold. "Parkman's Crack-Up: A Bostonian on the Oregon Trail." *New England Quarterly* 48 (March 1975): 84-103.
3848. Doughty, Howard. *Francis Parkman.* New York: Macmillan, 1962.
3849. Feltskog, E. N., ed. *The Oregon Trail.* Madison: University of Wisconsin Press, 1969.
3850. Hart, James D. "Patrician Among Savages: Francis Parkman's *The Oregon Trail.*" *Georgia Review* 10 (Spring 1956): 69-73.
3851. Jennings, F. P. "A Vanishing Indian: Francis Parkman versus His Sources." *Pennsylvania Magazine of History and Biography* 87 (July 1963): 306-23.
3852. Lee, Robert Edson. *From West to East.* Urbana: University of Illinois Press, 1966, pp. 69-81.
3853. Levin, David. "Francis Parkman: *The Oregon Trail.*" *Landmarks of American Writing.* Ed. Hennig Cohen. New York: Basic Books, 1969, pp. 79-89.
3854. ——. *History As Romantic Art.* Stanford, Calif.: Stanford University Press, 1959.
3855. Pease, Otis. *Parkman's History: The Historian as Literary Artist.* New Haven, Conn.: Yale University Press, 1953.

3856. Powers, William. "Bulkington as Henry Chatillon." *Western American Literature* 3 (Summer 1968): 153-55.
3857. Tribble, Joseph L. "The Paradise of the Imagination: The Journeys of The Oregon Trail." *New England Quarterly* 46 (December 1973): 523-42.
3858. Wade, Mason. *Francis Parkman: Heroic Historian.* New York: Viking, 1942.
3859. ——, ed. *The Journals of Francis Parkman.* 2 vols. New York: Harper, 1947.
3860. Walsh, J. E. *"The California and Oregon Trail:* A Bibliographical Study." *New Colophon* 3 (1950): 279-85.

VERNON LOUIS PARRINGTON

3861. Hall, Helen L. "Vernon Louis Parrington: The Genesis and Design of *Main Currents in American Thought.*" Doctoral dissertation, Yale University, 1979.
3862. Hofstadter, Richard. *The Progressive Historians: Turner, Beard, Parrington.* New York: Alfred A. Knopf, 1968.
3863. Houghton, D. E. "Vernon Louis Parrington's Unacknowledged Debt to Moses Coit Tyler." *New England Quarterly* 43 (March 1970): 124-30.
3864. Reinitz, Richard. "Vernon Louis Parrington as Historical Ironist." *Pacific Northwest Quarterly* 68 (July 1977): 113-19.
3865. Singer, Barnett. "Judging Vernon

Louis Parrington." *Research Studies* 43 (1975): 209-21.

San Francisco: Scrimshaw Press 1976.

KENNETH PATCHEN

3866. Clodd, Alan, ed. *Tribute to Kenneth Patchen.* London: Enitharmon, 1977. Includes reminiscences and essays.
3867. Detro, Gene. *Patchen: The Last Interview.* Santa Barbara, Calif.: Capra, 1976.
3868. Glicksberg, Charles I. "The World of Kenneth Patchen." *Arizona Quarterly* 7 (Autumn 1951): 263-75.
3869. Hack, Richard. "Memorial Poetry Reading for Kenneth Patchen. . . ." *Chicago Review* 24, No. 2 (1972): 65-80.
3870. Morgan, Richard G., ed. *Kenneth Patchen: A Collection of Essays.* New York: AMS, 1977.
3871. Nelson, Raymond John. "An American Mysticism: The Example of Kenneth Patchen." Doctoral dissertation, Stanford University, 1969.
3872. See, Carolyn. "The Jazz Musician as Patchen's Hero." *Arizona Quarterly* 17 (Summer 1961): 136-46.
3873. ——. "Kenneth Patchen, 1934-1958: A Partial Bibliography." *Bulletin of Bibliography* 23 (January-April 1961): 81-84.
3874. Smith, Larry R. *Kenneth Patchen.* Boston: Twayne, 1978.
3875. Veres, Peter. *The Argument of Innocence: A Selection from the Arts of Kenneth Patchen.*

JAMES KIRKE PAULDING

3876. Alderman, Ralph M. "James Kirke Paulding on Literature and the West." *American Literature* 27 (March 1955): 97-101.
3877. Person, Leland S., Jr. "James Kirke Paulding: Myth and the Middle Ground." *Western American Literature* 16 (Spring 1981): 39-54.

THOMAS BROWER PEACOCK

3878. Pady, Donald S. "Thomas Brower Peacock." *Bulletin of Bibliography* 28 (April-June 1971): 37-40.

GEORGE SESSIONS PERRY

3879. Alexander, Stanley G. *George Sessions Perry.* Southwest Writers Series, No. 13. Austin, Tex.: Steck-Vaughn, 1967.
3880. Bradford, M. E. "Making Time Run: The Rich Harvest of George Sessions Perry." *Southwestern American Literature* 1 (September 1971): 129-36.
3881. Cowser, Robert C. "A Biographical and Critical Interpretation of George Sessions Perry." Doctoral dissertation, Texas Christian University, 1965.
3882. Hairston, Maxine C. "The Development of George Sessions Perry as a Writer of Rural

Texas." Doctoral dissertation, University of Texas, 1968.

3883. ——. *George Sessions Perry: His Life and Works.* Austin, Tex.: Jenkins, 1973.
3884. ——. "The George Sessions Perry Manuscript Collection." *Library Chronicle of the University of Texas* 2 (November 1970): 63-71.
3885. ——. "Introduction" to George Sessions Perry, *Hold Autumn in Your Hand.* Albuquerque: University of New Mexico Press, 1975, pp. vii-xvi.

JOHN PHOENIX
See George H. Derby

ALBERT PIKE

3886. Allsopp, Frederick William. *Albert Pike: A Biography.* Little Rock, Ark.: Parke-Harper, 1928.
3887. Boyden, William L. *Bibliography of the Writings of Albert Pike: Prose, Poetry, Manuscript.* Washington, D.C.: n.p., 1921.
3888. Riley, Susan B. "The Life and Works of Albert Pike to 1860." Doctoral dissertation, George Peabody College, 1934.
3889. Shrell, Darwin H. "Albert Pike (1809-1891)." *A Bibliographical Guide to the Study of Southern Literature.* Baton Rouge: Louisiana State University Press, 1969, pp. 260-61.

CHIEF SIMON POKAGON

3890. Larson, Charles R. *American Indian Fiction.* Albuquerque: University of New Mexico Press, 1978, pp. 34-46, 62-65.

KATHERINE ANNE PORTER

3891. Allen, Charles A. "Southwestern Chronicle: Katherine Anne Porter." *Arizona Quarterly* 2 (Summer 1946): 90-95.
3892. Auchincloss, Louis. *Pioneers and Caretakers: A Study of American Women Novelists.* Minneapolis: University of Minnesota Press, 1965.
3893. Baker, Howard. "The Upward Path: Notes on the Work of Katherine Anne Porter." *Southern Review* 4 (January 1968): 1-19.
3894. Baldeshwiler, Eileen. "Structural Patterns in Katherine Anne Porter's Fiction." *South Dakota Review* 11 (Summer 1973): 45-53.
3895. Becker, Laurence A. "'The Jilting of Granny Weatherall': The Discovery of Pattern." *English Journal* 55 (December 1966): 1164-69.
3896. Core, George. "Katherine Anne Porter (1894-)." *A Bibliographical Guide to the Study of Southern Literature.* Baton Rouge: Louisiana State University Press, 1969, pp. 268-72.
3897. DeMouy, Jane Krause. "The Seeds of the Pomegranate: A Study of Katherine Anne

Porter's Women." Doctoral dissertation, University of Maryland, 1978.

3898. Emmons, Winfred S. *Katherine Anne Porter: The Regional Stories.* Southwest Writers Series, No. 6. Austin, Tex.: Steck-Vaughn, 1967.

3899. Farrington, Thomas Arthur. "The Control of Imagery in Katherine Anne Porter's Fiction." Doctoral dissertation, University of Illinois at Urbana, Champaign, 1972.

3900. Givner, Joan. "'Her Great Art, Her Somber Craft': Katherine Anne Porter's Creative Process." *Southwest Review* 62 (Summer 1977): 217-30.

3901. Groff, Edward. "'Noon Wine': A Texas Tragedy." *Descant* 22 (1977): 39-47.

3902. Hardy, John Edward. *Katherine Anne Porter.* New York: Frederick Ungar, 1973.

3903. Hartley, Lodwick, and George Core, eds. *Katherine Anne Porter: A Critical Symposium.* Athens: University of Georgia Press, 1969.

3904. Hendrick, George. *Katherine Anne Porter.* New York: Twayne, 1965.

3905. Kiernan, Robert F. *Katherine Anne Porter and Carson McCullers: A Reference Guide.* Boston: G. K. Hall, 1976.

3906. Liberman, M. M. *Katherine Anne Porter's Fiction.* Detroit: Wayne State University Press, 1971.

3907. Lugg, Bonelyn. "Mexican Influences on the Work of Katherine Anne Porter." Doctoral dissertation, Pennsylvania State University, 1976.

3908. Miles, Lee Robert. "Unused Possibilities: A Study of Katherine Anne Porter." Doctoral dissertation, University of California, Los Angeles, 1973.

3909. Mooney, Harry John, Jr. *The Fiction and Criticism of Katherine Anne Porter.* Pittsburgh: University of Pittsburgh Press, 1957; rev. ed., 1962.

3910. Nance, William L. "Katherine Anne Porter and Mexico." *Southwest Review* 55 (Spring 1970): 143-53.

3911. ——. *Katherine Anne Porter and the Art of Rejection.* Chapel Hill: University of North Carolina Press, 1964.

3912. Partridge, Colin. "'My Familiar Country': An Image of Mexico in the Work of Katherine Anne Porter." *Studies in Short Fiction* 7 (Fall 1970): 597-614.

3913. Porter, Katherine Anne. *The Collected Essays and Occasional Writings of Katherine Anne Porter.* New York: Delacorte Press, 1970.

3914. Schwartz, Edward. *Katherine Anne Porter: A Critical Bibliography.* New York: New York Public Library, 1953; Darby, Pa.: Darby Books, 1969.

3915. Shurbutt, S. "The Short Fiction of Katherine Anne Porter: *Momentos de Verdades.*" *Southwestern American Literature* 5 (1975): 40-46.

3916. Smith, J. Oates. "Porter's *Noon Wine*: A Stifled Tragedy."

Renascence 17 (Spring 1965): 157-62.

3917. Thompson, Barbara. "Katherine Anne Porter: An Interview." *Paris Review* 29 (Winter-Spring 1963): 87-114.

3918. Waldrip, Louise, and Shirley Ann Bauer. *A Bibliography of the Works of Katherine Anne Porter and A Bibliography of the Criticism of the Works of Katherine Anne Porter.* Metuchen, N.J.: Scarecrow Press, 1969.

3919. Warren, Robert Penn. "Uncorrupted Consciousness: The Stories of Katherine Anne Porter." *Yale Review* 55 (Winter 1966): 280-90.

3920. Welty, Eudora. "The Eye of the Story." *Yale Review* 55 (Winter 1966): 265-74.

3921. West, Ray B., Jr. *Katherine Anne Porter.* Minneapolis: University of Minnesota Press, 1963.

3922. ———. "Katherine Anne Porter and 'Historic Memory.'" *Hudson Review* 6 (Fall 1952): 16-27.

3923. ———. "Katherine Anne Porter: Symbol and Theme in 'Flowering Judas.'" *Accent* 7 (Spring 1947): 182-87.

3924. Wolfe, Peter. "The Problems of Granny Weatherall." *CLA Journal* 11 (December 1967): 142-48.

3925. Yosha, Lee William. "The World of Katherine Anne Porter." Doctoral dissertation, University of Michigan, 1961.

3926. Young, Vernon A. "The Art of Katherine Anne Porter." *New Mexico Quarterly* 15 (Autumn 1945): 326-41.

WILLIAM SYDNEY PORTER
(O. Henry)

3927. Clarkson, Paul S. *A Bibliography of William Sydney Porter (O. Henry).* Caldwell, Idaho: Caxton Printers, 1938.

3928. Current-Garcia, Eugene. *O. Henry.* New York: Twayne, 1965.

3929. ———. "William Sydney Porter ('O. Henry') (1862-1910)." *A Bibliographical Guide to the Study of Southern Literature.* Baton Rouge: Louisiana State University Press, 1969, pp. 272-74.

3930. Davis, Robert H., and Arthur B. Maurice. *The Caliph of Bagdad.* New York: D. Appleton, 1931.

3931. Gallegly, J. S. "Background and Pattern of O. Henry's Texas Badman Stories." *Rice Institute Pamphlets* 42 (October 1955): 1-32.

3932. ———. *From Alamo Plaza to Jack Harris's Saloon: O. Henry and the Southwest He Knew.* The Hague: Mouton, 1971.

3933. Harris, Richard C. *William Sydney Porter.* Boston: Twayne, 1980.

3934. Kramer, Dale. *The Heart of O. Henry.* New York: Rinehart, 1954.

3935. Langford, Gerald. *Alias O. Henry: A Biography of William Sydney Porter.* New York: Macmillan, 1957.

223

3936. Long, E. Hudson. "O. Henry (William Sydney Porter)." *American Literary Realism 1870-1910* 1 (Fall 1967): 93-99.

3937. ——. *O. Henry: American Regionalist.* Southern Writers Series, No. 3. Austin, Tex.: Steck-Vaughn, 1969.

3938. ——. *O. Henry: The Man and His Work.* Philadelphia: University of Pennsylvania Press, 1949; New York: A. J. Barnes, 1960.

3939. ——. "O. Henry as a Regional Artist." *Essays on American Literature in Honor of Jay B. Hubbell.* Ed. Clarence Gohdes. Durham, N.C.: Duke University Press, 1967, pp. 229-40.

3940. ——. "Social Customs in O. Henry's Texas Stories." *A Good Tale and a Bonnie Tune.* Texas Folklore Society Publication 32. Dallas: Southern Methodist University Press, 1964, pp. 148-67.

3941. Meats, Stephen E. "William Sidney Porter." *American Literary Realism 1870-1910* 8 (Autumn 1975): 322-23. Review of dissertations on Porter.

3942. O'Quinn, Trueman. "O. Henry in Austin." *Southwestern Historical Quarterly* 43 (October 1939): 143-57.

3943. Payne, L. W., Jr. "The Humor of O. Henry." *Texas Review* 4 (October 1918): 18-37.

3944. Peel, Donald F. "A Critical Study of the Short Stories of O. Henry." *Northwest Missouri State College Studies* 25 (November 1961): 3-24.

3945. Robinson, Duncan, et al. "O. Henry's Austin." *Southwest Review* 24 (July 1939): 388-410.

3946. Rollins, Hyder E. "O. Henry's Texas." *Texas Review* 4 (July 1919): 295-307.

3947. Sibley, M. A. "Austin's First National and the Errant Teller." *Southwestern Historical Quarterly* 74 (April 1971): 478-506.

3948. Van Doren, Carl. "O. Henry." *Texas Review* 2 (January 1917): 248-59.

CHARLES PORTIS

3949. Ditsky, John, "True 'Grit' and *True Grit.*" *Ariel* 4 (April 1973): 18-31.

3950. Shuman, R. Baird. "Portis' *True Grit*: Adventure Story or *Entwicklungsroman?*" *English Journal* 49 (March 1970): 367-70.

J. F. POWERS

3951. Hertzel, Leo J. "What About Writers in the North?" *South Dakota Review* 5 (Spring 1967): 3-19.

3952. Stewart, D. H. "J. F. Powers' *Morte D'Urban* as Western." *Western American Literature* 5 (Spring 1970): 31-44.

3953. Wedge, G. F. "Two Bibliographies: Flannery O'Connor, J. F. Powers." *Critic* 2 (Fall 1958): 59-70.

THOMAS PYNCHON

3954. Abernethy, Peter L. "Entropy in Pynchon's *The Crying of Lot 49.*" *Critique* 14, No. 2 (1972): 18-33.
3955. Carpenter, Richard C. "State of Mind: The California Setting of *The Crying of Lot 49.*" *Itinerary: Criticism, Essays on California Writers.* Ed. Charles L. Crow. Bowling Green, Ohio: University Press, 1978, pp. 105-13.
3956. Stark, John O. *Pynchon's Fictions: Thomas Pynchon and the Literature of Information.* Athens: Ohio University Press, 1981.
3957. Weixlmann, Joseph. "Thomas Pynchon: A Bibliography." *Critique* 14, No. 2 (1972): 34-43.

HERBERT QUICK

3958. Bogue, Allan G. "Herbert Quick's Hawkeye Trilogy." *Books at Iowa* 15 (April 1972): 3-13.
3959. Keen, Carl L. "The Fictional Writings of Herbert Quick." Doctoral dissertation, Michigan State University, 1968.
3960. Morain, Frederick G. "Herbert Quick, Iowa Democrat." Doctoral dissertation, Yale University, 1970.

WILLIAM MACLEOD RAINE

3961. "Git Along, Ol' Typewriter." *Time* 64 (July 19, 1954): 82-84.
3962. Loomis, C. Grant. "Folk Language in William MacLeod Raine's West." *Tennessee Folklore Society Bulletin* 24 (December 1958): 131-48.

OPIE READ

3963. Baird, Reed M. "Opie Read (1852-1939): An Introduction." *Mark Twain Journal* 19 (1977-78): 11-13.
3964. Baird, Reed M. "Opie Read (1852-1939): A Study in Popular Culture." Doctoral dissertation, University of Michigan, 1966.
3965. Linneman, William. "Opie Read and *The Arkansas-Traveler*: The Trials of a Regional Humor Magazine." *Midwest Folklore* 10 (Spring 1960): 5-10.
3966. Rascoe, Burton. "Opie Read and Zane Grey." *Saturday Review of Literature* 21 (November 11, 1939): 8.
3967. Sloane, David E. E. "Opie Read." *American Literary Realism 1870-1910* 8 (Autumn 1975): 323. Reviews dissertations on Read.

MAYNE REID

3968. Billington, Ray Allen. *Land of Savagery / Land of Promise: The European Image of the American Frontier in the Nineteenth Century.* New York: W. W. Norton, 1981, pp. 43-44, 46-47, 142-44 passim.

3969. Meyer, Roy W. "The Western Fiction of Mayne Reid." *Western American Literature* 3 (Summer 1968): 115-32.

3970. Steele, Joan. "Mayne Reid: A Revised Bibliography." *Bulletin of Bibliography* 29 (July-September 1972): 95-100.

FREDERIC REMINGTON

3971. Allen, E. Douglas. "Frederic Remington—Author and Illustrator—A List of His Contributions to American Periodicals." *Bulletin of the New York Public Library* 49 (December 1945): 895-912.

3972. Alter, Judith. "Frederic Remington's Major Novel: *John Ermine.*" *Southwestern American Literature* 2 (Spring 1972): 42-46.

3973. ——. "The Western Myth in American Painting and Fiction of the Late 19th and Early 20th Centuries." Doctoral dissertation, Texas Christian University, 1970.

3974. Dary, David A. "Frederic Remington." *Persimmon Hill* 6 (1976): 28-35.

3975. ——. "Frederic Remington in Kansas." *Prairie Scout* 1 (Abilene: Kansas Corral of the Westerners, 1973), pp. 78-94.

3976. Dippie, Brian W. "Frederic Remington's Wild West." *American Heritage* 26 (April 1975): 7-23, 76-79.

3977. Dykes, Jeff C. "Tentative Bibliographic Check Lists of West-ern Illustrators: 26, Frederic Remington (1861-1909)." *American Book Collector* 16 (November 1965): 20-31; (December 1965): 22-31; (January 1966): 26-31; (February 1966): 34-39; (March 1966): 21-27; (April 1966): 23-35.

3978. Erisman, Fred. *Frederic Remington.* Western Writers Series, No. 16. Boise, Idaho: Boise State University, 1975.

3979. ——. "Frederic Remington: The Artist as Local Colorist." *South Dakota Review* 12 (Winter 1974-75): 76-88.

3980. ——. "Remington the Author." *Persimmon Hill* 10, No. 3 (1980): 24-35.

3981. Hassrick, Peter H. *Frederic Remington.* New York: Abrams, 1973.

3982. ——. "Remington in the South-west." *Southwestern Historical Quarterly* 76 (January 1973): 297-314.

3983. McCracken, Harold. *Frederic Remington: Artist of the Old West.* Philadelphia: Lippincott, 1947.

3984. McKown, Robin. *Painter of the Wild West: Frederic Reming-ton.* New York: Messner, 1959.

3985. Manley, Atwood. *Frederic Remington in the Land of His Youth.* Ogdensburg, N.Y.: Northern New York Publishing Company, 1961.

3986. Randall, John. "Frederic Remington's Anglo-Saxon Indian." *American Transcendental Quarterly* 30 (Spring 1976): 22-27.

3987. Rush, N. Orwin. "Frederic

Remington and Owen Wister: The Story of a Friendship, 1893-1909." *Probing the American West: Papers from the Santa Fe Conference.* Ed. K. Ross Toole, et al. Santa Fe: Museum of New Mexico, 1962, pp. 148-57.

3988. Taft, Robert. *Artists and Illustrators of the Old West, 1850-1900.* New York: Charles Scribner's Sons, 1953.

3989. Vorpahl, Ben Merchant. *Frederick Remington and the West: With the Eye of the Mind.* Austin: University of Texas Press, 1978. A first-rate study.

3990. ——. *"My Dear Wister": The Frederic Remington-Owen Wister Letters.* Palo Alto, Calif.: American West, 1972.

3991. White, G. Edward. *The Eastern Establishment and the Western Experience: The West of Frederic Remington, Theodore Roosevelt, and Owen Wister.* New Haven, Conn.: Yale University Press, 1968.

KENNETH REXROTH

3992. Foster, Richard. "The Voice of a Poet: Kenneth Rexroth." *Minnesota Review* 2 (Spring 1962): 377-84.

3993. Garren, Samuel Baity. "Quest for Value: A Study of the Collected Longer Poems of Kenneth Rexroth." Doctoral dissertation, Louisiana State University, 1976.

3994. Gibson, Morgan. *Kenneth Rex-roth.* New York: Twayne, 1972.

3995. Grigsby, Gordon K. "The Presence of Reality: The Poetry of Kenneth Rexroth." *Antioch Review* 31 (Fall 1971): 405-22.

3996. Hartzell, James, and Richard Zumwinkle, comps. *Kenneth Rexroth: A Checklist of His Published Writings.* Los Angeles: Friends of the UCLA Library, 1967.

3997. "An Interview with Kenneth Rexroth." *Critique* 10 (Summer 1969): 313-31.

3998. Lipton, Lawrence. "The Poetry of Kenneth Rexroth." *Poetry* 90 (June 1957): 168-80.

3999. McKenzie, James J., and Robert W. Lewis. "'That Rexroth—He'll Argue You into Anything': An Interview with Kenneth Rexroth." *North Dakota Quarterly* 44 (Summer 1976): 7-33.

4000. Parkinson, Thomas. "Kenneth Rexroth, Poet." *Ohio Review* 17 (1976): 54-67.

4001. Rexroth, Kenneth. *The Alternative Society: Essays from the Other World.* New York: Herder and Herder, 1970.

4002. ——. *An Autobiographical Novel.* Garden City, N.Y.: Doubleday, 1966.

4003. Sakurai, Emiko. "The Oriental Tradition in the Poetry of Kenneth Rexroth." Doctoral dissertation, University of Alabama, 1973.

4004. Williams, W. C. "Two New Books

227

by Kenneth Rexroth." *Poetry* 90 (June 1957): 180-90.

4005. Woodcock, George. "Realms beyond the Mountains: Notes on Kenneth Rexroth." *Ontario Review* 6 (1977): 39-48.

EUGENE MANLOVE RHODES

4006. Busby, Mark. "Eugene Manlove Rhodes: Ken Kesey Passed by Here." *Western American Literature* 15 (Summer 1980): 83-92.

4007. Compton, Adele O. "Eugene Manlove Rhodes: A Critical Study." Master's thesis, Eastern New Mexico University, 1966.

4008. Day, Beth F. *Gene Rhodes, Cowboy.* New York: Julian Messner, 1954.

4009. Dearing, Frank V., ed. *The Best Novels and Stories of Eugene Manlove Rhodes.* Boston: Houghton Mifflin, 1949. See introductory remarks by J. Frank Dobie, pp. xi-xxii.

4010. DeVoto, Bernard. "The Novelists of the Cattle Country" in May Davison Rhodes, *The Hired Man on Horseback.* Boston: Houghton Mifflin, 1938, pp. xix-xliv.

4011. Dobie, J. Frank. "Gene Rhodes: Cowboy Novelist." *Atlantic* 183 (June 1949): 75-77.

4012. Fife, Jim Lawrence. "Eugene Manlove Rhodes: Spokesman for Romantic Frontier Democracy." Doctoral dissertation, University of Iowa, 1965.

4013. ——. "Two Views of the American West." *Western American Literature* 1 (Spring 1966): 34-43.

4014. Folsom, James K. "A Dedication to the Memory of Eugene Manlove Rhodes: 1869-1934." *Arizona and the West* 2 (Winter 1969): 310-14.

4015. Gaston, Edwin W., Jr. *Eugene Manlove Rhodes: Cowboy Chronicler.* Southwest Writers Series, No. 11. Austin, Tex.: Steck-Vaughn, 1967.

4016. Hutchinson, W. H. *A Bar Cross Liar. Bibliography of Eugene Manlove Rhodes Who Loved the West-That-Was When He Was Young.* Stillwater, Okla.: Redlands Press, 1959.

4017. ——. *A Bar Cross Man: The Life and Personal Writings of Eugene Manlove Rhodes.* Norman: University of Oklahoma Press, 1956.

4018. ——. "I Pay for What I Break." *Western American Literature* 1 (Summer 1966): 91-96.

4019. ——. "New Mexico Incident: An Episode in the Life of Western Writer Eugene Manlove Rhodes." *American West* 14 (November-December 1977): 4-7, 59-63.

4020. ——. "Virgins, Villains and Varmints." *Huntington Library Quarterly* 16 (August 1953): 381-92.

4021. ——. "The West of Eugene Manlove Rhodes." *Arizona and the West* 9 (Autumn 1967): 211-18.

4022. ——. *The Works of Eugene Manlove Rhodes.* Cassette.

Deland, Fla.: Everett/Edwards, 1974.

4023. ——, ed. *The Rhodes Reader: Stories of Virgins, Villains, and Varmints.* Norman: University of Oklahoma Press, 1957.

4024. Keleher, William A. *The Fabulous Frontier.* Santa Fe, N.Mex.: Rydal Press, 1945, pp. 137-49.

4025. Knibbs, Henry Herbert. "Gene Rhodes" in Eugene Manlove Rhodes, *The Proud Sheriff.* Boston: Houghton Mifflin, 1935, pp. iii-xxxviii.

4026. Powell, Lawrence Clark. "Southwest Classics Reread: From Cattle Kingdom Come." *Westways* 65 (April 1973): 30-35, 85.

4027. Raine, William MacLeod. "Eugene Manlove Rhodes, American." *1945 Brand Book.* Denver, 1946, pp. 47-58.

4028. Rhodes, May Davison. *The Hired Man on Horseback: My Story of Eugene Manlove Rhodes.* Boston: Houghton Mifflin, 1938.

4029. ——. "The Most Unforgettable Character I've Met." *Reader's Digest* 64 (January 1954): 21-26.

4030. Ristvedt, Helen Smith. "Eugene Manlove Rhodes as Social Historian and Literary Artist." Master's thesis, Drake University, 1937.

4031. Skillman, Richard, and Jerry C. Hoke. "The Portrait of the New Mexican in the Fiction of Eugene Rhodes." *Western Review* 6 (Spring 1969): 26-36.

4032. Work, Allene. "Eugene Manlove Rhodes: Chronicler of the Cow Country." Master's thesis, Southern Methodist University, 1948.

CONRAD RICHTER

4033. Barnard, Kenneth J. "Presentation of the West in Conrad Richter's Trilogy." *Northern Ohio Quarterly* 29 (Autumn 1957): 224-34.

4034. Barnes, Robert J. *Conrad Richter.* Southwest Writers Series, No. 14. Austin, Tex.: Steck-Vaughn, 1968.

4035. Bloodworth, William A. "Introduction" to Conrad Richter, *Early Americana and Other Stories.* Boston: Gregg Press, 1978, pp. v-x.

4036. Carpenter, Frederic I. "Conrad Richter's Pioneers: Reality and Myth." *College English* 12 (November 1950): 77-83.

4037. Edwards, Clifford D. *Conrad Richter's Ohio Trilogy: Its Ideas, Themes and Relationship to Literary Tradition.* The Hague: Mouton, 1971.

4038. Flanagan, John T. "Conrad Richter: Romancer of the Southwest." *Southwest Review* 43 (Summer 1958): 189-96.

4039. ——. "Folklore in the Novels of Conrad Richter." *Midwest Folklore* 2 (Spring 1952): 5-14.

4040. Gaston, Edwin W., Jr. *Conrad Richter.* New York: Twayne, 1965.

4041. Harris, Jim R. "New Mexico

History: A Transient Period in Conrad Richter's *The Sea of Grass*." *Southwestern American Literature* 5 (1975): 62-67.

4042. Kohler, Dayton. "Conrad Richter: Early Americana." *College English* 8 (February 1947): 221-27.

4043. LaHood, Marvin J. "Conrad Richter and Willa Cather: Some Similarities." *Xavier University Studies* 9 (Spring 1970): 33-44.

4044. ——. *Conrad Richter's America.* The Hague: Mouton, 1975.

4045. ——. *"The Light in the Forest*: History as Fiction." *English Journal* 55 (March 1966): 298-304.

4046. ——. "Richter's Early America." *University Review* 30 (June 1964): 311-16.

4047. Meldrum, Barbara. "Conrad Richter's Southwestern Ladies." *Women, Women Writers, and the West.* Eds. Lawrence L. Lee and Merrill E. Lewis. Troy, N.Y.: Whitston, 1978.

4048. Pearce, T. M. "Conrad Richter." *New Mexico Quarterly* 20 (Autumn 1950): 371-73.

4049. Richter, Conrad. "The Sea of Grass—A New Mexico Novel." *New Mexico Magazine* 43 (February 1965): 12-15.

4050. Sutherland, Bruce. "Conrad Richter's Americana." *New Mexico Quarterly Review* 15 (Winter 1945): 413-22.

4051. Wilson, Dawn M. "Conrad Richter: The Novelist as Philosopher." Doctoral dissertation, Kent State University, 1971.

4052. ——. "The Influence of the West on Conrad Richter's Fiction." *Old Northwest* 1 (1975): 375-89.

4053. Young, David Lee. "The Art of Conrad Richter." Doctoral dissertation, Ohio State University, 1964.

EDWARD F. RICKETTS

4054. Astro, Richard. *Edward F. Ricketts.* Western Writers Series, No. 21. Boise, Idaho: Boise State University, 1976.

4055. ——. *John Steinbeck and Edward Ricketts: The Shaping of a Novelist.* Minneapolis: University of Minnesota Press, 1973.

4056. ——. "Steinbeck and Ricketts: Escape or Commitment in the *Sea of Cortez?*" *Western American Literature* 6 (Summer 1971): 109-21.

4057. ——. "Steinbeck and Ricketts: The Morphology of a Metaphysic." *Windsor Review* 3 (Spring 1973): 24-33.

4058. Fontenrose, Joseph. "Sea of Cortez." *John Steinbeck: An Introduction and Interpretation.* New York: Holt, Rinehart and Winston, 1962, pp. 84-97.

4059. Hedgpeth, Joel W. "Philosophy on Cannery Row." *Steinbeck: The Man and His Work.* Eds. Richard Astro and Tetsumaro Hayashi. Corvallis: Oregon State University Press, 1971, pp. 89-129.

4060. Perez, Betty L. "The Collaborative Role of John Steinbeck and Edward F. Ricketts in the Narrative Section of *Sea of Cortez.*" Doctoral dissertation, University of Florida, 1972.

4061. ——. "Steinbeck, Ricketts and *Sea of Cortez*: Partnership or Exploitation?" *Steinbeck Quarterly* 7 (Summer-Fall 1974): 73-79.

4062. Steinbeck, John. "About Ed Ricketts." *The Log from the Sea of Cortez.* New York: Viking Press, 1951, pp. i-lxvii.

LYNN RIGGS

4063. Aughtry, Charles. "Lynn Riggs at the University of Oklahoma." *Chronicles of Oklahoma* 37 (Autumn 1959): 280-84.

4064. ——. "Lynn Riggs, Dramatist: A Critical Biography." Doctoral dissertation, Brown University, 1959.

4065. Benton, Joseph. "Some Personal Remembrances about Lynn Riggs." *Chronicles of Oklahoma* 34 (Autumn 1956): 296-301.

4066. Erhard, Thomas A. *Lynn Riggs: Southwest Playwright.* Southwest Writers Series, No. 29. Austin, Tex.: Steck-Vaughn, 1970.

4067. Roth, Henry. "Lynn Riggs and the Individual." *Folk-Say: A Regional Miscellany 1930.* Ed. B. A. Botkin. Norman: University of Oklahoma Press, 1930, pp. 386-95.

4068. Wentz, John C. "American Regional Drama, 1920-40: Frustration and Fulfillment." *Modern Drama* 6 (December 1963): 286-93.

4069. Wilson, Eloise. "Lynn Riggs: Oklahoma Dramatist." Doctoral dissertation, University of Pennsylvania, 1957.

TOMÁS RIVERA

4070. Grajeda, Ralph F. "Tomás Rivera's Appropriation of the Chicano Past." *Modern Chicano Writers.* Eds. Joseph Sommers and Tomás Ybarra-Frausto. Englewood Cliffs, N.J.: Prentice-Hall, 1979, pp. 74-85.

4071. Pino, Frank, Jr. "The Outsider and 'El Otro' in Tomás Rivera's '. . . *y no se lo tragó la tierra.*'" *Books Abroad* 49 (Summer 1975): 453-59.

4072. Rocard, Marcienne. "The Cycle of Chicano Experience in '. . . *and the earth did not part*' by Thomas Rivera." *Caliban* 10 (1974): 141-51.

4073. Rodríguez, Juan. "The Problematic in Tomás Rivera's *. . . And the Earth Did Not Part.*" *Revista Chicano-Riqueña* 6 (1978): 42-50.

4074. Sommers, Joseph. "Interpreting Tomás Rivera." *Modern Chicano Writers.* Eds. Joseph Sommers and Tomás Ybarra-Frausto. Englewood Cliffs, N.J.: Prentice-Hall, 1979, pp. 94-107.

4075. Testa, Daniel P. "Narrative

Technique and Human Experience in Tomás Rivera." *Modern Chicano Writers.* Eds. Joseph Sommers and Tomás Ybarra-Frausto. Englewood Cliffs, N.J.: Prentice-Hall, 1979, pp. 86-93.

TOM ROBBINS

4076. Anderson, Bette Bacon, and William Burke. "Tom Robbins' *Another Roadside Attraction* and the Second Coming." *Slackwater Review* 3 (Winter 1979-80): 69-76.
4077. Nadeau, Robert. "Physics and Cosmology in the Fiction of Tom Robbins." *Critique* 20 (1978): 63-74.
4078. Siegel, Mark. *Tom Robbins.* Western Writers Series, No. 42. Boise, Idaho: Boise State University, 1980.

THEODORE ROETHKE

4079. Alkalay, Karen. "The Poetry of Theodore Roethke." Doctoral dissertation, University of Rochester, 1974.
4080. Blessing, Richard A. *Theodore Roethke's Dynamic Vision.* Bloomington: Indiana University Press, 1974.
4081. ——. "Theodore Roethke's Sometimes Metaphysical Motion." *Texas Studies in Literature and Language* 14 (Winter 1973): 731-49.
4082. Breslin, Glenna Louise. "Form as Process in the Poetry of Theodore Roethke." Doctoral dissertation, University of Minnesota, 1973.
4083. Burke, Kenneth. "The Vegetal Radicalism of Theodore Roethke." *Language as Symbolic Action.* Berkeley: University of California Press, 1966, pp. 254-81.
4084. Dickey, James. "Theodore Roethke." *Poetry* 105 (November 1964): 120-24.
4085. Everette, Oliver. "Theodore Roethke: The Poet as Teacher." *West Coast Review* 3 (1968): 5-11.
4086. Ferry, David. "Roethke's Poetry." *Virginia Quarterly Review* 43 (Winter 1967): 169-73.
4087. Foster, Ann Tucker. "A Field for Revelation: Mysticism in the Poetry of Theodore Roethke." Doctoral dissertation, Florida State University, 1977.
4088. Freer, Coburn. "Theodore Roethke's Love Poetry." *Northwest Review* 11 (Summer 1971): 42-66.
4089. Heilman, Robert. "Theodore Roethke: Personal Notes." *Shenandoah* 16 (Autumn 1964): 55-64.
4090. Heron, Philip E. "The Vision of Meaning: Theodore Roethke's Frau Bauman, Frau Schmidt, and Frau Schwartze." *Western Speech* 34 (Winter 1970): 29-33.
4091. Heyen, William. "The Divine Abyss: Theodore Roethke's Mysticism." *Texas Studies in Literature and Language* 11 (Winter 1969): 1051-68.

4092. ——. *Profile of Theodore Roethke*. Columbus, Ohio: Charles E. Merrill Company, 1971.

4093. Hollenberg, S. W. "Theodore Roethke: Bibliography." *Twentieth-Century Literature* 12 (January 1967): 216-21.

4094. Kramer, Hilton. "The Poetry of Theodore Roethke." *Western Review* 18 (Winter 1954): 131-46.

4095. Kunitz, Stanley. "Roethke: Poet of Transformations." *New Republic* 152 (January 23, 1965): 23-29.

4096. LaBelle, Jenijoy. *The Echoing Wood of Theodore Roethke*. Princeton, N.J.: Princeton University Press, 1976.

4097. Lane, Gary, ed. *A Concordance to the Poems of Theodore Roethke*. Metuchen, N.J.: Scarecrow Press, 1972.

4098. Lee, Charlotte I. "The Line as a Rhythmic Unit in the Poetry of Theodore Roethke." *Speech Monographs* 30 (March 1963): 15-22.

4099. Lorimer, William Lund. "Ripples from a Single Stone: An Archetypal Study of Theodore Roethke's Poetry." Doctoral dissertation, University of Notre Dame, 1976.

4100. McLeod, James Richard. *Theodore Roethke: A Bibliography*. Kent, Ohio: Kent State University, 1973.

4101. ——. *Theodore Roethke: A Manuscript Checklist*. Kent, Ohio: Kent State University Press, 1971.

4102. McMichael, James. "The Poetry of Theodore Roethke." *Southern Review* 5 (Winter 1969): 4-25.

4103. ——. "Roethke's North America." *Northwest Review* 11 (Summer 1971): 149-59.

4104. Malkoff, Karl. *Theodore Roethke: An Introduction to the Poetry*. New York: Columbia University Press, 1966.

4105. Martz, William J. *The Achievement of Theodore Roethke*. Glenview, Ill.: Scott, Foresman, 1966.

4106. Matheson, John William. "Theodore Roethke: A Bibliography." Master's thesis, University of Washington, 1958.

4107. Mazzaro, Jerome. "Theodore Roethke and the Failures of Language." *Modern Poetry Studies* 1 (July 1970): 73-96.

4108. Meredith, William. "A Steady Storm of Correspondences: Theodore Roethke's Long Journey Out of the Self." *Shenandoah* 16 (Autumn 1964): 41-54.

4109. Mills, Ralph J., Jr. "Roethke's Garden." *Poetry* 100 (April 1962): 54-59.

4110. ——. *Theodore Roethke*. Minneapolis: University of Minnesota Press, 1963.

4111. ——. "Theodore Roethke: The Lyric of the Self." *Poets in Progress: Critical Prefaces to Ten Contemporary Americans*. Ed. Edward Hungerford. Evanston: Northwestern University Press, 1962, pp. 3-23.

4112. ——, ed. *On the Poet and His*

Craft: Selected Prose of Theodore Roethke. Seattle: University of Washington Press, 1965.

4113. ——, ed. *Selected Letters of Theodore Roethke*. Seattle: University of Washington Press, 1968.

4114. Moul, Keith R. *Theodore Roethke's Career: An Annotated Bibliography*. Boston: G. K. Hall, 1977.

4115. Pinsker, Sanford. "An Urge to Wrestle, A Need to Dance: The Poetry of Theodore Roethke." *CEA Critic* 41 (May 1979): 12-17.

4116. Schumacker, Paul J. "The Unity of Being: A Study of Theodore Roethke's Poetry." *Ohio University Review* 12 (1970): 20-40.

4117. Schwartz, Delmore. "The Cunning and the Craft of the Unconscious and the Preconscious." *Poetry* 94 (June 1959): 203-5.

4118. Scott, Nathan A. "The Example of Roethke." *The Wild Prayer of Longing and the Sacred*. New Haven, Conn.: Yale University Press, 1971, pp. 76-118.

4119. Seager, Allan. *The Glass House: The Life of Theodore Roethke*. New York: McGraw-Hill, 1968.

4120. ——, Stanley Kunitz, and John Ciardi. "An Evening with Ted Roethke." *Michigan Quarterly Review* 6 (Fall 1967): 227-45.

4121. Seymour-Smith, Martin. "Where Is Mr. Roethke?" *Black Mountain Review* 1 (Spring 1954): 40-47.

4122. Southworth, James G. "The Poetry of Theodore Roethke." *College English* 21 (March 1960): 326-30, 335-38.

4123. Staples, Hugh. "The Rose in the Sea-Wind: A Reading of Theodore Roethke's North American Sequence." *American Literature* 36 (May 1964): 189-203.

4124. Stein, Arnold, ed. *Theodore Roethke: Essays on the Poetry*. Seattle: University of Washington Press, 1965.

4125. Sullivan, Rosemary. "A Still Center: A Reading of Theodore Roethke's North American Sequence." *Texas Studies in Literature and Language* 16 (Winter 1975): 765-83.

4126. ——. *Theodore Roethke: The Garden Master*. Seattle: University of Washington Press, 1975.

4127. Vanderbilt, Kermit. "Theodore Roethke as a Northwest Poet." *Northwest Perspectives: Essays on the Culture of the Pacific Northwest*. Eds. Edwin R. Bingham and Glen A. Love. Seattle: University of Washington Press, 1979, pp. 187-216.

4128. Wain, John. "Theodore Roethke." *Critical Quarterly* 6 (Winter 1964): 322-38.

4129. Williams, Harry. *"The edge is what I have": Theodore Roethke and After*. Cranbury, N.J.: Bucknell University Press, 1977.

4130. Wilson, Matthew Thomas. "A. R. Ammons, Theodore Roethke, and American Nature Poetry." Doctoral dissertation, Rutgers University, 1978.

4131. Winters, Yvor. "The Poems of Theodore Roethke." *Kenyon Review* 3 (Autumn 1941): 514-16.

WILL ROGERS

4132. Alworth, E. Paul. *Will Rogers.* New York: Twayne, 1974.

4133. Brown, William R. *Imagemaker: Will Rogers and the American Dream.* New York: Columbia University Press, 1970.

4134. *Chronicles of Oklahoma* 57 (Fall 1979). Special issue of ten essays on Will Rogers.

4135. Clark, Blue. "The Literary Will Rogers." *Chronicles of Oklahoma* 57 (Fall 1979): 385-94. A useful bibliographical essay.

4136. Collins, Reba Neighbors. "Will Rogers: Writer and Journalist." Doctoral dissertation, Oklahoma State University, 1967.

4137. Day, Donald. *Will Rogers, A Biography.* New York: David McKay, 1962.

4138. Eitner, Walter H. "Will Rogers: Another Look At His Act." *Kansas Quarterly* 2 (Spring 1970): 46-52.

4139. Roach, Samuel Frederick, Jr. "Lariat in the Sun: The Story of Will Rogers." Doctoral dissertation, University of Oklahoma, 1972.

4140. Rogers, Will. *The Autobiogra-phy of Will Rogers.* Ed. Donald Day. Boston: Houghton Mifflin, 1949.

OLE RÖLVAAG

4141. Anderson, Carol Jane. "Narrative Techniques in Selected Novels by Ole Edvart Rölvaag." Doctoral dissertation, University of Arkansas, 1979.

4142. Baker, Joseph E. "Western Man Against Nature: *Giants in the Earth.*" *College English* 4 (October 1942): 19-26.

4143. Beck, Richard. "Rölvaag, Interpreter of Immigrant Life." *North Dakota Quarterly* 24 (Winter 1956): 26-30.

4144. Bjork, Kenneth O. "The Unknown Rölvaag: Secretary in the Norwegian-American Historical Association." *Norwegian-American Studies and Records* 11 (1940): 114-49.

4145. Boewe, Charles. "Rölvaag's America: An Immigrant Novelist's Views." *Western Humanities Review* 11 (Winter 1957): 3-12.

4146. Boynton, Percy H. "O. E. Rölvaag and the Conquest of the Pioneer." *English Journal* 18 (September 1929): 535-42.

4147. ——. "Ole Edvart Rölvaag." *America in Contemporary Fiction.* Chicago: University of Chicago Press, 1927, pp. 225-40.

4148. Dittmann, Erling. "The Immigrant Mind: A Study of Rölvaag." *Christian Liberty* 1 (October 1952): 7-47.

4149. Eckstein, Neil T. "*Giants in the Earth* as Saga." *Where the West Begins.* Eds. Arthur R. Huseboe and William Geyer. Sioux Falls, S.Dak.: Center for Western Studies Press, 1978, pp. 34-41.

4150. ———. "The Social Criticism of Ole Edvart Rölvaag." *Norwegian-American Studies* 24 (1970): 112-36.

4151. Fox, Maynard. "The Bearded Face Set Toward the Sun." *Ball State Teacher's College Forum* 1 (Winter 1960-61): 62-64.

4152. Geyer, Carolyn. "An Introduction to Ole Rölvaag (1876-1931)." *Big Sioux Pioneers.* Ed. Arthur R. Huseboe. Sioux Falls, S.Dak.: Norland Heritage Foundation, 1980, pp. 54-62.

4153. Grider, Sylvia. "Madness and Personification in *Giants in the Earth.*" *Women, Women Writers, and the West.* Eds. Lawrence L. Lee and Merrill E. Lewis. Troy, N.Y.: Whitston, 1978.

4154. Gvåle, Gudrun Hovde. *Ole Edvart Rölvaag: Nordmann og Amerikanar.* Oslo: Aschehoug, 1962.

4155. Hahn, Steve. "Vision and Reality in *Giants in the Earth.*" *South Dakota Review* 17 (Spring 1979): 85-100.

4156. Haugen, Einar. "O. E. Rölvaag: Norwegian-American." *Norwegian-American Studies and Records* 7 (1933): 53-73.

4157. Heitmann, John. "Ole Edvart Rölvaag." *Norwegian-American Studies and Records* 12 (1941): 144-66.

4158. Jordahl, O. "Folkloristic Influences upon Rölvaag's Youth." *Western Folklore* 34 (January 1975): 1-15.

4159. Jorgenson, Theodore. "The Main Factors in Rölvaag's Authorship." *Norwegian-American Studies and Records* 10 (1938): 135-51.

4160. ———, and Nora O. Solum. *Ole Edvart Rölvaag: A Biography.* New York: Harper and Brothers, 1939.

4161. Larsen, Erling. "The Art of O. E. Rölvaag." *Minnesota English Journal* 8 (Winter 1972): 17-29.

4162. Meyer, Roy W. *The Middle Western Farm Novel in the Twentieth Century.* Lincoln: University of Nebraska Press, 1965.

4163. Mortensen, Wayne F. "The Problem of the Loss of Culture in Rölvaag's *Giants in the Earth, Peder Victorious,* and *Their Fathers' God.*" *Minnesota English Journal* 8 (Winter 1972): 42-50.

4164. Nelson, Pearl. "Rölvaag." *Prairie Schooner* 3 (Spring 1929): 156-59.

4165. Olson, Julius E. "Ole Edvart Rölvaag, 1876-1931: In Memoriam." *Norwegian-American Studies and Records* 7 (1933): 121-30.

4166. ———. "Rölvaag's Novels of Norwegian Pioneer Life in the Dakotas." *Scandinavian Studies and Notes* 9 (1927): 45-55.

4167. Parrington, Vernon. "Ole Rölvaag's 'Giants in the Earth.'"

The Beginnings of Critical Realism in America: 1860–1920. New York: Harcourt, Brace and World, 1930, pp. 387–96.

4168. Paulson, Kristoffer F. "Ole Rölvaag, Herbert Krause, and the Frontier Thesis of Frederick Jackson Turner." Where the West Begins. Eds. Arthur R. Huseboe and William Geyer. Sioux Falls, S.Dak.: Center for Western Studies Press, 1978, pp. 24–33.

4169. Reigstad, Paul. "The Norwegians in Rölvaag's Novels." New America 3 (Summer–Fall 1977): 38–41.

4170. ———. Rölvaag: His Life and Art. Lincoln: University of Nebraska Press, 1972.

4171. Ruud, Curtis Duane. "The Dakota Prairie as Changing Force in Ole Rölvaag's Giants in the Earth." Doctoral dissertation, University of Nebraska, Lincoln, 1977.

4172. Simonson, Harold P. The Closed Frontier: Studies in American Literary Tragedy. New York: Holt, Rinehart and Winston, 1970, pp. 77–97.

4173. ———. "Rölvaag and Kierkegaard." Scandinavian Studies 49 (Winter 1977): 67–80.

4174. Solum, Nora O. "The Sources of the Rölvaag Biography." Norwegian-American Studies and Records 11 (1940): 150–59.

4175. Steensma, Robert. "Rölvaag and Turner's Frontier Thesis." North Dakota Quarterly 27 (Autumn 1959): 100–104.

4176. Stevens, Robert. "Ole Edvart Rölvaag: A Critical Study of His Norwegian-American Novels." Doctoral dissertation, University of Illinois, 1955.

4177. Storm, Melvin. "The Immigrant in Giants in the Earth: Conflict and Resolution." Heritage of Kansas 8 (Winter 1975): 36–40.

4178. Suderman, Elmer F. "An Experiment in Reading Giants in the Earth." Minnesota English Journal 8 (Winter 1972): 30–41.

4179. Thorson, Gerald, ed. Ole Rölvaag: Artist and Cultural Leader. Northfield, Minn.: St. Olaf College Press, 1975. A major collection of eight essays and a bibliographical listing.

4180. Tweet, Ella Valborg. "Recollections of My Father, O. E. Rölvaag." Minnesota English Journal 8 (Winter 1972): 4–16.

4181. White, George Leroy. "O. E. Rölvaag—Prophet of a People." Scandinavian Themes in American Fiction. Philadelphia: University of Pennsylvania Press, 1937, pp. 97–108.

THEODORE ROOSEVELT

4182. Barsness, John A. "Theodore Roosevelt as Cowboy: The Virginian as Jacksonian Man." American Quarterly 21 (Fall 1969): 609–19.

4183. Dornbusch, Clyde H. "Theodore Roosevelt's Literary Taste and Relationships with Authors." Doctoral dissertation, Duke University, 1957.

4184. Fenton, Charles. "Theodore Roosevelt as a Man of Letters." *Western Humanities Review* 13 (August 1959): 369-74.

4185. Lewis, Merrill E. "American Frontier History as Literature: Studies in Historiography of George Bancroft, Frederick Jackson Turner, and Theodore Roosevelt." Doctoral dissertation, University of Utah, 1968.

4186. Moers, Ellen. "Teddy Roosevelt: Literary Feller." *Columbia University Forum* 6 (Summer 1963): 10-16.

4187. Norton, Aloysius A. *Theodore Roosevelt.* Boston: Twayne, 1980.

4188. Walker, Don D. "Wister, Roosevelt and James: A Note on the Western." *American Quarterly* 12 (Fall 1960): 358-66.

4189. White, G. Edward. *The Eastern Establishment and the Western Experience: The West of Frederic Remington, Theodore Roosevelt, and Owen Wister.* New Haven, Conn.: Yale University Press, 1968.

JEROME ROTHENBERG

4190. Clements, William M. "Faking the Pumpkin: On Jerome Rothenberg's Literary Offenses." *Western American Literature* 16 (Fall 1981): 193-204.

JOSIAH ROYCE

4191. Clendenning, John, ed. *The Letters of Josiah Royce.* 2 vols. Chicago: University of Chicago Press, 1970.

4192. Pomeroy, Earl. "Josiah Royce, Historian in Quest of Community." *Pacific Historical Review* 40 (February 1971): 1-20.

4193. ———. "Josiah Royce, Philosopher of Community: An Essay Review." *Pacific Northwest Quarterly* 63 (April 1972): 69-70.

4194. Starr, Kevin. *Americans and the California Dream 1850-1915.* New York: Oxford University Press, 1973, pp. 142-71.

4195. Wells, Ronald Albert. "A Portrait of Josiah Royce." Doctoral dissertation, Boston University, 1967.

DAMON RUNYON

4196. Bayard, Charles J. "Me and Mr. Finch in Denver." *Colorado Magazine* 52 (Winter 1975): 22-33.

CHARLES M. RUSSELL

4197. Adams, Ramon F., and Homer E. Britzman. *Charles M. Russell, The Cowboy Artist.* Pasadena, Calif.: Trail's End Publishing, 1948.

4198. Brunvand, Jan Harold. "From Western Folklore to Fiction in the Stories of Charles M. Russell." *Western Review* 5 (Summer 1968): 41-49.

4199. Conrad, Barnaby, III. "C. M. Russell and the Buckskin Paradise of the West." *Horizon* 22 (May 1979): 42-49.

4200. Dippie, Brian W. "Charlie Russell's Lost West." *American Heritage* 24 (April 1973): [4]-21, 89.

4201. Ellsberg, William. "Charles, Thou Art a Rare Blade." *American West* 6 (March 1969): 4-9; (May 1969): 40-43, 62.

4202. Gale, Robert L. *Charles Marion Russell.* Western Writers Series, No. 38. Boise, Idaho: Boise State University, 1979.

4203. Linderman, Frank Bird. *Recollections of Charles Russell.* Norman: University of Oklahoma Press, 1963.

4204. McCracken, Harold. *The Charles M. Russell Book: The Life and Work of the Cowboy Artist.* Garden City, N.Y.: Doubleday, 1957.

4205. Renner, Frederic G. "Rangeland Rembrandt: The Incomparable Charles Marion Russell." *Montana: The Magazine of Western History* 7 (Autumn 1957): 15-28.

4206. Russell, Austin. *C. M. R.: Charles M. Russell: Cowboy Artist: A Biography.* New York: Twayne, 1957.

4207. Shelton, Lola. *Charles Marion Russell: Cowboy, Artist, Friend.* New York: Dodd, Mead, 1962.

4208. Yost, Karl, and Frederic G. Renner. *Bibliography of the Published Works of Charles M. Russell.* Lincoln: University of Nebraska Press, 1971.

GEORGE F. RUXTON

4209. Barrick, Mac E. "Ruxton's Western Proverbs." *Western Folklore* 34 (July 1975): 215-25.

4210. Cracroft, Richard H. "*The Big Sky*: A. B. Guthrie's Use of Historical Sources." *Western American Literature* 6 (Fall 1971): 163-76.

4211. ——. "'Half Froze for Mountain Doins': The Influence and Significance of George F. Ruxton's *Life in the Far West.*" *Western American Literature* 10 (May 1975): 29-43.

4212. Gaston, Edwin W., Jr. *The Early Novel of the Southwest.* Albuquerque: University of New Mexico Press, 1961.

4213. Grinnell, George Bird. "George Frederick Ruxton, Hunter." *Beyond the Old Frontier.* New York: Charles Scribner's Sons, 1913.

4214. Hafen, LeRoy, et al., eds. *Ruxton of the Rockies.* Norman: University of Oklahoma Press, 1950.

4215. Hubbard, Claude. "The Language of Ruxton's Mountain Men." *American Speech* 43 (October 1968): 216-21.

4216. Lambert, Neal. *George Frederick Ruxton.* Western Writers Series, No. 15. Boise, Idaho: Boise State University, 1974.

4217. Lehmberg, Paul. "Ruxton's *Life in the Far West* as Fiction." *Possible Sack* 5 (April 1974): 1-6; *Rendezvous* 11 (Spring 1976): 11-15.

4218. Poulsen, Richard L. "Black

George, Black Harris, and the Mountain Man Vernacular." *Rendezvous* 8 (Summer 1973): 15-23.

4219. Powell, Lawrence Clark. "Personalities of the West: The Adventurous Englishman." *Westways* 65 (November 1973): 18-22, 70-71.

4220. Sutherland, Bruce. "George Frederick Ruxton in North America." *Southwest Review* 30 (Autumn 1944): 86-91.

4221. Voelker, Frederic E. "Ruxton of the Rocky Mountains." *Missouri Historical Bulletin* 5 (January 1949): 79-90.

4222. Walker, Don D. "The Mountain Man as Literary Hero." *Western American Literature* 1 (Spring 1966): 15-25.

EDWARD L. SABIN

4223. Jordan, Philip D. "Edwin L. Sabin: Literary Explorer of the West." *Books at Iowa* 22 (April 1975): 3-19, 24-25.

MARI SANDOZ

4224. Barnes, Marian. "An Evaluation of the Novels of Mari Sandoz." Master's thesis, South Dakota State University, 1968.

4225. Clark, Felie Woodrow. "Mari Sandoz: Daughter of Old Jules." Master's thesis, University of Florida, 1956.

4226. Clark, LaVerne Harrell. "The Indian Writings of Mari Sandoz: 'A Lone One Left from the Old Times.'" *American Indian*

Quarterly 1 (Autumn 1974): 183-92; (Winter 1974-75): 269-80.

4227. ——. *Re-visiting the Plains Indian Country of Mari Sandoz.* Marvin, S.Dak.: Blue Cloud Quarterly Chapbook, No. 5, 1977.

4228. Doher, Pam. "The Idioms and Figures of *Cheyenne Autumn.*" *Where the West Begins.* Eds. Arthur R. Huseboe and William Geyer. Sioux Falls, S.Dak.: Center for Western Studies Press, 1978, pp. 143-51.

4229. Greenwell, Scott L. "Fascists in Fiction: Two Early Novels of Mari Sandoz." *Western American Literature* 12 (August 1977): 133-43.

4230. ——. "The Literary Apprenticeship of Mari Sandoz." *Nebraska History* 57 (Summer 1976): 248-72.

4231. Lowe, David. "A Meeting with Mari Sandoz." *Prairie Schooner* 42 (Spring 1968): 21-26.

4232. "Mari Sandoz: 1935." *Prairie Schooner* 41 (Summer 1967): 172-77.

4233. Moon, Myra Jo, and Rosemary Whitaker. "A Bibliography of Works by and about Mari Sandoz." *Bulletin of Bibliography* 38 (April-June 1981).

4234. Morton, Beatrice K. "A Critical Appraisal of Mari Sandoz' *Miss Morissa*: Modern Woman on the Western Frontier." *Heritage of Kansas* 10 (Fall 1977): 37-45.

4235. Nicoll, Bruce H. "Mari Sandoz: Nebraska Loner." *American*

West 2 (Spring 1965): 32-36.

4236. Overing, Robert. "Willa Cather and Mari Sandoz: Differing Viewpoints of the Early West." Master's thesis, University of South Carolina, 1971.

4237. Pifer, Caroline Sandoz. *Making of an Author: From the Mementoes of Mari Sandoz.* Gordon, Nebr.: Mari Sandoz Corporation, 1972.

4238. Rice, Minnie C. "Mari Sandoz: Biographer of the Old West." *Midwest Review* (Spring 1960): 44-49.

4239. Stauffer, Helen. "Mari Sandoz and Western Biography." *Heritage of Kansas* 10 (Fall 1977): 3-15.

4240. ——. "Mari Sandoz and Western Biography." *Women, Women Writers, and the West.* Eds. Lawrence L. Lee and Merrill E. Lewis. Troy, N.Y.: Whitson, 1978.

4241. ——. "Mari Sandoz: A Study of the Artist as Biographer." Doctoral dissertation, University of Nebraska, 1974.

4242. ——. *Mari Sandoz, Story-Catcher of the Plains.* Lincoln: University of Nebraska Press, 1982.

4243. ——. "Two Authors and a Hero: Neihardt, Sandoz, and Crazy Horse." *Great Plains Quarterly* 1 (January 1981): 54-66.

4244. Switzer, Dorothy. "Mari Sandoz's Lincoln Years." *Prairie Schooner* 45 (Summer 1971): 107-15.

4245. Walton, Kathleen O'Donnell.

"Mari Sandoz: An Initial Critical Appraisal." Doctoral dissertation, University of Delaware, 1970.

4246. Whitaker, Rosemary. "Violence in *Old Jules* and *Slogum House.*" *Western American Literature* 16 (Fall 1981): 217-24.

ROSS SANTEE

4247. Dykes, Jeff C. "Tentative Bibliographic Check Lists of Western Illustrators: 28, Ross Santee (1888-1965)." *American Book Collector* 16 (Summer 1966): 23-28.

4248. Ford, Moselle A. "Ross Santee: Author and Artist of the Southwest." Master's thesis, Texas Western College, 1966.

4249. Houston, Neal B. *Ross Santee.* Southwest Writers Series, No. 18. Austin, Tex.: Steck-Vaughn, 1968.

4250. Powell, Lawrence Clark. "Southwest Classics Reread: How He Pictured the West." *Westways* 65 (March 1973): 46-50, 84.

WILLIAM SAROYAN

4251. Burgum, Edwin B. "The Lonesome Young Man on the Flying Trapeze." *Virginia Quarterly Review* 20 (Summer 1944): 392-403.

4252. Carpenter, Frederic I. "The Time of Saroyan's Life." *Pacific Spectator* 1 (Winter 1947): 88-96.

4253. Everding, Robert George. "The

Dissolution Process in the Early Plays of William Saroyan." Doctoral dissertation, Stanford University, 1976.

4254. Fisher, William J. "What Ever Happened to Saroyan?" *College English* 16 (March 1955): 336-40.

4255. Floan, Howard R. *William Saroyan.* New York: Twayne, 1966.

4256. Hatcher, Harlan. "William Saroyan." *English Journal* 28 (March 1939): 169-77.

4257. Kherdian, David. *A Bibliography of William Saroyan, 1934-1964.* San Francisco: Roger Beacham, 1965.

4258. Krickel, Edward. "Cozzens and Saroyan: A Look at Two Reputations." *Georgia Review* 24 (Fall 1970): 281-96.

4259. LaCroix, Paul-Henri. "William Saroyan and the Short Story." Master's thesis, University of Montreal, 1959.

4260. Morris, David W. "A Critical Analysis of William Saroyan." Doctoral dissertation, Denver University, 1960.

4261. Nathan, George Jean. "Saroyan: Whirling Dervish of Fresno." *American Mercury* 51 (November 1940): 303-8.

4262. Rahv, Philip. "William Saroyan: A Minority Report." *American Mercury* 57 (September 1943): 371-77.

4263. Remenyi, Joseph. "William Saroyan: A Portrait." *College English* 6 (November 1944): 92-100.

4264. Schulberg, Budd. "Saroyan: Ease and Unease on the Flying Trapeze." *Esquire* 54 (October 1960): 85-91.

4265. Shinn, Thelma J. "William Saroyan: Romantic Existentialist." *Modern Drama* 15 (September 1972): 185-94.

4266. Singer, Felix. "Saroyan at 57: The Daring Young Man After the Fall." *Trace* 15 (Spring 1966): 2-5.

4267. Wilson, Edmund. "The Boys in the Back Room." *A Literary Chronicle: 1920-1950.* Garden City, N.Y.: Doubleday, 1956, pp. 222-27.

DOROTHY SCARBOROUGH

4268. Beard, Joyce J. "Dorothy Scarborough: Texas Regionalist." Master's thesis, Texas Christian University, 1965.

4269. Heavens, Jean. "Dorothy Scarborough–Fictional Historian." Master's thesis, University of Texas, El Paso, 1968.

4270. Muncy, Elizabeth R. "Dorothy Scarborough: A Literary Pioneer." Master's thesis, Baylor University, 1940.

4271. Neatherlin, James William. "Dorothy Scarborough: Form and Milieu in the Work of a Texas Writer." Doctoral dissertation, University of Iowa, 1973.

4272. Quissell, Barbara. "Dorothy Scarborough's Critique of the Frontier Experience in *The Wind." Women, Women Writers, and the West.* Eds. Lawrence L. Lee and Merrill E.

Lewis. Troy, N.Y.: Whitston, 1978.

4273. Whitcomb, Virginia Roland. "Dorothy Scarborough: Biography and Criticism." Master's thesis, Baylor University, 1945.

JACK SCHAEFER

4274. Cleary, Michael. "Jack Schaefer: The Evolution of Pessimism." *Western American Literature* 14 (Spring 1979): 33-47.

4275. Dieter, Lynn. "Behavioral Objectives in the English Classroom: A Model." *English Journal* 59 (December 1970): 1258-62, 1271.

4276. Erisman, Fred. "Growing Up With the American West: Fiction of Jack Schaefer." *Journal of Popular Culture* 7 (Winter 1973): 710-16.

4277. ——. "Jack Schaefer: The Writer as Ecologist." *Western American Literature* 13 (Spring 1978): 3-13.

4278. Folsom, James K. "*Shane* and *Hud*: Two Stories in Search of a Medium." *Western Humanities Review* 24 (Autumn 1970): 359-72.

4279. Haslam, Gerald. *Jack Schaefer.* Western Writers Series, No. 20. Boise, Idaho: Boise State University, 1975.

4280. ——. "Jack Schaefer's Frontier: The West as Human Testing Ground." *Rocky Mountain Review* 4 (1967): 59-71.

4281. ——. "Sacred Sources in *The Canyon.*" *Western American*

Literature 14 (Spring 1979): 49-55.

4282. ——. "*Shane*: Twenty-five Years Later." *Western American Literature* 9 (November 1974): 215-16.

4283. ——. *The Works of Jack Schaefer.* Cassette. Deland, Fla.: Everett/Edwards, 1974.

4284. Johnson, Dorothy M. "Jack Schaefer's People" in Jack Schaefer, *The Short Novels of Jack Schaefer.* Boston: Houghton Mifflin, 1967.

4285. Marsden, Michael T. "Savior in the Saddle: The Sagebrush Testament." *Illinois Quarterly* 36 (December 1973): 5-15.

4286. ——. "*Shane*: From Magazine Serial to American Classic." *South Dakota Review* 15 (Winter 1977-78): 59-69.

4287. Mikkelsen, Robert. "The Western Writer: Jack Schaefer's Use of the Western Frontier." *Western Humanities Review* 8 (Spring 1954): 151-55.

4288. Nuwer, Hank. "An Interview with Jack Schaefer." *South Dakota Review* 11 (Spring 1973): 48-58.

4289. Simmons, Marc. "A Salute to *Shane.*" *Roundup* 23 (May 1974): 1-2, 9-11.

4290. Work, James C. "Settlement Waves and Coordinate Forces in *Shane.*" *Western American Literature* 14 (Fall 1979): 191-200.

MARK SCHORER

4291. Bluefarb, Sam. "What We Don't

Know *Can* Hurt Us." *Studies in Short Fiction* 5 (Spring 1968): 269-74.

HARVEY SCOTT

4292. Nash, Lee. "Scott of the *Oregonian*: Literary Frontiersman." *Pacific Historical Review* 45 (August 1976): 357-78.

4293. ———. "Scott of the *Oregonian*: The Editor as Historian." *Oregon Historical Quarterly* 70 (1969): 197-232.

JOHN SEELYE

4294. Cleary, Michael. "John Seelye's *The Kid*: Western Satire and Literary Reassessment." *South Dakota Review* 17 (Winter 1979-80): 23-43.

CHESTER SELTZER
(Amado Jesus Muro)

4295. Bode, Elroy. "The Making of a Legend." *Texas Observer* 65 (March 30, 1973): 1, 3-5.

4296. Gegenheimer, Albert F. "'Amado Muro.'" *Arizona Quarterly* 34 (Autumn 1978): 197-203.

4297. Haslam, Gerald. "The Enigma of Amado Jesus Muro." *Western American Literature* 10 (May 1975): 3-9.

4298. "The Short Stories of 'Amado Muro': A Checklist." *Arizona Quarterly* 34 (Autumn 1978): 217-18.

ROBERT W. SERVICE

4299. Bucco, Martin. "Folk Poetry of Robert W. Service." *Alaska Review* 2 (Fall 1965): 16-26.

RICHARD SHELTON

4300. Contoski, Victor. "Richard Shelton: A Voice in the Wilderness." *Western American Literature* 14 (Spring 1979): 3-17.

LUKE SHORT
See Frederick Glidden

LESLIE MARMON SILKO

4301. Blicksilver, Edith. "Traditionalism vs. Modernity: Leslie Silko on American Indian Women." *Southwest Review* 64 (Spring 1979): 149-60.

4302. Evers, Lawrence J., and Dennis W. Carr, eds. "A Conversation with Leslie Marmon Silko." *Sun Tracks* 3 (Fall 1976): 28-33.

4303. Grenier, Kate Parker. "Folklore, Poetry, and Identity: A Study of the Archetypes in the Poetry of Leslie Silko." Master's thesis, Western Kentucky University, 1978.

4304. Hoilman, Dennis R. "'A World Made of Stories': An Interpretation of Leslie Silko's *Ceremony*." *South Dakota Review* 17 (Winter 1979-80): 54-66.

4305. Larson, Charles R. *American Indian Fiction.* Albuquerque:

University of New Mexico Press, 1978, pp. 150-61.

4306. Ruoff, A. LaVonne. "Ritual and Renewal: Keres Traditions in the Short Fiction of Leslie Silko." *MELUS* 5 (Winter 1978): 2-17.

4307. Sands, Kathleen M., ed. "A Special Symposium Issue on Leslie Marmon Silko's *Ceremony*." *American Indian Quarterly* 5 (February 1979): 1-75. An important special issue.

4308. Seyersted, Per. *Leslie Marmon Silko*. Western Writers Series, No. 45. Boise, Idaho: Boise State University, 1980.

JOHN L. SINCLAIR

4309. Waters, Frank. "Introduction" to John L. Sinclair, *In Time of Harvest*. Albuquerque: University of New Mexico Press, 1971, pp. vii-x.

UPTON SINCLAIR

4310. Becker, George J. "Upton Sinclair: Quixote in a Flivver." *College English* 21 (December 1959): 133-40.

4311. Bloodworth, William A., Jr. *Upton Sinclair*. Boston: Twayne, 1977.

4312. Blumenthal, W. A. "Prolific: Writer's Cramp versus Literary Fecundity." *American Book Collector* 8 (May 1958): 3-10.

4313. Brooks, Van Wyck. "The Novels of Upton Sinclair." *Emerson and Others*. New York: E. P. Dutton, 1958, pp. 209-17.

4314. Duram, James C. "Upton Sinclair's Realistic Romanticism." *University Studies* 83 (May 1970): 1-11.

4315. Gottesman, Ronald. *Upton Sinclair: An Annotated Checklist*. Kent, Ohio: Kent State University Press, 1973.

4316. ——, and Charles L. P. Silet. *The Literary Manuscripts of Upton Sinclair*. Columbus: Ohio State University Press, 1972.

4317. Graham, John. "Upton Sinclair and the Ludlow Massacre." *Colorado Quarterly* 21 (Summer 1972): 55-67.

4318. Gross, Dalton. "George Sterling's Letters to the Upton Sinclairs: A Selection." *American Book Collector* 24 (September-October 1973): 16-20.

4319. Harris, Leon. *Upton Sinclair: American Rebel*. New York: Thomas Y. Crowell, 1975.

4320. Hicks, Granville. "The Survival of Upton Sinclair." *College English* 4 (January 1943): 213-20.

4321. Koerner, J. D. "The Last of the Muckrake Men." *South Atlantic Quarterly* 55 (April 1956): 221-32.

4322. Remley, David. "The Correspondence of H. L. Mencken and Upton Sinclair: 'An Illustration of How Not to Agree.'" Doctoral dissertation, Indiana University, 1967.

4323. Silet, Charles L. P. "The Upton

Sinclair Archives." *Southern California Quarterly* 4 (Winter 1974): 407-14.

4324. ——, ed. "Upton Sinclair to Jack London: A Literary Friendship." *Jack London Newsletter* 5 (May–August 1972): 49-76.

4325. Soderbergh, Peter A. "Upton Sinclair and Hollywood." *Midwest Quarterly* 11 (January 1970): 173-91.

4326. Yoder, Jon. "Decades of Decay: Upton Sinclair and American Liberalism After World War II." Doctoral dissertation, University of New Mexico, 1970.

4327. ——. *Upton Sinclair.* Modern Literature Monographs. New York: Frederick Ungar, 1975.

4328. ——. "Upton Sinclair, Lanny and the Liberals." *Modern Fiction Studies* 20 (Winter 1974-75): 483-504.

CHARLES A. SIRINGO

4329. Adams, Clarence Siringo. "Fair Trial at Encinoso." *True West* 5 (March–April 1966): 32 ff.

4330. Clark, Neil M. "Close Calls: An Interview with Charles A. Siringo." *American Magazine* 107 (January 1929): 38 ff.

4331. Hammond, John Hays. "Strong Men of the West." *Scribner's Magazine* 77 (February, March 1925): 115-25, 246-56.

4332. Nolen, O. W. "Charley Siringo." *Cattleman* 38 (December 1951): 50 ff.

4333. Peavy, Charles D. *Charles A. Siringo: A Texas Picaro.* South-

west Writers Series, No. 3. Austin, Tex.: Steck-Vaughn, 1967.

4334. Sawey, Orlan. *Charlie Siringo.* Boston: Twayne, 1981.

4335. ——. "Charlie Siringo: Reluctant Propagandist." *Western American Literature* 7 (Fall 1972): 203-10.

4336. Thorp, Raymond W. "Cowboy Charley Siringo." *True West* 12 (January–February 1965): 32 ff.

JEDEDIAH SMITH

4337. Morgan, Dale. *Jedediah Smith and the Opening of the West.* Indianapolis: Bobbs-Merrill, 1953; Lincoln: University of Nebraska Press, 1964.

4338. Walker, Don D. "The Western Explorer as a Literary Hero: Jedediah Smith and Ludwig Leichhardt." *Western Humanities Review* 29 (Summer 1975): 243-59.

GARY SNYDER

4339. Almon, Bert. "Buddhism and Energy in the Recent Poetry of Gary Snyder." *Mosaic* 11 (Fall 1977): 117-25.

4340. ——. *Gary Snyder.* Western Writers Series, No. 37. Boise: Boise State University, 1979.

4341. ——. "The Imagination of Gary Snyder." Doctoral dissertation, University of New Mexico, 1971.

4342. Altieri, Charles. "Gary Snyder's Lyric Poetry: Dialectic as

Ecology." *Far Point* 4 (Spring-Summer 1970): 55-65.

4343. ——. "Gary Snyder's *Turtle Island*: The Problem of Reconciling the Roles of Seer and Prophet." *Boundary 2* 4 (Spring 1976): 761-77.

4344. Bartlett, Lee. "Interview: Gary Snyder." *California Quarterly* 9 (Spring 1975): 43-50.

4345. Benoit, Raymond. "The New American Poetry." *Thought* 44 (Summer 1969): 201-18.

4346. Bly, Robert. "The Work of Gary Snyder." *The Sixties* 6 (Spring 1962): 25-42.

4347. Cheng, Lok Chua, and N. Sasaki. "Zen and the Title of Gary Snyder's 'Marin-An.'" *Notes on Contemporary Literature* 8 (May 1978): 2-3.

4348. Faas, Ekbert. *Towards a New American Poetics: Essays and Interviews.* Santa Barbara, Calif.: Black Sparrow Press, 1978, pp. 87-142.

4349. Folsom, L. Edwin. "Gary Snyder's Descent to Turtle Island: Searching for Fossil Love." *Western American Literature* 15 (Summer 1980): 103-21.

4350. Geneson, Paul. "An Interview with Gary Snyder." *Ohio Review* 18 (Fall 1977): 67-105.

4351. Gitzen, Julian. "Gary Snyder and the Poetry of Compassion." *Critical Quarterly* 15 (Winter 1973): 341-57.

4352. Hayman, Ronald. "From Hart Crane to Gary Snyder." *Encounter* 32 (February 1969): 72-79.

4353. Howard, Richard. *Alone with America: Essays on the Art of Poetry in the United States.* New York: Atheneum, 1969, pp. 485-98.

4354. Hunt, Anthony. "'Bubbs Creek Haircut': Gary Snyder's 'Great Departure' in *Mountains and Rivers Without End.*" *Western American Literature* 15 (Fall 1980): 163-75.

4355. Jungels, William J. "The Use of Native-American Mythologies in the Poetry of Gary Snyder." Doctoral dissertation, State University of New York, Buffalo, 1973.

4356. Kern, Robert. "Clearing the Ground: Gary Snyder and the Modernist Imperative." *Criticism* 19 (Spring 1977): 158-77.

4357. ——. "Recipes, Catalogues, Open Form Poetics: Gary Snyder's Archetypal Voice." *Contemporary Literature* 18 (Spring 1977): 173-97.

4358. Kherdian, David. *A Biographical Sketch and Descriptive Checklist of Gary Snyder.* Berkeley, Calif.: Oyez, 1965. Some of this material was worked into Kherdian, ed., *Six San Francisco Poets,* Fresno, Calif.: Giligia Press, 1969.

4359. Leach, Thomas James, Jr. "Gary Snyder: Poet as Mythographer." Doctoral dissertation, University of North Carolina, Chapel Hill, 1974.

4360. Lewis, Peter Elfred. "Robert Creeley and Gary Snyder: A

British Assessment." *Stand* 13 (1972): 42-47.

4361. Lewis, Tom, and Chuck Simmons. "Gary Snyder: A Trilogy." *Mountain Gazette* 36 (August 1975): 20-28.

4362. Lyon, Thomas J. "The Ecological Vision of Gary Snyder." *Kansas Quarterly* 2 (Spring 1970): 117-24.

4363. ——. "Gary Snyder, a Western Poet." *Western American Literature* 3 (Fall 1968): 207-16.

4364. McNeill, Don. "Gary Snyder, Doubter of Cities." *Moving Through Here.* New York: Alfred A. Knopf, 1970.

4365. Nelson, Rudolph L. "'Riprap on the Slick Rock of Metaphysics': Religious Dimensions in the Poetry of Gary Snyder." *Soundings* 57 (Summer 1974): 206-21.

4366. Okade, Roy. "Zen and the Poetry of Gary Snyder." Doctoral dissertation, University of Wisconsin, 1973.

4367. Parkinson, Thomas. "After the Beat Generation." *Colorado Quarterly* 17 (Summer 1968): 45-56.

4368. ——. "The Poetry of Gary Snyder." *Southern Review* 4 (Summer 1968): 616-32.

4369. ——. "The Theory and Practice of Gary Snyder." *Journal of Modern Literature* 2 (1971-72): 448-52.

4370. Paul, Sherman. "From Lookout to Ashram: The Way of Gary Snyder." *Repossessing and Renewing: Essays in the Green American Tradition.* Baton Rouge: Louisiana State University Press, 1976, pp. 195-235.

4371. Peach, Linden. "*Earth House Hold*: A Twentieth Century *Walden*?" *Anglo-Welsh Review* 25 (1975): 108-14.

4372. Rothberg, Abraham. "A Passage to More Than India: The Poetry of Gary Snyder." *Southwest Review* 61 (Winter 1976): 26-38.

4373. Steuding, Bob. *Gary Snyder.* Boston: Twayne, 1976.

4374. Williamson, Alan. "Gary Snyder, An Appreciation." *New Republic* 173 (November 1, 1975): 11-21.

4375. Windham, Steve. "Unity and Power of Imagination in Gary Snyder's 'The Elwha River.'" *Western American Literature* 14 (Winter 1980): 317-19.

C. L. SONNICHSEN

4376. Roach, Joyce Gibson. *C. L. Sonnichsen.* Western Writers Series, No. 40. Boise, Idaho: Boise State University, 1979.

4377. Walker, Dale. *C. L. Sonnichsen, Grassroots Historian.* El Paso: Texas Western Press, 1972.

VIRGINIA SORENSEN

4378. Bradford, Mary L. "Virginia Sorensen: A Saving Remnant." *Dialogue* 4 (Autumn 1969): 56-64.

4379. Hunsaker, Kenneth B. "The Twentieth Century Mormon Novel." Doctoral dissertation, Pennsylvania State University, 1968.

4380. Lambert, Neal. "Saints, Sinners and Scribes: A Look at the Mormons in Fiction." *Utah Historical Quarterly* 36 (Winter 1968): 63-76.

4381. Lee, L. L. and Sylvia B. *Virginia Sorensen.* Western Writers Series, No. 31. Boise, Idaho: Boise State University, 1978.

4382. Lee, Sylvia B. "The Mormon Novel: Virginia Sorensen's *The Evening and the Morning.*" *Women, Women Writers, and the West.* Eds. Lawrence L. Lee and Merrill E. Lewis. Troy, N.Y.: Whitston, 1978.

4383. Lythgoe, Mary. "Virginia Sorensen: An Introduction." Master's thesis, University of Utah, 1956.

JACK SPICER

4384. Herndon, James. *Everything as Expected.* San Francisco: Small Press Distribution, 1973.

4385. "Jack Spicer." *Boundary* 6 (1977). Special issue on Spicer.

4386. Sadler, Frank. "The Frontier in Jack Spicer's 'Billy the Kid.'" *The Westering Experience in American Literature: Bicentennial Essays.* Eds. Merrill Lewis and L. L. Lee. Bellingham: Bureau for Faculty Research, Western Washington University, 1977, pp. 154-60.

JEAN STAFFORD

4387. Burns, Stuart L. "Counterpoint in Jean Stafford's *The Mountain Lion.*" *Critique* 9, No. 2 (1967): 20-32.

3288. Flagg, Nancy. "People to Stay." *Shenandoah* 30, No. 3 (1979): 65-76.

4389. Gelfant, Blanche H. "*The Mountain Lion* by Jean Stafford." *New Republic* 172 (May 10, 1975): 22-25.

4390. Hassan, Ihab H. "Jean Stafford: The Expense of Style and the Scope of Sensibility." *Western Review* 19 (Spring 1955): 185-203.

4391. Jensen, Sid. "The Noble Wicked West of Jean Stafford." *Western American Literature* 7 (Winter 1973): 261-70.

4392. Oates, Joyce Carol. "The Interior Castle: The Art of Jean Stafford's Short Fiction." *Shenandoah* 30, No. 3 (1979): 61-64.

4393. Sheed, Wilfred. "Miss Jean Stafford." *Shenandoah* 30, No. 3 (1979): 92-99.

4394. Straus, Dorothea. "Jean Stafford." *Shenandoah* 30, No. 3 (1979): 85-91.

4395. Taylor, Peter. "A Comemorative Tribute to Jean Stafford. . . ." *Shenandoah* 30, No. 3 (1979): 56-60.

4396. Vickery, Olga W. "The Novels of Jean Stafford." *Critique* 5 (Spring-Summer 1962): 14-26.

WILLIAM STAFFORD

4397. Benoit, Raymond. "The New American Poetry." *Thought* 44 (Summer 1969): 201-18.

4398. "A Conversation between William Stafford and Primus St. John." *Voyages* 3 (Spring 1970): 70-79.

4399. Dickinson-Brown, Roger. "The Wise, the Dull, the Bewildered: What Happens in William Stafford." *Modern Poetry Studies* 6 (Spring 1975): 30-38.

4400. Ellsworth, Peter. "A Conversation with William Stafford." *Chicago Review* 30 (Summer 1978): 94-100.

4401. Gerber, Philip L., and Robert J. Gemmett, eds. "Keeping the Lines Wet: A Conversation with William Stafford." *Prairie Schooner* 44 (Summer 1970): 123-36.

4402. Greiner, Charles F. "Stafford's 'Traveling Through the Dark': A Discussion of Style." *English Journal* 55 (November 1966): 1015-18.

4403. Heyen, William. "William Stafford's Allegiances." *Modern Poetry Studies* 1, No. 6 (1970): 307-18.

4404. Holden, Jonathan. *The Mark to Turn: A Reading of William Stafford's Poetry.* Lawrence: University Press of Kansas, 1976.

4405. Howard, Richard. *Alone with America: Essays on the Art of Poetry in the United States.* New York: Atheneum, 1969, pp. 499-506.

4406. Hugo, Richard. "Problems with Landscapes in Early Stafford Poems." *Kansas Quarterly* 2 (Spring 1970): 33-38.

4407. ——, and William Stafford. "The Third Time the World Happens: A Dialogue in Writing." *Northwest Review* 13 (March 1973): 26-47.

4408. "An Interview with William Stafford." *Crazy Horse* 7 (June 1971): 36-41.

4409. Kelley, Patrick. "Legend and Ritual." *Kansas Quarterly* 2 (Spring 1970): 28-31.

4410. Kramer, Lawrence. "In Quiet Language." *Parnassus* 6 (Spring-Summer 1978): 101-17.

4411. Kyle, Carol. "Point of View in 'Returned to Say' and the Wilderness of William Stafford." *Western American Literature* 7 (Fall 1972): 191-201.

4412. Lauber, John. "World's Guest— William Stafford." *Iowa Review* 5 (Spring 1974): 88-101.

4413. Lensing, George S. "William Stafford: Mythmaker." *Modern Poetry Studies* 6 (Spring 1975): 1-18.

4414. Lofsness, Cynthia. "An Interview with William Stafford." *Iowa Review* 3 (Summer 1972): 92-107.

4415. Lynch, Dennis Daley. "Journeys in Search of Oneself: The Metaphor of the Road in William Stafford's *Traveling through the Dark* and *The Rescued Year.*" *Modern Poetry*

Studies 7 (Autumn 1976): 122-31.

4416. McMillan, Samuel H. "On William Stafford and His Poems: A Selected Bibliography." *Tennessee Poetry Journal* 2 (Spring 1969): 21-22.

4417. Miller, Tom P. "'In Dear Detail, by Ideal Light': The Poetry of William Stafford." *Southwest Review* 56 (Autumn 1971): 341-45.

4418. Moran, Ronald, and George Lensing. "The Emotive Imagination: A New Departure in American Poetry." *Southern Review* 3 (January 1967): 51-67.

4419. *Northwest Review* 13, No. 3 (1973): 1-92. Special issue on William Stafford.

4420. Pinsker, Sanford. "Finding What the World is Trying to Be: A Conversation with William Stafford." *American Poetry Review* 4 (July/August 1975): 28-30.

4421. Ramsey, Paul. "What the Light Struck." *Tennessee Poetry Journal* 2 (Spring 1969): 17-20.

4422. Roberts, J. Russell, Sr. "Listening to the Wilderness with William Stafford." *Western American Literature* 3 (Fall 1968): 217-26.

4423. Stafford, William E. "A Poet Responds." *Oregon Historical Quarterly* 81 (Summer 1980): 172-79.

4424. Stewart, David, and Michael Smetzer. "Interview with William Stafford." *Cottonwood*

Review (Fall 1975): 21-34.

4425. Sumner, D. Nathan. "The Poetry of William Stafford." *Research Studies* 36 (September 1968): 187-95.

4426. Turco, Lewis, and Gregory Fitz Gerald. "Keeping the Lines Wet: A Conversation with William Stafford." *Prairie Schooner* 44 (Summer 1970): 123-36.

4427. Turner, A. T. "William Stafford and the Surprise Cliche." *South Carolina Review* 7 (April 1975): 28-33.

4428. Wagner, Linda W. "William Stafford's Plain-Style." *Modern Poetry Studies* 6 (Spring 1975): 19-30.

PATIENCE STAPLETON

4429. Dalton, Joann. "Patience Stapleton: A Forgotten Frontier Writer." *Colorado Magazine* 53 (Summer 1976): 261-76.

WILBUR DANIEL STEELE

4430. Bucco, Martin. *Wilbur Daniel Steele.* New York: Twayne, 1972.

WALLACE STEGNER

4431. Ahearn, Kerry. "*The Big Rock Candy Mountain* and *Angle of Repose*: Trial and Culmination." *Western American Literature* 10 (May 1975): 11-27.

4432. ———. "Heroes vs. Women: Conflict and Duplicity in Stegner." *Women, Women Writers, and the West.* Eds. Lawrence L. Lee and Merrill E. Lewis. Troy, N.Y.: Whitston, 1978.

4433. ——. "Wallace Stegner and John Wesley Powell: The Real—And Maimed—Western Spokesman." *South Dakota Review* 15 (Winter 1977-78): 33-48.

4434. Canzoneri, Robert. "Wallace Stegner: Trial by Existence." *Southern Review* 9 (Autumn 1973): 796-827.

4435. ——. Clayton, James L. "From Pioneers to Provincials: Mormonism as Seen by Wallace Stegner." *Dialogue* 1 (Winter 1966): 105-14.

4436. Dillon, David. "Time's Prisoners: An Interview with Wallace Stegner." *Southwest Review* 61 (Summer 1976): 252-67.

4437. Eisinger, Chester E. *Fiction of the Forties.* Chicago: University of Chicago Press, 1963, pp. 324-28.

4438. ——. "Twenty Years of Wallace Stegner." *College English* 20 (December 1958): 110-16.

4439. Etulain, Richard W. "Western Fiction and History: A Reconsideration." *The American West: New Perspectives, New Dimensions.* Ed. Jerome O. Steffen. Norman: University of Oklahoma Press, 1979, pp. 152-74.

4440. Ferguson, J. M., Jr. "Cellars of Consciousness: Stegner's 'The Blue-Winged Teal.'" *Studies in Short Fiction* 14 (Spring 1977): 180-82.

4441. Flora, Joseph M. "Vardis Fisher and Wallace Stegner: Teacher and Student." *Western Ameri-can Literature* 5 (Summer 1970): 122-28.

4442. Hairston, Joe B. "Wallace Stegner and the Great Community." *South Dakota Review* 12 (Winter 1974-75): 31-42.

4443. ——. "The Westerner's Dilemma." Doctoral dissertation, University of Minnesota, 1971.

4444. Hofheins, Roger, and Dan Tooker. "Interview with Wallace Stegner." *Southern Review* 11 (Autumn 1975): 794-801.

4445. Hudson, Lois Phillips. "*The Big Rock Candy Mountain*: No Roots and No Frontier." *South Dakota Review* 9 (Spring 1971): 3-13.

4446. "Interview [with] Wallace Stegner." *Great Lakes Review* 2 (Summer 1975): 1-25.

4447. Jensen, Sid [Sydney LaMarr]. "The Compassionate Seer: Wallace Stegner's Literary Artist." *BYU Studies* 14 (Winter 1974): 248-62.

4448. ——. "The Middle Ground: A Study of Wallace Stegner's Use of History in Fiction." Doctoral dissertation, University of Utah, 1972.

4449. Lewis, Merrill. *The Works of Wallace Stegner.* Cassette. Deland, Fla.: Everett/Edwards, 1974.

4450. —— and Lorene. *Wallace Stegner.* Western Writers Series, No. 4. Boise, Idaho: Boise State College, 1972.

4451. Milton, John. "Conversation with Wallace Stegner." *South Dakota Review* 10 (Spring 1971): 45-57.

4452. Mosley, Richard. "First-Person Narration in Wallace Stegner's *All the Little Live Things.*" *Notes on Contemporary Literature* 3 (March 1973): 12-13.

4453. Otis, John Whitacre. "The Purified Vision: The Fiction of Wallace Stegner." Doctoral dissertation, Drake University, 1977.

4454. Peterson, Audrey C. "Narrative Voice in Wallace Stegner's *Angle of Repose.*" *Western American Literature* 10 (August 1975): 125-33.

4455. Putnam, Jackson K. "Wallace Stegner and Western History: Some Historiographical Problems in *Angle of Repose.*" *vis-a-vis* 3 (September 1975): 51-60.

4456. Robertson, Jamie. "Henry Adams, Wallace Stegner, and the Search for a Sense of Place in the West." *The Westering Experience in American Literature: Bicentennial Essays.* Eds. Merrill Lewis and L. L. Lee. Bellingham: Bureau for Faculty Research, Western Washington University, 1977, pp. 135-43.

4457. Robinson, Forrest G., and Margaret G. *Wallace Stegner.* Boston: Twayne, 1977.

4458. ——. "Wallace Stegner: An Interview." *Quarry* 4 (1975): 72-84.

4459. Saporta, Marc. "Wallace Stegner." *Informations et documents* 187 (September 15-October 1, 1963): 23-36.

4460. Singer, Barnett. "The Historical Ideal in Wallace Stegner's Fiction." *South Dakota Review* 15 (Spring 1977): 28-44.

4461. Tyler, Robert L. "The I.W.W. and the West." *American Quarterly* 12 (Summer 1960): 175-87.

4462. White, Robin, and Ed McClanahan. "An Interview with Wallace Stegner." *Per Se* 3 (Fall 1968): 28-35.

4463. Willey, Jill Lucas. "Wallace Stegner: An Annotated Bibliography." Master's thesis, California State University, San Jose, 1975.

JOHN STEINBECK

4464. Alexander, Stanley. "*Cannery Row*: Steinbeck's Pastoral Poem." *Western American Literature* 2 (Winter 1968): 281-95.

4465. ——. "The Conflict of Form in *Tortilla Flat.*" *American Literature* 40 (March 1968): 58-66.

4466. ——. "Primitivism and Pastoral Form in John Steinbeck's Early Fiction." Doctoral dissertation, University of Texas, 1965.

4467. Anderson, Arthur Commins. "The Journey Motif in the Fiction of John Steinbeck—The Traveler Discovers Himself." Doctoral dissertation, Fordham University, 1976.

4468. Antico, John. "A Reading of

Steinbeck's 'Flight.'" *Modern Fiction Studies* 11 (Spring 1965): 45-53.

4469. Astro, Richard. "From the Tidepool to the Stars: Steinbeck's Sense of Place." *Steinbeck Quarterly* 10 (Winter 1977): 5-11.

4470. ——. "Into the Cornucopia: Steinbeck's Vision of Nature and the Ideal Man." Doctoral dissertation, University of Washington, 1969.

4471. ——. *John Steinbeck and Edward F. Ricketts: The Shaping of a Novelist.* Minneapolis: University of Minnesota Press, 1973.

4472. ——. "John Steinbeck and the Tragic Miracle of Consciousness." *San Jose Studies* 1 (November 1975): 61-72.

4473. ——. "Something That Happened: A Non-Teleological Approach to 'The Leader of the People.'" *Steinbeck Quarterly* 6 (Winter 1973): 19-23.

4474. ——. "Steinbeck and Ricketts: Escape or Commitment in *The Sea of Cortez*." *Western American Literature* 6 (Summer 1971): 109-21.

4475. ——. "Steinbeck and Ricketts: The Morphology of a Metaphysic." *University of Windsor Review* 8 (Spring 1973): 24-33.

4476. ——. "Steinbeck's Bittersweet Thursday." *Steinbeck Quarterly* 4 (Spring 1971): 36-48.

4477. ——. "Steinbeck's Post-War Trilogy: A Return to Nature and Natural Man." *Twentieth Century Literature* 16 (April 1970): 109-22.

4478. ——. "Travels With Steinbeck: The Laws of Thought and the Laws of Things." *Steinbeck Quarterly* 8 (Spring 1975): 35-44.

4479. ——, and Tetsumaro Hayashi, eds. *Steinbeck: The Man and His Work.* Corvallis: Oregon State University Press, 1971.

4480. Autrey, Max L. "Men, Mice and Moths: Gradation in Steinbeck's 'The Leader of the People.'" *Western American Literature* 10 (November 1975): 195-204.

4481. Beebe, Maurice, and Jackson R. Bryer. "Criticism of John Steinbeck: A Selected Checklist." *Modern Fiction Studies* 11 (Spring 1965): 90-103.

4482. Benson, Jackson J. "Environment as Meaning: John Steinbeck and the Great Central Valley." *Steinbeck Quarterly* 10 (Winter 1977): 12-20.

4483. ——. "John Steinbeck: Novelist as Scientist." *Novel: A Forum on Fiction* 10 (Spring 1977): 248-64.

4484. ——. "John Steinbeck's *Cannery Row*: A Reconsideration." *Western American Literature* 12 (May 1977): 11-40.

4485. ——. "'To Tom, Who Lived It': John Steinbeck and the Man from Weedpatch." *Journal of Modern Literature* 5 (April 1976): 151-94. See also "An Afterword and An Introduction," pp. 194-210.

4486. ——, and Anne Loftis. "John

Steinbeck and Farm Labor Unionization: The Background of *In Dubious Battle.*" *American Literature* 52 (May 1980): 194-223.

4487. Benton, Robert M. "Realism, Growth, and Contrast in 'The Gift.'" *Steinbeck Quarterly* 6 (Winter 1973): 3-9.

4488. Bleeker, Gary Wallace. "Setting and Animal Tropes in the Fiction of John Steinbeck." Doctoral dissertation, University of Nebraska, 1969.

4489. Bowron, Bernard. *"The Grapes of Wrath*: A 'Wagons West' Romance." *Colorado Quarterly* 3 (Summer 1954): 84-91.

4490. Bracher, Frederick. "Steinbeck and the Biological View of Man." *Pacific Spectator* 2 (1948): 14-29.

4491. Brasch, James D. *"The Grapes of Wrath* and Old Testament Skepticism." *San Jose Studies* 3 (1977): 16-27.

4492. Brown, D. Russell. "The Natural Man in John Steinbeck's Non-Teleological Tales." *Ball State University Forum* 7 (Spring 1966): 47-52.

4493. Brown, Joyce D. "Animal Symbolism and Imagery in John Steinbeck's Fiction from 1929 through 1939." Doctoral dissertation, University of Southern Mississippi, 1972.

4494. Burns, Stuart L. "The Turtle or the Gopher: Another Look at the Ending of *The Grapes of Wrath.*" *Western American Literature* 9 (May 1974): 53-57.

4495. Carpenter, Frederic I. "The Philosophic Joads." *College English* 2 (December 1941): 315-25.

4496. Carr, Duane Ralph. "John Steinbeck: Twentieth Century Romantic: A Study of the Early Works." Doctoral dissertation, University of Tulsa, 1975.

4497. ——. "Steinbeck's Blakean Vision in *The Grapes of Wrath.*" *Steinbeck Quarterly* 8 (Summer-Fall 1975): 67-73.

4498. Caselli, Jaclyn. "John Steinbeck and the American Patchwork Quilt." *San Jose Studies* 1 (November 1975): 83-87.

4499. Casimar, Louis J. "Human Emotion and the Early Novels of John Steinbeck." Doctoral dissertation, University of Texas, 1966.

4500. Chametzky, Jules. "The Ambivalent Endings of *The Grapes of Wrath.*" *Modern Fiction Studies* 11 (Spring 1965): 34-44.

4501. Champney, Freeman. "John Steinbeck, Californian." *Antioch Review* 7 (1947): 345-62.

4502. Cox, Martha Heasley. "The Conclusion of *The Grapes of Wrath*: Steinbeck's Conception and Execution." *San Jose Studies* 1 (November 1975): 73-81.

4503. ——. "In Search of John Steinbeck: His People and His Land." *San Jose Studies* 1 (November 1975): 41-60.

4504. ——. "Remembering John Steinbeck." *San Jose Studies* 1 (November 1975): 109-27.

4505. Crouch, Steve. *"Cannery Row."* *American West* 10 (September 1973): 18-27.

4506. ——. *Steinbeck Country.* Palo Alto, Calif.: American West, 1973.

4507. Davis, Robert M., ed. *Steinbeck: A Collection of Critical Essays.* Englewood Cliffs, N.J.: Prentice-Hall, 1972.

4508. De Mott, Robert. "Toward a Redefinition of *To a God Unknown.*" *University of Windsor Review* 8 (Spring 1973): 34-53.

4509. Ditsky, John. "The Ending of *The Grapes of Wrath*: A Further Commentary." *Agora* 2 (Fall 1973): 41-50.

4510. ——. *Essays on "East of Eden."* Steinbeck Monograph Series, No. 7. Muncie, Ind.: Ball State University, 1977.

4511. ——. *"The Grapes of Wrath*: A Reconsideration." *Southern Humanities Review* 13 (Summer 1979): 215-20.

4512. ——. "Music from a Dark Cave: Organic Form in Steinbeck's Fiction." *Journal of Narrative Technique* 1 (January 1971): 59-67.

4513. ——. "Steinbeck's 'Flight': The Ambiguity of Manhood." *Steinbeck Quarterly* 5 (Summer-Fall 1972): 80-85.

4514. ——. "Steinbeck's *Travels With Charley*: The Quest That Failed." *Steinbeck Quarterly* 8 (Spring 1975): 45-50.

4515. ——. *"The Wayward Bus*: Love and Time in America." *San Jose Studies* 1 (November 1975): 89-101.

4516. Donohue, Agnes McNeill, ed. *A Casebook on The Grapes of Wrath.* New York: Thomas Y. Crowell, 1968. Useful collection of essays on Steinbeck's best-known novel.

4517. Eddy, Darlene. "To Go A-Buccaneering and Take a Spanish Town: Some Seventeenth-Century Aspects of *A Cup of Gold.*" *Steinbeck Quarterly* 8 (Winter 1975): 3-12.

4518. Falkenberg, Sandra. "A Study of Female Characterization in Steinbeck's Fiction." *Steinbeck Quarterly* 8 (Spring 1975): 50-56.

4519. Feied, Frederick. "Steinbeck's Depression Novels: The Ecological Basis." Doctoral dissertation, Columbia University, 1968.

4520. Fensch, Thomas. *Steinbeck and Covici: The Story of a Friendship.* Middlebury, Vt.: Paul S. Eriksson, 1979.

4521. Fossey, W. Richard. "The End of the Western Dream: *The Grapes of Wrath* and Oklahoma." *Cimarron Review* 22 (January 1973): 25-34.

4522. French, Warren G. "After *The Grapes of Wrath.*" *Steinbeck Quarterly* 8 (Summer-Fall 1975): 73-78.

4523. ——. "Another Look at *The Grapes of Wrath.*" *Colorado Quarterly* 3 (Winter 1955): 337-43.

4524. ——. "The 'California Quality' of Steinbeck's Best Fiction." *San Jose Studies* 1 (November 1975): 9-19.

4525. ——. "'Johnny Bear'–Steinbeck's 'Yellow Peril' Story." *Steinbeck Quarterly* 5 (Summer-Fall 1972): 101-7.

4526. ——. *John Steinbeck.* 2d ed., rev. New York: Twayne, 1975.

4527. ——. "John Steinbeck." *Fifteen Modern American Authors.* Ed. Jackson R. Bryer. Durham, N.C.: Duke University Press, 1969, pp. 369-87; *Sixteen Modern American Authors.* New York: W. W. Norton, 1973, pp. 499-527.

4528. ——, ed. *A Companion to The Grapes of Wrath.* New York: Viking, 1963.

4529. Garcia, Reloy. "Steinbeck's 'The Snake': An Explication." *Steinbeck Quarterly* 5 (Summer-Fall 1972): 85-90.

4530. Gerstenberger, Donna. "Steinbeck's Waste Land." *Modern Fiction Studies* 11 (Spring 1965): 59-65.

4531. Goboni, Mark William. "'Symbols for the Wordlessness': A Study of John Steinbeck's *East of Eden.*" Doctoral dissertation, Ohio University, 1978.

4532. Goldhurst, William. "*Of Mice and Men*: John Steinbeck's Parable of the Curse of Cain." *Western American Literature* 6 (Summer 1971): 123-35.

4533. Goldsmith, Arnold L. "Thematic Rhythm in *The Red Pony.*" *College English* 26 (February 1965): 391-94.

4534. Goldstone, Adrian H., and John R. Payne. *John Steinbeck: A Bibliographical Catalogue of the Adrian H. Goldstone Collection.* Austin: University of Texas, Humanities Research Center, 1974.

4535. Golemba, Henry L. "Steinbeck's Attempt to Escape the Literary Fallacy." *Modern Fiction Studies* 15 (Summer 1969): 231-39.

4536. Gordon, Walter K. "Steinbeck's 'Flight': Journey *to* or *from* Maturity?" *Studies in Short Fiction* 3 (Summer 1966): 453-55.

4537. Gray, James. *John Steinbeck.* Minneapolis: University of Minnesota Press, 1971.

4538. Griffin, R. J., and W. A. Freedman. "Machines and Animals: Pervasive Motifs in *The Grapes of Wrath.*" *Journal of English and Germanic Philology* 62 (July 1963): 569-80.

4539. Grommon, A. H. "Who Is 'The Leader of the People'?" *English Journal* 48 (November 1959): 449-61.

4540. Gurko, Leo. "*Of Mice and Men*: Steinbeck as Manichean." *University of Windsor Review* 8 (Spring 1973): 11-23.

4541. Hartrangt, Marshall V. *Grapes of Gladness.* Los Angeles: DeVorss, 1939. An "answer" to *Grapes of Wrath.*

4542. Hayashi, Tetsumaro. "A Brief Survey of John Steinbeck Bibliographies." *Kyushu American Literature* 9 (July 1966): 54-61.

4543. ——. *John Steinbeck: A Concise Bibliography (1930-1965).* Metuchen, N.J.: Scarecrow Press, 1967.

4544. ——. *John Steinbeck: A Dictionary of His Fictional Characters.* Metuchen, N.J.: Scarecrow Press, 1976.

4545. ——. *John Steinbeck: A Guide to the Doctoral Dissertations (1946-1969).* Steinbeck Monograph Series, No. 1. Muncie, Ind.: Ball State University, 1971.

4546. ——. *A New Steinbeck Bibliography, 1929-1971.* Metuchen, N.J.: Scarecrow Press, 1973.

4547. ——. "Recent Steinbeck Studies in the United States." *Steinbeck Quarterly* 4 (Summer 1971): 73-76.

4548. ——. *Steinbeck's Literary Dimension: A Guide to Comparative Studies.* Metuchen, N.J.: Scarecrow Press, 1973.

4549. ——. *Steinbeck's Women: Essays in Criticism.* Muncie, Ind.: Steinbeck Society of America, 1979.

4550. ——. *A Study Guide to Steinbeck: A Handbook of His Major Works.* Metuchen, N.J.: Scarecrow Press, 1974.

4551. ——. *A Study Guide to Steinbeck (Part II).* Metuchen, N.J.: Scarecrow Press, 1979. A guide to the lesser-known works. Companion to *A Handbook to His Major Works* (1974).

4552. ——, ed. *Steinbeck Quarterly* 1 (1968-). Ball State University, Muncie, Ind.

4553. Hedgpeth, Joel W. "Genesis of the *Sea of Cortez.*" *Steinbeck Quarterly* 6 (Summer 1973): 74-80.

4554. Hilton, William C. "John Steinbeck: An annotated Bibliography of Criticism, 1936-1963." Master's thesis, Wayne State University, 1965.

4555. Hopkins, Karen J. "Steinbeck's *East of Eden*: A Defense." *Itinerary: Criticism, Essays on California Writers.* Ed. Charles L. Crow. Bowling Green, Ohio: University Press, 1978, 63-78.

4556. Houghton, Donald E. "'Westering' in 'Leader of the People.'" *Western American Literature* 4 (Summer 1969): 117-24.

4557. "Interview with John Steinbeck." *Paris Review* 63 (Fall 1975): 180-94.

4558. Jain, Sunita. *John Steinbeck's Concept of Man: A Critical Study of His Novels.* New Delhi: New Statesman Publishers, 1979.

4559. Johnson, Curtis L. "Steinbeck: A Suggestion for Research." *Modern Fiction Studies* 11 (Spring 1965): 75-78.

4560. Jones, Lawrence William. "'A Little Play in Your Head': Parable Form in John Steinbeck's Post-War Fiction." *Genre* 3 (March 1970): 55-63.

4561. Justus, James H. "The Transient World of *Tortilla Flat.*" *Western Review* 7 (Spring 1970): 55-60.

4562. Karsten, Ernest E., Jr. "Thematic Structure in *The Pearl.*" *English Journal* 54 (January 1965): 1-7.

4563. Kiernan, Thomas. *The Intricate Music: A Biography of John*

Steinbeck. Boston: Little, Brown, 1979.

4564. Kinney, Arthur F. "The Arthurian Cycle in *Tortilla Flat.*" *Modern Fiction Studies* 11 (Spring 1965): 11-20.

4565. Koloc, Frederick Joseph. "John Steinbeck's *In Dubious Battle*: Backgrounds, Reputation, and Artistry." Doctoral dissertation, University of Pittsburgh, 1974.

4566. Krause, Sydney J. "*The Pearl* and 'Hadleyburg': From Desire to Renunciation." *Steinbeck Quarterly* 7 (Winter 1974): 3-18.

4567. ——. "Steinbeck and Mark Twain." *Steinbeck Newsletter* 6 (Fall 1973): 104-11.

4568. Levant, Howard. *The Novels of John Steinbeck: A Critical Study*. Columbia: University of Missouri Press, 1974.

4569. ——. "*Tortilla Flat*: The Shape of John Steinbeck's Career." *PMLA* 85 (October 1970): 1087-95.

4570. ——. "The Unity of *In Dubious Battle*: Violence and Dehumanization." *Modern Fiction Studies* 40 (Spring 1965): 21-33.

4571. Lieber, Todd M. "Talismanic Patterns in the Novels of John Steinbeck." *American Literature* 44 (May 1972): 262-75.

4572. Lisca, Peter. "*Cannery Row* and the *Tao Teh Ching.*" *San Jose Studies* 1 (November 1975): 21-27.

4573. ——. "John Steinbeck: A Literary Biography." *Steinbeck and His Critics: A Record of Twenty-five Years.* Eds. E. W. Tedlock, Jr., and C. V. Wicker. Albuquerque: University of New Mexico Press, 1957, pp. 3-22.

4574. ——. *John Steinbeck: Nature and Myth.* New York: Thomas Y. Crowell, 1978.

4575. ——. "New Perspectives in Steinbeck Studies." *University of Windsor Review* 8 (Spring 1973): 6-10.

4576. ——. "Steinbeck and Hemingway: Suggestions for a Comparative Study." *Steinbeck Newsletter* 2 (Spring 1969): 9-17.

4577. ——. "Steinbeck's Image of Man and His Decline as a Writer." *Modern Fiction Studies* 11 (Spring 1965): 3-10.

4578. ——. *The Wide World of John Steinbeck.* New Brunswick, N.J.: Rutgers University Press, 1958.

4579. ——, ed. *John Steinbeck, The Grapes of Wrath: Text and Criticism.* New York: Viking Press, 1972.

4580. ——, et al. "John Steinbeck Special Number." *Modern Fiction Studies* 11 (Spring 1965): 3-103.

4581. McCarthy, Paul. "House and Shelter as Symbol in *The Grapes of Wrath.*" *South Dakota Review* 5 (Winter 1967-68): 48-67.

4582. ——. *John Steinbeck.* Modern Literature Monographs. New York: Frederick Ungar, 1979.

4583. McDaniel, Barbara Albrecht.

"Self-Alienating Characters in the Fiction of John Steinbeck." Doctoral dissertation, North Texas State University, 1974.

4584. McMahan, Elizabeth E. "The Chrysanthemums': Study of a Woman's Sexuality." *Modern Fiction Studies* 14 (Winter 1968-69): 453-58.

4585. McTee, James David. "Underhill's Mystic Way and the Initiation Theme in the Major Fiction of John Steinbeck." Doctoral dissertation, East Texas State University, 1975.

4586. McWilliams, Carey. "A Man, A Place, and a Time." *American West* 7 (May 1970): 4-8, 38-40, 62-64.

4587. Marcus, Mordecai. "The Lost Dream of Sex and Childbirth in 'The Chrysanthemums.'" *Modern Fiction Studies* 11 (Spring 1965): 54-58.

4588. Marks, Lester Jay. "*East of Eden*: 'Thou Mayest.'" *Steinbeck Quarterly* 4 (Winter 1971): 3-18.

4589. ——. *Thematic Design in the Novels of John Steinbeck.* The Hague: Mouton, 1970.

4590. Marovitz, Sanford E. "The Cryptic Raillery of 'Saint Katy the Virgin.'" *Steinbeck Quarterly* 5 (Summer-Fall 1972): 107-12.

4591. ——. "The Expository Prose of John Steinbeck." *Steinbeck Quarterly* 7 (Spring 1974): 41-53; (Fall 1974): 88-102.

4592. Martin, Bruce K. "'The Leader of the People' Reexamined." *Studies in Short Fiction* 8 (Summer 1971): 423-32.

4593. May, Charles E. "Myth and Mystery in Steinbeck's 'The Snake': A Jungian View." *Criticism* 15 (Fall 1973): 322-35.

4594. Metzger, C. R. "Steinbeck's Version of the Pastoral." *Modern Fiction Studies* 6 (Summer 1960): 115-24.

4595. Miller, William V. "Sexual and Spiritual Ambiguity in 'The Chrysanthemums.'" *Steinbeck Quarterly* 5 (Summer-Fall 1972): 68-75.

4596. Mitchell, Marilyn L. "Steinbeck's Strong Women: Feminine Identity in the Short Stories." *Southwest Review* 61 (Summer 1976): 303-15.

4597. Moore, Harry Thornton. *The Novels of John Steinbeck: A First Critical Study.* Chicago: Normandie House, 1939; Port Washington, N.Y.: Kennikat, 1968.

4598. Morsberger, Robert E. "In Defense of 'Westering.'" *Western American Literature* 5 (Summer 1970): 143-46.

4599. Nelson, H. S. "Steinbeck's Politics Then and Now." *Antioch Review* 27 (Spring 1967): 118-33.

4600. Nimitz, Jack. "Ecology in *The Grapes of Wrath*." *Hartford Studies in Literature* 2 (No. 2): 165-68.

4601. Nossen, Evon. "The Beast-Man Theme in the Work of John Steinbeck." *Ball State University Forum* 7 (Spring 1966): 52-64.

4602. O'Connor, Richard. *John Steinbeck.* American Writers Series. New York: McGraw-Hill, 1970.

4603. Okerland, Arlene N., ed. "Steinbeck Special Issue." *San Jose Studies* 1 (November 1975).

4604. Ortego, Philip D. "Fables of Identity: Stereotype and Caricature of Chicanos in Steinbeck's *Tortilla Flat.*" *Journal of Ethnic Studies* 1 (Spring 1973): 39-43.

4605. Owens, Louis D. "Steinbeck's 'Flight': Into the Jaws of Death." *Steinbeck Quarterly* 10 (Summer-Fall 1977): 103-8.

4606. Pearce, Howard D. "Steinbeck's 'Leader of the People': Dialectic and Symbol." *Publications in Language and Literature* 8 (Fall 1972): 415-26.

4607. Peterson, Richard F. "The Grail Legend and Steinbeck's 'The Great Mountains.'" *Steinbeck Quarterly* 6 (Winter 1973): 9-15.

4608. Powell, Lawrence Clark. "Toward a Bibliography of John Steinbeck." *Colophon* N.S., 3 (Autumn 1938): 558-68.

4609. Pratt, John Clark. *John Steinbeck.* Contemporary Writers in Christian Perspective. Grand Rapids, Mich.: William B. Eerdmans, 1970.

4610. Pratt, Linda Ray. "Imagining Existence: Form and History in Steinbeck and Agee." *Southern Review* 11 (Winter 1975): 84-98.

4611. ———. "In Defense of Mac's Dubious Battle." *Steinbeck Quarterly* 10 (Spring 1977): 36-44.

4612. Ross, Woodburn O. "John Steinbeck: Naturalism's Priest." *College English* 10 (May 1949): 432-37.

4613. Rundell, Walter, Jr. "Steinbeck's Image of the West." *American West* I (Spring 1964): 4-17, 79.

4614. Schmitz, Anne-Marie. *In Search of Steinbeck.* Los Altos, Calif.: Hermes Publications, 1978.

4615. Scoville, Samuel. "The *Weltanschauung* of Steinbeck and Hemingway: An Analysis of Themes." *English Journal* 56 (January 1967): 60-63, 66.

4616. Scrota, Steve. "The Function of the Grotesque in the Works of John Steinbeck." Doctoral dissertation, Oklahoma State University, 1973.

4617. Shockley, Martin. "Christian Symbolism in *The Grapes of Wrath.*" *College English* 18 (November 1956): 87-90.

4618. Short, John D., Jr. "John Steinbeck: A 1930's Photo-Recollection." *San Jose Studies* 2 (May 1976): 74-82.

4619. Shuman, R. Baird. "Initiation Rites in Steinbeck's *The Red Pony.*" *English Journal* 59 (December 1970): 1252-55.

4620. Simmons, Roy S. *Steinbeck's Literary Achievement.* Muncie, Ind.: Ball State University, 1976.

4621. Slade, Leonard A., Jr. "The Use of Biblical Allusions in *The Grapes of Wrath.*" *CLA Journal* 11 (March 1968): 241-47.

4622. Spies, George Henry, III. "John Steinbeck's *The Grapes of Wrath* and Frederick Manfred's *The Golden Bowl*: A Comparative Study." Doctoral dissertation, Ball State University, 1973.

4623. Spilka, Mark. "Of George and Lennie and Curley's Wife: Sweet Violence in Steinbeck's Eden." *Modern Fiction Studies* 20 (Summer 1974): 169-79.

4624. Steele, Joan. "John Steinbeck: A Checklist of Biographical, Critical, and Bibliographical Material." *Bulletin of Bibliography* 24 (May-August 1965): 149-52, 162-63.

4625. Steinbeck, Elaine, and Robert Wallsten, eds. *Steinbeck: A Life in Letters*. New York: Viking Press, 1975.

4626. Street, Webster. "Remembering John Steinbeck." Ed. Martha Heasley Cox. *San Jose Studies* 1 (November 1975): 109-27.

4627. Taylor, Horace P., Jr. "John Steinbeck: The Quest." *McNeese Review* 16 (1965): 33-45.

4628. Taylor, Walter Fuller. *"The Grapes of Wrath* Reconsidered." *Mississippi Quarterly* 12 (Summer 1959): 136-44.

4629. Tedlock, E. W., Jr., and C. V. Wicker, eds. *Steinbeck and His Critics: A Record of Twenty-Five Years*. Albuquerque: University of New Mexico Press, 1957.

4630. TeMaat, Agatha. "John Steinbeck: On the Nature of the Creative Process in the Early Years." Doctoral dissertation, University of Nebraska, Lincoln, 1975.

4631. Trachtenberg, Stanley. "John Steinbeck: The Fate of Protest." *North Dakota Quarterly* 41 (Spring 1973): 5-11.

4632. Tuttleton, James W. "Steinbeck in Russia: The Rhetoric of Praise and Blame." *Modern Fiction Studies* 11 (Spring 1965): 79-89.

4633. Valjean, Nelson. *John Steinbeck the Errant Knight: An Intimate Biography of His California Years*. San Francisco: Chronicle Books, 1975.

4634. Wallis, Prentiss Bascom. "John Steinbeck: The Symbolic Family." Doctoral dissertation, University of Kansas, 1966.

4635. Watt, F. G. *John Steinbeck*. New York: Grove Press; Edinburgh: Oliver and Boyd, 1962.

4636. West, Philip J. "Steinbeck's 'The Leader of the People': A Crisis in Style." *Western American Literature* 5 (Summer 1970): 137-41.

4637. Woodress, James. "John Steinbeck: Hostage to Fortune." *South Atlantic Quarterly* 63 (Summer 1964): 385-97.

4638. Woodward, Robert H. "Steinbeck's 'The Promise.'" *Steinbeck Quarterly* 6 (Winter 1973): 15-19.

4639. Wyatt, Bryant N. "Experimentation as Technique: The Protest Novels of John Steinbeck." *Discourse* 12 (Spring 1969): 143-53.

4640. Yano, Shigeharu. *The Current*

of *Steinbeck's World*. Steinbeck Study Series, No. 1. Tokyo: Seibido, 1978.
4641. Yarmus, Marcia D. "John Steinbeck and the Hispanic Influence." *Steinbeck Quarterly* 10 (Summer-Fall 1977): 97-102.

ALLAN STEVENS

4642. Markos, Donald W. "Allan Stephens: The Lineaments of the Real." *Southern Review* 11 (Spring 1975): 331-56.

GEORGE STERLING

4643. Angoz, Charles, ed. *George Sterling: A Centenary Memoir Anthology*. South Brunswick, Maine: A. S. Barnes, 1969.
4644. Benediktsson, Thomas E. *George Sterling*. Boston: Twayne, 1980.
4645. Bouwman, Fred. "George Sterling and Jack London: A Literary Friendship." *Jack London Newsletter* 5 (May-August 1972): 108-10.
4646. Brazil, John R. "Ambrose Bierce, Jack London, and George Sterling: Victorians between Two Worlds." *San Jose Studies* 4 (February 1978): 19-33.
4647. ———. "George Sterling: Art, Politics, The Retreat to Carmel." *Markham Review* 8 (Winter 1979): 27-33.
4648. Coblentz, S. A. "George Sterling: Western Phenomenon." *Arizona Quarterly* 13 (Spring 1957): 54-60.

4649. Cross, Dalton, ed. "Seventeen George Sterling Letters." *Jack London Newsletter* 1 (July-December 1968): 41-61.
4650. Duke, Maurice. "Letters of George Sterling to James Branch Cabell." *American Literature* 44 (March 1972): 146-53.
4651. Dunbar, John R. "Letters of George Sterling to Carey McWilliams." *California Historical Society Quarterly* 46 (September 1967): 235-52.
4652. Fleming, Donald R. "The Last Bohemian." *Book Club of California Quarterly News-Letter* 37 (Fall 1972): 75-95.
4653. Gross, Dalton. "George Sterling's Letters to William Stanley Braithwaite: The Poet Versus the Editor." *American Book Collector* 24 (November-December 1973): 18-20.
4654. ———. "George Sterling's Life at Carmel: Sterling's Letters to Witter Bynner." *Markham Review* 4 (October 1973): 12-16.
4655. Johnson, Cecil, ed. *A Bibliography of the Writing of George Sterling*. Folcroft, Pa.: Folcroft Press, 1969.
4656. Longtin, Ray C. *Three Writers of the Far West: A Reference Guide*. Boston: G. K. Hall, 1980.
4657. Slade, Joseph W. "George Sterling, 'Prophet of the Suns.'" *Markham Review* 1 (May 1968): 4-10.
4658. ———, ed. "The Testament of an

American Schopenhauer: George Sterling's 'Pleasure and Pain!'" *Resources for American Literary Study* 3 (Autumn 1973): 230-48.

4659. Stevenson, Lionel. "George Sterling's Place in Modern Poetry." *University of California Chronicle* 31 (October 1929): 401-21.

JAMES STEVENS

4660. Clare, Warren L. "Big Jim Stevens: A Study in Pacific Northwest Literature." Doctoral dissertation, Washington State University, 1967.

4661. ——. "James Stevens: The Laborer and Literature." *Research Studies* 4 (December 1964): 355-67.

4662. ——. "'Posers, Parasites, and Pismires': *Status Rerum*, by James Stevens and H. L. Davis." *Pacific Northwest Quarterly* 61 (January 1970): 22-30.

4663. Maunder, Elwood R. "An Interview with James Stevens: The Making of a Folklorist." *Forest History* 7 (Winter 1964): 2-19.

4664. [Stevens, James.] "Footnote to History: Jim Stevens at the Intermountain Institute." *Idaho Yesterdays* 23 (Winter 1980): 18-19.

ROBERT LOUIS STEVENSON

4665. Baumgarten, Murray. "Between Geology and History: An Interpretation of Robert Louis Stevenson's *Silverado Squat-* *ters*." *Book Club of California Quarterly News-Letter* 38 (Fall 1973): 75-83.

4666. Issler, Anne Roller. "Robert Louis Stevenson in Monterey." *Pacific Historical Review* 34 (August 1965): 305-21.

4667. Thomas, Phillip D. "From Old World to New with Robert Louis Stevenson: The Famous Scottish Author Reports on Life in Steerage and Emigrant Train During an 1879 Trip to the Far West." *American West* 12 (May 1975): 28-31, 60-61.

GEORGE R. STEWART

4668. Beeler, Madison S. "George R. Stewart, Toponymist." *Names* 24 (June 1976): 77-85.

4669. Caldwell, John. *George R. Stewart*. Western Writers Series, No. 46. Boise, Idaho: Boise State University, 1981.

4670. ——. "George R. Stewart, Jr.: A Checklist." *Bulletin of Bibliography* 36 (April–June 1979): 99-104.

4671. Cogell, Elizabeth Cummins. "The Middle-Landscape Myth in Science Fiction." *Science Fiction Studies* 5 (July 1978): 134-42.

4672. Egan, Ferol. "In a World of Creation." *Westways* 72 (July 1980): 16-19, 80.

CHARLES WARREN STODDARD

4673. Baird, James R. "The Noble Polynesian." *Pacific Spectator* 4 (Autumn 1950): 452-65.

4674. Bentzon, Théodore. [Marie Thérèse Blanc] "Un Loti américain: Charles Warren Stoddard." *Revue des Deux Mondes* 138 (December 1, 1896): 615-44.

4675. Gale, Robert L. *Charles Warren Stoddard.* Western Writers Series, No. 30. Boise, Idaho: Boise State University, 1977.

4676. Grenander, M. E. "Ambrose Bierce and Charles Warren Stoddard: Some Unpublished Correspondence." *Huntington Library Quarterly* 23 (May 1960): 261-92.

4677. Hubbell, Jay B. "George Henry Boker, Paul Hamilton Hayne, and Charles Warren Stoddard: Some Unpublished Letters." *American Literature* 5 (May 1933): 146-65.

4678. Longtin, Ray C. *Three Writers of the Far West: A Reference Guide.* Boston: G. K. Hall, 1980.

4679. McGinty, Brian. "Charles Warren Stoddard: The Pleasure of His Company." *California Historical Quarterly* 52 (Summer 1973): 153-69.

4680. Stroven, Carl G. "A Life of Charles Warren Stoddard." Doctoral dissertation, Duke University, 1939.

HYEMEYOHSTS STORM

4681. Larson, Charles R. *American Indian Fiction.* Aubuquerque: University of New Mexico Press, 1978, pp. 112-27, 130-32, 165-72.

4682. ———. *"Seven Arrows*: Sage of the American Indian." *Books Abroad* 47 (1973): 88-92.

4683. Peyer, Bernd. "Reconsidering Native American Fiction." *Amerikastudien/American Studies* 24, No. 2 (1979): 264-74.

MICHAEL STRAIGHT

4684. Graham, Don. "Tragedy and Western American Literature: The Example of Michael Straight's *A Very Small Remnant.*" *Denver Quarterly* 12 (Winter 1978): 59-66.

4685. Milton, John R. *Three West: Conversations with Vardis Fisher, Max Evans, Michael Straight.* Vermillion, S.Dak.: Dakota Press, 1970.

IDAH MEACHAM STROBRIDGE

4686. Amaral, Anthony. "Idah Meacham Strobridge: First Woman of Nevada Letters." *Nevada Historical Society Quarterly* 10 (Fall 1967): 5-12.

RUTH SUCKOW

4687. Baker, Joseph E. "Regionalism in the Middle West." *American Review* 5 (March 1935): 603-14.

4688. Frederick, John T. "Ruth Suckow and the Middle Western Literary Movement." *English Journal* 20 (January 1931): 1-8.

4689. Hamblen, Abigail Ann. *Ruth Suckow.* Western Writers Series,

No. 34. Boise, Idaho: Boise State University, 1978.

4690. Kiesel, Margaret Matlack. "Iowans in the Arts: Ruth Suckow in the Twenties." *Annals of Iowa* 45 (Spring 1980): 257-87.

4691. Kissane, Leedice. "D. H. Lawrence, Ruth Suckow and Modern Marriage." *Rendezvous* 4 (Spring 1969): 39-45.

4692. ——. *Ruth Suckow.* New York: Twayne, 1969.

4693. McAlpin, Sister Sara. "Enlightening the Commonplace: The Art of Sarah Jewett, Willa Cather and Ruth Suckow." Doctoral dissertation, University of Pennsylvania, 1971.

4694. Mohr, Martin. "Ruth Suckow: Regionalism and Beyond." Master's thesis, University of Iowa, 1955.

4695. Mott, Frank Luther. "Ruth Suckow." *A Book of Iowa Authors.* Ed. Johnson Brigham. Des Moines: Iowa State Teachers Association, 1930, pp. 215-24.

4696. Muehl, Lois B. "Ruth Suckow's Art of Fiction." *Books at Iowa* 13 (November 1970): 3-12.

4697. Nuhn, Ferner. "The Orchard Aviary: Ruth Suckow in Earlville." *Iowan* 20 (Summer 1972): 21-54.

4698. ——, ed. "Cycle of the Seasons in Iowa: Unpublished Diary of Ruth Suckow." *Iowan* 9 (October-November 1960, December-January 1960-61, April-May 1961).

4699. Oehlschlaeger, Fritz. "The Art of Ruth Suckow's 'A Start in Life.'" *Western American Literature* 15 (Fall 1980): 117-86.

4700. Omrcanin, Margaret Stewart. *Ruth Suckow: A Critical Study of Her Fiction.* Philadelphia: Dorrance, 1972.

4701. Paluka, Frank. "Ruth Suckow: A Calendar of Letters." *Books at Iowa* 1 (October 1964): 34-40; 2 (April 1965): 31-40.

RONALD SUKENICK

4702. Bellamy, Joe David. "Imagination as Perception: An Interview with Ronald Sukenick." *Chicago Review* 23 (Winter 1972): 59-72.

4703. Cheuse, Alan. "Way Out West: The Exploratory Fiction of 'Ronald Sukenick.'" *Itinerary: Criticism, Essays on California Writers.* Ed. Charles L. Crow. Bowling Green, Ohio: University Press, 1978, pp. 115-21.

4704. Klinkowitz, Jerome. "Getting Real: Making It (up) with Ronald Sukenick." *Chicago Review* 23 (Winter 1972): 73-82.

4705. Noel, Daniel C. "Tales of Fictive Power: Dreaming and Imagination in Ronald Sukenick's Postmodern Fiction." *Boundary* 5 (Fall 1976): 117-35.

MARTHA SUMMERHAYES

4706. Powell, Lawrence C. "Martha

Summerhays' *Vanished Arizona.*" *Westways* 63 (July 1971): 16-19, 60-61.

ALAN SWALLOW

4707. Claire, William F., ed. *Publishing in the West: Alan Swallow.* Santa Fe, N.Mex.: Lightning Tree, 1974.
4708. Harris, Mark. "Obituary Three for Alan Swallow." *Modern Fiction Studies* 15 (Summer 1969): 187-90.
4709. McConnell, Virginia. "Alan Swallow and Western Writers." *South Dakota Review* 5 (Summer 1967): 88-97.
4710. Manfred, Frederick. "Alan Swallow: Poet and Publisher." *Denver Quarterly* 2 (Spring 1967): 27-31.
4711. North, Dennis D. "Alan Swallow: A Bibliographical Checklist." *Denver Quarterly* 2 (Spring 1967): 63-72.
4712. Ross, Morton L. "Alan Swallow and Modern, Western American Poetry." *Western American Literature* 1 (Summer 1966): 97-104.
4713. Waters, Frank. "Notes on Alan Swallow." *Denver Quarterly* 2 (Spring 1967): 16-25.
4714. Winters, Yvor. "Alan Swallow: 1915-1966." *Southern Review* 3 (July 1967): 796-98.

GLENDON SWARTHOUT

4715. Robertson, Richard. "Book's End: The Modern Western Hero and Glendon Swarthout's

The Shootist." *Heritage of the Great Plains* 13 (Winter 1980): 20-27.

ALEXANDER SWEET

4716. Speck, Ernest B. "Alex. Sweet, Texas Humorist." *Southwestern American Literature* 3 (1973): 49-60.

JOHN SWETT

4717. Polos, Nicholas C. "Early California Poetry." *California Historical Society Quarterly* 48 (September 1969): 243-55.

BELLA FRENCH SWISHER

4718. Dickey, Imogene. "Bella French Swisher: Texas Editor and Litterateur." *Southwestern American Literature* 1 (January 1971): 8-11.

BAYARD TAYLOR

4719. Doughty, Nanelia S. "Bayard Taylor: First California Booster." *Western Review* 7 (Spring 1970): 22-27.
4720. ———. "Bayard Taylor's Second Look at California (1859)." *Western Review* 8 (Winter 1971): 51-55.
4721. Luedtke, Luther S., and Patrick D. Morrow. "Bret Harte on Bayard Taylor: An Unpublished Tribute." *Markham Review* 3 (May 1973): 101-5.
4722. Schwartz, Thomas D. "Bayard

Taylor's 'The Prophet': Mormonism as Literary Taboo." *BYU Studies* 14 (Winter 1974): 235-47.

4723. Wermuth, Paul C. *Bayard Taylor.* New York: Twayne, 1973.

JOHN WILLIAM THOMASON, JR.

4724. Dykes, Jeff C. "Tentative Bibliographic Check Lists of Western Illustrators: XXXV, John William Thomason, Jr. (1893-1944)." *American Book Collector* 17 (April 1967): 17-20.

4725. Graves, John. "The Old Breed: A Note on John W. Thomason, Jr." *Southwest Review* 54 (Winter 1969): 36-46.

4726. Norwood, W. D. *John W. Thomason, Jr.* Southwest Writers Series, No. 25. Austin, Tex.: Steck-Vaughn, 1969.

4727. Perkins, Maxwell. *Editor to Author.* New York: Charles Scribner's Sons, 1950. Contains letters to and about Thomason.

4728. Willock, Roger. *Lone Star Marine: A Biography of the Late Colonel John W. Thomason, Jr., U.S.M.C.* Princeton, N.J.: Roger Willock, 1961.

THOMAS BANGS THORPE

4729. Blair, Walter. "The Technique of 'The Big Bear of Arkansas.'" *Southwest Review* 28 (Summer 1943): 426-35.

4730. Current-Garcia, Eugene. "Thomas Bangs Thorpe and the Literature of the Ante-Bellum Southwestern Frontier." *Louisiana Historical Quarterly* 39 (April 1956): 199-222.

4731. Estes, David C. "Thomas Bangs Thorpe's Sketches of the Old West: A Critical Edition." Doctoral dissertation, Duke University, 1980.

4732. Lemay, J. A. Leo. "The Text, Tradition, and Themes of 'The Big Bear of Arkansas.'" *American Literature* 47 (November 1975): 321-42.

4733. Rickels, Milton. "Thomas Bangs Thorpe (1815-1878)." *A Bibliographical Guide to the Study of Southern Literature.* Baton Rouge: Louisiana State University Press, 1969, pp. 308-9.

4734. ———. *Thomas Bangs Thorpe: Humorist of the Old Southwest.* Baton Rouge: Louisiana State University Press, 1962.

4735. Simoneaux, Katherine G. "Symbolism in Thorpe's 'The Big Bear of Arkansas.'" *Arkansas Historical Quarterly* 25 (Fall 1966): 240-47.

WALLACE THURMAN

4736. Haslam, Gerald. "Wallace Thurman: A Western Renaissance Man." *Western American Literature* 6 (Spring 1971): 53-59.

4737. Perkins, Huel D. "Renaissance 'Renegade'? Wallace Thurman." *Black World* 25 (1976): 29-35.

4738. West, Dorothy. "Elephant's Dance: A Memoir of Wallace Thurman." *Black World* 20 (1970): 77-85.

JEAN TOOMER

4739. Quirk, Tom, and Robert E. Eleming. "Jean Toomer's Contributions to the *New Mexico Sentinel*." *CLA Journal* 29 (June 1976): 524-32.

BERICK TRAVEN TORSVAN (B. Traven)

4740. Baumann, Michael L. *B. Traven: An Introduction.* Albuquerque: University of New Mexico Press, 1976.

4741. ——. "B. Traven: Realist and Prophet." *Virginia Quarterly Review* 53 (Winter 1977): 73-85.

4742. Chankin, Donald O. *Anonymity and Death: The Fiction of B. Traven.* University Park: Pennsylvania State University Press, 1975.

4743. Gutierrez, Donald. "Maker Versus Profit-Maker: B. Traven's 'Assembly Line.'" *Studies in Short Fiction* 17 (Winter 1980): 9-14.

4744. Mezo, Richard Eugene. "The Journey to Solipaz: A Study of B. Traven's Fiction." Doctoral dissertation, University of North Dakota, 1978.

4745. Miller, Charles, and R. E. Lujan, eds. "B. Traven." *Texas Quarterly* 6 (1963): 161-211.

4746. Olafson, Robert B. "B. Traven's *Northamericanos* in Mexico." *Markham Review* 4 (October 1973): 1-5.

4747. Pearson, Sheryl Marie Sherman. "The Anglo-American Novel of the Mexican Revolution, 1910-1940: D. H. Lawrence, B. Traven, Graham Greene." Doctoral dissertation, University of Michigan, 1976.

4748. Ponick, Terrence Lee. "The Novels of B. Traven: Literature and Politics in the American Editions." Doctoral dissertation, University of South Carolina, 1976.

4749. Stone, Judy. "The Mystery of B. Traven." *Ramparts* 6 (1967): 31-49, 55-69 ff.

4750. Warner, John M. "Tragic Vision in B. Traven's 'The Night of the Visitor.'" *Studies in Short Fiction* 7 (Summer 1970): 377-84.

4751. Wyatt, Will. *The Secret of the Sierra Madre: The Man Who Was B. Traven.* New York: Doubleday, 1980.

JOHN K. TOWNSEND

4752. Walker, Don D. "Townsend's *Narrative*: A Note on Its Literary Features." *Possible Sack* 4 (October 1973): 15-20.

FREDERICK JACKSON TURNER

4753. Bennett, James D. *Frederick Jackson Turner.* Boston: Twayne, 1975.

4754. Billington, Ray A. *The American Frontier Thesis: Attack and Defense.* Washington, D.C.: American Historical Association, 1971. An extended essay summarizing and analyzing Turner's thesis, its proponents, and dissenters.

4755. ——. *Frederick Jackson Turner: Historian, Scholar, Teacher.* New York: Oxford University Press, 1973. A magnificent biography.

4756. ——. "Frederick Jackson Turner: The Image and the Man." *Western Historical Quarterly* 3 (April 1972): 137-52.

4757. Boyle, Thomas E. "Frederick Jackson Turner and Thomas Wolfe: The Frontier as History and Literature." *Western American Literature* 4 (Winter 1970): 273-85.

4758. Carpenter, Ronald H. "Frederick Jackson Turner and the Rhetorical Impact of the Frontier Thesis." *Quarterly Journal of Speech* 63 (April 1977): 117-29.

4759. ——. "Style in Discourse as an Index of Frederick Jackson Turner's Historical Creativity: Conceptual Antecedents of the Frontier Thesis in His 'American Colonization.'" *Huntington Library Quarterly* 40 (May 1977): 269-77.

4760. Ducey, Cathryn Annette. "The Development of a Frontier Thesis: Mark Twain, Domingo Faustino Sarmineto, and Frederick Jackson Turner." Doctoral dissertation, University of Hawaii, 1975.

4761. Jacobs, Wilbur R. "The Many-Sided Frederick Jackson Turner." *Western Historical Quarterly* 1 (October 1970): 363-72.

4762. Jensen, Richard. "On Modernizing Frederick Jackson Turner:

The Historiography of Regionalism." *Western Historical Quarterly* 11 (July 1980): 307-22.

4763. Lewis, Merrill E. "American Frontier History as Literature: Studies in Historiography of George Bancroft, Frederick Jackson Turner, and Theodore Roosevelt." Doctoral dissertation, University of Utah, 1968.

4764. ——. "The Art of Frederick Jackson Turner: The Histories." *Huntington Library Quarterly* 35 (May 1972): 241-55.

4765. ——. "Language, Literature, Rhetoric, and the Shaping of the Historical Imagination of Frederick Jackson Turner." *Pacific Historical Review* 45 (August 1976): 399-424.

4766. Nichols, David A. "Civilization over Savage: Frederick Jackson Turner and the Indian." *South Dakota History* 2 (Fall 1972): 383-405.

4767. Paulson, Kristoffer F. "Ole Rölvaag, Herbert Krause, and the Frontier Thesis of Frederick Jackson Turner." *Where the West Begins.* Eds. Arthur R. Huseboe and William Geyer. Sioux Falls, S.Dak.: Center for Western Studies Press, 1978, pp. 24-33.

4768. Putnam, Jackson K. "The Turner Thesis and the Westward Movement: A Reappraisal." *Western Historical Quarterly* 7 (October 1976): 377-404.

4769. Simonson, Harold P. "Frederick Jackson Turner: Frontier History as Art." *Antioch Review* 24 (Summer 1964): 201-11.

4770. Steiner, Michael C. "The Significance of Turner's Sectional Thesis." *Western Historical Quarterly* 10 (October 1979): 437-66.

MARK TWAIN
See Samuel Clemens

I. L. UDELL

4771. Jason, Rick. "Udell." *South Dakota Review* 7 (Spring 1969): 5-7.

4772. Milton, John R. "Udell—The Taos Man." *South Dakota Review* 7 (Spring 1969): 107-23.

ALBERTO URISTA
(Alurista)

4773. Ybarra-Frausto, Tomás. "Alurista's Poetics: The Oral, The Bilingual, The Pre-Columbian." *Modern Chicano Writers.* Eds. Joseph Sommers and Tomás Ybarra-Frausto. Englewood Cliffs, N.J.: Prentice-Hall, 1979, pp. 117-32.

FRANCES FULLER VICTOR

4774. Mills, Hazel Emery. "The Emergence of Frances Fuller Victor—Historian." *Oregon Historical Quarterly* 62 (December 1961): 309-36.

JOSÉ ANTONIO VILLARREAL

4775. Bruce-Novoa, [Juan]. "*Pocho* as Literature." *Aztlán* 7 (Spring 1976): 65-77.

4776. Luedtke, Luther S. "*Pocho* and the American Dream." *Minority Voices* 1 (1977): 1-16.

DAVID WAGONER

4777. Cording, Robert Kenneth. "A New Lyricism: David Wagoner and the Instructional Voice." Doctoral dissertation, Boston College, 1976.

4778. Peters, Robert. "Thirteen Ways of Looking at David Wagoner's New Poems." *Western Humanities Review* 35 (Autumn 1981): 267-72.

4779. Pinsker, Sanford. "The Achievement of David Wagoner." *Connecticut Review* 8 (October 1974): 42-47.

4780. ——. "On David Wagoner." *Salmagundi* 22-23 (Spring-Summer 1973): 306-14.

4781. Schafer, William J. "David Wagoner's Fiction: In the Mills of Satan." *Critique* 9, No. 1 (1966): 71-89.

STANLEY WALKER

4782. Milner, Jay. "Stanley Walker: The Retread Texan." *Arlington Quarterly* 2 (Summer 1969): 7-21.

ARTEMUS WARD
See Charles Farrar Browne

MAY WARD

4783. Snipes, Helen Joann. "May Ward: Poet of the Prairie and its People." Doctoral dissertation, Kansas State University, 1973.

4784. Suran, Irene. "May Williams Ward: Kansas Poet." Master's thesis, Fort Hays Kansas State College, 1951.

EUGENE FITCH WARE

4785. Malin, James C. "The Burlington, Iowa, Apprenticeship of the Kansas Poet Eugene Fitch Ware, 'Ironquill.'" *Iowa Journal of History* 57 (July 1959): 193-230.

4786. ——. "Eugene F. Ware, Master Poet. . . ." *Kansas Historical Quarterly* 32 (Winter 1966): 401-25.

4787. ——. "Eugene F. Ware's Literary Chronology." *Kansas Historical Quarterly* 37 (August 1971): 314-32.

4788. ——. "Notes on the Poetic Debts of Eugene F. Ware—Ironquill." *Kansas Historical Quarterly* 35 (Summer 1969): 165-81.

FRANK WATERS

4789. Bucco, Martin. *Frank Waters.* Southwest Writers Series, No. 22. Austin, Tex.: Steck-Vaughn, 1969.

4790. Davis, Jack L. and June H. "Frank Waters and the Native American Consciousness." *Western American Literature* 9 (May 1974): 33-44.

4791. "Frank Waters Issue." *South Dakota Review* 15 (Autumn 1977): 5-153. A major collection of essays and photographs.

4792. Grigg, Quay. "The Kachina Characters of Frank Waters' Novels." *South Dakota Review* 11 (Spring 1973): 6-16.

4793. Hoy, Christopher. "The Archetypal Transformation of Martiniano in *The Man Who Killed The Deer.*" *South Dakota Review* 13 (Winter 1975-76): 43-56.

4794. ——. "A Study of *The Man Who Killed the Deer.*" Master's thesis, Colorado State University, 1970.

4795. Huntress, Diana. "The Man Who Resurrected the Deer." *South Dakota Review* 6 (Winter 1968-69): 69-71.

4796. Lyon, Thomas J. "An Ignored Meaning of the West." *Western American Literature* 3 (Spring 1968): 51-59.

4797. ——. *Frank Waters.* New York: Twayne, 1973.

4798. ——. *The Works of Frank Waters.* Cassette. Deland, Fla.: Everett/Edwards, 1974.

4799. McCann, Garth. "Patterns of Redemption and the Failure of Irony: *The Ox-Bow Incident* and *The Man Who Killed the Deer.*" *Southwestern American Literature* 4 (1974): 62-67.

4800. Malpezzi, Frances. "A Study of the Female Protagonist in Frank Waters' *People of the Valley* and Rudolfo Anaya's *Bless Me, Ultima.*" *South Dakota Review* 14 (Summer 1976): 102-10.

272

4801. Milton, John R. "Conversation with Frank Waters." *South Dakota Review* 9 (Spring 1971): 16-27.

4802. ——. "The Land as Form in Frank Waters and William Eastlake." *Kansas Quarterly* 2 (Spring 1970): 104-9.

4803. ——. *The Novel of the American West.* Lincoln: University of Nebraska Press, 1980, pp. 264-97.

4804. ——, ed. *Conversations with Frank Waters.* Chicago: Swallow Press, 1972.

4805. Pilkington, William T. "Character and Landscape: Frank Waters' Colorado Trilogy." *Western American Literature* 2 (Fall 1967): 183-93.

4806. Powell, Lawrence C. "A Writer's Landscape." *Westways* 66 (January 1974): 24-27, 70-72.

4807. Swallow, Alan. "The Mavericks." *Critique* 2 (Winter 1959): 74-92.

4808. Waters, Frank, ed. "Bibliography of the Works of Frank Waters." *South Dakota Review* 4 (Summer 1966): 77-78.

4809. Young, Vernon. "Frank Waters: Problems of the Regional Imperative." *New Mexico Quarterly Review* 19 (Autumn 1949): 353-72.

WINSTON WEATHERS

4810. Kidney-Wells, Jennifer. "The Writer in His Region: An Interview with Winston Weathers." *Kansas Quarterly* 9 (Spring 1977): 11-18.

4811. Sale, Richard B. "The Several Worlds of Winston Weathers." *Southwestern American Literature* 1 (May 1971): 93-97.

WALTER PRESCOTT WEBB

4812. Friend, Llerena. "Walter Prescott Webb and Book Reviewing." *Western Historical Quarterly* 4 (October 1973): 381-404.

4813. Furman, Necah Stewart. *Walter Prescott Webb: His Life and Impact.* Albuquerque: University of New Mexico Press, 1976.

4814. Morris, Margaret. "Walter Prescott Webb, 1888-1963: A Bibliography." *Essays in the American Civil War.* Eds. William F. Holmes and Harold M. Hollingsworth. Austin: University of Texas Press, 1968.

4815. Philp, Kenneth R., and Elliott West, eds. *Essays on Walter Prescott Webb.* Austin: University of Texas Press, 1976.

4816. Rundell, Walter, Jr. *Walter Prescott Webb.* Austin, Tex.: Steck-Vaughn, 1971.

4817. ——. "Walter Prescott Webb: Product of Environment." *Arizona and the West* 5 (Spring 1963): 4-28.

4818. Shannon, Fred A. *An Appraisal of Walter Prescott Webb's The Great Plains: A Study in Institutions and Environment.* New York: Social Sciences Research Council, 1940.

4819. Tobin, Gregory M. "Landscape, Region, and the Writing of History: Walter Prescott Webb in the 1920s" *American Studies International* 16 (Summer 1978): 7-18.

4820. ——. *The Making of a History: Walter Prescott Webb and "The Great Plains."* Austin: University of Texas Press, 1976.

NATHAN WALLENSTEIN
WEINSTEIN
(Nathanael West)

4821. Atheneos, Michael Anthony. "Nathanael West: Progressive Pessimist." Doctoral dissertation, University of Northern Colorado, 1976.

4822. Banta, Martha. "American Apocalypses: Excrement and Ennui." *Studies in Literary Imagination* 7 (Spring 1974): 1-30.

4823. Baxter, Charles Morley. "Black Hole in Space. The Figure of the Artist in Nathanael West's *Miss Lonely Hearts,* Djuana Barnes' *Nightwood,* and Malcolm Lowry's *Under the Volcano.*" Doctoral dissertation, State University of New York, Buffalo, 1974.

4824. ——. "Nathanael West: Dead Letters and the Martyred Novelist." *West Coast Review* 9 (October 1974): 3-11.

4825. Briggs, Arlen John. "Nathanael West and Surrealism." Doctoral dissertation, University of Oregon, 1972.

4826. Brown, Daniel R. "The War Within Nathanael West: Naturalism and Existentialism." *Modern Fiction Studies* 20 (Summer 1974): 181-202.

4827. Clark, Neill Wilson, III. "The Metaphor of Apocalypse in the Fiction of Nathanael West." Doctoral dissertation, Emory University, 1976.

4828. Comerchero, Victor. *Nathanael West: The Ironic Prophet.* Syracuse, N.Y.: Syracuse University Press, 1964; Seattle: University of Washington Press, 1967.

4829. Cramer, Carter M. *The World of Nathanael West: A Critical Interpretation.* Emporia: Kansas State Teachers College, 1971.

4830. Dardis, Tom. "Nathanael West: The Scavenger of the Back Lots." *Some Time in the Sun.* New York: Charles Scribner's Sons, 1976, pp. 151-81. Emphasizes his work with films.

4831. Fine, David M. "Landscape of Fantasy: Nathanael West and Los Angeles Architecture of the Thirties." *Itinerary: Criticism, Essays on California Writers.* Ed. Charles L. Crow. Bowling Green, Ohio: University Press, 1978, pp. 49-62.

4832. Galloway, David D. "Nathanael West's Dream Dump." *Critique* 6 (Winter 1963-64): 46-63.

4833. Gerkey, Stephen Joseph. "You Only Have Time to Explode: Technique and Structure in Nathanael West's Narratives." Doctoral dissertation, Indiana University, 1977.

4834. Herbst, Josephine. "Nathanael West." *Kenyon Review* 23 (Autumn 1961): 611-30.

4835. Hyman, Stanley Edgar. *Nathanael West.* Pamphlets on American Writers. Minneapolis: University of Minnesota Press, 1962.

4836. Keyes, John McDonald. "Nathanael West: A Technical View." Doctoral dissertation, University of Toronto, 1972.

4837. Light, James F. *Nathanael West: An Interpretive Study.* 2d ed. Evanston: Northwestern University Press, 1971.

4838. ——. "Varieties of Satire in the Art of Nathanael West." *Studies in American Humor* 2 (April 1975): 46-60.

4839. Madden, David, ed. *Nathanael West: The Cheaters and the Cheated: A Collection of Critical Essays.* Deland, Fla.: Everett/Edwards, 1973. Includes an annotated bibliography by Helen R. Taylor, pp. 323-41.

4840. Malin, Irving. *Nathanael West's Novels.* Carbondale: Southern Illinois University Press, 1972.

4841. Martin, Jay. *Nathanael West: The Art of His Life.* New York: Farrar, Straus and Giroux; London: Secker and Warburg, 1971.

4842. ——, ed. *Nathanael West: A Collection of Critical Essays.* Englewood Cliffs, N.J.: Prentice-Hall, 1971.

4843. Michaels, I. Lloyd. "A Particular Kind of Joking: Nathanael West and Burlesque." Doctoral dissertation, State University of New York, Buffalo, 1972.

4844. Reid, Randall. *The Fiction of Nathanael West: No Redeemer, No Promised Land.* Chicago: University of Chicago Press, 1971.

4845. Ross, Alan. "The Dead Centre: An Introduction to Nathanael West." *Horizon* 18 (October 1948): 284-96.

4846. Schoenewolf, Carroll Robert. "The Novels of Nathanael West." Doctoral dissertation, University of Oklahoma, 1973.

4847. Scott, Nathan A., Jr. *Nathanael West: A Critical Essay.* Grand Rapids, Mich.: Eerdmans, 1971.

4848. Smith, Marcus. "Religious Experience in *Miss Lonelyhearts.*" *Contemporary Literature* 9 (Spring 1968): 172-88.

4849. Trachtenberg, Stanley. "West's Locusts: Laughing at the Laugh." *Michigan Quarterly Review* 14 (1975): 187-98.

4850. Vannatta, Dennis P. *Nathanael West: An Annotated Bibliography of the Scholarship and Works.* New York: Garland, 1976.

4851. White, William. "Nathanael West: A Bibliography. *Serif* 2 (March 1965): 5-18; 2 (September 1965): 28-31.

4852. ——. *Nathanael West: A Comprehensive Bibliography.* Kent, Ohio: Kent State University Press, 1975.

4853. Zlotnick, Joan. "Nathanael West and the Pictorial Imagination." *Western American Literature* 9 (November 1974): 177-85.

JAMES WELCH

4854. Barnett, Louise K. "Alienation and Ritual in *Winter in the Blood.*" *American Indian Quarterly* 4 (May 1978): 123-30.

4855. Barry, Nora Baker. *"Winter in the Blood* as Elegy." *American Indian Quarterly* 4 (May 1978): 149-57.

4856. Beidler, Peter G., ed. "A Special Symposium Issue on James Welch's *Winter in the Blood*." *American Indian Quarterly* 4 (May 1978). Includes nine essays and other materials.

4857. ——, and A. LaVonne Ruoff, eds. "A Discussion of *Winter in the Blood*." *American Indian Quarterly* 4 (May 1978): 159-68.

4858. Horton, Andrew. "The Bitter Humor of *Winter in the Blood*." *American Indian Quarterly* 4 (May 1978): 131-39.

4859. Kunz, Don. "Lost in the Distance of Winter: James Welch's *Winter in the Blood*." *Critique* 20, No. 1 (1978): 93-99.

4860. Larson, Charles R. *American Indian Fiction*. Albuquerque: University of New Mexico Press, 1978, pp. 140-49.

4861. Rhodes, Geri. *"Winter in the Blood*: Bad Medicine in the Blood." *New America* 2 (Summer-Fall 1976): 44-49.

4862. Ruoff, A. LaVonne. "Alienation and the Female Principle in *Winter in the Blood*." *American Indian Quarterly* 4 (May 1978): 107-22.

4863. ——. "History in *Winter in the Blood*: Backgrounds and Bibliography." *American Indian Quarterly* 4 (May 1978): 169-72.

4864. Sands, Kathleen M. "Alienation and Broken Narrative in *Winter in the Blood*." *American Indian Quarterly* 4 (May 1978): 97-105.

4865. Smith, William F. *"Winter in the Blood*: The Indian Cowboy as Everyman." *Michigan Academician* 10 (1978): 299-306.

4866. Thackeray, William W. "'Crying for Pity' in *Winter in the Blood*." *MELUS* 7 (Spring 1980): 61-78.

4867. Velie, Alan R. "James Welch's Poetry." *American Indian Culture and Research Journal* 3 (1979): 19-38.

4868. ——. *"Winter in the Blood* as Comic Novel." *American Indian Quarterly* 4 (May 1978): 141-47.

LEW WELCH

4869. Allen, Donald, ed. *I Remain: The Letters of Lew Welch and The Correspondence of His Friends*. Vol. I: 1949-1960; Vol. II: Bolinas, Calif.: Grey Fox Press, 1980.

4870. Saroyan, Aram. *Genesis Angels: The Saga of Lew Welch and the Beat Generation*. New York: William Morrow, 1979.

JESSAMYN WEST

4871. Shivers, Alfred S. "Jessamyn West." *Bulletin of Bibliography* 28 (January-March 1971): 1-3.

4872. ——. *Jessamyn West*. New York: Twayne, 1972.

NATHANAEL WEST
See Nathan Wallenstein Weinstein

ALBERT RICHARD WETJEN

4873. Corning, Howard McKinley. "A. R. Wetjen: British Seaman in the Western Sunrise." *Oregon Historical Quarterly* 74 (June 1973): 145-78.

STEWART EDWARD WHITE

4874. Alter, Judy. *Stewart Edward White*. Western Writers Series, No. 18. Boise, Idaho: Boise State University, 1975.
4875. Aufderheide, Lawrence Richard. "American Literary Primitivists: Owen Wister, Stewart Edward White and Jack London." Doctoral dissertation, University of Michigan, 1973.
4876. Butte, Edna Rosemary. "Stewart Edward White: His Life and Literary Career." Doctoral dissertation, University of Southern California, 1960.
4877. Jones, Howard Mumford. *The Age of Energy: Varieties of American Experience, 1865-1915*. New York: Viking Press, 1971, pp. 303-6.
4878. McCall, Margery Stewart. "The Life and Works of Stewart Edward White." Master's thesis, Louisiana State University, 1939.
4879. Powell, Lawrence Clark. "Southwest Classics Reread: A Land to Know, A West to Love." *Westways* 64 (December 1972):

28-31, 50, 52-53.
4880. Saxton, Eugene F. *Stewart Edward White*. New York: Doubleday, Page, n.d.
4881. Underwood, John Curtis. "Stewart Edward White and All Outdoors." *Literature and Insurgency: Ten Studies in Racial Evolution*. New York: Michell Kinnerley, 1914, pp. 254-98.

WILLIAM ALLEN WHITE

4882. Dubbert, Joe L. "William Allen White: Reflections on an American Life." *Markham Review* 4 (May 1974): 41-47.
4883. ——. "William Allen White's American Adam." *Western American Literature* 7 (Winter 1973): 271-78.
4884. Elkins, William R. "William Allen White's Early Fiction." *Heritage of Kansas* 8 (Winter 1975): 5-17.
4885. Groman, George L. "The Political Fiction of William Allen White: A Study in Emerging Progressivism." *Midwest Quarterly* 8 (October 1966): 79-93.
4886. Johnson, W., and P. Pantle. "Bibliography of the Published Works of William Allen White." *Kansas Historical Quarterly* 15 (February 1947): 22-41.
4887. McKee, John DeWitt. *William Allen White: Maverick in Main Street*. Westport, Conn.: Greenwood Press, 1975.
4888. Pady, Donald S. "A Bibliography

277

of the Poems of William Allen White." *Bulletin of Bibliography* 25 (January-April 1971): 44-46.

4889. Resh, Richard W. "GLR Bibliography: William Allen White." *Great Lakes Review* 5 (Summer 1978): 49-66.

4890. ——. "A Vision in Emporia: William Allen White's Search for Community." *Midcontinent American Studies Journal* 10 (Fall 1969): 19-35.

OPAL WHITELEY

4891. Bede, Elbert. *Fabulous Opal Whiteley: From Logging Camp to Princess of India.* Portland, Oreg.: Binfords and Mort, 1954.

4892. Holbrook, Stewart H. *Far Corner: A Personal View of the Pacific Northwest.* New York: Macmillan, 1952, pp. 209-19.

4893. Whiteley, Opal. *Opal/Opal Whiteley.* Arranged and adapted by Jane Boulton. New York: Macmillan, 1976.

WALT WHITMAN

4894. Allen, Gay Wilson. *The Solitary Singer: A Critical Biography of Walt Whitman.* New York: Macmillan, 1955.

4895. ——. *Walt Whitman Handbook.* New York: Packard, 1946.

4896. Bulow, Ernest. "The Poet of the West: Walt Whitman and the Native American Voice." *Possi-*

ble Sack 3 (November 1971): 7-10.

4897. Canby, Henry Seidel. *Walt Whitman: An American.* Boston: Houghton Mifflin, 1943.

4898. Coffman, S. K., Jr. "Form and Meaning in Whitman's 'Passage to India.'" *PMLA* 70 (June 1955): 337-49.

4899. Eitner, Walter H. *Walt Whitman's Western Jaunt.* Lawrence: Regent's Press of Kansas, 1981.

4900. Fussell, Edwin. *Frontier: American Literature and the American West.* Princeton University Press, 1965, pp. 397-441.

4901. Hubach, Robert R. "Walt Whitman and the West." Doctoral dissertation, Indiana University, 1943.

4902. ——. "Western Newspaper Accounts of Whitman's 1879 Trip to the West." *Walt Whitman Review* 18 (June 1972): 56-62.

4903. Huffstickler, Star. "Walt Whitman as a Precursor of Frederick Jackson Turner." *Walt Whitman Review* 8 (March 1962): 3-8.

4904. Lehmberg, P. S. "That Vast Something': A Note on Whitman and the American West." *Studies in the Humanities* (Indiana, Pa.) 6 (1978): 50-53.

4905. Lovell, John, Jr. "Appreciating Whitman: 'Passage to India.'" *Modern Language Quarterly* 21 (June 1960): 131-41.

4906. Miller, James E., Jr. *A Critical Guide to Leaves of Grass.* Chicago: University of Chicago Press, 1957.

4907. Nelson, Herbert B. "Walt Whitman and the Westward Movement." Doctoral dissertation, University of Washington, 1945.

4908. Smith, Henry Nash. *Virgin Land: The American West as Symbol and Myth.* Cambridge, Mass.: Harvard University Press, 1950.

4909. Steensma, Robert C. "Whitman and General Custer." *Walt Whitman Review* 10 (June 1964): 41-42.

4910. Thorp, Willard. "Whitman." *Eight American Authors.* Ed. Floyd Stovall. New York: W. W. Norton, 1963, pp. 271-318, 445-51.

4911. Trimble, Martha Scott. "The Westering of Walt Whitman." *Heritage of Kansas* 10 (Summer 1977): 42-51.

LAURA INGALLS WILDER

4912. Erisman, Fred. "The Regional Vision of Laura Ingalls Wilder." *Studies in Medieval, Renaissance, and American Literature: A Festschrift.* Ed. Betsy Colquitt. Fort Worth: Texas Christian Press, 1971, pp. 165-71.

4913. Jacobs, W. J. "Frontier Faith Revisited: The Little House Books of Laura Ingalls Wilder." *Horn Book Magazine* 41 (October 1965): 465-73.

4914. Moore, Rosa Ann. "Laura Ingalls Wilder's Orange Notebooks and the Art of the Little House Books." *Children's Literature* 4 (1975): 105-19.

4915. Rosenblum, Dolores. "'Intimate Immensity': Mythic Space in the Works of Laura Ingalls Wilder." *Where the West Begins.* Eds. Arthur R. Huseboe and William Geyer. Sioux Falls, S.Dak.: Center for Western Studies Press, 1978, pp. 72-79.

4916. St. John, Katherine E. "A Bio-Bibliography of Laura Ingalls Wilder (1867-1957)." Master's thesis, Catholic University, 1968.

4917. Zochert, Donald. *Laura: The Life of Laura Ingalls Wilder.* Chicago: Regnery, 1976.

JOHN WILLIAMS

4918. Brenner, Jack. *"Butcher's Crossing*: The Husks and Shells of Exploitation." *Western American Literature* 7 (Winter 1973): 243-59.

4919. Morrow, Patrick. "Introduction" to John Williams, *Butcher's Crossing.* Boston: Gregg Press, 1978, pp. vii-xiii.

HERBERT WILNER

4920. Wilner, Herbert. "Dovisch: Things, Facts, and Rainbows." *The Art of Writing Fiction.* Ed. Ray B. West, Jr. New York: Thomas Y. Crowell, 1968, pp. 110-16.

HARRY LEON WILSON

4921. Kummer, George. *Harry Leon Wilson: Some Accounts of the Triumphs and Tribulations of*

279

an *American Popular Writer.*
Cleveland: Press of Western
Reserve University, 1963.

YVOR WINTERS

4922. Abood, Edward. "Some Observations on Yvor Winters." *Chicago Review* 11 (Autumn 1957): 51-66.

4923. Barish, Jonas A. "Yvor Winters and the Antimimetic Prejudice." *New Literary History* 2 (Spring 1971): 419-44.

4924. Davie, Donald. "Winters and Leavis: Memories and Reflections." *Sewanee Review* 87 (Fall 1959): 608-18.

4925. Fraser, Shirley S. "Yvor Winters: The Critic as Moralist." Doctoral dissertation, Louisiana State University, 1972.

4926. Graff, Gerald. "Yvor Winters of Stanford." *American Scholar* 44 (Spring 1975): 291-98.

4927. Hobsbaum, Philip. "The Discovery of Form." *Michigan Quarterly Review* 12 (Summer 1973): 235-42.

4928. Holloway, John. "The Critical Theory of Yvor Winters." *Critical Quarterly* 7 (Spring 1965): 54-66.

4929. Kaye, Howard. "The Post-Symbolist Poetry of Yvor Winters." *Southern Review* 7 (January 1971): 176-97.

4930. Levin, David. "Yvor Winters at Stanford." *Virginia Quarterly Review* 54 (Summer 1978): 454-73.

4931. Lohf, Kenneth A., and E. P. Sheehy. "Yvor Winters: A Bibliography." *Twentieth Century Literature* 5 (April 1959): 27-51.

4932. Marsh, Robert. "Observations on the Criticism of Ivor Winters." *Spectrum* 4 (Fall 1960): 146-62.

4933. Parkinson, Thomas. "The Hart Crane-Yvor Winters Correspondence." *Ohio Review* 16 (Fall 1974): 5-24.

4934. ——, ed. *Hart Crane and Yvor Winters: Their Literary Correspondence.* Berkeley: University of California Press, 1978.

4935. Powell, Grosvenor E. "Mythical and Smoky Soil: Imagism and the Aboriginal in the Early Poetry of Yvor Winters." *Southern Review* 11 (April 1975): 300-317.

4936. ——. "Solipsism and the Absolute in Yvor Winters' Poetry." *Compass* 1 (1977): 44-59.

4937. ——. "Yvor Winters' Greek Allegories." *Southern Review* 14 (Spring 1978): 262-80.

4938. Ramsey, Paul. "Yvor Winters: Some Abstractions Against Abstraction." *Sewanee Review* 73 (Summer 1965): 451-64.

4939. Robson, W. W. "The Literary Criticism of Yvor Winters." *Cambridge Quarterly* 6, No. 2 (1973): 189-200.

4940. Sexton, Richard J. "The Complex of Yvor Winters Criticism." Doctoral dissertation, Fordham University, 1965.

4941. Stephens, Alan. "The *Collected Poems* of Yvor Winters." *Twentieth Century Literature* 9 (October 1963): 127-39.

4942. Van Deusen, Marshall. "In Defense of Yvor Winters." *Thought* 32 (Autumn 1957): 409-36.

4943. Wellek, René. "Yvor Winters Rehearsed and Reconsidered." *Denver Quarterly* 10 (Autumn 1975): 1-27.

4944. Zaniello, Thomas A. "The Early Career of Yvor Winters: The Imagist Movement and the American Indian." *Studies in the Humanities* 6 (1977): 5-10.

SOPHUS K. WINTHER

4945. Meldrum, Barbara. "Duality and Dream in S. K. Winther's Grimsen Trilogy." *Prairie Schooner* 49 (Winter 1975-76): 311-19.

4946. ———. "Structure and Meaning in S. K. Winther's *Beyond the Garden Gate.*" *Western American Literature* 6 (Fall 1971): 191-202.

4947. Mossberg, Christer Lennart. *Scandinavian Immigrant Literature.* Western Writers Series, No. 47. Boise, Idaho: Boise State University, 1981.

4948. Powell, Desmond. "Sophus Winther: The Grimsen Trilogy." *American Scandinavian Review* 36 (June 1948): 144-47.

4949. Whicher, George F. "Dane in America." *Forum* 106 (November 1946): 450-54.

OWEN WISTER

4950. Agnew, S. M. "Destry Goes on Riding: *The Virginian.*" *Publisher's Weekly* 157 (August 23, 1952): 746-51.

4951. Alter, Judy. "The Virginian Rides On." *Southwestern American Literature* 5 (1975): 68-72.

4952. Aufderheide, Lawrence Richard. "American Literary Primitivists: Owen Wister, Stewart Edward White, and Jack London." Doctoral dissertation, University of Michigan, 1973.

4953. Baldwin, Charles C. "Owen Wister." *The Men Who Make Our Novels.* New York: Dodd, Mead, 1925, pp. 590-600.

4954. Barsness, John A. "Theodore Roosevelt as Cowboy: The Virginian as Jacksonian Man." *American Quarterly* 21 (Fall 1969): 609-19.

4955. Boatright, Mody C. "The American Myth Rides the Range: Owen Wister's Man on Horseback." *Southwest Review* 36 (Summer 1951): 157-63.

4956. Bode, Carl. "Henry James and Owen Wister." *American Literature* 26 (May 1954): 250-52.

4957. Branch, Douglas. *The Cowboy and His Interpreters.* New York: D. Appleton, 1926.

4958. Bratcher, James T. "Owen Wister." *American Literary Realism 1870-1910* 8 (Autumn 1975): 341. Review of dissertations on Wister.

4959. Cady, Edwin H. *The Light of Common Day: Realism in American Fiction.* Bloomington: Indiana University Press, 1971, pp. 171-73, 182-92.

4960. Cawelti, John G. *Adventure, Mystery, and Romance: Formula Stories as Art and Popular Culture.* Chicago: University of Chicago Press, 1976, pp. 230–41.

4961. Cooper, Frederic Taber. "Owen Wister." *Some American Story Tellers.* New York: Henry Holt, 1911, pp. 265–94.

4962. Durham, Philip. "Introduction" and "Textual Note" to Owen Wister, *The Virginian: A Horseman of the Plains.* Riverside Edition. Boston: Houghton Mifflin Company, 1968.

4963. Etulain, Richard W. *Owen Wister.* Western Writers Series, No. 7. Boise, Idaho: Boise State College, 1973.

4964. ——. "Owen Wister, the West, and the Cowboy Hero." *Idaho Humanities Forum,* Spring 1981, pp. 3–4.

4695. Fiske, Horace Spencer. *Provincial Types in American Fiction.* Chautauqua, N.Y.: Chautauqua Press, 1903, pp. 215–41.

4966. Frantz, Joe B., and Julian Ernest Choate, Jr. *The American Cowboy: The Myth and the Reality.* Norman: University of Oklahoma Press, 1955.

4967. Gripp, Gary. "Point of View in Wister's *Red Man and White.*" *Possible Sack* 5 (April 1974): 7–17.

4968. Houghton, Donald E. "Two Heroes in One: Reflections Upon the Popularity of *The Virginian.*" *Journal of Popular Culture* 4 (Fall 1970): 497–506.

4969. Hubbell, Jay B. "Owen Wister's Work." *South Atlantic Quarterly* 29 (October 1930): 440–43.

4970. Kaye, Frances W. "Cooper, Sarmiento, Wister, and Hernández: The Search for a New World Literary Hero." *College Language Association Journal* 19 (1976): 404–11.

4971. Lambert, Neal. "A Cowboy Writes to Owen Wister." *American West* 2 (Fall 1965): 31–36.

4972. ——. "Owen Wister—The 'Real Incident' and the 'Thrilling Story.'" *The American West: An Appraisal.* Ed. Robert G. Ferris. Santa Fe: Museum of New Mexico Press, 1963, pp. 191–200.

4973. ——. "Owen Wister's 'Hank's Woman': The Writer and His Comment." *Western American Literature* 4 (Spring 1969): 39–50.

4974. ——. "Owen Wister's Lin McLean: The Failure of the Vernacular Hero." *Western American Literature* 5 (Fall 1970): 219–32.

4975. ——. "Owen Wister's Virginian: The Genesis of a Cultural Hero." *Western American Literature* 6 (Summer 1971): 99–107.

4976. ——. "The Values of the Frontier: Owen Wister's Final Assessment." *South Dakota Review* 9 (Spring 1971): 76–87.

4977. ——. "The Western Writing of Owen Wister: The Conflict of East and West." Doctoral dissertation, University of Utah, 1966.

4978. Lewis, Marvin. "Owen Wister: Caste Imprints in Western Letters." *Arizona Quarterly* 10 (Summer 1954): 147-56.

4979. Morovitz, Sanford E. "Owen Wister: An Annotated Bibliography of Secondary Material." *American Literary Realism 1870-1910* 7 (Winter 1974): 1-110. The beginning place for commentary on Wister.

4980. ——. "Testament of a Patriot: The Virginian, the Tenderfoot, and Owen Wister." *Texas Studies in Literature and Language* 15 (Fall 1973): 551-75.

4981. Mason, Julian. "Owen Wister and World War I: Appeal for Pentecost." *Pennsylvania Magazine of History and Biography* 101 (January 1977): 89-102.

4982. ——. "Owen Wister, Boy Librarian." *Quarterly Journal of the Library of Congress* 26 (October 1969): 201-12.

4983. [Mayfield, John S.] "A Note about Owen Wister." *Courier* [Syracuse University Library] 26 (1966): 29-36.

4984. Mogen, David. "Owen Wister's Cowboy Heroes." *Southwestern American Literature* 5 (1975): 47-61.

4985. Robinson, Forrest G. "The Roosevelt-Wister Connection: Some Notes on the West and the Uses of History." *Western American Literature* 14 (Summer 1979): 95-114.

4986. Rush, N. Orwin. "Frederic Remington and Owen Wister: The Story of Friendship." *Probing the American West*. Eds. K. Ross Toole, et al. Santa Fe: Museum of New Mexico Press, 1962, pp. 154-57.

4987. Solensten, John M. "Richard Harding Davis, Owen Wister, and *The Virginian*: Unpublished Letters and a Commentary." *American Literary Realism 1870-1910* 5 (Spring 1972): 122-33.

4988. Sherman, Dean. "Owen Wister: An Annotated Bibliography." *Bulletin of Bibliography* 28 (January-March 1971): 7-16.

4989. Seelye, John. "When West Was Wister." *New Republic* 167 (September 2, 1972): 28-33.

4990. Stokes, Frances Kemble Wister. *My Father, Owen Wister, and Ten Letters Written by Owen Wister to his Mother during his First Trip to Wyoming in 1885.* Laramie: University of Wyoming Library, 1952.

4991. Trimmer, Joseph F. *"The Virginian*: Novel and Films." *Illinois Quarterly* 35 (December 1972): 5-18.

4992. Trombley, W. "Another Western: Owen Wister's Virginian." *Saturday Evening Post* 234 (December 23, 1961): 98-101.

4993. Vorpahl, Ben M. "Ernest Hemingway and Owen Wister." *Library Chronicle* 36 (Spring 1970): 126-37.

4994. ——. "Henry James and Owen Wister." *Pennsylvania Magazine of History and Biography* 95 (July 1971): 291-338.

4995. ——. *"My Dear Wister"*: The Frederic Remington–Owen Wister Letters. Palo Alto, Calif.: American West, 1972.

4996. ——. "Very Much Like a Fire-cracker: Owen Wister on Mark Twain." *Western American Literature* 6 (Summer 1971): 83-98.

4997. Walbridge, Earl F. *"The Virginian* and Owen Wister: A Bibliography." *Papers of the Bibliographical Society of America* 46 (1952): 117-20.

4998. Walker, Don D. "Essays in the Criticism of Western Literary Criticism: II. The Dogmas of DeVoto." *Possible Sack* 3 (November 1971): 1-7.

4999. ——. "Wister, Roosevelt and James: A Note on the Western." *American Quarterly* 22 (Fall 1960): 358-66.

5000. Watkins, George T. "Owen Wister and the American West: A Biographical and Critical Study." Doctoral dissertation, University of Illinois, 1959.

5001. ——. "Wister and 'The Virginian.'" *Pacific Northwesterner* 2 (Fall 1958): 49-52.

5002. Weber, Richard Charles. "Owen Wister: An Annotated Bibliography." Master's thesis, University of Northern Iowa, 1971.

5003. Westbrook, Max. "Afterword" to Owen Wister, *The Virginian.*

New York: Signet Books, 1979, pp. 318-31.

5004. White, G. Edward. *The Eastern Establishment and the Western Experience: The West of Frederic Remington, Theodore Roosevelt, and Owen Wister.* New Haven, Conn.: Yale University Press, 1968.

5005. White, John I. "Owen Wister and the Dogies." *Journal of American Folklore* 82 (January-March 1969): 66-69.

5006. ——. "The Virginian." *Montana: Magazine of Western History* 16 (October 1966): 2-11.

5007. Wister, Fanny K. "Letters of Owen Wister, Author of *The Virginian.*" *Pennsylvania Magazine of History and Biography* 83 (January 1959): 3-28.

5008. ——. "Owen Wister Out West." *Midway* 10 (April 1962): 24-49.

5009. ——. "Owen Wister's West." *Atlantic Monthly* 195 (May 1955): 29-35; (June 1955): 52-57.

5010. ——, ed. *That I May Tell You: Journals and Letters of the Owen Wister Family.* Wayne, Pa.: Haverford House, 1979.

5011. Wister, Owen. *Owen Wister Out West: His Journals and Letters.* Ed. Fanny Kemble Wister. Chicago: University of Chicago Press, 1958.

5012. ——. "Strictly Hereditary." *Musical Quarterly* 22 (January 1936): 1-7.

5013. Witkowsky, Paul William. "The Idea of Order: Frontier Societies in the Fiction of Cooper,

Simms, Hawthorne, and Wister." Doctoral dissertation, University of North Carolina, Chapel Hill, 1978.

THOMAS WOLFE

5014. Boyle, Thomas E. "Frederick Jackson Turner and Thomas Wolfe: The Frontier as History and Myth." *Western American Literature* 4 (Winter 1970): 273-85.
5015. Chittick, V. L. O. "Thomas Wolfe's Farthest West." *Southwest Review* 48 (Spring 1963): 93-110.
5016. Cracroft, Richard H. "Through Utah and the Western Parks: Thomas Wolfe's Farewell to America." *Utah Historical Quarterly* 37 (Summer 1969): 291-306.
5017. Powell, Desmond. "Of Thomas Wolfe." *Arizona Quarterly* 1 (Spring 1945): 28-36.
5018. Wolfe, Thomas. *A Western Journal.* Pittsburgh: University of Pittsburgh Press, 1951. Includes a helpful introductory note by Edward Aswell.

CHARLES ERSKINE SCOTT WOOD

5019. Bingham, Edwin R. "Experiment in Launching a Biography: Three Vignettes of Charles Erskine Scott Wood." *Huntington Library Quarterly* 35 (May 1972): 221-39.
5020. ——. "Oregon's Romantic Rebels: John Reed and Charles Erskine Scott Wood." *Pacific Northwest Quarterly* 50 (July 1959): 77-90.
5021. ——. "Shaping a Region's Culture: Charles Erskine Scott Wood in Oregon." *Oregon Rainbow* 1 (Number 4): 13-20.

STANLEY WOOD

5022. Kedro, Milan James. "Stanley Wood and the Great Divide: Rocky Mountain Literary Promotion in the Late Nineteenth Century." Doctoral dissertation, University of Denver, 1977.

JOHN WOODS

5023. Smith, Dave. "Fifty Years, Mrs. Carter: The Poetry of John Woods." *Midwest Quarterly* 17 (Summer 1976): 410-31.

DAVID WRIGHT

5024. Jorgensen, Bruce W. "The Vocation of David Wright: An Essay in Analytic Biography." *Dialogue* 11 (Summer 1978): 38-52.

HAROLD BELL WRIGHT

5025. Arnold, Oren. "Knowing the Wright People." *Writer's Digest* 21 (February 1941): 26-28.
5026. Gaston, Edwin W., Jr. *The Early Novel of the Southwest.* Albuquerque: University of New Mexico Press, 1961.
5027. Ifkovic, Edward. "Harold Bell

Wright and The Minister of Man: The Domestic Romancer at The End of the Genteel Age." *Markham Review* 4 (February 1974): 21-26.

JAMES ARLINGTON WRIGHT

5028. McMaster, Belle M. "James Arlington Wright: A Checklist." *Bulletin of Bibliography* 31 (April-June 1974): 71-82, 88.

BRIGHAM YOUNG

5029. Jessee, Dean C. "The Writings of Brigham Young." *Western Historical Quarterly* 4 (July 1973): 273-94.

RAY A. YOUNG BEAR

5030. Gish, Robert F. "Memory and Dream in the Poetry of Ray A. Young Bear." *Minority Voices* 2 (1978): 21-29.

INDEX

Abbott, Carl, 3592
Abernethy, Francis Edward, 2268
Abernethy, Peter L., 3954
Abood, Edward, 4922
Adamic, Louis, 2924
Adams, Andy, 379
Adams, Clarence Siringo, 4329
Adams, John H., 2125
Adams, Ramon F., 1-3, 2480, 4197
Adelman, Irving, 4
Adkins, Nelson F., 3700
Agnew, Seth M., 891-93, 4950
Ahearn, Kerry D., 184, 3459, 4431-33
Ahnebrink, Lars, 185, 2481, 3732
Ahouse, John, 2944
Albers, Randall K., 3628
Albertini, Virgil, 1712, 2821
Alberts, S. S., 2926
Alderman, Ralph M., 3876
Alderman, Taylor, 3695
Aldrich, Ann R., 2449
Alexander, Franklyn, 1614
Alexander, John R., 2927
Alexander, Stanley G., 3879, 4464-66
Alexander, William, 1024
Alkalay, Karen, 4079
Allen, Carolyn J., 2680
Allen, Charles, 790, 3165
Allen, Charles A., 3891
Allen, Donald, 1336, 4869
Allen, E. Douglas, 3971
Allen, Eliot D., 3045
Allen, Elizabeth, 3460
Allen, Gay Wilson, 4894-95
Allen, John L., 380
Allen, Martha Mitten, 186
Allen, Merritt P., 3567
Allen, Michael, 2844-45
Allen, Paula Gunn, 1110-12

Allen, T. D., 1113
Allison, James, 2198
Allred, Jared Rulon, 2642-43, 2928
Allsopp, Frederick William, 3886
Almon, Bert, 3421, 4339-41
Alpert, Barry, 2291
Alsen, Eberhard, 2482
Alsmeyer, Henry Louis, Jr., 5, 2269
Alt, Jon, 1871-72
Alter, Judith, 187, 3035-36, 3972-73,
    4874, 4951
Altieri, Charles, 4342-43
Altrocchi, J. C., 381
Alworth, E. Paul, 4132
Aly, Lucile F., 3701-6
Amaral, Anthony, 2920-21, 4686
Anaya, Rudolfo A., 1488
Andersen, Kenneth, 1873-74
Anderson, Arthur Commins, 4467
Anderson, Bette Bacon, 4076
Anderson, Carol Jane, 4141
Anderson, David D., 791, 2284
Anderson, Frederick, 1919, 2018
Anderson, John Q., 8, 382, 2310
Andrews, Clarence A., 9, 188
Andrews, Thomas F., 10
Andrews, William D., 2044
Angell, Richard C., 2315
Angoz, Charles, 4643
Antico, John, 4468
Antone, Evan H., 3198
Antoninus, Brother. See Everson, William
Apple, Max, 113
Arbuckle, Donald Redmond, 894
Ardinger, Richard K., 1337
Arlt, G. O., 3537
Armas, José, 1239
Armato, Philip M., 2861
Armitage, Shelley, 383-84, 2466

Armitage, Susan H., 385
Armstrong, George M., 2204-5
Arnold, Marilyn, 1713, 2282
Arnold, Oren, 5025
Arpin, Roger C., 2644
Arrington, Leonard J., 386-87, 2409
Arthur, Anthony, 2238, 3037, 3503, 3707
Arvidson, Lloyd A., 2483-84
Ashliman, D. L., 388-89
Askew, Melvin W., 3046
Astre, Georges-Albert, 1025
Astro, Richard, 2645, 3490, 4054-57, 4469-79
Astrov, Margot, 1114
Athearn, Robert G., 390-91
Atheneos, Michael Anthony, 4821
Atherton, L. E., 392
Attebery, Louis, 393
Auchincloss, Louis, 1714, 3892
Aufderheide, Lawrence Richard, 4875, 4952
Aughtry, Charles, 4063-64
Austin, Allen, 3238
Austin, James C., 394, 1660-61, 3504
Austin, Mary, 792, 1115, 1516
Autor, Hans, 395
Autrey, Max L., 4480
Avery, Emmett L., 3294-96
Axelrad, Allan M., 2053, 2285

Babcock, C. Merton, 114
Backus, Joseph M., 1681
Badé, William F., 3679
Baender, Paul, 1920
Bahr, H. W., 1581
Bain, Robert, 2206
Baird, James R., 4673
Baird, Newton D., 11
Baird, Reed M., 3963-64
Bakeless, John E., 3227
Baker, Bruce, II, 1715
Baker, Gail, 1868
Baker, Howard, 3893
Baker, J. Wayne, 2286
Baker, Joseph E., 793-96, 3239, 4142, 4687
Bakerville, Barnet, 3820
Baldanza, Frank, 1921
Baldeshwiler, Eileen, 3894
Baldwin, Charles C., 2367, 4953
Baldwin, R. G., 1383

Bales, Kent, 1644
Ball, Gordon, 2565
Ball, Lee, Jr., 2610
Ball, Vernon Francis, 3047
Ballard, Rae Galbraith, 1517
Ballotti, Geno A., 1116
Ballou, Robert, 1548
Bangs, Carol Jane, 396
Banks, Loy Otis, 397
Bankston, Darena, 189
Banning, Evelyn I., 2909
Bannon, John Francis, 1631-32
Banta, Martha, 4822
Barish, Jonas A., 4923
Baritz, Loren, 398
Barker, Warren J., 895
Barltrop, Robert, 3305
Barnard, Kenneth J., 4033
Barnes, Marian, 4224
Barnes, Robert J., 190, 4034
Barnett, Linda D., 2699-2701
Barnett, Louise K., 191, 1117-18, 4854
Barrett, Charles M., 2862
Barrick, Mac E., 4209
Barry, James D., 3240
Barry, Nora Baker, 1635, 3598, 4855
Barsness, John A., 192, 399, 896, 1026, 3083, 3491, 4182, 4954
Bartlett, Lee, 2347, 4344
Barton, Sandra L., 1468
Bashford, Herbert, 400
Baskett, Sam S., 3306-9
Bates, Barclay W., 1875
Bauer, Erwin A., 2611
Bauer, Shirley Ann, 3918
Bauer, Walter John, Jr., 3733
Baum, Bernard, 1716
Baumann, Michael L., 4740-41
Baumbach, Jonathan, 3629
Baumgarten, Murray, 4665
Baurecht, William C., 401
Baxter, Charles Morley, 4823-24
Bay, Jens C., 12-15
Bayard, Charles J., 4196
Baym, Nina, 2054
Bazin, André, 1027
Beach, J. W., 2930
Beach, Leonard B., 2870
Beard, James Franklin, 2055-57
Beard, Joyce J., 4268
Beaver, Harold, 3847

288

Bebeau, Don, 3505
Beck, Richard, 4143
Beck, Warren, 3241
Becker, George J., 4310
Becker, Laurence A., 3895
Becker, May L., 115
Bede, Elbert, 4891
Bedichek, Roy, 1560
Beebe, Beatrice B., 3568
Beebe, Maurice, 2140, 4481
Beeler, Madison S., 4668
Beer, Thomas, 2141
Beeton, Beverly, 402
Beggs, Nancy Marie Kyker, 797
Beidler, Peter G., 1119-20, 1922, 2134,
 2196, 3084, 4856-57
Beilke, Marlan, 2931
Beisman, Emmeline B., 2702
Bell, Robert G., 3500
Bell, Vereen M., 2846
Bellamy, Gladys Carmen, 1923
Bellamy, Joe David, 4702
Beller, Hilliard Irwin, 3734
Bellman, S. I., 2400-401
Benediktsson, Thomas E., 4644
Benn, Mary Lou, 2467-69
Bennett, James D., 4753
Bennett, Kenneth I., 3310
Bennett, M. H., 897
Bennett, Melba B., 2932-33
Bennett, Mildred R., 1717
Bennett, Patrick, 3199
Benoit, Raymond, 3311, 4345, 4397
Benson, Ivan, 1924
Benson, Jackson J., 4482-86
Benson, Peter Edward, 798
Benton, Joseph, 4065
Benton, Robert M., 1454, 4487
Benton, Thomas H., 799
Bentzon, Théodore, 4674
Bergon, Frank, 116, 2142-43
Berkhofer, Robert F., Jr., 1121
Berkman, Brenda, 1122
Bernard, Harry, 800
Bernard, Kenneth, 2144
Berner, Robert L., 3486, 3599
Bernstein, Suzy Jahss, 3735
Berrigan, Ted, 3048
Berry, J. Wilkes, 1518-19
Berryman, John, 2145
Berthoff, Warner, 193

Bett, Carolyn E., 2566
Bevis, William, 1123
Bewley, Marius, 2058-59, 2551, 3228
Biebel, Charles D., 2786
Bieber, Ralph P., 2552
Bier, Jesse, 2060
Billingsley, Ronald G., 3085, 3600
Billington, Ray Allen, 194, 403, 3968,
 4754-56
Bingham, Edwin, 141, 195, 3430, 5019-21
Bingham, June, 1338
Birney, Hoffman, 898
Bishop, John Peale, 2410-11
Bixler, Paul H., 3736
Bjork, Kenneth O., 4144
Black, W. E., 3708
Blackburn, Philip C., 2116
Blacker, Irwin R., 117
Blaine, Harold A., 196
Blair, Walter, 197, 1662, 1925-26, 3821,
 4729
Blanck, Jacob, 16
Blatt, Gloria T., 1240
Blatt, Muriel Rosen, 198
Bleeker, Gary Wallace, 4488
Blessing, Richard, 3086, 3729, 4080-81
Bleufarb, San. See Bluefarb, Sam
Blicksilver, Edith, 4301
Blodgett, E. D., 1384
Bloodworth, William, 899, 1124-25, 1636,
 2353, 3601, 3696, 3709, 4035, 4311
Bloom, Edward A., 1718-21
Bloom, Lillian D., 1718-22
Bluefarb, Sam, 2402, 3630, 4291
Blues, Thomas, 1927
Bluestone, George, 900, 1028, 1876
Blumenthal, W. A., 4312
Bly, Robert, 4346
Boatright, James, 2856
Boatright, Mody C., 199, 404-9, 901-3,
 1029-30, 4955
Bode, Carl, 3164, 4956
Bode, Elroy, 4295
Bode, Winston, 2270
Boewe, Charles, 4145
Bogard, William J., 200
Bogdanovich, Peter, 1031
Boggan, J. R., 2703
Bogue, Allan G., 3501, 3958
Bohlke, L. Brent, 1723
Boies, J. J., 904

289

Booth, Bradford A., 2704
Booth, Wayne C., 3631-32
Boquet, Sarah, 410
Borgman, Paul, 1724
Botkin, Benjamin Albert, 118, 801-2
Bouwman, Fred, 4645
Bovee, John R., 2287
Bowen, Catherine Drinker, 2239
Bowen, James K., 3312
Bowman, John Scott, 1694
Bowron, Bernard, 4489
Boyden, William L., 3887
Boyer, Mary G., 119, 2684, 3210
Boyers, Robert, 2934
Boyle, Thomas E., 4757, 5014
Boyling, Mary Ellen F., 2240
Boynton, Henry W., 2061, 2705
Boynton, Percy H., 201, 803, 4146-47
Bracher, Frederick, 411, 804, 4490
Braddy, Haldeen, 3200
Bradford, Curtis, 1725
Bradford, M. E., 2601-2, 3880
Bradford, Mary L., 4378
Brady, Duer S., 2706
Brady, H. Jennifer, 2259
Bragin, Charles, 17
Branch, E. Douglas, 202, 905, 4957
Branch, Edgar M., 1928-32
Brandon, William, 1126
Brasch, James D., 4491
Brashear, Minnie M., 412, 805, 1933
Brashers, Howard C., 906
Bratcher, James T., 4958
Brauer, Ralph, 1032-33
Bray, Robert, 1934
Brazil, John R., 4646-47
Bredeson, Robert, 413
Brendemuhl, Gabriella C., 3569
Brennan, Joseph X., 1726
Brenner, Jack, 203, 414, 3633, 4918
Brenni, Vito Joseph, 18, 2360
Brenzo, Richard Allen, 1127-28
Breslin, Glenna Louise, 4082
Brett, Dorothy E., 1654, 3426
Bridges, Emily, 204
Brier, Howard, 205
Briggs, Arlen John, 4825
Britzman, Homer E., 4197
Brodin, Pierre, 806
Brokaw, Zoanne S., 3166
Bromfield, Louis, 3201

Brooks, Cleanth, 807
Brooks, Van Wyck, 206, 1935, 4313
Brophy, Robert J., 2935-44
Brown, Allen B., 2707
Brown, Carl R. V., 1710
Brown, D. Russell, 4492
Brown, Daniel R., 3242, 4826
Brown, E. K., 1727-29
Brown, Joyce D., 4493
Brown, Marion Marsh, 1730-31
Brown, Russell M., 1385
Brown, William R., 4133
Browne, Lina Fergusson, 1674-75
Brownlow, Kevin, 1034
Bruce-Novoa, John [Juan], 1241-44, 4775
Brumble, H. David, III, 1129
Brune, Ruth E., 2823
Brunvand, Jan Harold, 416, 1469-70, 2207,
    4198
Bryant, Paul T., 417, 2208-9
Bryer, Jackson R., 19, 2485, 4481
Bucco, Martin, 2339, 2822, 3243, 4299,
    4430, 4789
Buchanan, L. E., 3570
Buckland, Roscoe, 2708
Budd, Louis J., 1936-37
Bukalski, Peter J., 1035
Bukey, E. B., 2557
Bullen, John S., 20
Buller, Galen Mark, 1130-31
Bulow, Ernest L., 3176, 4896
Bunker, Robert, 3167
Burack, A. S., 907
Burgum, Edwin B., 4251
Burke, John Gordon, 808
Burke, Kenneth, 4083
Burke, William, 4076
Burkhardt, Peggy Craven, 2062
Burkom, Selma, 3837
Burlingame, Robert, 3422
Burnet, R. A., 1938
Burns, Glen, 1132
Burns, Leslie Edward, 3634
Burns, Shannon, 2146
Burns, Stuart L., 2343, 4387, 4494
Burton, Wilfred C., 3131
Busby, Mark, 3087, 3461, 4006
Bush, Alfred L., 21
Buske, Frank E., 3313
Butler, Frank A., 1339
Butler, J. A., 2382

Butler, Michael D., 207, 418-19, 2063
Butte, Edna Rosemary, 4876
Butterick, George F., 2292
Byers, John R., Jr., 2910-12
Byington, Robert, 420
Bynner, Witter, 2778
Byrd, Charles Lively, 3168
Byrd, Forrest Mickey, 3506
Byrne, Kathleen D., 1732-33

Cady, Edwin H., 2147, 4959
Calder, Jenni, 208, 908, 1036, 3207
Caldwell, John, 4669-70
Cameron, Donald, 1386
Camp, James E., 1939
Campbell, Jeff H., 2271, 2639
Campbell, Robert A., 44
Campbell, Walter S., 209
Canby, Henry Seidel, 1940, 4897
Cansler, Loman D., 2232
Cantú, Robert, 1245, 1489
Canzoneri, Robert, 4434
Capell, Letita Lee, 2307
Capps, Benjamin, 909, 1471
Cárdenas de Dwyer, Carlota, 1246-48
Cardwell, Guy A., 1941
Carey, Larry Lee, 1133
Cargas, H. J., 2348
Carillo, Loretta, 1249-50
Carl, Sister M. Hildalita, 3442
Carlisle, E. Fred, 2334
Carlson, Roy, 120
Carnes, Bruce, 3088
Carpenter, David, 1387
Carpenter, Frederic I., 1877, 2945-51,
    3244, 3635, 4036, 4252, 4495
Carpenter, Richard C., 3955
Carpenter, Ronald H., 4758-59
Carr, Dennis W., 4302
Carr, Duane Ralph, 4496-97
Carroll, John Alexander, 421
Carson, W. G. B., 22
Carstensen, Vernon, 422, 1942
Carter, Albert Howard, III, 3453
Carter, Alfred, 2787
Carter, Harvey C., 423
Carter, Joseph L., 2488-89
Carter, Paul J., Jr., 1943
Carver, Wayne, 424
Caselli, Jaclyn, 4498
Casimar, Louis J., 4499

Cassady, Carolyn, 1707, 3049
Cassai, Marianne, 1734
Castañeda Shular, Antonia, 1251
Castro, Donald F., 1252
Cather, Willa, 2148
Caughey, John W., 121, 425-27, 1552
Caughey, LaRee, 121
Cawelti, John G., 428-30, 910-16, 1037-
    40, 2612, 4960
Cestre, Charles, 2952
Chabot, C. Barry, 2260
Chambers, Robert, 1388
Chametsky, Jules, 809, 4500
Champney, Freeman, 4501
Chankin, Donald O., 4742
Chaplin, W. E., 3822
Chapman, Abraham, 1134
Chapman, Edgar L., 2354
Chappell, Fred, 3151
Charles, Sister Peter Damian, 1735-37
Charters, Ann, 1340, 3050-51
Chase, Don M., 3538
Chase, Richard, 210, 2064, 3737
Chatfield, Hale, 2953
Chatterton, Wayne, 2412
Chavez, John R., 1253
Cheng, Lok Chua, 4347
Chenoweth, Richard R., 1869
Cherewick, Janice, 1389
Cherkovski, Neeli, 2383
Cheuse, Alan, 4703
Chittick, V. L. O., 211, 5015
Choate, Julian Ernest, Jr., 242, 4966
Christensen, J. A., 431
Ciardi, John, 1341
Claire, William F., 4707
Clare, Warren L., 2210, 4660-62
Clark, Blue, 4135
Clark, Felie Woodrow, 4225
Clark, Harry, 1553
Clark, Harry Hayden, 1944
Clark, LaVerne Harrell, 1135, 4226-27
Clark, M. Bruce, 212
Clark, Neil M., 4330
Clark, Neill Wilson, III, 4827
Clark, Thomas D., 432
Clark, Thomas L., 433
Clark, Walter Van Tilburg, 2954
Clark, William Bedford, 2871
Clarkson, Paul S., 3927
Clavel, Marcel, 2065

291

Clayton, James L., 4435
Clayton, Lawrence Ray, 3042, 3303-304
Cleary, Michael, 917, 1568, 4274, 4294
Clemens, Cyril, 3539
Clemens, Samuel L., 1945
Clements, Marshall, 3443
Clements, William M., 434, 918, 1041, 4190
Clendenning, John, 4191
Clevenger, Darnell Haines, 213
Clifford, John, 214
Clodd, Alan, 3866
Clough, Wilson O., 215, 435
Clymer, Kenton J., 2755
Coan, Otis W., 23
Coblentz, S. A., 4648
Cochran, Alice C., 3191
Cochran, Robert W., 1878
Coffin, Arthur B., 2955
Coffman, S. K., Jr., 4898
Cogell, Elizabeth Cummins, 4671
Coggeshall, William T., 122
Cohen, B. J., 436
Cohen, Edward H., 1879
Cohen, Lester H., 437
Cohen, Michael P., 3680
Cohen, Saul, 2368
Cohn, Jack Rice, 3636
Colby, William E., 3681
Cole, Wendell, 24
Coleman, Rufus A., 25, 123, 810
Collier, Ned, 124
Collins, Billy Gene, 3314
Collins, Reba Neighbors, 4136
Colony, Horatio, 1687
Colquitt, Betsy F., 216
Comeau, Paul, 1738
Comerchero, Victor, 4828
Commager, Henry Steele, 438, 2956
Compton, Adele O., 4007
Conrad, Barnaby, III, 4199
Conrow, Robert W., 2406
Conroy, Jack, 1695
Conroy, Stephen S., 3245
Contoski, Victor, 4300
Cook, Bruce, 1342, 2136, 2384, 2567, 3052
Cook, Robert G., 2149
Cooley, Dennis, 2303
Coon, Delia M., 1549
Coon, Gilbert D., 2646-47
Cooper, Frederic Taber, 1501, 4961
Cooper, Guy L., 2788

Cooperman, Stanley, 3738
Copeland, Marion W., 2323
Cording, Robert Kenneth, 4777
Core, George, 3896, 3903
Corning, Howard McKinley, 439, 1483, 2211, 4873
Corser, Cristin D., 2135
Cosbey, Robert C., 3682
Cosgrove, Robert William, 2824
Couch, William, Jr., 3246
Cousins, Norman, 2241
Covici, Pascal, Jr., 1946
Cowley, Malcolm, 3089
Cowser, Robert C., 3881
Cox, James M., 1947
Cox, James Trammell, 2150
Cox, Martha Heasley, 4502-4
Cracroft, Richard H., 26, 440, 1880, 1948-49, 2648, 2872-73, 4210-11, 5016
Cragg, Barbara, 2470
Crain, Mary Beth, 1881
Cramer, Carter M., 4829
Crandall, Allen, 2413
Crisler, Jessee Shattuck, 3739-40
Criswell, Elijah H., 3229
Crone, Ruth, 1730-31
Cronin, Con P., 919
Crooks, Alan Franklin, 217, 3462
Crosby, Harry, 3134
Cross, Dalton, 4649
Crouch, Steve, 4505-6
Crow, Charles L., 218, 3221, 3741
Crowell, Chester T., 441
Crump, G. B., 3637-38
Culbert, Gary Allen, 2490
Culmsee, Carlton F., 219
Cummings, D. Duane, 125
Cunliffe, Marcus, 1950
Cunningham, Eugene, 920
Cunningham, Keith, 442
Cunningham, Mary, 2066
Current-Garcia, E., 443, 3928-29, 4730
Curti, Merle, 921
Curtin, William M., 1739-40

Dahl, Curtis, 1741
Daiches, David, 1742
Dale, Edward E., 444-46
Dalton, Joann, 4429
Dardess, George, 3053-54
Dardis, Tom, 4830

Dary, David A., 3974-75
Davidson, Donald, 811
Davidson, Levette J., 28, 126-28, 447-50, 922, 1136, 1472, 3823
Davidson, Michael, 2293
Davidson, Robert M., 2304
Davie, Donald, 3222, 4924
Davis, David B., 451, 923, 2414
Davis, Harold L., 2957
Davis, Jack L., 2491, 3602-3, 4790
Davis, Joseph Addison, 220
Davis, June H., 4790
Davis, Kenneth W., 3463, 3556
Davis, Robert H., 3930
Davis, Robert M., 4507
Davis, Robert Murray, 452
Davis, Ronald L., 453
Davison, Richard Allan, 3742-43
Davison, Stanley R., 1637
Day, A. Grove, 129, 1137, 3559
Day, Beth F., 4008
Day, Donald, 4137
Day, George F., 2415
Day, James M., 2789
Day, Robert, 454
Deahl, William Evans, Jr., 221
Deamer, Robert Glen, 2151-53
Dean, James L., 2153, 2841
Deane, Paul, 1882
Dearing, Frank V., 4009
De Casseres, Benjamin, 2958
DeFlyer, Joseph Eugene, 1138
Degenfelder, E. Pauline, 3464
Dekker, George, 2067
Delaney, Paul, 1951
Delano, Alonzo, 2234
DeLowry, Linda Diane, 3710
De Menil, Alexander Nicholas, 222
Deming, Caren Joy, 1042
DeMott, Robert, 2959, 4508
Demouy, Jane Krause, 3897
Dennis, Larry R., 1952
Derleth, August W., 924, 3247
Dervin, James Allen, 2874
De Shong, Charles Thomas, 223
Dessain, Kenneth, 455
Detro, Gene, 3867
Deutsch, Babette, 2960
DeVoto, Bernard, 925-27, 1953-54, 2760, 3230, 3248, 4010
Dewey, Evelyn G., 1554

Dick, Everett, 2825
Dickason, David H., 3135-36
Dickey, Imogene, 4718
Dickey, James, 4084
Dickinson, Donald C., 224
Dickinson-Brown, Roger, 3604, 4399
Dieter, Lynn, 4275
Dike, Donald A., 812
Dill, Vicky Schreiber, 2349
Dillingham, Peter, 1139, 3605
Dillingham, William B., 3744-46
Dillon, David, 2847, 4436
Dillon, Richard H., 1676-77, 1867, 3231
Dinn, James M., 1743
Dippie, Brian W., 456, 1569, 3976, 4200
Disbrow, Jimmie L., 3562
Ditsky, John M., 457, 1744, 3949, 4509-15
Dittmann, Erling, 4148
Divorkin, Rita, 4
Djwa, Sandra, 1390-91
Dobie, Bertha, 2272
Dobie, J. Frank, 29, 225, 458, 813, 1473, 2311, 4011
Dockstader, Alice W., 1140
Dockstader, Frederick J., 1140
Dodd, Wayne, 1615
Dodson, Mary Kay, 3315
Doher, Pam, 4228
Donald, David, 459, 2689
Donaldson, Scott, 3055
Donchak, Stella Cassano, 2790
Dondore, Dorothy Anne, 30, 226, 460, 814
Donelson, Kenneth L., 31, 461-62
Donohue, Agnes McNeill, 4516
Dooley, D. J., 3249
Dooley, Nelly, 815
Dornbusch, Clyde, 4183
Dorris, Michael, 1141
Dougherty, Charles T., 32
Doughty, Howard, 3848
Doughty, Nanelia S., 4719-20
Douglas, George H., 3250
Douglass, Thomas E., 2450
Dowden, George, 2568
Dowell, Faye Nell, 1256
Downey, Linda K., 2799
Downs, Alexis, 3563
Doyle, Helen McKnight, 1520
Dresman, Paul C., 2294
Drizari, Nelo, 3316
Dubbert, Joe L., 4882

293

DuBois, Arthur E., 816, 1521
Dubose, Thomas, 3465
Ducey, Cathryn Annette, 1955, 4760
Duckett, Margaret, 1956, 2709-13
Duffey, Bernard, 2492, 3056
Dugger, Ronnie, 1561
Duke, Maurice, 4650
Dula, Martha, 2875
Dullea, Gerard J., 2137
Dunbar, John R., 4651
Duncan, Erika, 2592
Duncan, Janice K., 1544
Dunnivant, James, 3090
Duram, James C., 4314
Durham, Philip, 130-31, 227, 463-64, 928-33, 2775, 3697, 4962
Dussere, David Philip, 1870
Dykes, Jeff C., 33, 465, 934, 2273, 3202, 3977, 4247, 4724
Dykes, Mattie M., 3573
Dymond, Richard Bruce, 3639

Easton, Robert, 2355
Easy, Peter, 1142
Eckman, Frederick, 2569
Eckstein, Neil T., 4149-50
Eddy, Darlene, 4517
Edwards, Clifford D., 4037
Effinger, Cecil, 2388
Egan, Ferol, 4672
Egge, Marion F., 1120
Eggleston, Wilfrid, 1392-93
Ehrlich, J. W., 2570
Eichelberger, Clayton, 34, 817, 2826-27
Eifner, Walter H., 466
Eisinger, Chester E., 1883-84, 3640, 4437-38
Eitel, Edmund H., 3824
Eitner, Walter H., 4138, 4899
Elder, A. T., 1394
Elder, Gary, 132
Elizondo, Sergio D., 1257
Elkins, William R., 4884
Ellingsen, Melva G., 2312
Elliot, William D., 467
Ellis, James, 3317
Ellsberg, William, 4201
Ellsworth, Peter, 4400
Emblidge, David, 2283
Emerson, O. B., 35
Emmons, David M., 228

Emmons, Winfred S., 3898
Engel, Bernard F., 3449
Engel, Mary Frances, 1395
Engen, Orrin A., 1638
England, D. Gene, 3466
Erbentraut, Edwin B., 3318
Erhard, Thomas A., 4066
Erisman, Fred, 36-37, 229, 468-71, 818-21, 1455, 2649-51, 2695, 3978-80, 4276-77, 4912
Erno, Richard B., 472
Erskine, John, 2714
Eschholz, Paul A., 91
Eshleman, H. D., 473
Espey, David B., 1143, 3144
Esselman, Kathryn C., 1043
Estes, David C., 4731
Etulain, Richard W., 38-41, 84, 229-30, 474-87, 822-23, 935-41, 1642, 1699, 1885, 2212, 2233, 2416, 2465, 2471-72, 2613, 2652-53, 2762-64, 3208, 3319-21, 3440, 4439, 4963-64
Evans, James Leroy, 231
Evans, Max, 1044
Evans, Robley, 2784
Evans, T. Jeff, 2493
Evans, Timothy, 3488
Everding, Robert George, 4253
Everette, Oliver, 4085
Evers, Lawrence J., 1144-46, 3606, 4302
Everson, William, 488, 824, 1046, 1343, 2929

Faas, Ekbert, 1616-17, 4348
Faderman, Lillian, 1314
Fadiman, Clifton, 489
Falk, Armand, 2654
Falke, Anne, 1484-85
Falkenberg, Sandra, 4518
Fallis, Guadalupe Valdés, 1258
Fargo, James, 2765
Farley, Marie Breniman, 3540
Farrington, Thomas Arthur, 3899
Fatout, Paul, 1582-84, 1663, 1957-58
Fay, Julie, 2302
Feger, Lois, 1745
Feied, Frederick, 3057, 4519
Feinstein, Herbert, 2403
Feldman, Gene, 1344
Feltskog, E. N., 3849
Fender, Stephen, 490, 1045, 1959

294

Fenin, George N., 1046
Fensch, Thomas, 4520
Fenton, Charles, 4184
Ferguson, DeLancey, 1960
Ferguson, J. M., Jr., 1746, 4440
Fergusson, Erna, 2369
Ferlinghetti, Lawrence, 232, 1345
Ferry, David, 4086
Fetrow, Fred M., 1570
Fetty, Audrey Mae Shelly, 1747
Fiedler, Leslie A., 233, 1147, 3091, 3492
Fielding, Lavina, 234-35
Fielding, Raymond, 1047
Fields, Kenneth, 1148
Fife, Alta, 491
Fife, Austin, 491
Fife, Jim L., 3251, 4012-13
Filler, Louis, 3211-12, 3541-42
Findley, Sue, 3322
Fine, David M., 1692, 4831
Finestone, Harry, 1748
Firebaugh, Joseph J., 2389
Fisher, Laura, 1149
Fisher, Vardis, 492, 825, 2417
Fisher, William J., 4254
Fishwick, Marshall, 236, 493, 826, 942-43
Fiske, Horace S., 827, 4965
Fiske, Turbesé Lummis, 3431
Fite, Gilbert, 2494
Fitz Gerald, Gregory, 4426
Fitzmaurice, James Earl, 237
Flagg, Nancy, 4388
Flanagan, John T., 42, 134, 494-97, 828-
    30, 2068, 2690, 3145, 3252-53, 3641,
    3711, 4038-39
Flanner, Hildegarde, 1688
Fleck, Byron Y., 238
Fleck, Richard F., 43-44, 238, 3683
Fleeger, Wayne Robert, 2495
Fleischmann, Wolfgang B., 1346
Fleming, Becky London, 3323
Fleming, Donald R., 4652
Fleming, Esther, 3254
Fleming, Patricia Jean, 1749
Fleming, Robert E., 3254, 3432, 4739
Flint, Timothy, 2453
Floan, Howard R., 4255
Flora, Joseph M., 2418-23, 3092, 3507-8,
    4441
Flores, Vetal, 498
Foerster, Norman, 3684

Folsom, James K., 239-40, 499-501, 944,
    1048, 1886, 2370, 2454, 2655, 3467,
    3747, 4014, 4278
Folsom, L. Edwin, 4349
Foner, Philip S., 1961, 3324
Fontana, Ernest L., 2785
Fontenrose, Joseph, 4058
Foote, Arthur B., 2473
Footman, Robert H., 1750
Ford, Charles, 1049
Ford, Edsel, 2301
Ford, John, 1050
Ford, Moselle A., 4248
Ford, Thomas W., 1522, 2656-57
Forman, Henry James, 1502, 1751
Forrey, Carolyn, 1503-4
Forrey, Robert, 3093
Fortenberry, George E., 1585
Fossey, W. Richard, 4521
Foster, Ann Tucker, 4087
Foster, Edward Halsey, 2553, 2603
Foster, John Wilson, 3094
Foster, Joseph, 3193
Foster, Richard, 3992
Fox, Maynard, 1752-53, 4151
Fracchia, Charles A., 3325
Franklin, Wayne, 241, 2876
Frantz, Joe B., 242, 4966
Fraser, Shirley S., 4925
Frayling, Christopher, 1051
Frear, Samuel Thomas, 1497
Frederick, John T., 502-4, 945, 2069,
    4688
Freedman, W. A., 4538
Freeman, Martha Doty, 505
Freer, Coburn, 4088
French, Carole Anne, 506
French, Philip, 1052
French, Warren, 507-8, 946-47, 2496,
    3748-49, 4522-28
Frey, Susan A., 2795
Freydberg, Margaret Howe, 1754
Friar, Natasha A., 1053, 1150
Friar, Ralph E., 1053, 1150
Friberg, Ingegerd, 1618
Fried, Martin B., 1962
Friend, Llerena, 4812
Frohock, W. M., 3058, 3750
Frost, O. W., 3574
Fujii, Gertrude Sugioka, 2497
Fuller, Daniel J., 1963

Furman, Necah Stewart, 4813
Furness, Edna L., 509
Fuson, Ben W., 510
Fussell, Edwin, 243, 2070, 4900

Gaer, Joseph, 1523, 1586, 3751
Gale, Robert, 1755
Gale, Robert L., 1964, 2199, 2586, 2756, 4202, 4675
Galinski, Hans, 244
Gallagher, Thomas Augustus, Jr., 1054
Gallagher, William D., 135
Gallegly, J. S., 3931-32
Galloway, David D., 4832
Garber, Frederick, 2848-49
Garcia, Reloy, 4529
Garcia, Ricardo, 1259
García-Girón, Edmundo, 1260
Gard, Wayne, 245
Gardner, Erle Stanley, 948
Gardner, J. H., 2877
Gardner, Joseph H., 2716, 3752
Garfield, Brian, 949-51, 2766
Garland, Hamlin, 511-12, 2154, 2498
Garren, Samuel Baity, 3993
Garrett, George, 3642
Gartenberg, Max, 1344
Garza, Mario, 1261
Gaston, Edwin W., Jr., 8, 45, 246, 513, 2800, 4015, 4040, 4212, 5026
Geary, Edward A., 514-15, 831
Gebhardt, Eike, 1347
Gegenheimer, Albert F., 4296
Geherin, David J., 2261
Geismar, Maxwell, 1756, 1965, 2640, 3256, 3326, 3753
Gelfant, Blanche H., 1757, 3059, 4389
Gemmett, Robert J., 4401
Geneson, Paul, 4350
Gentles, Ruth G., 2164
Georgakas, Dan, 1055
Gerber, Philip L., 1758, 4401
Gerdes, Dick, 1329
Gerkey, Stephen Joseph, 4833
Gerlach, John, 2071
Gernes, Sonia Grace, 1966
Gerstenberger, Donna, 46-47, 4530
Geuder, Patricia A., 1557
Geyer, Carolyn, 4152
Geyer, William, 265, 3155
Giannone, Richard, 1759-60

Gibbs, Barbara, 2572
Gibson, Donald, 2155-56
Gibson, Michael D., 952
Gibson, Morgan, 3994
Gibson, William M., 1967, 2019
Gierasch, Walter, 2961
Gifford, Barry, 1708, 3060-61
Gilbert, Julie Goldsmith, 2361
Gilbert, Rudolph, 2962
Gilbert, Susan Hull, 2072
Giles, James R., 3468
Gilliard, Frederick W., 516
Gilliland, Marshall A., 3297
Gillis, Everett A., 517, 3169, 3304
Gillmor, Frances, 518
Ginanni, Francis Ralph, 3754
Gingerich, Willard, 3841
Ginsberg, Allen, 2571
Gish, Robert F., 2499-502, 2791, 5030
Gitzen, Julian, 4351
Givner, Joan, 3900
Gladsky, Thomas S., 2073
Gleason, G. Dale, 953
Glicksberg, Charles I., 3868
Glover, Donald E., 2717-18
Goble, Danney, 2615-16
Goboni, Mark William, 4531
Goetzmann, William H., 519
Gohdes, Clarence, 48-49, 520, 832
Goldhurst, William, 4532
Goldman, Suzy Bernstein, 3755
Goldsmith, Adrian H., 4534
Goldsmith, Arnold L., 3731, 3756-57, 4533
Goldstein, Bernice, 1056
Goldstein, Jessie Sidney, 1587, 3543-46
Goldstone, Adrian H., 4534
Golemba, Henry L., 4535
Golffing, Francis, 2572
Gonzalez, Arturo F., Jr., 3177
González, Sylvia A., 1262
Goodwyn, Frank, 521
Gordon, Dudley C., 3433-35
Gordon, Walter K., 4536
Gossett, Louise Y., 2593
Gottesman, Ronald, 4315-16
Gottfried, Herbert Wilson, 247
Goudie, Andrea, 1968
Goulart, Ron, 954
Gower, Calvin W., 522
Gower, Ronald A., 3327
Graber, Kay, 2328

Graff, Gerald, 4926
Graham, Don, 523, 1087, 1474, 1700, 2316, 3209, 3328, 3758-62, 4684
Graham, Ina Agnes, 2046
Graham, John, 4317
Grahame, Pauline, 2801
Grajeda, Ralph F., 4070
Grant, George Paul, 3712
Granzow, Barbara, 3469
Grattan, C. Hartley, 1588
Graves, John, 4725
Gray, James, 4537
Gray, Richard H., 2802
Greb, Gordon, 1613
Grebstein, Sheldon Norman, 3257-59
Green, Douglas B., 524
Green, Timothy, 525
Greenan, Edith, 2963
Greenberg, David B., 136
Greene, Donald, 1396
Greenway, John, 137
Greenwell, Scott L., 4229-30
Greenwood, Robert, 11
Gregg, Barbara, 138
Gregg, John J., 138
Gregg, Josiah, 2604
Gregory, Horace, 955
Greiner, Charles F., 4402
Greiner, Francis F., 2213
Grenander, M. E., 1589-92, 4676
Grenier, Kate Parker, 4303
Grey, Zane, 2617
Gribben, Alan, 1969
Grider, Sylvia, 4153
Griego y Maestas, José, 139
Griffin, R. J., 4538
Griffin, Robert J., 3260
Griffith, Doris, 50
Grigg, Quay, 4792
Grigsby, Gordon K., 3995
Grimm, Clyde L., Jr., 2594
Grinnell, George Bird, 4213
Gripp, Gary, 4967
Groff, Edward, 3901
Groman, George L., 4885
Grommon, A. H., 4539
Gronewold, Benjamin F., 2503
Grose, G. R., 3547
Gross, Barry, 2447
Gross, Dalton, 4318, 4653-54
Gross, Konrad, 1397

Grossman, James, 2074
Grove, F. P., 1398
Grover, Dorys C., 526, 2424-27, 2803-4, 3043
Gruber, Frank, 956-58, 2618
Guettinger, Roger J., 3643
Gullason, Thomas A., 2140, 2157
Gurian, Jay, 248, 527-29, 1571, 1887, 2214, 3329
Gurko, Leo, 4540
Guthrie, A. B., Jr., 530-31, 2554, 2658
Gutierrez, Donald, 4743
Gvåle, Gudrun Hovde, 4154

Haaland, C. Carlyle, 3548
Hack, Richard, 3869
Hadley, Edith, 3685
Hafen, LeRoy, 4212
Hafer, Jack, 3644
Hafer, John William, 249
Hahn, Stephen, 2573, 4155
Haight, Mary M., 3575
Hairston, Joe B., 250, 2659, 4442-43
Hairston, Maxine C., 3882-85
Hakac, John, 833
Hale, Edward E., 532
Hall, Helen L., 3861
Hallwas, John E., 3298
Halperin, Irving, 3194
Hamblen, Abigail Ann, 4689
Hamilton, Cynthia A., 959
Hamilton, David Mike, 3330
Hamilton, John A., 2455
Hamilton, W. I., 1151
Hamilton, Wynette, 1152
Hammond, John Hays, 4331
Hamner, Eugenie Lambert, 1761
Hancock, Joel, 1264
Hanks, Ida Mae, 2428
Hanna, Archibald, 51
Hansen, Klaus J., 533
Hanson, Irene, 1399
Harding, Eugene, 2485-87
Hardwick, Bonnie Skell, 251
Hardy, John Edward, 3902
Harkness, David James, 252-54, 834
Harmsen, Tyrus, 2964
Harper, Robert D., 3645
Harpham, Geoffrey, 3331
Harrington, John, 1057
Harris, Charles W., 960

297

Harris, Elbert L., 2504
Harris, Jim, 4041
Harris, Leon, 4319
Harris, Mark, 4708
Harris, Richard Casey, 1762-63, 3933
Harrison, Dick, 1400-1406
Harrison, Joseph B., 2719
Harrison, Stanley R., 2505
Hart, James D., 255, 2200, 3763, 3850
Hart, John E., 3062
Hart, William S., 1058
Harte, Bret, 2720
Harte, John Bret, 2721
Hartley, Lodwick, 3903
Hartrangt, Marshall V., 4541
Hartwick, Harry, 3261
Hartzell, James, 3996
Harver, Hyla Hope, 2506
Harvey, Alice G., 52
Harvey, Charles M., 961
Haslam, Gerald, 53, 140, 534-38, 1153-57,
  1265, 1456, 2317-18, 3445, 4279-83,
  4297, 4736
Hasley, Louis, 3825-26
Hassan, Ihab H., 4390
Hassrick, Peter H., 3981-82
Hatcher, Harlan, 4256
Hauck, Richard B., 3095
Haugen, Einar, 4156
Haupt, Jon, 386-87, 2409
Hauptman, Laurence M., 539
Havlice, Patricia Pate, 54
Hayashi, Tetsumaro, 4479, 4542-52
Haycox, Ernest, Jr., 2767
Haycox, Jill Marie, 2768-70
Haycraft, Howard, 1467
Haydock, James, 3332
Hayman, Ronald, 4352
Hays, John Q., 1970
Hazard, Lucy Lockwood, 256, 2722
Hazel, Erick R., 257
Healey, James W., 3039
Hearron, Thomas, 1645
Heatherington, Madelon E., 540
Heavans, Jean, 4269
Hedgpeth, Joel W., 4059, 4553
Heestand, Diane Elissa, 3827
Hegbloom, Kirk, 2215
Heilman, Robert B., 541, 4089
Heitmann, John, 4157
Helle, Anita, 1555

Helmick, Evelyn Thomas, 1764-66
Henderson, Katherine Usher, 2262
Henderson, Sam H., 2584
Hendon, Telfair, 162
Hendrick, George, 46-47, 3904
Hendricks, George D., 1888
Hendricks, King, 3333-34
Henley, Joan Asher, 1158
Henry, Jeanette, 1159-60
Henry, Stuart, 2805
Hensley, Dennis E., 3335-36
Henson, Clyde E., 3146-48
Herbert, Janis, 3558
Herbst, Josephine, 4834
Herndon, James, 4384
Herndon, Jerry A., 1457
Hernlund, Patricia, 1646
Heron, Philip E., 4090
Herrmann, John, 1889
Herron, Ima Honaker, 258, 2863, 3213,
  3564
Hertzel, Leo J., 542, 1619, 3839, 3951
Heyen, William, 1620, 4091-92, 4403
Hicks, Granville, 1767, 3646-47, 4320
Higgins, J. E., 2507
Hilfer, Anthony Channell, 259, 3262
Hill, Douglas B., Jr., 2201
Hill, Eldon C., 2508
Hill, Gertrude, 55
Hill, Hamlin, 1971-73
Hill, John S., 3764
Hill, Richard Allen, 3096
Hilton, William C., 4554
Hinds, Harold E., Jr., 3178
Hine, Robert V., 141
Hingston, Edward P., 1664
Hinojosa, Rolando, 1266
Hin-Smith, Joan, 1407
Hinz, Evelyn J., 1768
Hipkiss, Roberta, 3063
Hirschfelder, Arlene B., 1161
Hiscoe, David W., 2509
Hitt, Helen, 544, 2216
Hoarau, Albert-Patrick, 1025
Hosbaum, Philip, 4927
Hodgins, Francis E., Jr., 260, 2217, 2660
Hoebzema, Loren, 3137
Hoffman, Hans A., 142
Hoffmann, Charles G., 3765
Hoffmann, Frederick J., 2857
Hofheins, Roger, 359, 3223, 4444

298

Hofstadter, Richard, 3862
Hoge, James O., 3097
Hogue, Alexandre, 2274
Hoilman, Dennis R., 4304
Hoke, Jerry C., 4031
Holaday, Clayton A., 3149
Holbrook, Stewart H., 143, 545, 4892
Holden, Jonathan, 4404
Hollander, John, 3493
Hollenberg, S. W., 4093
Hollister, Marian E., 2390
Holloway, Jean, 2510
Holloway, John, 4928
Holmes, John Clellon, 1348
Holsinger, Paul M., 2511
Holtz, William, 3159
Homans, Peter, 1059
Hood, Charles E., 2661-62
Hopkins, Karen J., 4555
Horgan, Paul, 546, 835, 2605-6
Hornberger, Theodore, 547
Horton, Andrew, 4858
Horton, Andrew S., 962
Horton, T. D., 3263
Hotchkiss, Jeannette, 56
Hotchkiss, William, 2965
Hough, Emerson, 548
Hougland, Willard, 1526
Houghton, Donald E., 1890-91, 3863, 4556, 4968
House, Julian T., 3713
House, Kay Seymour, 2075
Houston, James D., 140
Houston, Neal B., 2512, 4249
Howard, Helen Addison, 1162-63
Howard, Leon, 549, 3648
Howard, Patsy C., 57
Howard, Richard, 261, 2138, 2850, 3152-53, 4353, 4405
Howe, E. W., 2828
Howell, Elmo, 1974
Howells, William Dean, 1975
Hoy, Christopher, 4793-94
Hoy, Helen Elizabeth, 1408
Hubach, Robert R., 4901-2
Hubbard, Claude, 4215
Hubbard, George U., 2047
Hubbell, Jay B., 262, 550, 836, 4677, 4969
Hudson, Lois Phillips, 4445
Hudson, Ruth, 263, 1976, 2878
Hudson, Wilson M., 1475-77

Hudspeth, Robert N., 2158
Huebel, Harry Russell, 1349, 1709, 3064
Huffstickler, Star, 4903
Hugo, Richard, 2851-52, 4406-7
Hull, Keith N., 3065
Humphrey, William, 264
Humphries, Rolfe, 3214
Hunsaker, Kenneth B., 551, 2429, 4379
Hunt, Anthony, 4354
Hunt, John W., 3084
Hunt, John W., Jr., 3649
Hunt, Tim, 3066
Huntress, Diana, 4795
Hurst, Lannie, 2048
Huseboe, Arthur R., 265, 3155, 3509
Hutchens, John K., 2218
Hutchinson, Phyllis Martin, 1769
Hutchinson, W. H., 552-55, 963-65, 2806-7, 4016-23
Hutton, Paul A., 1060
Hyde, Mary Marra, 3607
Hylton, Marion Willard, 3608
Hyman, Stanley Edgar, 4835
Hymes, Dell, 1164

Ianni, L. A., 2385
Ifkovic, Edward Joseph, 266, 5027
Inada, Lawson Fusao, 3836
Inge, M. Thomas, 144
Inglis, Fred, 3224
Innis, Kenneth, 1409
Irving, Pierre M., 2879
Irving, Washington, 2880-81
Issler, Anne Roller, 4666

Jacks, L. V., 1770
Jackson, Carlton, 2619
Jackson, Donald, 3232
Jackson, Joseph Henry, 145
Jacobs, Elijah L., 268
Jacobs, Fred Rue, 2263
Jacobs, John Tobias, 2882
Jacobs, W. J., 4913
Jacobs, Wilbur R., 1633, 4761
Jacobson, Angeline, 58
Jacobson, Harvey K., 269
Jacobson, Larry King, 966
Jain, Sunita, 4558
James, Eleanor, 1562
James, Elizabeth, 3038
James, G. W., 1977

James, Overton Philip, 2159
James, Stuart B., 557
Jamison, Blanche Noma Miller, 1166
Janssen, Judith M., 3156
Janssens, G. A. M., 1621
Jarrod, Keith, 3179
Jarvis, Charles D., 3068
Jason, Rick, 4771
Jaynes, Bryson L., 1665
Jenkins, Eli Seth, 2219
Jennings, Ann S., 3337
Jennings, F. P., 3851
Jensen, Merrill, 837
Jensen, Oliver, 3698
Jensen, Sid [Sydney LaMarr], 4391, 4447–48
Jenson, Richard, 4762
Jeranko, Mildred, 558
Jerome, Judson, 2966
Jessee, Dean C., 5029
Jett, Stephen C., 2479
Jewett, Isaac Appleton, 559
Jimenez, Francesco, 1267
Johannsen, Albert, 270, 967
Johannsen, Robert W., 2329
Johnson, Carole M., 2808–10
Johnson, Cecil, 4655
Johnson, Curtis L., 4559
Johnson, Dorothy M., 4284
Johnson, George W., 3766–67
Johnson, Kenneth, 271
Johnson, Lee Ann, 2474
Johnson, Merle, 1978
Johnson, Thomas, 838
Johnson, W., 4886
Johnson, William Savage, 2967
Johnston, Kenneth C., 2776
Jones, Alfred Haworth, 2242
Jones, Daryl E., 968–71
Jones, Everett L., 130, 227
Jones, Granville, 3069
Jones, Harry H., 560
Jones, Howard Mumford, 59, 272, 561, 2076, 4877
Jones, Joel M., 273, 2754
Jones, Lawrence William, 4560
Jones, Margaret Ann, 562
Jones, Phillip L., 2220
Jones, Stephen R., 1647
Jordahl, O., 4158
Jordan, Lois B., 1268

Jordan, Philip D., 4223
Jorgensen, Bruce W., 563, 5024
Jorgenson, Theodore, 4159–60
Josephy, Alvin M., Jr., 564
Jungels, William J., 4355
Juricek, John T., 565
Justin, Jeffrey Arthur, 1622
Justus, James H., 4561

Kafka, Robb, 2968
Kaminsky, Stuart M., 1061
Kaplan, Charles, 3768
Kaplan, Justin, 1979
Kardell, Margaret M., 3338
Karolides, Nicholas J., 274
Karp, Walter, 1062
Karr, Jean, 2620
Karsten, Ernest E., Jr., 4562
Kassebaum, L. Harvey, 2335
Katz, Joseph, 2160–62, 3769–71
Kaufman, Donald L., 1167
Kaul, A. N., 2077
Kay, Arthur Murray, 275, 3714
Kaye, Frances W., 566, 2193, 2513–14, 4970
Kaye, Howard, 1865, 4929
Kedro, M. James, 567, 5022
Keeler, Clinton, 568, 1771
Keen, Carl L., 3959
Kehde, Martha, 839
Kehl, D. G., 1892
Keim, Charles J., 569
Keiser, Albert, 276, 1168, 2883
Keith, W. J., 1410
Keleher, Julia, 570
Keleher, William A., 4024
Keller, Karl, 571, 2969–70
Keller, Richard, 60
Keller, Richard Morton, 840
Kelley, Patrick, 4409
Kellock, Katherine, 841
Kellogg, George, 2221, 2430, 3510–11
Kelly, William Patrick, III, 2078
Kelton, Elmer, 842
Kennedy, Sister Patricia, 277
Kennedy, X. J., 1939
Kern, Robert, 1648, 4356–57
Kerr, Blaine, 3609
Kesey, Ken, 3098–99
Kesterson, David B., 3828
Keyes, John McDonald, 4836

300

Kherdian, David, 61, 1350, 4257, 4358
Kidney-Wells, Jennifer, 4810
Kiefer, Gordon B., 1893
Kiernan, Robert F., 3905
Kiernan, Thomas, 4563
Kiesel, Margaret Matlack, 4690
Kiley, George B., 2971
Killoh, Ellen, 3225
Kimball, Richard R., 62
Kime, Wayne R., 2884-87, 2913
King, James T., 572
King, Kimball, 843
King, Scottie, 1643
Kingman, Russ, 3339
Kings, John, 3560
Kinnamon, Jon M., 2163
Kinney, Arthur F., 4564
Kirby, David K., 63
Kirkpatrick, John Ervin, 2456
Kissane, Leedice M., 4691-92
Kite, Merilyn, 2663
Kitses, Jim, 1063
Kittredge, William, 573
Kizer, Carolyn, 574
Klaschus, Candace, 3180
Klein, Marcus, 1593, 3650
Kleis, David John, 1894
Klinkowitz, Jerome, 4704
Klotman, Phyllis R., 575
Knapp, James F., 3100
Knibbs, Henry Herbert, 4025
Knight, Arthur, 1064, 1351-52
Knight, Damon, 972
Knight, Glee, 1351
Knight, Kit, 1352
Knoll, Robert E., 3651
Kobler, Turner S., 3551-52
Koenig, Jacqueline, 3340
Koerner, J. D., 4321
Koerner, James D., 2515
Kohler, Dayton, 2222, 2664, 4042
Kolb, Alfred, 2558-60
Koloc, Frederick Joseph, 4565
Kolodzie, Christine, 1653
Kopp, Jane, 146
Kopp, Karl, 146
Kosofsky, Rita Nathalie, 3494
Koszarski, Diane Kaiser, 1065
Kousaleos, Peter G., 3610
Kraft, James, 2792-93
Kramer, Dale, 3934

Kramer, Hilton, 4094
Kramer, Jane, 2574
Kramer, Lawrence, 4410
Kramer, Mary D., 576
Krassner, Paul, 3101
Kraus, Michelle P., 2575
Krause, Herbert, 577
Krause, Janet Boettcher, 1772
Krause, Sydney J., 1980-82, 4566-67
Krauzer, Steven M., 573
Kreisel, Henry, 1411
Krickel, Edward, 4258
Krim, Seymour, 1353-54
Kroeber, Clifton B., 377
Krupat, Arnold, 578
Kruse, Horst H., 973
Kuehl, John R., 1895
Kuhlman, Susan, 2723
Kuhlman, Thomas A., 579
Kummer, George, 4921
Kunitz, Stanley, 4095
Kunz, Don R., 3102, 4859
Kuperman, David Arnold, 1983
Kurtz, Kenneth, 64
Kwiat, Joseph J., 3772-73
Kyle, Carol, 4411

La Belle, Jenijoy, 4096
Labor, Earle, 3341-45
Lachtman, Howard, 3346-53
Lacroix, Paul-Henri, 4259
La Farge, Oliver, 2778
Lahmen, Peter Robert, 1066
LaHood, Marvin, 1773, 4043-46
Laing, Wesley, 3181
Laird, W. David, 224
Lamar, Howard R., 278
Lambert, Maude Eugenie, 1774
Lambert, Neal E., 580-82, 1458, 4216,
    4971-77
Lambert, Patricia J. B., 583
Landess, Thomas, 3470
Lane, Gary, 4097
Langford, Gerald, 3935
Langum, David J., 1269
Lanier, Doris, 3829
Lansaw, Paul, 2665
Larkin, Sharon, 2516
Larsen, Erling, 4161
Larson, Charles R., 1169, 2404, 3487, 3554,
    3611, 3842, 3890, 4305, 4681-82, 4860

301

Larson, Clinton, 147
Larson, T. A., 3830-31
Lathrop, JoAnna, 1775
Lattin, Vernon E., 1270-71, 1558
Lauber, John, 2223, 4412
Lauriston, Victor, 1412
Lavender, David, 584
Lawrence, D. H., 2079
Lawson, Benjamin S., Jr., 844, 3576-77
Lawson, Lewis A., 2923
Leab, Daniel J., 974
Leach, Joseph, 289, 585, 975
Leach, Thomas James, Jr., 4359
Leal, Luis, 1272
Leary, Lewis, 65-67, 1924
Lease, Benjamin, 3150
Leavitt, Harvey, 1649
LeDuc, Thomas H., 3502
Lee, Billy C., 3044
Lee, Charles, 148
Lee, Charlotte I., 4098
Lee, Fred L., 3715
Lee, Hector, 586-87
Lee, James W., 8, 2858, 3512
Lee, John Thomas, 2607
Lee, L. L., 280, 1572, 1896-97, 4381
Lee, Robert Edson, 281, 1776, 1985,
   2242-43, 2457, 2691, 2888, 3233,
   3852
Lee, Sylvia B., 4381-82
Lee, W. Storrs, 149-50
Lee, Wayne C., 3182
Leeds, Barry H., 3103
Leer, Norman, 3070
Legris, Maurice, 1612
Lehman, Anthony L., 3160
Lehmberg, Paul S., 4217, 4904
Leisy, Ernest E., 282
Leithead, J. Edward, 588, 976
Le Master, J. R., 2972
Lemay, J. A. Leo, 4732
Lemons, William Everett, Jr., 2245, 3716
Lenihan, John H., 1067
Lensing, George S., 1623, 4413, 4418
Le Pellec, Yves, 3071
Lepper, Gary M., 68
LeRoy, Bruce, 3553
Levant, Howard, 4568-70
Levernier, James A., 1170-72, 2146
Levin, David, 3853-54, 4930
Levitas, Gloria, 1173

Levy, Alfred J., 1986
Lewandowska, M. L., 589
Lewis, Edith, 1777
Lewis, Grace Hegger, 3264
Lewis, Lorene, 4450
Lewis, Marvin A., 590, 1498, 3557, 4978
Lewis, Merrill E., 280, 283-84, 1696, 2080,
   4185, 4449-50, 4763-65
Lewis, Peter Elfred, 4360
Lewis, Robert W., 3265, 3999
Lewis, Tom, 4361
Lewis, Tom J., 1273
Liberman, M. M., 3906
Lieber, Todd M., 4571
Light, James F., 4837-38
Light, Martin, 3266-69
Lillard, Richard G., 23
Lin, Maurice Yaofu, 2386
Lincoln, Kenneth, 1174-75
Linden, George W., 1176
Linden, Stanton J., 3652
Linderman, Frank Bird, 4203
Lindsay, Robert O., 1689
Lindsey, Ethel Leona, 3832
Lindstrom, Naomi, 591
Linneman, William, 3965
Lipton, Lawrence, 1355-56, 3998
Lisca, Peter, 4572-80
Lish, Gordon, 3104
Littlefield, Daniel F., 1177, 2517, 2544-45
Lockwood, William J., 1624, 2295, 2853
Lofsness, Cynthia, 4414
Loftis, Anne, 4486
Logasa, Hannah, 69
Lohf, Kenneth A., 3774, 4931
Lomax, John A., 151
Lombard, C., 2458
Lomelí, Francisco A., 1274-75
London, Charmian, 3354
London, Jack, 3355-56
London, Joan, 3357
Long, Barbara N. Messner, 3138
Long, E. Hudson, 1987, 3936-40
Long, Louise, 2431
Longtin, Ray C., 3578, 4656, 4678
Loomis, C. Grant, 1988, 3962
Lorch, Fred W., 1666, 1989-90
Lord, Glenn, 2818
Lorentz, Pare, 2224
Lorimer, William Lund, 4099
Lounsbury, Thomas R., 2081

302

Love, Glen A., 195, 1577, 3270, 3775
Lovelace, Lisabeth, 3203
Lovell, John, Jr., 4905
Loveman, S., 1594
Lowe, David, 4231
Lucia, Ellis, 152
Lucid, Robert Francis, 2202-3
Ludovici, Paola, 1178
Ludwig, Edward W., 1276
Luedtke, Luther S., 4721, 4776
Lugg, Bonelyn, 3907
Lujan, R. E., 4745
Lummis, Keith, 3431
Lund, Mary Graham, 3220
Lundquist, James, 3271-74
Lundy, Robert D., 3776
Lyday, Jo W., 1524-25
Lynch, Dennis Daley, 4415
Lynch, Michael, 3444
Lynn, Kenneth S., 1991-92, 3358, 3777
Lyon, Horace, 2973
Lyon, Peter, 285, 592
Lyon, Thomas J., 70, 593, 2889, 3686,
    4362-63, 4796-98
Lyon, Zoë, 3441
Lyons, Richard, 153
Lythgoe, Mary, 4383

Mabie, Hamilton W., 845
McAllister, H. S. [Mick], 1179, 2432,
    3612-14
MacAlpin, Sister Sara, 1778, 4693
McBride, Joseph, 1069-71
McCabe, John D., 1779
McCaffery, Larry, 2319, 3454
McCall, Margery Stewart, 4878
McCann, Garth, 1459, 1898, 4799
McCard, Nancy Wilson, 3513
McCarthy, John Alan, 1072
McCarthy, Paul, 4581-82
McClanahan, Ed, 4462
McClanahan, Muriel H., 1527
McClintock, James I., 3359-60
McClure, Charlotte S., 1505-9, 1528, 1780
McCluskey, Sally, 3717-18
McConnell, Richard M. M., 2795-96
McConnell, Virginia, 2914, 4709
McCourt, Edward, 1413
McCown, Robert A., 2133
McCracken, Harold, 1862, 3983, 4204
McCullough, Joseph B., 2518-20

McDaniel, Barbara Albrecht, 4583
McDermott, John Francis, 286, 2890
Macdonald, Dwight, 2974
McDonnell, T. P., 2350
McDonnell, Thomas P., 2641
McDowell, Tremaine, 594, 848
McElderry, Bruce R., 1510
McElhiney, Annette Bennington, 287
McElrath, Joseph R., Jr., 3778-85
McFarland, Dorothy Tuck, 1751
McGinity, Sue Simmons, 1277, 2371
McGinty, Brian, 2975, 4679
McGrath, Thomas, 3450
Machann, Ginny Brown, 3653
Machen, Meredith R., 1782-83
McHenry, Carol S., 3170
Mack, Effie Mona, 1993
McKee, Irving, 1667
McKee, John DeWitt, 1994, 4887
McKenna, Teresa, 1278
McKenzie, James J., 3999
McKinney, Doug, 1073
McKnight, Jeannie, 595
McKown, Robin, 3984
McLay, Catherine M., 1414, 1784
McLean, Austin J., 2564
Maclean, H. N., 2164
McLean, Malcolm, 71
McLeod, Gordon Duncan, 1415
McLeod, James Richard, 4100-101
Macleod, Norman, 847
McMahan, Elizabeth E., 1495, 4584
McMaster, Belle M., 5028
McMichael, James, 4102-3
McMillan, Marilyn Johnson, 3361
McMillan, Sammuel H., 4416
McMillan, Scott R., 3183
McMullen, Lorraine, 1416-17
McMullin, Stanley E., 1418
McMurtry, Larry, 288, 596, 1074
McNally, Dennis, 3072
McNamee, Lawrence F., 72
Macnaughton, William R., 1996
McNeill, Don, 4364
McNickle, D'Arcy, 3171
McReynolds, Douglas J., 597
McTaggart, Fred, 1180
McTee, James David, 4585
McVicker, Mary Louise, 2275
McWilliams, Carey, 598-99, 849-50, 1595-
    97, 4586

303

Madden, David, 3652, 3654-59, 4839
Madrid-Barela, Arturo, 1279
Magnaghi, R. M., 1634
Maguire, James H., 73, 2475
Mahon, Robert Lee, 289
Mailer, Norman, 1357
Major, Mabel, 74, 154
Malin, Irving, 3105, 4840
Malin, James C., 4785-88
Malkoff, Karl, 4104
Malley, Terence, 1650
Mallon, Thomas, 2264
Malloy, Jean Norris, 1899
Malpezzi, Frances, 1490, 4800
Manchel, Frank, 1075
Manchester, John, 1655
Mandel, Eli, 1419
Mane, Robert, 2521
Manfred, Frederick, 600, 3275, 4710
Manley, Atwood, 3985
Manley, Francis, 2864
Mann, John S., 3362
Mann, Ralph, 601
Mansfield-Kelley, Deane, 3172
Manzo, Flournoy Davis, 3215-16
Marberry, M. Marion, 3579
Marchand, Ernest, 602, 3786
Marcus, Mordecai, 4587
Mares, E. A., 1280
Margolis, John D., 3161
Marín, Mariana, 1499
Marken, Jack W., 1181-83
Markos, Donald W., 4642
Marks, Barry, 603, 1997
Marks, Lester Jay, 4588-89
Marovitz, Sanford E., 290, 604-6, 2165,
   4590-91, 4579-80
Márquez, Antonio, 3730
Marsden, James Douglas, 3106
Marsden, Michael T., 941, 977-79, 1076,
   2915, 3184-87, 3844, 4285-86
Marsh, Robert, 4932
Martin, Bruce K., 4592
Martin, Jay, 291, 4841-42
Martin, Minerva L., 2916
Martin, Terence, 1785, 2082-83, 2891,
   3107
Martinec, Barbara, 2522
Martinez, Diana, 307
Martínez, Eliud, 1500
Martínez, Max, 1281

Martz, William J., 4105
Marx, Leo, 1998-99
Mason, Julian, 4981-82
Mason, Kenneth C., 3615
Mass, Roslyn, 1077
Massa, Ann, 3299
Matheson, John William, 4106
Mathews, Sue, 3039
Matlack, Anne, 2338
Matthews, Eleanor H., 2688
Mattingly, Garrett, 2246
Mattson, Jeremy, 292
Maule, Harry E., 155
Maunder, Elwood R., 4663
Maurice, Arthur B., 3930
Mawer, Randall Ray, 846
Maxwell, Margaret F., 224
Maxwell, Richard, 3108
May, Charles E., 2724, 4593
May, Ernest, 2725-26
May, Judith Stinson, 2084
Mayer, Charles W., 2829
Mayfield, John S., 4983
Mazzaro, Jerome, 4107
Meador, John, 3002
Meador, Roy, 2696
Mearns, Hughes, 1690
Meats, Stephen E., 3941
Medicine, Bea, 2783
Medoff, Jeslyn, 1786
Mehl, R. F., 3217, 3363
Meier, A. Mabel, 1482
Meine, Franklin J., 197
Meinzer, Helen Abbott, 2922
Meldrum, Barbara, 607-11, 2433, 4047,
   4945-46
Meltzer, David, 156, 1358
Mencken, H. L., 2225
Menkin, E. Z., 2576
Meredith, Scott, 157-58
Meredith, William, 4108
Merren, John, 2258
Merriam, H. G., 3289-90
Merrild, Knud, 3195
Merrill, Thomas F., 2577
Merritt, J. I., 3687
Merwin, Henry C., 2727-28
Messenger, Christian, 3787
Messer, Richard, 2976
Metzger, C. R., 4594
Meyer, George, 3788

Meyer, Harold, 2000
Meyer, Roy W., 75, 293, 612–15, 1639, 2523, 2555, 3969, 4162
Meyer, William Claus, 2085
Meyer, William R., 1078
Mezo, Richard Eugene, 4744
Michael, Larry A., 3514
Michael, Marion C., 35
Michaels, I. Lloyd, 4843
Michener, James, 3561
Micklus, Robert, 3789
Mikkelsen, Hubert Aage, 2086
Mikkelsen, Robert J., 4287
Miles, Elton, 294, 616
Miles, Josephine, 617
Miles, Lee Robert, 3908
Millbrook, Minnie D., 618
Miller, Alexander, 980
Miller, Bruce E., 1787
Miller, Charles, 4745
Miller, Charles T., 2525
Miller, David Reed, 2324
Miller, Edwin Haviland, 3790
Miller, James E., Jr., 1788–90, 3660, 4906
Miller, John H., 2811
Miller, Jordan Y., 2865
Miller, Juanita, 3580
Miller, Ralph N., 3661
Miller, Tom P., 4417
Miller, William V., 4595
Millichap, Joseph R., 1863
Mills, Gordon, 2087, 3364–66
Mills, Hazel Emery, 4774
Mills, Ralph J., Jr., 4109–13
Mills, Randall V., 1564
Milner, Jay, 4782
Milton, John R., 76, 159, 295, 619–31, 981, 1184–85, 1900–903, 2320, 2344–45, 2372–73, 2434–36, 2616, 3535–21, 3719, 4451, 4685, 4772, 4801–4
Mitchell, Carol, 1491
Mitchell, Lee Clark, 296
Mitchell, Marilyn, 2866
Mitchell, Marilyn L., 4596
Mitchell, Mildred, 2667
Mitten, Irma Catherine, 2685
Miura, Tokuhiro, 2977
Mobley, Lawrence E., 2001
Moen, Ole O., 3522
Moers, Ellen, 4186
Mogen, David, 4984

Mohr, Martin, 4694
Molen, Dayle H., 1478
Molesworth, Charles, 1625–26, 2578
Momaday, Natachee Scott, 1186
Monaghan, Jay, 632, 982
Money, Mary Alice, 1079
Monjian, Mercedes C., 2978
Monteiro, George, 2166–68, 2736
Moon, Myra Jo, 4233
Mooney, Harry John, Jr., 3909
Moore, Harry Estill, 853
Moore, Harry Thornton, 4597
Moore, J. B., 1904
Moore, Rosa Ann, 4914
Moorhead, Elizabeth, 1791
Morain, Frederick G., 3960
Moran, Ronald, 1623, 4418
Morgan, Dale L., 633, 4337
Morgan, David Lee, 297
Morgan, H. Wayne, 298, 2525, 3791
Morgan, Paul, 1187
Morgan, Richard G., 3870
Morley, S. Griswold, 634
Morrill, Claire, 1656, 3427
Morris, David W., 4260
Morris, Lawrence S., 2979
Morris, Margaret, 4814
Morris, Robert L., 2459
Morris, Wright, 299, 3662
Morrow, Patrick D., 635, 851, 2049, 2729–35, 4721, 4919
Morsberger, Robert E., 1682–85, 3792, 4598
Mortensen, Wayne F., 4163
Morton, Beatrice K., 2437–38, 4234
Morton, Bruce, 2451
Morton, W. L., 1420
Moseley, Ann, 1792–93
Mosley, Richard, 4452
Moss, James Davidson, 1578
Moss, Sidney P., 2980
Mossberg, Krister [Christer] Lennart, 300, 636–37, 4947
Mott, Frank Luther, 4695
Moul, Keith R., 4114
Movalli, Charles Joseph, 2088
Moynihan, Ruth Barnes, 2308
Muehl, Lois B., 4696
Muncy, Elizabeth R., 4270
Munden, Kenneth J., 983
Murphy, Brenda, 2736

Murphy, John J., 1794–97
Murphy, Michael Walter, 1798
Murphy, Miriam B., 1704
Murthy, S. S., 3793
Musick, Gerald Donald, 3794
Muszynska-Wallace, E. Soteris, 2089
Myers, Andrew B., 2892
Myers, John Myers, 2782
Myers, Samuel L., 2686

Nachbar, Jack, 1080–82, 2356
Nadeau, Robert, 4077
Nance, William L., 3910–11
Nash, Lee, 4292–93
Nash, Roderick, 301–2, 3688
Nathan, George Jean, 4261
Neale, Walter, 1598
Neatherlin, James William, 4271
Needham, Arnold E., 1486
Neihardt, John G., 3720–21
Neinstein, Raymond L., 852, 3471, 3663
Nelson, Carl, 2090
Nelson, Carolyn W., 3664
Nelson, F. C., 638
Nelson, H. S., 4599
Nelson, Herbert B., 303, 1545–47, 1565, 4907
Nelson, Jane, 2340
Nelson, Margaret Faye, 3616
Nelson, Mary Carroll, 984
Nelson, Pearl, 4164
Nelson, Raymond John, 3871
Nelson, Rudolph L., 4365
Nelson, Solveig Leraas, 304
Nemanic, Gerald, 3665–66
Nesbitt, John D., 2771, 3188–89
Neumann, Edwin J., 2526
Nevins, Allan, 2917
Nevius, Blake, 2091
New, W. H., 1421–23
Newman, May W., 160
Newmark, Marco, 3436
Newton, D. B., 1705, 2772–73
Nibbelink, Harman, 2002
Nichol, John, 3367
Nicholas, Charles A., 3617
Nicholl, James R., 639
Nichols, David A., 4766
Nichols, Roger L., 640, 1188
Nichols, William, 3234
Nickerson, Edward A., 2981–85

Nicoll, Bruce H., 4235
Nilon, Charles H., 78
Nimitz, Jack, 4600
Nisonger, Thomas Evans, 3074
Noble, David W., 305, 2092
Nock, A. J., 1668
Noel, Daniel C., 4705
Noel, Mary, 306
Nolan, Paul T., 2187
Nolen, O. W., 4332
Nolte, William H., 2986–90
Norell, Irene P., 641
North, Dennis D., 4711
Norton, Aloysius A., 4187
Norwood, W. D., 4726
Nossen, Evon, 4601
Noto, Sal, 3368–69
Nuhn, Ferner, 4696–98
Nussbaum, Martin, 985–86
Nutt, Francis Dorothy, 2687
Nuwer, Henry [Hank], 2991, 4288
Nye, Frank Wilson, 3833
Nye, Russel, 987, 1640, 2587

Oaks, Priscilla, 80, 1189, 3555
Oates, Joyce Carol, 4392
O'Brien, Dominic Vincent, 2737
O'Brien, Lynne Woods, 1190, 2325
O'Connor, John Joseph William, 1424
O'Connor, Margaret Anne, 1799
O'Connor, Richard, 1599, 2738, 3276, 3370, 4602
O'Dell, Charles A., 2190
Odell, Ruth, 2918
Odland, N., 1658
Odum, Howard W., 853
Oehlschlaeger, Fritz, 4699
Okada, Roy K., 2296, 4366
Okerland, Arlene N., 4603
Olafson, Robert B., 4746
Olderman, Raymond Michael, 3109
Oldham, John N., 853
Oleson, Carole, 3618
Oliva, Leo E., 1191, 1573
Oliver, Egbert S., 642, 2739
Olsen, T. V., 2588
Olson, Alan M., 1711
Olson, James C., 643
Olson, Julius E., 4165
Omrcanin, Margaret Stewart, 4700
Oppewall, Peter, 3523

306

O'Quinn, Trueman, 3942
Orians, G. Harrison, 882
Ortega, Adolpho, 1283
Ortego, Philip D., 1284-88, 4604
Ortego y Gasca, Felipe de, 1289
Ossman, David, 1359
Otis, John Whitacre, 4453
Overing, Robert, 4236
Overland, Örm, 2093, 3075
Overton, Grant, 2362
Owens, Louis D., 4605
Owens, William A., 644, 1563, 3845
Ownbey, Ray Wilson, 3371

Pacey, Desmond, 1425-26
Packer, Warren M., 645
Pady, Donald S., 81, 3878, 4888
Paine, Albert Bigelow, 2003
Paine, Doris M., 307
Paine, Gregory, 646, 2094
Palmer, Frederick A., 459
Paluka, Frank, 82, 4701
Pankake, Jon Allan, 3372-73
Pantle, P., 4886
Papanikolas, Zeese, 116
Paredes, Américo, 1290-92, 2860
Paredes, Raymund A., 1293-94, 2169
Parker, Jean Louise, 2992
Parker, Robert Brown, 308
Parkinson, Linda F. L., 2439
Parkinson, Thomas, 1360-62, 4000, 4367-69, 4933-34
Parks, B. K., 1800
Parr, Carmen Salazar, 1295
Parrington, Vernon Louis, 4167
Partridge, Colin, 3912
Patrick, A., 2621
Pattee, Fred Lewis, 2741-42
Patterson, John, 2288
Patterson-Black, Gene, 83
Patterson-Black, Sheryll, 83
Paul, Jay S., 2595
Paul, Rodman W., 84, 2476-77
Paul, Sherman, 2297, 2305, 4370
Paulson, Kristoffer F., 3157, 4168, 4767
Pauly, Thomas H., 1083-84
Pavich, Paul N., 3162, 3594
Payne, John R., 4534
Payne, Leonidas W., 309, 3943
Peach, Linden, 4371
Pearce, Howard D., 4606

Pearce, Roy Harvey, 310, 1192, 2095
Pearce, T. M., 74, 154, 161-62, 647-48, 1529-32, 2779, 3173, 4048
Pearsall, Robert Brainard, 3374
Pearson, Carol, 3110
Pearson, Edmund, 988
Pearson, Lorene, 2375
Pearson, Sheryl Marie Sherman, 4747
Peary, Gerald, 1085
Pease, Otis, 3855
Peavy, Charles D., 3472-75, 4333
Peck, H. Daniel, 2096
Peel, Donald F., 3944
Peet, Howard, 3524
Penglase, John Dols, 2579
Percy, Walker, 989
Perez, Betty L., 4060-61
Perham, Joseph A., 3699
Perkins, Huel D., 4737
Perkins, Maxwell, 4727
Perry, George Sessions, 163
Pers, Mona, 1801
Person, Leland S., Jr., 3877
Perucci, Robert, 1056
Peters, E. Roxanne, 2842-43
Peters, J. U., 649
Peters, Nancy J., 232
Peters, Robert, 4778
Petersen, Lance, 1659
Peterson, Audrey C., 4454
Peterson, Clell T., 3132, 3375-76
Peterson, Levi S., 311, 650-51, 1905
Peterson, Martin Severin, 3581
Peterson, Richard F., 4607
Peterson, Richard K., 1193
Peterson, Vernon, 2276
Petrullo, Helen B., 3277-78
Petry, Alice Hall, 855-56
Pettit, Arthur G., 1086, 1296, 2004-5
Peverly, Carlos Francis, 990
Peyer, Bernd, 4683
Peyroutet, Jean A., 652
Phillips, Billie, 3476
Phillips, James E., 653
Phillips, Raymond C., Jr., 3477
Phillips, Robert, 2596-99
Philp, Kenneth R., 4815
Piacentino, Edward J., 1802
Piccione, Anthony, 1627
Pickett, Calder M., 2830-32
Pifer, Caroline Sandoz, 4237

Pike, Donald G., 2191
Pilkington, John, 2527
Pilkington, William T., 312-14, 654-55,
    1087, 1460-61, 2237, 2277, 2376-77,
    3478-79, 3846, 4805
Pino, Frank, 1297-98
Pino, Frank, Jr., 1299, 4071
Pinsker, Sanford, 3111, 4115, 4420, 4779-
    80
Pizer, Donald, 315, 2170, 2528-33, 3795-
    803
Place, J. A., 1088
Plante, Patricia R., 2363
Pochmann, Henry A., 2893
Podhoretz, Norman, 1363
Pogel, Nancy H., 1089
Pohlmann, John Ogden, 316
Polk, Noel, 85
Polk, Stella Gipson, 2585
Pollard, Lancaster, 86, 656
Polos, Nicholas C., 657, 4717
Pomeroy, Earl, 658-60, 4192-93
Poncet, Andre, 3804
Ponick, Terrence Lee, 4748
Pope, Bertha, 1600
Porter, Katherine Anne, 3913
Porter, Kenneth, 1579
Porter, Mark, 661, 1194
Porter, Willard H., 2043
Portillo, Estella, 1301
Portz, John, 1906
Potter, Richard Harold, 317
Potts, James Thompson, 2226-27
Poulsen, Richard C., 318, 662, 1566, 2097,
    4218
Pound, Louise, 2098, 2919
Povey, John F., 1195-96
Powell, Desmond, 4948, 5017
Powell, Grosvenor E., 4935-37
Powell, Lawrence Clark, 87, 164, 319-20,
    1462, 1533-34, 1678, 2045, 2365,
    2378, 2556, 2608, 2622-23, 2797,
    2993-94, 3163, 3174, 3423, 3437-38,
    4026, 4219, 4250, 4608, 4706, 4806,
    4879
Powers, Alfred, 321, 1550, 1567, 2313,
    3582
Powers, Richard, 2833
Powers, William, 3856
Pownall, David, 87
Pratt, John Clark, 3112-13, 4609

Pratt, Linda Ray, 4610-11
Price, Carol, 2192
Price, Starling, 3377
Primeau, Ronald, 991, 3076
Prince, Richard John, 322
Pruessing, Peter Skiles, 2247
Pry, Elmer, 3446
Pugh, David William, 324
Pullen, John J., 1669
Putnam, Jackson K., 663, 2668, 4455, 4768

Quantic, Diane Dufva, 664-65
Quinn, Roland Joseph, 325
Quirk, Tom, 4739
Quissell, Barbara, 1480, 4272

Rackleff, Julia, 3565
Radke, Merle L., 857
Rahv, Philip, 4262
Railton, Stephen, 2099
Raine, Kathleen, 2562
Raine, William MacLeod, 4027
Rainey, Buck, 960
Ramsey, Jarold, 1197-1202
Ramsey, Paul, 4421, 4938
Randall, John, 3986
Randall, John H., 1803-4
Randall, Randolph C., 2692
Randel, William Pierce, 2330-32
Rans, Geoffrey, 1203
Ransom, John C., 858
Rao, Vimala C., 1365
Rascoe, Burton, 3966
Rasky, Frank, 1427
Rather, Lois, 3378
Ravitz, Abe C., 3218
Rawls, James J., 2248
Ray, Charles Eugene, 2669
Raymond, Catherine E., 859
Reade, Frank R., 3583
Reamer, Own J., 2534-35
Reaver, J. Russell, 1805
Reck, Tom S., 1693
Reddin, Paul Laverne, 326
Redekip, Ernest, 1204
Redinger, Ellsworth L., 2995
Reed, John Q., 1670, 2006
Reeve, Frank D., 2798
Reeve, Kay Aiken, 327
Reid, Randall, 4844
Reigelman, Milton M., 861

Reigstad, Paul M., 4169-70
Rein, David, 2440
Reinitz, Richard, 3864
Reiter, Joan Govan, 2448
Remenyi, Joseph, 4263
Remley, David A., 2366, 3425, 4322
Reninger, H. Williard, 3805
Renner, Frederick G., 4205, 4208
Resh, Richard W., 4889-90
Rexroth, Kenneth, 1366-68, 4001-2
Reynard, Grant, 1806
Reynolds, Helen Louise, 2780
Reynolds, Quentin, 992, 2357
Rhode, Robert D., 862-63
Rhodelhamel, Josephine DeWitt, 2050
Rhodes, Geri Marlane, 1205, 4861
Rhodes, May Davison, 4028-29
Rice, Minnie C., 4238
Richards, John S., 3584
Richards, John Thomas, 3722-23
Richards, Robert F., 2391-95
Richardson, Darrell C., 2358
Richey, Elinor, 1511
Richman, Sidney, 3495
Richter, Conrad, 4049
Rickels, Milton, 4733-34
Ricou, Laurence, 1428-29
Rideout, Walter B., 1697
Ridge, Martin, 2289
Ridgeway, Ann N., 2228, 2996
Rieupeyrout, Jean-Louis, 1090-91
Riley, Susan B., 3888
Ringe, Donald A., 2100-2102
Ringler, Donald P., 1535
Rios-C, Herminio, 1301, 1312
Ristvedt, Helen Smith, 4030
Ritchie, Ward, 2997-98
Rivera, Tomás, 1302-3
Rizzo, Fred F., 2351
Roach, Joyce Gibson, 4376
Roach, Samuel Frederick, Jr., 4139
Robb, Kenneth A., 3597
Robbins, J. Albert, 89
Roberts, J. Russell, Sr., 4422
Robertson, Jamie, 2171, 4456
Robertson, Richard, 4715
Robinson, Barbara J., 1304
Robinson, Cecil, 328, 1305-6, 2379-80
Robinson, Chandler A., 2683
Robinson, Duncan, 3945
Robinson, Forrest G., 2007, 4457-58, 4985

Robinson, J. Cordell, 1304
Robinson, John W., 666
Robinson, Margaret G., 4457-58
Robinson, Ruth Williard, 329
Robinson, William Hedges, Jr., 2008
Robson, W. W., 4939
Rocard, Marcienne, 4072
Rock, Francis John, 1679
Rodenberger, M. Lou, 667, 2591, 3204
Rodgers, John William, 330
Rodgers, Paul C., Jr., 2009
Rodríguez, Juan, 4073
Rodríguez, Raymond J., 1307-8
Roe, Margie M., 2396
Roemer, Kenneth M., 90, 1206, 3649
Rogers, Covington, 3001-2
Rogers, Douglas G., 1907
Rogers, Franklin R., 2010-11
Rogers, Jane, 1492
Rogers, Will, 4140
Rohrbach, Sister Charlotte, 1807
Rojas, Guillermo, 1309
Rolfe, Lionel, 331
Rollins, Hyder E., 3946
Rollins, Myrth W., 1310
Romano-V, Octavio Ignacio, 1301, 1311-12
Ronald, Ann, 668-69, 2624
Rook, Constance Merriam, 3667
Ropp, Philip H., 2834
Rosa, Alfred F., 91
Rosa, Joseph G., 332, 993
Rose, Ellen Cronan, 3838
Rosen, Kenneth, 1207-9
Rosenberg, Betty, 994, 1487
Rosenberg, Charles E., 3279
Rosenblum, Dolores, 4915
Rosenthal, M. L., 2580
Rosenus, A. H., 3585-86
Rosenzwig, Paul Jonathan, 333
Rosowski, Susan J., 1808-10
Ross, Alan, 4845
Ross, John F., 2103
Ross, Marvin C., 1864
Ross, Morton L., 2104, 4712
Ross, Nancy Wilson, 2309
Ross, Woodburn O., 4612
Roth, Henry, 4067
Roth, John D., 2333
Roth, Russell, 1601, 3525
Rothberg, Abraham, 3379, 4372
Rothenberg, Jerome, 1210-11

Rothwell, Kenneth S., 3724
Roulston, Robert, 1811
Rovit, Earl H., 864
Rowland, Connie M. Payne, 165
Rowlette, Robert, 2012
Roy, Gregor, 1369
Rubin, Louis D., 92, 2859, 3077
Rucker, Mary E., 2105
Rudnick, Lois, 3428-29
Rudolph, Earle Leighton, 670
Ruehlmann, William, 2697
Ruggles, Eleanor, 3300
Rumaker, Michael, 2581
Rundell, Walter, Jr., 93, 671, 4613, 4816-17
Ruoff, A. LaVonne Brown, 4306, 4862-63
Ruppert, James, 1212
Rusch, Lana Koepp, 672
Rush, N. Orwin, 3834, 3987, 4986
Rusk, Ralph Leslie, 94, 334
Russell, Austin, 4206
Russell, Jason A., 2106, 2894
Rust, Richard D., 2895
Ruud, Curtis Duane, 4171
Ryan, Pat M., Jr., 2013
Ryan, Patrick Edward, 335

Saciuk, Olena H., 336
Sackett, S. J., 95, 2835, 3133
Sadler, Frank, 4386
Sage, Frances Kellogg, 673, 1628
Sage, Leland L., 674
St. John, Katherine E., 4916
Sakurai, Emiko, 4003
Sale, Richard B., 4811
Salinas, Judy, 1313
Salinas, Luis Omar, 1314
Sanchez, George I., 1315
Sanchez, Rita, 1316
Sandburg, Carl, 2229
Sands, Kathleen M., 4307, 4864
Sanford, Geraldine A. J., 3595-96
Santibanez, James, 1276
Saporta, Marc, 4459
Saroyan, Aram, 1370, 4870
Sarris, Andrew, 1092
Sarton, May, 3424
Sasaki, N., 4347
Satterwhite, Joseph N., 2172
Sattlemeyer, Robert, 3205
Saucerman, James R., 675

Saum, Lewis O., 865, 2536
Saunders, Thomas E., 1213-14
Savage, George Howard, 2537
Savage, William W., Jr., 337, 676
Sawey, Orlan, 2249-50, 4334-35
Saxton, Eugene F., 4880
Sayre, Robert F., 1215
Schaefer, Jack, 166, 3040
Schaefer, William J., 4781
Scheick, William J., 2743, 2896
Schein, Harry, 1093
Scherting, Jack, 2397-98
Schlissel, Lillian, 677
Schmidt, Dorey, 3480
Schmitt, Peter J., 338
Schmitz, Anne-Marie, 4614
Schmitz, Neil, 1651, 2014
Schneider, Jack, 525
Schneider, Jack W., 1216-17
Schneider, Norris F., 2625
Schneider, Robert W., 3806-7
Schneider, Sister Lucy, 1812-16
Schoenewolf, Carroll Robert, 4846
Schoolcraft, John, 2359
Schopf, William, 678, 3114
Schorer, C. E., 2836
Schorer, Mark, 3280-82
Schroder, Fred E. H., 679, 2744
Schroeter, James Marvin, 1817
Schulberg, Budd, 4264
Schultz, Max F., 2405, 3496
Schumacker, Paul J., 4116
Schwartz, Delmore, 3003, 4117
Schwartz, Edward, 3914
Schwartz, James M., 2336-37
Schwartz, Joseph, 680
Schwartz, Marilyn M., 1371
Schwartz, Narda Lacey, 96
Schwartz, Thomas, 3835
Schwartz, Thomas D., 4722
Schweitzer, Darrell, 2819
Scott, James F., 1372
Scott, John Charles, 1818
Scott, Kenneth W., 2626-27
Scott, Nathan A., Jr., 4118, 4847
Scott, Robert I., 3004-7
Scott, Winfield Townley, 3175
Scoville, Samuel, 4615
Scrota, Steve, 4616
Scullin, George, 681
Seager, Allan, 4119-20

Seal, Robert, 1152
See, Carolyn P., 339, 3872-73
Seelye, John D., 682, 2460, 4989
Segade, Gustavo, 1317
Seibel, George, 1819
Seitz, Don C., 1671
Sellars, Richard West, 683
Sequeira, Isaac, 2107
Sergeant, Elizabeth Shepley, 1820
Seshachari, Candadai, 684, 996
Sessions, George, 3008
Settle, William A., 997
Sewell, Ernestine, 2341-42
Sexton, Richard J., 4940
Seydor, Paul, 1094
Seyersted, Per, 4308
Seymour-Smith, Martin, 4121
Shadoian, Jack, 685
Shames, Priscilla, 1218
Shannon, Fred A., 4818
Sharnik, John, 998
Shaughnessy, Mary Rose, 2364
Shaul, Lawana J., 686
Shebl, James M., 3009, 3139
Sheean, Vincent, 3283-84
Sheed, Wilfred, 1373, 4393
Sheehy, E. P., 3794, 4931
Sheller, Harry L., 1602
Shelton, Frank W., 1821
Shelton, Lola, 4207
Sheppard, Keith S., 2108
Sherman, Caroline B., 687-89
Sherman, Dean, 4988
Sherman, Joan R., 3380
Sherman, Stuart P., 3587
Sherman, W. D., 3115
Sherwood, Terry G., 3116
Shetty, M. Nalini, 3668-70
Shiglas, Jerry Ashburn, 3010
Shinn, Thelma J., 4265
Shively, James R., 1822
Shivers, Alfred S., 3381-83, 4871-72
Shockley, Martin, 167, 4617
Short, John D., Jr., 4618
Short, Julee, 2897
Short, Luke, 2589
Short, R. W., 3011
Shrell, Darwin H., 3889
Shulenberger, Arvid, 2109
Shuman, R. Baird, 2867, 3950, 4619
Shurbutt, S., 3915

Sibley, M. A., 3947
Siegel, Mark, 4078
Silber, Irwin, 168
Silet, Charles L. P., 2538-39, 3384, 4323-24
Silver, Charles, 1095
Silver, Marilyn Brick, 340
Simmen, Edward, 1318
Simmons, Chuck, 4361
Simmons, Marc, 3439, 4289
Simmons, Michael K., 999-1000
Simmons, Roy S., 4620
Simon, Tobin, 3285
Simoneaux, Katherine G., 4735
Simonson, Harold P., 341, 690, 3689, 4172-73, 4769
Simpson, Claude M., 866, 2540, 2837
Sinclair, Andrew, 1096, 3385-86
Singer, Barnett, 691, 1580, 3117, 3497, 3865, 4460
Singer, Felix, 4266
Singleton, M. K., 1430
Sisk, J. P., 1001
Sisk, John P., 1374
Skårdal, Dorothy Burton, 342, 692
Skau, Michael Walter, 1375, 2387
Skelley, Grant Teasdale, 867
Skillman, Richard, 4031
Skipp, Frances E., 3388
Skjelver, Mabel R., 1003
Slade, Joseph W., 3549, 4657-58
Slade, Leonard A., Jr., 4621
Sloane, David E. E., 2757, 3967
Slote, Bernice, 1823-31, 2173-74, 3725
Slotkin, Richard, 343
Smeall, Joseph F. S., 3451
Smetzer, Michael, 4424
Smith, Alfred, 3012
Smith, Bob L., 3196
Smith, Caroline, 344
Smith, Dave, 2563, 5023
Smith, Duane Allan, 693, 2407
Smith, Dwight L., 97, 1219
Smith, Edwin B., 694
Smith, Goldie Capers, 695
Smith, Gregory, 2251
Smith, Henry Nash, 345, 696-705, 1004, 1536, 2016-19, 2110-12, 4908
Smith, Herbert F., 3690
Smith, J. Oates, 3916
Smith, Jean P., 3291

Smith, Larry R., 3874
Smith, Marcus, 4848
Smith, Marie, 3620
Smith, Norman D., 1466
Smith, Norman David, 1319
Smith, Rebecca W., 706
Smith, Stephen, 3041
Smith, William F., 4865
Smith, William F., Jr., 1220-21
Snell, George, 2441
Snell, Joseph W., 1005
Sniffen, Jimmie Clifton, 3481
Snipes, Helen Joann, 4783
Snook, Donald Gene, 2113
Snyder, Gary, 707
Snyder, Lucy, 1152
Soderbergh, Peter A., 4325
Solensten, John M., 4987
Solomon, Andrew, 2020
Solomon, Eric, 2175
Solomon, Roger B., 2021
Solotaroff, Theodore, 3498
Solum, Nora O., 4160, 4174
Sommers, Joseph, 1320-22, 4074
Sondrup, Steven P., 708
Sonnichsen, C. L., 169, 346-47, 709-14,
    1006-8, 1097, 1222, 1323, 1701, 2346,
    3482
Southworth, James G., 4122
Spaulding, George E., 2898
Spaulding, Kenneth A., 2899
Spears, Jack, 1098
Speck, Ernest B., 1630, 1702-3, 4716
Speir, Jerry, 1866, 3447
Spence, Clark C., 170
Spencer, Benjamin T., 869-71
Spencer, Betty Lee, 2360
Spencer, Marcia C., 423
Spettigue, Douglas, 1431
Spies, George Henry, III, 3527, 4622
Spilka, Mark, 4623
Spiller, Robert E., 2114-16
Spinner, Jonathan S., 3388
Spinning, Bruce, 715
Spotts, Carl B., 348
Springer, Haskell, 2900
Squires, Radcliffe, 3013-14
Stafford, Bart Lanier, III, 146
Stafford, William E., 147, 349, 2352, 4423
Stall, Lindon, 2194
Stallman, R. W., 2176-77

Standiford, Lester A., 1223, 1463
Staples, Hugh, 4123
Stark, John O., 3956
Starr, Kevin, 350, 1512, 2267, 3015, 4194
Starrett, Vincent, 1603-4, 2186
Stasz, Clarice, 3389-90
Stauffer, Helen, 4239-43
Stearns, Bertha-Monica, 872
Steckmesser, Kent L., 716-17, 1009
Steele, Frank, 1629
Steele, Joan, 3970, 4624
Steensma, Robert C., 718, 3158, 4175, 4909
Steeves, Harrison R., 2561
Steffen, Jerome O., 3235
Steffens, Lincoln, 1537
Stegner, Wallace, 351, 719-22, 1432, 1832-
    33, 1908, 2252-56, 2670, 2745
Stein, Arnold, 4124
Stein, Howard F., 3118
Stein, Paul, 1909
Stein, Rita, 352
Stein, Robert A., 2195
Stein, W. B., 2117
Steinbeck, Elaine, 4625
Steinbeck, John, 4062
Steinberg, Alan L., 2118
Steinbrink, Jeffrey Carl, 2119
Steiner, Michael C., 4770
Steiner, Stan, 1237, 1332
Stensland, Anna Lee, 1224-26, 2326
Stephan, Peter M., 2671
Stephens, Alan, 4941
Stephens, D. G., 1433
Stephens, Edna Buell, 2452
Stephens, George D., 3016
Sterling, George, 171, 3017
Stern, Daniel, 2600
Stern, Frederick C., 3452
Steuding, Bob, 4373
Stevens, A. Wilbur, 172
Stevens, James, 2230-31, 4664
Stevens, Peter, 1432
Stevens, Robert, 4176
Stevenson, Dorothy, 723
Stevenson, Elizabeth, 3236
Stevenson, Lionel, 4659
Stewart, D. H., 1834, 3952
Stewart, David, 4424
Stewart, Donald C., 2672-73
Stewart, George R., 724, 873, 2235, 2746-
    49

Stich, Klaus Peter, 1435
Stimson, Frederick S., 2461
Stineback, David C., 1835, 2265, 2674
Stobie, Margaret, 1436
Stokes, Frances Kemble Wister, 4990
Stone, Albert E., Jr. 2022
Stone, Irving, 3391
Stone, Judy, 4749
Stone, Lee Alexander, 2812
Storm, Melvin, 4177
Story, Norah, 1437
Stott, Graham St. John, 2628
Stouck, David, 1836-44
Stouck, Mary-Ann, 1843-44
Stout, Janis P., 3483
Straight, Michael, 725, 1011
Straus, Dorothea, 4394
Street, Webster, 4626
Streeter, Thomas W., 98
Strelow, Michael, 173, 3119
Strenski, Ellen, 2784
Strickland, Arney L., 3843
Stronks, James B., 99, 2541-42, 2838
Stroven, Carl G., 4680
Stubbs, John C., 1605
Suckow, Ruth, 874
Suderman, Elmer F., 4178
Sullivan, Patrick J., 1895
Sullivan, Rosemary, 4125-26
Sullivan, Ruth, 3120
Sullivan, Sherry Ann, 1227
Summerlin, Tim, 3484
Sumner, D. Nathan, 4425
Suran, Irene, 4784
Surette, P. L., 1438
Sutherland, Bruce, 4050, 4220
Sutherland, Janet, 3121
Sutherland, Ronald, 1439
Sutton, Ann, 353
Sutton, Myron, 353
Sutton, Walter, 2178
Swados, Harvey, 1698
Swallow, Alan, 726-28, 1910, 3226, 3528, 4807
Sweeney, J. Gray, 354
Switzer, Dorothy, 4244
Synnestvedt, Sigfried T., 3550
Szasz, Ferenc M., 1228
Szasz, Margaret C., 1228

Taber, Ronald W., 2314, 2442-45

Taft, Robert, 355, 2478, 3988
Tallman, Warren, 1440-41, 3078
Tanner, Stephen L., 3122
Tanner, Tony, 3123-24
Taper, Bernard, 2023
Targ, William, 174
Tate, Allen, 875
Tate, George S., 729
Tatum, Charles M., 1325-27
Taylor, Archer, 1481
Taylor, Frajan, 3018
Taylor, Horace P., Jr., 4627
Taylor, J. Golden, 175-76, 730, 2024
Taylor, Marjorie Anne, 3301
Taylor, Peter, 4395
Taylor, Samuel W., 731
Taylor, Walter Fuller, 2543, 3808, 4628
Teale, Edwin May, 3691
Tebbel, John, 356
Tedlock, E. W., Jr., 4629
Teich, Nathaniel, 3392
TeMaat, Agatha, 4630
Tenefelde, Nancy L., 732
Tenney, Thomas Asa, 2025-27
Ter Matt, Cornelius John, 3529
Terrell, Dahlia Jewel, 2901
Testa, Daniel P., 1493, 4075
Thackeray, William W., 4866
Thayer, William Roscoe, 2758
Theisz, R. D., 1229
Thoburn, Joseph B., 2902
Thomas, Alfred Krupp, 2446
Thomas, Clara, 1442-43
Thomas, Jeffrey F., 1606, 2750-51, 3140
Thomas, Phillip D., 2590, 4667
Thomason, A. P., 161
Thompson, Barbara, 3917
Thompson, Bernita Lonette Arnold, 1846
Thompson, Dorothy, 3287
Thompson, Eric Callum, 1444
Thompson, H. C., 3588
Thompson, Mrs. Launt, 2236
Thompson, Thomas, 1012
Thoroughgood, Inez, 1538
Thorp, N. Howard, 177
Thorp, Raymond W., 4336
Thorp, Willard, 4910
Thorson, Gerald, 4179
Thrift, Bonnie B. R., 2381
Thurman, Kelley, 2759
Thwaites, Reuben Gold, 3237

313

Tibbetts, A. M., 2179
Tierney, William, 3393
Tiessen, Hildegarde, 1445
Timpe, Eugene F., 2752
Tinker, Edward Larocque, 357
Tinkle, Lon, 2278
Tobin, Gregory M., 4819-20
Todd, Edgeley W., 358, 733-34, 2693-94, 2903, 3726
Toler, Sister Colette, 1847
Tonsfeldt, Ward, 100
Tooker, Dan, 359, 3223, 4444
Topping, Gary, 1013-14, 1686, 2629-33
Torres-Rioseco, Arturo, 735
Tovar, Inez Hernandez, 3485
Towers, Tom H., 2028-29
Trachtenberg, Alan, 3671
Trachtenberg, Stanley, 4631, 4849
Trejo, Arnulfo D., 1328
Treviño, Albert D., 1494
Tribble, Joseph L., 3857
Trilling, Diana, 2582
Trimble, Martha Scott, 3621, 4911
Trimmer, Joseph F., 1099, 3622, 4991
Trombley, W., 4992
Trombly, A. E., 3302
Trusky, A. Thomas, 178, 2399, 3457
Tucker, Martin, 3672
Tuppet, Mary M., 877
Turco, Lewis, 4426
Turlish, Molly S., 3019
Turner, A. T., 4427
Turner, Arlin, 2462
Turner, E. S., 1015
Turner, Frederick W., III, 1230, 1574
Turner, Joseph William, 1575
Turner, Martha Anne, 2279
Turner, Steve, 1706
Turner, Steven, 3566
Turner, Tressa, 3219
Turner, William O., 1016
Tuska, Jon, 1100-1102
Tuttleton, James W., 4632
Twain, Mark, 2120
Tweet, Ella Valborg, 4180
Twining, Edward S., 1464
Twitchell, Ralph Emerson, 2609
Tyler, Robert L., 4461
Tynan, Kathleen, 736
Tyo, Jane, 558

Tyree, Donald W., 1231
Tytell, John, 1377-78, 2583, 3079

Ulibarrí, Sabine R., 1329
Ulph, Owen, 2052
Underhill, Lonnie, 1177, 2517, 2544-45
Underwood, John Curtis, 1513, 4881
Urioste, Donaldo W., 1275
Uzendoski, Emily Jane, 101

Vaca, Nick Corona, 1330
Valdes, Ricardo, 1331
Valdez, Luis, 1332
Valentin, David, 1244
Valjean, Nelson, 4633
Van Antwerp, Richard Fenn, 2121
Van Becker, David, 1559
Vance, William L., 2122, 3809
Van Dam, Denis, 3020
Van Der Beets, Richard, 1232, 2180, 3394
Vanderbilt, Kermit, 4127
Van Derhoff, Jake, 102
Vanderwerken, David L., 1652
Van Deusen, Marshall, 4942
Van de Water, F. F., 3292
Van Doren, Carl, 1539, 3948
Van Doren, Mark, 737
Van Ghent, Dorothy, 1848
Vannatta, Dennis P., 4850
Vanouse, Donald, 2181
Vardamis, Alex A., 3021
Vaughn, Eric, 3022
Velie, Alan R., 1233, 3623, 4867-68
Venable, William H., 360
Venn, George, 738
Veres, Peter, 3875
Veysey, Laurence R., 739, 878
Vickery, Olga W., 4396
Vigil, Ralph H., 1849
Vivelo, Frank R., 1173
Vivelo, Jacqueline J., 1173
Vlach, Gordon R., 2123
Voelker, Frederic E., 4221
Vogelbaum, Alexandra Doris van Ophuijsen, 2546, 3810
Von Frank, Albert James, 361, 2904
Vopat, Carole Gottlieb, 3080
Vore, Elizabeth, 2781
Vorpahl, Ben M., 2030, 2182, 2463, 3989-90, 4993-96
Voss, Ralph Frederick, 2868

314

Wadden, Anthony T., 2299–3000
Wade, Mason, 3858–59
Wagenaar, Dick, 3288
Wagenknecht, Edward, 1540, 1850, 2031, 2905
Wages, Jack D., 3304
Waggoner, Amy, 1495
Waggoner, Hyatt Howe, 3023–24
Wagner, H. R., 103
Wagner, Harr, 3589
Wagner, Linda W., 4428
Wagner, William D., 2547
Wahlstrom, Billie Joyce, 3727
Wain, John, 4128
Walbridge, Earl F., 4997
Walcutt, Charles Child, 879–80, 2548, 3395–96, 3811–14
Wald, Alan, 3458
Waldeland, Lynne, 3673–74
Walden, Keith, 1446
Waldmeir, J. J., 740
Waldmeir, Joseph J., 3125
Waldrip, Louise, 3918
Walker, Dale L., 1607, 2820, 3397–99, 4377
Walker, Don D., 362, 741–55, 1017–18, 1851, 2041, 2257, 2675–77, 3815, 4188, 4222, 4338, 4752, 4998–99
Walker, Franklin, 363–65, 756, 1608, 1680, 3400–403, 3590, 3816–18
Walker, Lennie Merle, 2464
Walker, Robert H., 366, 757
Walker, Warren S., 2124–26
Walker, William S., 758
Walkover, Andrew, 1379
Walle, Alf Howard, III, 2634
Wallenstein, Barry, 1380
Wallis, Prentiss Bascom, 4634
Wallsten, Robert, 4625
Walsh, J. E., 3860
Walterhouse, Roger R., 881, 2753, 3591
Walton, Kathleen O'Donnell, 4245
Wanless, James, 1653
Waples, Dorothy, 2127
Ward, Don, 179–80
Ward, John William, 2839
Ward, Susan Eileen, 3404–5
Warfel, Harry R., 882
Warner, John M., 4750
Warner, Richard H., 3406
Warren, R. P., 3025

Warren, Robert Penn, 883, 2032, 3919
Warren, Sidney, 759
Warshow, Robert, 1103
Wasserstrom, William, 2128
Waterman, Arthur E., 3675–76
Waters, Frank, 1234, 3197, 4309, 4713, 4808
Watkins, Eric, 367
Watkins, Floyd C., 3624
Watkins, George T., 5000–5001
Watkins, T. H., 2033
Watt, F. G., 4635
Watt, Frank W., 1447
Watts, Harold H., 3026–27
Weales, Gerald, 1852, 2869
Weathers, Winston, 884
Weaver, John D., 760
Webb, Howard W., Jr., 3081
Webb, Walter Prescott, 368, 761–62
Weber, Daniel B., 3692
Weber, F. J., 104
Weber, Harley R., 369
Weber, Richard Charles, 5002
Weber, Robert C., 2306
Wecter, Dixon, 370, 2034–35
Wedge, G. F., 3953
Weedin, Everett K., Jr., 3028
Weigant, Leo Augustus, 885
Weir, Sybil, 1514
Weisenburger, Francis Phelps, 2197
Weixlmann, Joseph, 3126, 3957
Welch, Dennis M., 3455
Wellek, René, 4943
Wells, Ronald Albert, 4195
Wells, Walter, 886
Welty, Eudora, 3920
Wentz, John C., 4068
Wermuth, Paul C., 4723
Wertheim, Stanley, 2183
Wesling, Donald, 2298
West, Dorothy, 4738
West, Elliott, 4815
West, Gordon, 1641
West, John O., 3206
West, Philip J., 4636
West, Ray B., Jr., 105, 181, 763, 1911, 2036, 2184, 3921–23
Westbook, Max, 764–70, 1912–15, 3531–32, 5003
Westdal, Lincoln Wesley, 3677
Westermeier, Clifford P., 771–72

315

Wexman, Virginia, 2037
Wheeler, Eva F., 106
Wheeler, Joseph Lawrence, 2635
Wheeler, Leslie, 1515, 3456
Whetton, Betty, 773
Whicher, George F., 4949
Whipple, T. K., 2636
Whisenhunt, Donald W., 774
Whitaker, Rosemary, 4233, 4246
Whitcomb, Virginia Roland, 4273
White, Barbara, 107
White, C., 3293
White, G. Edward, 372, 3991, 4189, 5004
White, George Leroy, 4181
White, Harry, 3666
White, Hayden, 775
White, Helen C., 776
White, John I., 1556, 3840, 5005-6
White, Kenneth, 3029
White, Robin, 4462
White, Trentwell Mason, 1019
White, Victor, 2280
White, William, 3030, 4851-52
White, William Gee, 125
Whitehall, Richard, 1104
Whiteley, Opal, 4893
Whitfield, Stephen J., 3407
Whitford, Kathryn, 2549-50
Whitley, John S., 2698
Whitney, Blair, 3728
Wicker, C. V., 4629
Widmer, Kingsley, 1381, 3127
Wiebe, Rudy, 1448-49
Wiget, Andrew, 777, 1235
Wiggins, Robert A., 1609-10, 2038
Wilcox, Earl J., 3408-11
Wild, Barbara, 1853
Wild, Peter, 3141, 3593
Wilder, Amos, 3031
Wilentz, Elias, 1382
Wiley, Leonard, 1551
Wilgus, D. K., 778
Wilkins, Thurman, 3142
Willett, Ralph, 1105
Willey, Jill Lucas, 4463
Williams, Ames W., 2186
Williams, Bruce Keith, 3082
Williams, Cecil B., 887-88
Williams, Harry, 4129
Williams, James Gary, 2129
Williams, John, 779, 1020, 2678

Williams, Margaret, 3837
Williams, Stanley T., 1672, 2906-8
Williams, W. C., 4004
Williamson, Alan, 4374
Willock, Roger, 4728
Willson, Carolyn Johnston, 3412-14
Willson, Lawrence, 780
Wilner, Herbert, 1916, 4920
Wilson, Carter, 1496
Wilson, Daniel J., 1021, 2637
Wilson, Dawn M., 4051-52
Wilson, Edmund, 373, 4267
Wilson, Eloise, 4069
Wilson, J. C., 3678
Wilson, James R., 2681
Wilson, Jennie Lee, 2130
Wilson, Matthew Thomas, 4130
Wilson, Norma Jean Clark, 1236
Wilson, Raymond, 2327
Wilson, Richard B., 3143
Wilson, Robert, 2139
Winchell, Mark Royden, 2266
Windham, Steve, 4375
Winslow, Cedric Reimers, 3415, 3819
Winslow, Richard, 2777
Winston, Robert Paul, 374
Winters, Yvor, 183, 3032, 3625, 4131,
   4714
Winther, Sophus K., 781, 889
Wister, Fanny Kemble, 5007-10
Wister, Owen, 2039, 5011-12
Witherington, Paul, 3499
Witke, Charles, 3128
Witkowsky, Paul William, 5013
Witt, Grace, 3489
Witt, Shirley H., 1237
Wittington, Curtis, Jr., 1855
Wojahn, David, 2302
Wolf, Bobi, 782
Wolfe, Hilton John, 375
Wolfe, Linnie Marsh, 3693-94
Wolfe, Peter, 3448
Wolfe, Thomas, 3924, 5018
Wolfe, Tom, 3129
Wolford, Chester L., 2185
Wolverton, Forrest E., 268
Wood, Ann D., 890
Wood, Raymund Francis, 2050-51
Wood, Robin, 1106
Wood, Susan, 1450-53
Woodbridge, Hensley C., 3033, 3416-19

Woodcock, George, 4005
Woodhouse, William Lloyd, 2840
Woodress, James, 109-11, 1856-57, 4637
Woodruff, Stuart C., 1611
Woods, Richard D., 1333
Woodward, Charles Lowell, 3626
Woodward, Robert H., 4638
Woolf, Douglas, 2321
Work, Allene, 4032
Work, James C., 4290
Wright, David E., 2290
Wright, Frances Valentine, 112
Wright, Robert C., 3533-34
Wright, Will, 1107
Wright, William, 1673
Wu, William F., 376
Wyatt, Bryant N., 4639
Wyatt, Will, 4751
Wylder, Delbert E., 784-85, 1022-23,
   1465, 1576, 2322, 2813-17, 3535-
   36
Wyman, Walker D., 377
Wynn, Dudley, 1541-42

Yano, Shigeharu, 4640
Yarborough, Ralph W., 2281

Yarmus, Marcia D., 4641
Yasuna, Edward Carl, 2131
Ybarra-Frausto, Tomás, 1334, 4773
Yoder, Jon A., 786, 3420, 4326-28
Yongue, Patricia Lee, 1858-61
Yosha, Lee William, 3925
Yost, Karl, 4208
Young, David Lee, 4053
Young, Mary, 787
Young, Vernon, 788, 1108, 1543, 1917-18,
   2679, 3034, 3926, 4809

Zabilski, Carol, 3154
Zachrau, Thekla, 3627
Zamora, Bernice, 1335
Zanger, Jules, 789
Zaniello, Thomas A., 4944
Zashin, Elliot M., 3130
Ziff, Larzer, 378, 2040
Zlotnick, Joan, 4853
Zochert, Donald, 2042, 4917
Zoellner, Robert H., 2132
Zolla, Elémire, 1238
Zolotow, Maurice, 1109
Zumwinkle, Richard, 3996
Zytaruk, George J., 1657